HAUNTED AMERICA

Terrifying Tales of Paranormal Phenomena

WEST
SIDE
PUBLISHING

Contributing Writers: Jeff Bahr, Mary Fons, Linda Godfrey, J. K. Kelley, Suzanne Reisman, Michael Riedlinger, Russell Roberts, Adam Selzer, Sue Sveum, Donald Vaughan, James Willis

Factual Verification: Hollie Deese, Kathryn L. Holcomb, Carl Miller, Christy Nadalin

Cover Illustration: Adrian Chesterman

Interior Illustrations: Dan Grant, iStockphoto, Jupiterimages, Robert Schoolcraft, Shutterstock, Thinkstock, John Zielinski

Louis Weber, CEO
Publications International, Ltd.
7373 North Cicero Avenue
Lincolnwood, Illinois 60712

Permission is never granted for commercial purposes.

ISBN-13: 978-1-4508-3182-6
ISBN-10: 1-4508-3182-6

Manufactured in USA.

8 7 6 5 4 3 2 1

Contents

Check Under the Bed!

Being scared can be kind of fun. Remember how cool it was to experience that little shiver when you'd hear or read a creepy story or watch a scary movie when you were younger? With *Armchair Reader™: Haunted America,* we re-create that thrill with a whole host of ghost stories and terrifying tales of the supernatural.

These are true tales (or so we're told) of the weird and wicked, the spectral and spirited, the creepy and cryptic. Some are intriguing, and some are befuddling. But don't say we didn't warn you: The stories in this book may give you goose bumps or make the hairs on the back of your neck stand up. Heck, after reading a tale or two, you may even feel the urge to look under your bed or double-check that the closet door is closed before you go to sleep—you know, *just in case.*

Inside *Haunted America,* you'll find plenty of fascinating and frightening facts as well as harrowing tales of visits from the "Other Side." We've also consulted paranormal experts who share what their job is *really* like and answer some burning questions about ghosts.

Still skeptical? Here's a taste of what we have in store for you:

- Restless spirits of slaves who were tortured and maimed by their mistress continue to haunt the LaLaurie Mansion in New Orleans. Several apparitions have been spotted there, including the ghost of a naked slave in chains that reportedly attacked a former tenant before vanishing into thin air.

- In Tennessee in the early 1800s, an entity that's come to be known as "the Bell Witch" terrorized a family for nearly three years and eventually caused the death of the family patriarch.

- Many people have died and lived to tell about it, including Baptist minister Don Piper, who was killed in a car accident and spent several minutes visiting deceased loved ones in heaven before being sent back to his earthly vessel.

See what we mean? *Armchair Reader™: Haunted America* is packed with tales of paranormal phenomena and unexplained events. So sit back, relax, and get ready for a scary ride.

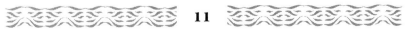

Ghosts 101: Everything You Always Wanted to Know About Ghosts but Were Afraid to Ask

When it comes to the paranormal, there are believers and nonbelievers, but no matter where you stand, you have to admit that the thought of an afterlife is intriguing. But how much do you really know about the spirit world? Read on as our experts answer some of the most common questions about ghosts.

So What *Is* a Ghost, Anyway?

A ghost is simply the spirit of a person who has died but has not yet made it to the "Other Side." In other words, it's caught between this world and the next. Ghosts are made up of energy and exist on this plane without a corporeal body. They are often the spirits of people who died suddenly as a result of murder, suicide, or tragic accidents and, thus, were not prepared for death. Sometimes ghosts appear to warn or guide family members, or to share in times of joy, such as the birth of a child.

Why Can Children See Ghosts More Easily than Adults?

Children are more sensitive to seeing spirits for several reasons. First, they are generally more open-minded and willing to accept things that are new and different. Also, studies have shown that kids are better able to see wavelengths in the lower-light spectrum than adults. Spiritually, children are more closely connected to their heavenly origins than adults. And adults may not be as willing to admit that they saw a ghost for fear of being ridiculed.

Can Ghosts Cross Water?

The relationship between ghosts and water is the subject of great debate, but the short answer is yes. In fact, most experts agree that ghosts are actually *attracted* to water. After all, spirits are made up of energy, and there's no better conductor of energy than water. That's why you'll often see a great deal of paranormal activity on and near bodies of water.

Can Ghosts Really Float Above the Ground?

Yep. Ghosts are made up of energy, and from what we understand, the spirit world works a bit like electricity. Specters appear to float because when they touch the ground, they are absorbed by the earth—or, electrically speaking, "grounded." That doesn't mean that all ghosts float through the air: Some apparitions seem to be walking without their feet touching the ground. The sound of ghostly footsteps? Well, that's a different mystery entirely.

Can Ghosts Attach Themselves to People?

Definitely. When spirits remain earthbound, it is often because they have unfinished business. They are usually drawn to specific locations—such as places where they lived, worked, or died—or to people who conjure up strong emotions—either good or bad. Occasionally, a ghost will attach itself to a stranger because that person is able to see or hear it, but that relationship generally only lasts until the spirit's earthly issues are resolved and it crosses over. So don't worry—the chances of a ghost stalking you are pretty slim.

How Do Ghosts Move Objects or Manipulate Electrical Devices?

Ghosts use energy—both their own essence and borrowed power—to move objects, make noises, play tricks, and get people's attention. Because spirits are made up of energy, they can gather additional fuel from electronic and battery-powered objects. It takes a lot of energy for spirits to communicate, so they need to "charge their batteries" in order to make their presence known. That's why a person living in or visiting a haunted location will sometimes notice that fully charged batteries are drained and other electronic equipment malfunctions. By the same token, ghosts can use their energy to control other technology.

Where Is the Best Place to See a Ghost?

Ghosts can be found just about anywhere, but some of the places where they are most commonly seen are cemeteries, old houses, battlefields, hospitals, colleges, and restaurants. Happy hunting!

The Angry Spirits of the Old Slave House

In 1818, Illinois entered the union as a free state; therefore, slave trading was never legal there. However, that did not stop John Hart Crenshaw of Equality, Illinois, from kidnapping free black men and women and turning them into slaves. That was in the 1830s and '40s, but it seems that the spirits of the people Crenshaw abused are resting anything but peacefully in the house known as Hickory Hill.

Not Exactly the Salt of the Earth

Salt was the fine white foundation upon which John Hart Crenshaw built his empire. Today, salt is known primarily as a seasoning and as the culprit in cases of high blood pressure. But before refrigeration, salt had many uses: It was a valuable commodity that was sometimes even used in place of money.

In the 19th century, working in the salt mines was difficult, dangerous, and physically exhausting. Crenshaw accumulated a number of salt mines in southern Illinois, but he had trouble finding workers. Fortunately for him, even though slavery was illegal in Illinois, a quirk in the law allowed slaves to be *leased* in the county where his mine holdings were located. And so Crenshaw began leasing slaves so that he would always have a ready supply of workers. However, not content with what the law allowed him, Crenshaw expanded his slavery practice to include the kidnapping of free black men and women and runaway slaves. Some of those he put to work in his mines, others he sold into slavery.

Over time, Crenshaw became a wealthy man. In 1817, he had married Sinia Taylor, and in the early 1830s, he began building a proper home for her. The three-story house that he called Hickory Hill was built high on a hill and had massive columns out front, which was typical of the Greek-revival style that was popular at the time. However, the most important feature of the house was not readily seen: A secret passageway actually allowed wagons to bring their cargo of slaves directly into the house. The property also reputedly included a secret tunnel that connected the home's basement to

the nearby Saline River; this was used to unload slaves brought there by boat and get them into the house without being seen.

Once inside the home, Crenshaw's human cargo was led up a narrow flight of stairs to the third floor, where the slaves were chained inside tiny, dirty, cell-like spaces smaller than closets. A whipping post—which was used far too often—occupied a prominent place nearby.

There on the virtually airless third floor, Crenshaw kept the men and women who he would either put to work in his mines or sell into slavery. Not content with just stealing human beings, Crenshaw also began a breeding program. One large slave named "Uncle Bob" allegedly fathered 300 children.

We're on to You...

In 1842, Crenshaw was arrested for orchestrating the kidnapping of a free black woman and her children. He was indicted on criminal charges, but unfortunately, the prosecuting attorney couldn't prove the allegations, and Crenshaw went free.

But soon after, rumors about Crenshaw's business activities began to circulate. These rumblings, combined with the earlier indictment, upset many local residents. In March 1842, one of Crenshaw's steam mills burned to the ground; it is believed that a group of free black men—who were fed up with Crenshaw's actions—took matters into their own hands.

In 1846, Crenshaw's business began to fail as demand for Illinois salt started to decline. After Crenshaw was attacked by one of his employees (which resulted in Crenshaw losing a leg), he closed down most of his salt operations.

Attic Antics

John Hart Crenshaw died in 1871. In 1913, the Sisk family purchased the house, and later, in the mid-1920s, started giving tours of the home. Considering the evil and human suffering that took place at Hickory Hill (aka "the Old Slave House"), it is no surprise that the

building is haunted. Visitors have often heard disembodied moans, cries, and whispers coming from the third floor. Rattling chains have also been heard, as have the shuffling of feet and the soft sounds of comforting spirituals being sung.

People have also reported that they've been touched by icy hands or felt someone—or something—momentarily brush past them, even though nobody else was around. Visitors have spoken of feeling like they were being watched, and some folks have been overcome by intense feelings of sadness or fear.

Hickory Hill gained a reputation as the house in which no one could stay overnight on the third floor. These stories began in the 1920s, when a famous ghost hunter/spiritualist named Hickman Whittington decided to exorcize the third floor of its ghosts. He reportedly fled from the premises after just a few hours and died shortly thereafter.

In 1966, two Marines attempted to spend the night on the third floor, but after hearing moaning and screaming and seeing indistinguishable shapes all about, they quickly fled the scene.

In 1978, as part of a Halloween ratings stunt, a television reporter named David Rogers managed to spend a night on the third floor of the Old Slave House, although he did say that his experience was extremely unsettling. He reported hearing many strange, unexplained sounds, and later discovered voices on his tape recorder that he did not hear during his stay.

Before the Sisks finally gave up the house in 1996, Mrs. Sisk would not stay alone in the dwelling. Even on the warmest days, an unexplained chill inhabited its rooms.

The Story Continues...

Although Hickory Hill is listed on the National Register of Historic Places, it was closed to the public after the Sisks left, and its fate remains uncertain. The state of Illinois subsequently bought it and is determining whether or not to open it as a historical attraction. But whatever ultimately happens to the Old Slave House, it seems almost certain that its tortured souls cannot, and will not, rest in peace, and they'll continue to protest the terrible violence that was done to them until the end of time.

Spirits Aboard the *Queen Mary*

🪦 🪦 🪦 🪦

Once one of the world's most luxurious cruise liners, the Queen
Mary *played host to rich and famous guests such as Clark Gable,
Charlie Chaplin, and Elizabeth Taylor. But since 1967, the
stately ship has been permanently docked at the Port of Long
Beach in California. In the early 1970s, she was transformed
into a luxury hotel that includes several restaurants, bars, and
lounges. She remains a very popular tourist attraction today.*

What many patrons may not know, however, is that this former grande
dame of the sea has a history of paranormal activity that has been
witnessed by passengers and crew members alike. In the early 1980s,
Tom Hennessy, a columnist for the *Long Beach Press-Telegram*,
decided to check out the ship's alleged hauntings for himself. An
avowed skeptic, Hennessy didn't expect to find much, but after just one
rather frightening night aboard the ship, he left a believer.

Bizarre Activity
Hennessy interviewed several people who had worked aboard the
Queen Mary, and many of them talked candidly about their experiences with the ship's ghosts. A security guard told Hennessy that it
wasn't uncommon for lights to mysteriously switch on and off and for
doors to slam shut on G Deck, which is where some believe the ship's
morgue was located. The guard also described bizarre activity in the
ship's artifacts section, such as motion sensors being tripped despite
the fact that the room was empty and locked up tight.

Other individuals who had worked on the ship told Hennessy that
they'd heard odd clanging noises in the engine room, as if someone
was hard at work. But the noises almost always occurred after hours,
when the room was unoccupied.

Face to Face with Ghosts
Another security officer revealed to Hennessy that once, while she
was standing on the stairs leading to the swimming pool, she saw a

woman in an old-fashioned swimsuit preparing to dive into the empty pool. When the guard hollered to stop her, the woman vanished.

Another time, the same guard was riding the escalator from the engine room exhibit when she had the eerie feeling that she was being watched. When she turned around, she saw a man dressed in gray overalls standing on the escalator directly behind her. Assuming that the man was a maintenance worker, she stepped aside to let him pass, but instead, he mysteriously disappeared.

Other witnesses have also encountered this spectral man in overalls. He has dark hair and a long beard and is believed to be a mechanic or maintenance worker from the 1930s.

The *Queen Mary* also has its own resident "Lady in White." Who this woman was in life is unknown, but she haunts the Queen's Salon. She wears a long white evening gown, and witnesses say that she dances alone near the grand piano as if listening to music that only she can hear.

Tour guides aboard the *Queen Mary* have also reported frightening phenomena, including hearing odds noises and seeing weird lights. One guide said that he heard an unseen man clear his throat, and then he watched as the chain across the entryway to the engine room began to shake violently.

Phantom voices, disembodied footsteps, cold spots, and inexplicable breezes that blow through closed-off areas are some of the other eerie occurrences that take place aboard the *Queen Mary.* While touring the ship, one guest felt someone tugging at her purse, pulling her sweater, and stroking her hair. Cold chills crept down her spine when she realized that no one was near her at the time.

Made a Believer

Hennessy's personal experience aboard the *Queen Mary* was equally odd. During the half hour he spent alone in the portion of the ship that houses its propeller shafts, the journalist heard weird clanging noises that ceased when he ran toward them and then started again when he walked away. He also reported finding an oil drum blocking an entryway where no oil drum had been before. Later, upon returning to the same passageway, he found two drums blocking the way. Hennessy also experienced rushing air in a supposedly airtight room, mysterious vibrations on a metal catwalk, and the sounds of a nearby conversation—despite the fact that the closest crew members were two decks away.

It is natural to assume that the spooks that haunt the *Queen Mary* are former guests and crew members, but their exact identities are unknown. Some speculate that the sounds of rolling metal that are occasionally heard in a particular hatchway may be related to a crewman who was crushed to death in the area when the *Queen Mary* was used as a troopship during World War II. And odd activity in one kitchen, including disappearing utensils, is believed to be the antics of an unpopular Navy cook who was killed during a riot aboard the ship. During the melee, the cook was allegedly shoved into a hot oven, where he burned to death.

The ghosts of the *Queen Mary* are apparently more into mischief than mayhem. No one has been hurt or threatened by the spirits, and press reports of the ship's paranormal activity have only served to attract more tourists. The *Queen Mary* may no longer be seafaring, but thanks in part to the spirits who remain on board, she's as popular as ever.

The *Queen Mary* was fast—at the outbreak of World War II, she was the world's fastest transatlantic liner. With a cruising speed of 28.5 knots, she often sailed unescorted, as German subs could not catch or keep up with her. The *Queen Mary* is also huge: In July 1943, she set the still-standing record for the most people on a single voyage with 16,683 soldiers and crew members on board.

Bobby Mackey's:
Ghosts That Like Country Music

Just over the Ohio River from downtown Cincinnati is the town of Wilder, Kentucky, home of Bobby Mackey's—a country-music nightclub and allegedly one of the most haunted locations in the United States. Over the years, the property is said to have seen such atrocities as a beheading, a poisoning, a suicide, numerous unsolved murders, and even a case of possession. On top of all that, some say there's an entrance to hell in the basement.

Hell's Gate

The first building that is believed to have stood on the property now occupied by Bobby Mackey's was a slaughterhouse, which operated from the 1850s until the late 1880s. During that time, it was said to have been so busy that the ground floor was often literally coated with blood. To alleviate that, a well was dug in the basement, which allowed the blood to be washed off the floor and carried out to the nearby river. Needless to say, gallons upon gallons of blood and other assorted matter were dumped into that well. Perhaps that's why legend has it that after the slaughterhouse closed, a satanic cult used the well as part of its rituals. Some even claim that these rituals opened a portal to the Other Side, a portal that—to this day—has yet to be closed.

An Unspeakable Crime

On February 1, 1896, the headless body of Pearl Bryan was found less than two miles from the site of the former slaughterhouse. It was later discovered that Bryan's boyfriend, Scott Jackson, and his friend, Alonzo Walling, had murdered her after a botched abortion attempt. The two men were arrested, but they refused to reveal the location of Bryan's head. Both men were hanged for the crime in March 1897, without ever disclosing the location of Bryan's head. But the consensus was that the head was probably thrown into the old slaughterhouse well. Perhaps that's why Pearl Bryan's ghost is seen wandering around inside Bobby Mackey's, both with and without her head. And although Jackson and

Walling did not take their last breaths on the property, it is believed that their ghosts are stuck there too; they have both been seen throughout the building, but Jackson's ghost seems to be more active . . . and angry. Those who have encountered his ghost—usually around the well in the basement—say that it is a dark and unhappy spirit.

Gangsters and Unsolved Murders

Shortly after the executions of Jackson and Walling, the former slaughterhouse was torn down, leaving only the well. In the 1920s, the building now known as Bobby Mackey's was built on the property directly over the well. During Prohibition, it functioned as a ruthless speakeasy and gambling den where several people lost their lives. Eventually, the building was shut down and cleared out—presumably of everything except the restless spirits.

In 1933, after Prohibition was lifted, E. A. "Buck" Brady purchased the building and renamed it The Primrose. Brady was competing with powerful gangsters who began showing up at The Primrose trying to scare him into giving them a cut of the profits. But Brady refused to be intimidated and continually turned them down. All this came to a head on August 5, 1946, when Brady and gangster Albert "Red" Masterson were involved in a shootout. After that, Brady decided that he was done. After many years of having to continually (and often forcibly) reject advances by Cincinnati-area gangsters, Brady sold the building. But if the stories are to be believed, as he handed over the keys, he cursed the building, saying that because he couldn't run a successful business there, no one should.

Today, the ghosts of both Buck Brady and Red Masterson are seen inside Bobby Mackey's. Brady's ghost has been identified from photographs taken of him when he was alive. And even though he cursed the building, his ghost seems harmless enough. Masterson's ghost, on the other hand, has been described as "not friendly" and has been blamed for some of the alleged attacks on bar patrons.

Johanna

After Brady sold the building, it reopened as The Latin Quarter. According to legend, Johanna, the daughter of The Latin Quarter's owner, fell in love with (and became pregnant by) Robert Randall, one of the singers at the nightclub. After Johanna's father found out

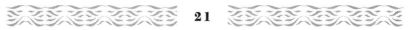

about the pregnancy, he ordered Randall killed. When Johanna learned of her father's involvement in her boyfriend's death, she first unsuccessfully tried to poison him and then committed suicide in the basement of the building.

Johanna's ghost is seen throughout the building, but it is most often reported on the top floor and in the stairwells, where she will either push or hug people. She is also said to hang out in the Spotlight Room, a secret place in the attic where she allegedly wrote a poem on the wall before committing suicide. Even those who cannot see her apparition can always tell that Johanna is around by the scent of roses.

One of the strangest phenomena attributed to Johanna's ghost is that the turned-off (and unplugged) jukebox sometimes springs to life by playing "The Anniversary Waltz"—despite the fact that the song is not even a selection on the device's menu and the record is not even in the machine.

Bobby Mackey's Music World

In the spring of 1978, musician Bobby Mackey purchased the building, and it has been in operation ever since. Besides operating as a bar, Bobby Mackey's has a stage and a dance floor and has featured performances by many popular country music acts over the years.

Shortly after her husband purchased the building, Janet Mackey was working in the upstairs apartment when she was shoved out of the room toward the stairs while being told to "Get out" by a spirit that she later identified as Alonzo Walling. After that, Janet refused to set foot in the room. So Bobby hired Carl Lawson as a caretaker and allowed him to stay in the upstairs apartment. Upon moving in, Lawson reportedly heard strange noises and saw shadowy figures moving around the bar late at night. Believing that the spirits were coming in through the well in the basement, Lawson threw holy water down the hole. As a result, Lawson claimed that he became possessed and was only able to break free from the demon's grasp after an exorcism was performed on him.

In 1993, a man sued Bobby Mackey's alleging that while he was in the bar's men's room, he was punched and kicked by a "dark-haired apparition" wearing a cowboy hat. The victim stated that he might have angered the ghost because he dared it to appear shortly before being attacked. While the suit was thrown out, it did result

in the now-famous sign that hangs above the front doors of Bobby Mackey's, which alerts guests to the possibility that the building may be haunted and that they are entering at their own risk.

Prime-Time Ghosts

Bobby Mackey repeatedly turned down requests to have his bar investigated; however, in 2008, he allowed the TV show *Ghost Adventures* to film an episode at his nightclub, which yielded some interesting and controversial footage. Among other things, investigators encountered odd cold spots and claimed to have heard the voice of a woman. While using the men's room, investigator Nick Groff also heard banging noises, which startled him so much that he ran out of the restroom without zipping up his pants. The team also captured some odd video of what appeared to be a man in a cowboy hat moving around in the basement.

But the episode will forever be remembered as the one in which overly dramatic ghost hunter Zak Bagans claimed to have been attacked by a demonic entity after challenging the evil forces in the basement. As proof, Bagans proudly displayed three scratch marks on his back. Bagans was so shaken by the event that he proclaimed it to be one of the scariest things he had ever encountered. But that didn't stop *Ghost Adventures* from returning to Bobby Mackey's in 2010.

Investigators spending time at Bobby Mackey's might be a bit disappointed if they don't experience as much paranormal activity as the *Ghost Adventures* team, but that doesn't mean that the place isn't active. For example, when the organization Ghosts of Ohio visited Bobby Mackey's, the investigation seemed uneventful. But when the team members reviewed their audio afterward, they found that a recorder set up near the infamous well picked up a voice clearly saying, "It hurts."

They're Waiting for You

While Bobby Mackey states that he does not believe in ghosts and doesn't think that his bar is haunted, reports of paranormal activity still continue to pour in. So should you ever find yourself sitting at the bar at Bobby Mackey's late at night, make sure you take a look around and keep in mind that just because the barstool next to you appears to be empty, you may not be drinking alone.

The Smurl Incident

*In the 1970s, the "Amityville Horror" story ignited a
firestorm of controversy that's still debated today.
The Smurl haunting is another incident that's
not as well known but is equally divisive.*

Spirit Rumblings

In 1973, Jack and Janet Smurl and their daughters Dawn and
Heather moved into a duplex in West Pittston, Pennsylvania. Jack's
parents occupied half of the home and Jack and Janet took the other.
Nothing out of the ordinary occurred during the first 18 months that
they lived there, but then odd things started to happen: Water pipes
leaked repeatedly, even though they had been soldered and resoldered;
claw marks were found on the bathtub, sink, and woodwork; an
unexplained stain appeared on the carpet; a television burst into
flames; and Dawn saw people floating in her bedroom.

In 1977, Jack and Janet welcomed twin daughters Shannon and
Carin to the family. By then, the family's home had become Spook
Central: Unplugged radios played, drawers opened and closed with
no assistance, toilets flushed on their own, empty porch chairs rocked
back and forth, and putrid smells circulated throughout the house.

Unfortunately, by 1985, events at the Smurl home had taken an
ominous turn. The house was always cold, and Jack's parents often
heard angry voices coming from their son's side of the home, even
though Jack and Janet were not arguing.

In February of that year, Janet was alone in the basement doing
laundry when something called her name several times. A few days
later, she was alone in the kitchen when the room became frigid;
suddenly, a faceless, black, human-shaped form appeared. It then
walked through the wall and was witnessed by Jack's mother.

At this point, the situation began to get even more bizarre. On
the night Heather was confirmed into the Catholic faith, Shannon
was nearly killed when a large light fixture fell from the ceiling and
landed on her. On another night, Janet was violently pulled off the

bed as Jack lay next to her, paralyzed and unable to help his wife as a foul odor nearly suffocated him. Periodically, heavy footsteps were heard in the attic, and rapping and scratching sounds came from the walls. Not even the family dog escaped: It was repeatedly picked up and thrown around.

"Who You Gonna Call?"

Unwilling to be terrorized out of their home, in January 1986, the Smurls contacted psychic researchers and demonologists Ed and Lorraine Warren, who confirmed that the home was possessed by four evil spirits, including a powerful demon. The Warrens theorized that the emotions generated as the older Smurl daughters entered puberty had somehow awoken a dormant demon.

The Warrens tried prayer and playing religious music, but this only angered the demon even more. It spelled out "You filthy bastard. Get out of this house" on a mirror, violently shook drawers, filled the TV set with an eerie white light, and slapped and bit Jack and Janet.

One day, Janet decided to try communicating with the demon on her own. She told it to rap once for "yes" if it was there to harm them; it rapped once. Next, the entity unleashed a new weapon: sexual assault. A red-eyed, green-gummed succubus with an old woman's face and a young woman's body raped Jack. An incubus sexually assaulted Janet, Dawn was nearly raped, and Carin fell seriously ill with an unusual fever. Pig noises—which supposedly signal a serious demonic infestation—emanated from the walls.

The Smurls could not escape even by leaving their home. The creature followed them on camping trips and even bothered Jack at his job, giving new meaning to the phrase "work is hell." The family appealed to the Catholic Church for help but to no avail. However, a renegade clergyman named Robert F. McKenna did try to help the Smurls by performing an exorcism in the spring of 1986, but even that didn't help.

Going Public

Finally, in August 1986, the family went to the media with their story. The incidents continued, but the publicity drew the attention of Paul Kurtz, chairman of the Buffalo-based Committee for the Scientific Investigation of Claims of the Paranormal (CSICOP). He

offered to investigate, but the Smurls turned him down, stating that they wanted to stay with the Warrens and the Church. They were also concerned that CSICOP had already concluded that their story was a hoax.

The Smurls did, however, contact a medium, who came to the same conclusion as the Warrens—that there were four spirits in the home: One she couldn't identify, but she said that the others were an old woman named Abigail, a murderer named Patrick, and a very strong demon.

Another exorcism was performed in the summer of 1986, and that seemed to do the trick because the incidents stopped. But just before Christmas of that year, the black form appeared again, along with the banging noises, foul odors, and other incidents.

Surrender

The Smurls finally moved out of the home in 1988; the next owner said that she never experienced any supernatural events while she lived there.

That same year, *The Haunted,* a book based on the Smurl family's experiences, was released. And in 1991, a TV movie with the same title aired.

But the controversy surrounding the alleged haunting was just beginning. In an article written for *The Skeptical Inquirer,* CSICOP's official magazine, Paul Kurtz cited financial gains from the book deal as a reason to doubt that the incidents were authentic. He also said that for years, residents in the area had complained about foul odors coming from a sewer pipe. He cited other natural explanations for some of the incidents and raised questions about Dawn Smurl's accounts of some of the events. He further claimed that the Warrens gave him a number of conflicting reasons why he couldn't see the video and audio evidence that they said they'd compiled.

And that's where matters stand today, with the true believers in the Smurl family's account on one side and the doubters on the other. Like the Amityville incident, the Smurl haunting is likely to be debated for a long time to come.

Ghosts on the Small Screen

*Fictional ghosts have been television favorites
since the medium's earliest days.*

Topper (1953–1955)

Topper was one of the first TV shows to feature ghosts. Based on a 1937 movie, the show starred Leo G. Carroll as Cosmo Topper, a man who moved into a house haunted by its previous owners, the Kerbys (Robert Sterling and Anne Jeffreys), who perished in an avalanche. Every week, the fun-loving Kerbys—along with the ghost of Neil, the St. Bernard that tried to save them—attempted to bring some joy and humor into Topper's stodgy life.

Tru Calling (2003–2005)

One of the first modern TV series to feature a psychic who could talk to the dead, *Tru Calling* starred Eliza Dushku as morgue worker Tru Davies, who had the ability to relive the previous day so that she could prevent murders and other wrongful deaths.

Ghost Whisperer (2005–2010)

As a child, Melinda Gordon's (Jennifer Love Hewitt) grandmother taught her how to communicate with spirits. As an adult, she used her unique gift to help troubled souls resolve issues from their former lives so that they could move on to the afterlife.

Medium (2005–2011)

Medium featured Patricia Arquette as Allison Dubois—a medium who used her ability to commune with the dead to help the District Attorney of Phoenix solve difficult crimes.

Being Human (2011–????)

Can a ghost, a vampire, and a werewolf get along as roommates? That's the question posed by *Being Human,* a series that features three supernatural twenty-somethings who struggle to keep their dark secrets from the world of the living.

The Hockey Hall of Fame—
Where Legends Live On ... and On and On

The Hockey Hall of Fame in Toronto was created to showcase all things hockey: the best players, games, and coaches. It's no surprise that legends come alive there— it's a place where stars of the sport live on forever. So you probably wouldn't be surprised to find a ghost hanging around its hallowed halls, but you might be surprised to learn that she has absolutely nothing to do with hockey.

Dorothy Who?

Situated on the corner of Yonge and Front Streets in downtown Toronto, the Hockey Hall of Fame resides in a beautiful old building that has the look of a cathedral, complete with a stained-glass dome. Built in 1885, the structure was home to the Bank of Montreal before it closed in 1982; the Hall moved into the building a decade later.

Over the years, there have been many theories regarding the building's resident ghost, Dorothy. As you can imagine, a lot of speculation has surrounded how the young woman died ... and why she stayed. Some thought that she was the victim of a robbery gone wrong. Others thought she was involved in an embezzling scheme and that she took her own life when the crime was uncovered. But most believed she was caught up in a tragic love affair. One version of the tale suggested that her boyfriend left to take "a job on the boats"; another told of her involvement with a married coworker.

In 2009, the *Toronto Star* conducted a thorough investigation of Dorothy and her mysterious demise. With that, the pieces started coming together.

In 1953, 19-year-old Dorothea Mae Elliott was working at the Bank of Montreal as a teller. She was a vivacious brunette, popular with coworkers and customers alike. Orphaned at nine years old, Dorothy didn't let her sad childhood get her down; in fact, friends and coworkers described her as "the most popular girl in the bank" and "the life of the party."

But on March 11, 1953, when Dorothy arrived at the bank, she appeared to be distressed and her clothing was disheveled. It would later be discovered that she had been involved in a romantic liaison with her bank manager—a married man—and when he chose to end the relationship, she was heartbroken. At some point, she discreetly removed the bank's .38-caliber revolver from a drawer and headed to the women's restroom on the second floor. At around 9 A.M., another female employee entered the room and began to scream: Dorothy had shot herself in the head and no one had even heard the gunshot. She died the next morning at a local hospital.

Cold Spots

Over the years, many employees, customers, and other visitors to the building have experienced odd phenomena, all of which have been attributed to Dorothy. Lights turn on and off on their own, and locked doors open by themselves when no one is around. People working in the building late at night have heard mysterious footsteps, and many have reported hearing moans and screams.

One worker who was setting up for an event witnessed a chair spinning around and around until it moved right into his hand. And while performing at an event in the building, harpist Joanna Jordan actually saw Dorothy's ghost along the second-floor ceiling. When she was invited to play there again, Jordan refused to venture onto that floor alone.

So attached was Dorothy to the old bank building that she remained there even after it was taken over by hockey fans and memorabilia. One young boy visiting the Hall also saw Dorothy's apparition; he screamed after glimpsing a woman with long dark hair gliding back and forth through the walls. Isn't there a penalty for that?

"There are some human beings who are dimly aware of their own deaths, yet have chosen to stay on in what used to be their homes, to be close to surroundings they once held dear."

—Hans Holzer

Ghostly Guests Stay for Free at the Hotel del Coronado

If you're like most people, you love to get extras during a hotel stay: Complimentary breakfast, Wi-Fi, and fancy shampoo are all welcome. But how about an extra guest? At the Hotel del Coronado in Coronado, California, you get all the usual amenities plus the chance to share your room with resident ghost Kate Morgan.

Guests and Ghosts

Any building that dates back to 1888 is certainly rich with history, and the Hotel del Coronado is no exception. For more than a century, travelers—many with stories and secrets of their own—have passed through its elegant doors. When it was built, this grandiose structure—which is perched right next to the Pacific Ocean—was the largest building outside of New York City to feature electric lighting. Today, Coronado is a rather affluent town, but in the late 1800s, it was filled with crime and debauchery. "The Del," as the hotel is affectionately known, offered its guests a peaceful escape where they could relax and forget their troubles. The building was named a National Historic Landmark in 1977, and it is still in operation today.

Over the years, the Del became a vacation hot spot for celebrities and politicians. Marilyn Monroe stayed there while filming *Some Like It Hot* (1959), and author L. Frank Baum is said to have written much of *The Wonderful Wizard of Oz* in his room at the famous hotel. In fact, it is believed that the Emerald City was inspired by the Del's architecture. But the hotel's most notable guest may be Kate Morgan—a young woman who checked into the Del in November 1892 . . . and never left.

Many stories have been told about Kate Morgan, but most accounts agree that the 24-year-old woman checked into Room 302 under the alias Lottie Bernard. Strikingly beautiful, she appeared to be either ill or upset, and she had no luggage. She said that she was planning to meet her "brother" for the Thanksgiving holiday, but

several days later, she was found on the hotel steps…with a bullet in her head. Her death was ruled a suicide.

The Background

The story behind the story is that Kate and her husband, Tom, had been staging a bit of a con game. They traveled the rails setting up card games that Tom invariably won. While Kate pretended to be Tom's sister, she flirted shamelessly with men who tried to impress her with their card-playing skills. She was impressed all right—to the tune of hundreds of dollars.

Kate finally tired of the scheming and the traveling, and like other young women her age, she longed to settle down in a home and start a family. For a brief time, Tom and Kate lived in Los Angeles, but Tom grew restless and headed back out on the rails. Shortly thereafter, when Kate discovered that she was pregnant, she made the mistake of telling this joyous news to her husband while on a train to San Diego. They quarreled, and he went on to another city, while she continued to her final destination: the Hotel del Coronado.

Evidence suggests that Kate may have tried to abort her baby by drinking large amounts of quinine. When that didn't work, she traveled across the bay to San Diego, where she purchased a gun and some bullets. Those who saw her reported that she seemed pale and sickly; they weren't surprised when she was found dead.

The Spirited Kate

Guests and employees alike have felt Kate's presence in several places around the Del, including her guest room, the beach, and

some of the hotel shops. One boutique, known as Established in 1888, has been the site of some particularly unusual activity. A display of Marilyn Monroe memorabilia was often targeted—items literally flew off the shelves. Staff members came to the conclusion that Kate was jealous of the famous starlet. When the Marilyn souvenirs were moved to a corner and replaced with mugs, both areas settled down and no more unusual activity was reported.

An apparition dressed in a long black dress has been seen around the shop and in the hallways. And a maintenance man at the hotel reports that there is one light on the property that will never stay lit: It's the one over the steps where Kate's lifeless body was found.

The most notable haunting, however, is in the room where Kate stayed in 1892. The room number has since changed from 302 to 3312, and recently to 3327. Possibly confused as to which room is hers, Kate also seems to make frequent visits to Room 3502, which is thought to be haunted as well. Strange, unexplained events have occurred in both of these rooms. Guests staying in these rooms have reported toilets flushing by themselves, lights flickering on and off, curtains blowing when the windows are closed, and a lingering floral scent. Ashtrays have been seen flying through the air, temperatures mysteriously dip and surge, and televisions blare one minute and are silent the next. Several visitors have also reported seeing a ghostly figure standing by the window of Kate's room, and a strange glow has been observed just inside that window from the outside. The screen on that same window has fallen off mysteriously more than once, and hotel guests have reported hearing soft murmurs inside the room. Is it the ocean...or the sound of a young woman reliving her distress over and over again?

Room 3519 at the Del is also thought to be haunted, perhaps even more intensely than Kate's room. In 1983, a Secret Service agent stayed in Room 3519 while guarding then–Vice President George H.W. Bush. The agent bolted from the room in the middle of the night claiming that he'd heard unearthly gurgling noises and that the entire room seemed to glow.

Remember the Alamo!

While no one knows for certain why ghosts choose particular places to haunt, one explanation suggests that many earthbound spirits are victims of tragedy. One of the greatest tragedies in American history occurred when General Santa Anna's Mexican army slaughtered nearly 200 Texans during the Battle of the Alamo. The tales of those gallant men who refused to give up the mission-turned-fortress still resonate with us today. In fact, it seems as though many of those brave souls haven't left.

Standing Their Ground

By early February 1836, the fledgling government of Texas was in disarray, and its army couldn't muster much in the way of reinforcements. As a result, when Colonel James Bowie, Colonel William Travis, and Davy Crockett arrived in San Antonio, they knew that little help was on the way, so their scant garrison of around 180 soldiers prepared to face a Mexican army of more than 1,800.

General Santa Anna shelled the mission for 12 days before ordering his men to charge. The brave soldiers inside the fort were hopelessly outnumbered, but they fought valiantly, killing or wounding hundreds of Mexican soldiers. The battle was over in less than 90 minutes, and only a handful of the fighting Texans survived (they were later executed), along with the women and children who Santa Anna spared from the slaughter.

Protective Phantoms

Several weeks after the fateful battle took place, Santa Anna ordered his men to raze the Alamo, thus erasing any evidence of the Texans' brave stand. The task fell to Colonel Sanchez, who rode with his men to dismantle the old church. As they set about their task, however, six phantom monks appeared from the walls of the Alamo. The monks, armed with flaming swords, made their demands clear. "Do not touch the walls of the Alamo!" the spirits shrieked. Colonel Sanchez and his men—frightened for their lives and their very

souls—retreated to camp to report to General Andrade. The general was not impressed by the story, so he brought a contingent of soldiers and a cannon back to the mission to finish the job himself. No sooner had he ordered the cannon aimed at the chapel door than the monks appeared again. Armed with their flaming swords and screaming their singular demand, they startled the troops and spooked their horses. General Andrade was thrown from his mount, and when he regained control of his horse, he turned his attention back to the Alamo. It was then that a wall of fire appeared to erupt from the ground, preventing him from getting any closer to the mission. To his further horror, the thick black smoke produced by the fire quickly took the form of a large man with a ball of fire in each of his spectral hands. The general ran and never returned, but this was only the beginning of the Alamo's supernatural history.

Guarding Ghosts

In the years after the Battle of the Alamo, the fort was used as a jail. During this time, newspapers reported sightings of a sentry patrolling the roof. The guard was spotted walking east to west and back again each night; however, the authorities claimed that they'd never stationed a man there. In fact, anyone who bothered to watch the guard for more than a moment noticed that he quickly vanished. Most guards and officers refused to patrol the building at night because they kept hearing horrible moans in the darkness. It sounded as if a soldier's final moments—perhaps being stabbed to

death by bayonet-wielding Mexican soldiers—were being reenacted over and over again each night. The men also reported feeling as though eyes were following them throughout the building. This ominous presence seems to stalk visitors to the Alamo to this day.

Wandering Wraiths

The spirits guarding the Alamo aren't the only specters that make themselves known at the site. Visitors often report seeing a young blond-haired boy in a window over what is now a gift shop. Every year in early March, near the anniversary of the massacre, neighbors say that a horse can be heard galloping on the pavement at dawn; perhaps it's a spectral courier who is still trying to reach Colonel Travis. Artilleryman Anthony Wolfe's young sons, who died at the hands of the Mexican army like their father, are said to go along on the daily tours of the Alamo: Many tour groups have reported seeing the two young boys following them and have noted that the boys vanish when the groups reach the chapel. Park rangers have also seen a man dressed in period clothing; when they followed him across the grounds, he faded from view when he reached the chapel.

Celebrity Specters

Not all the ghosts at the Alamo are unknown figures. One spirit that is often spotted on the grounds wears a buckskin shirt, moccasins, and a coonskin cap. Sometimes he stands at attention, a flintlock rifle at his side; other times he's leaning on a wall near the chapel, dying from his wounds. One ranger even claimed that he got close enough to determine that it was definitely Davy Crockett and that he watched as phantom soldiers in Mexican uniforms attacked the famed frontiersman. Multiple people have even reported seeing Crockett from different vantage points at the same time.

Finally, there's the case of John Wayne, who became obsessed with the old mission while he was directing his epic western *The Alamo* (1960) on location. Since his death in 1979, "The Duke" has been spotted at the Alamo on more than one occasion. He usually just wanders the grounds, but occasionally he is seen conversing with the other restless spirits. If John Wayne did indeed choose to haunt the Alamo, he certainly has plenty of company.

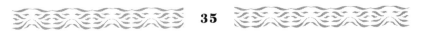

Here Lie the Ghosts of Prisoners Past

There's something about a prison that's a little scary... to most of us, anyway. But add the elements of murder, brutal assault, suicide, and riots, and you have an atmosphere ripe for paranormal activity. Society wanted these hardened criminals to remain behind bars for life, but some are bound there for eternity.

Burlington Prison (Mount Holly, New Jersey)

Architect Robert Mills designed the Burlington Prison to accommodate just 40 convicts when it was built in 1811. Like most other prisons, however, it eventually became overcrowded: By 1965, when it closed, nearly 100 inmates were living there.

The prison is now a museum, and when remodeling began in 1999, ghosts started making their presence known. Not surprisingly, workers weren't too thrilled to be sharing the building with the spirits of the dead, so paranormal investigators were called in to quell their fears. Unfortunately, that strategy backfired when the ghost hunters declared the place to be haunted. Some of the unexplained activity included missing tools showing up in different locations, unusual noises, and two visible ghosts—one in the shower area and another that is thought to be a prisoner who hung himself in a maximum-security cell. Before it closed, Burlington Prison was the oldest operating prison in the United States. Many of the former inmates are still there to welcome visitors—at least in spirit.

Idaho State Penitentiary (Boise, Idaho)

The early inmates at the Idaho State Penitentiary (which opened around 1870) were model prisoners, but by the 1930s, the convicts admitted there were much more violent and cunning. The prison closed in the 1970s due to riots brought on by the prison's pitiful living conditions. Where there is violence, there's also a good chance that spirits will linger behind. It's no surprise that a tremendous feeling of sadness is experienced in the execution chamber, but visitors' reactions to it are unusually strong: Some have become agitated and overcome with a feeling of dread, while others have dissolved into tears and reported feeling physically ill. And then

there are the noises—crying, moaning, and the sounds of guards walking the halls emanate from this facility's walls. The prison, which is now an official historic site, is used as a museum and is open for public tours.

Old City Jail (Charleston, South Carolina)

Before Charleston's city jail was built in 1802, the land on which it stands was designated for public use. Runaway slaves were held at a workhouse there, and the homeless came by for free meals and medical care. The area became less gentrified after the jail was built and hardened criminals and the criminally insane moved in. Over the years, the facility held pirates of the high seas and a great number of slaves who were involved in a revolt in 1822. With its long history and unusual combination of residents, it's no surprise that the Old City Jail has more than a few ghosts hanging around.

One of the specters frequently observed at the jail is an African American male, who probably worked on the premises as a slave. His clothing is ragged and he appears to be carrying a heavy load on his shoulders; he seems oblivious to his living counterparts. But a more violent presence also resides at the jail. Visitors have experienced the sensation that they were being pushed, tugged, or tapped by an unseen force, and many have actually felt physically ill. Today, the Old City Jail building houses the American College of the Building Arts and is an official "Save America's Treasures" project.

Southern Ohio Correctional Facility (Lucasville, Ohio)

One of the worst prison riots in history took place in April 1993 at the Southern Ohio Correctional Facility. For ten days, some 450 prisoners staged an uprising in Cellblock L of this maximum-security prison. In the end, five prisoners were sentenced to death for their roles in the fracas that left nine prisoners and one guard dead. Since then, guards patrolling Cellblock L have reported seeing apparitions in the area. They've also heard doors slam and seen shadows when no one else was around. One guard followed a prisoner who was walking the halls after lockdown, only to watch the man vanish before his very eyes.

The Lemp Mansion: A Favorite Haunt in St. Louis

Enormous success and unspeakable tragedy befell the Lemp family over the course of several generations. Fortunes were made and lives were destroyed, with much of the misfortune centered on the Lemp Mansion. So it comes as no surprise that the home has been listed on at least three "most haunted" lists. Today, the mansion is open to the public as a restaurant and bed-and-breakfast, catering mainly to those who love a good ghost story.

Pursuing the American Dream

Adam Lemp left Germany in 1836 to pursue the American dream. By 1838, he had settled in St. Louis, where he opened a grocery store that sold his homemade beer. Customers flocked to the store to buy his light, crisp lager, which became so popular that Adam opened his own brewery in 1840. By the time Adam Lemp died in 1862, he was a self-made millionaire.

Adam's wealth was passed down to his son William, who built up the brewery and was perhaps the first spirit to reside in the mansion.

The Tragedies Begin

In 1868, William's father-in-law built the house that would come to be known as the Lemp Mansion. William bought the dwelling outright in 1876, and he spared no expense in making it his own, expanding it to 33 rooms and adding an underground tunnel that connected the house to the brewery located just a couple blocks away.

Although William had four sons, his heir apparent was his beloved son Frederick. Hardworking and ambitious, Frederick devoted himself to the family business, but he may have worked himself too hard: In 1901, Frederick died of heart failure at age 28.

William took his son's death hard and was never the same. He kept to himself and lost interest in the brewery, and his health began to decline. Finally, his suffering became unbearable: Shortly after

breakfast on February 13, 1904, William retired to his bedroom and shot himself in the head with a .38-caliber revolver. No suicide note was ever found.

Where There's a Will, There's a Way

William Lemp Jr. succeeded his father as president of the brewery. Will and his wife Lillian spent their money extravagantly. Lillian, who was partial to all things lavender, became known as the "Lavender Lady." The couple had a son, William III, and all seemed right with the world.

But as much as Will liked to show off his beautiful wife, he also desired the company of other women. Wild parties with plenty of beer and "female entertainment" were held in the tunnels.

Allegedly, Will fathered a child during one of his trysts. The boy was said to have been born with Down's syndrome, and it is rumored that Will—perhaps angry that his son was not perfect—kept the boy secluded in the attic of the Lemp Mansion. One St. Louis historian reported that a former nanny and chauffeur both confirmed the existence of this boy, and a psychic claimed to have felt his presence in the attic.

In 1911, Will and Lillian divorced after a long and public trial that caused quite a scandal in town and forced the "Lavender Lady" into seclusion.

Following in Father's Footsteps

In the early 20th century, several independent brewers combined to create competition for the Lemp Brewing Company, which, for the first time in its existence, saw a decline in sales. In 1919, the passage of the 18th Amendment—which prohibited the manufacture, transport, and sale of alcohol in the United States—proved to be the final nail in the coffin for the Lemp Brewing Company, which simply closed its doors one morning.

Fortunately for the Lemp family, the business had been good to them and they were financially secure. But money can't buy happiness, and that was certainly true for the Lemps. On March 20, 1920, Will's sister Elsa—the wealthiest woman in St. Louis after inheriting her share of her father's estate—shot herself with a .38 revolver, just like her father. Once again, no suicide note was found.

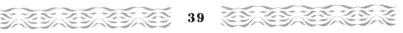

The death of his sister and the loss of the family business proved to be too much for Will to handle. Like his father, he became depressed and withdrawn, and on December 29, 1922, he was found dead in his office, the victim of a self-inflicted gunshot wound to the chest.

With Will gone and his brothers Charles and Edwin involved in their own endeavors, it seemed that the days of the Lemp empire had come to an end. But the specter of tragedy had not left the family just yet.

After Will's death, Charles, a lifelong bachelor, moved into the mansion; he remodeled the home and hired two live-in servants for company. By age 77, Charles was an eccentric and arthritic recluse. Because of the history of the place, his brother Edwin encouraged him to move out of the house, but Charles had developed a morbid attachment to the family home and refused to leave.

Instead, Charles became the fourth member of the Lemp family to take his own life in the mansion. Sometime during the early morning hours of May 10, 1949, he went to the basement and shot his beloved Doberman. Then he went upstairs to his second-floor bedroom and shot himself. He was the only member of the Lemp family to leave a suicide note, in which he wrote, "In case I am found dead, blame it on no one but me."

The Ghosts Come Out

The Lemp family, once so large and prosperous, had been nearly destroyed in less than a century. Only Edwin Lemp remained, and for years, he had shunned the family business and the home that had been the site of so much tragedy for the rest of his family. In 1970, at age 90, he died of natural causes at his secluded estate, Cragwold.

After the death of Charles Lemp, the mansion was sold and turned into a boarding house but with little success. The neighborhood declined and the mansion fell into disrepair; that's when the ghosts came out. The eerie sounds of unexplainable knocks and phantom footsteps sent tenants running, and new ones were hard to find.

In 1975, Dick Pointer and his family bought the Lemp Mansion and converted it into a restaurant and bed-and-breakfast. The Pointers undertook a massive renovation to restore the Victorian beauty of the old house and honor its history.

And that history has certainly made itself known. Throughout the restoration, workers reported strange and eerie incidents: Cold spots, feelings of being watched, odd noises, and missing tools were enough to send more than one worker running.

Now the Pointers embrace the ghosts of the past. People come to see the mansion in its original glory, and the ghosts do not disappoint. The Lemp Mansion has been named one of the ten most haunted houses in America, one of *Life* magazine's ten most haunted places, and Missouri's most haunted house.

Staff members and guests alike report brushes with the paranormal: Toiletries are rearranged, cell phones disappear or ring when no one is on the other end, lights turn on and off by themselves, and doors lock and unlock on their own. Inexplicable sounds and the smell of lavender have also been noted. Visitors have watched as glasses fly though the air, chairs move on their own, and candles ignite by themselves. Ghostly apparitions have also been seen: A face has been spotted looking out from a room in the attic; Charles Lemp and his phantom pooch have been seen; and a ghostly "Lavender Lady" has made appearances as well. One guest awoke to see the specter of a woman standing next to her bed. The ghost raised a finger to her lips, as if asking the sleepy guest not to scream, and then she quickly vanished.

In a 2010 episode of the TV show *Ghost Hunters,* Jason Hawes and Grant Wilson spent the night at the Lemp Mansion to investigate claims of paranormal activity. The investigators witnessed the lights of a K-2 meter (which is used to detect changes in electromagnetic fields) flashing in response to their questions. And then there was the word game. The researchers split up and went to separate rooms, after which Hawes uttered a single word to the spirits and asked them to say that word to Wilson. In his room, Wilson heard the word whispered in his ear. Whether this was a trick, the power of suggestion, or the real deal may never be known, but at the end of the visit, Hawes was ready to declare the house haunted. Wilson wasn't as sure, but he did admit that something "weird" was going on there.

The Pointer family accepts these resident ghosts as part of the character, charm, and ambiance of the historic home, which attracts many visitors hoping to have paranormal encounters. As Paul Pointer (Dick's son) once said, "Fortunately for us, they are rarely disappointed."

Ghosts of Higher Education

Colleges and universities are some of the oldest institutions in America, so it's not surprising that they might harbor ghosts of those who passed through their hallowed halls in times past. College buildings and their surrounding grounds are often home to eternal residents that give new meaning to the term school spirit.

Eastern Illinois University (Charleston, Illinois)

The resident ghost of Eastern Illinois University's Pemberton Hall was a young woman who was brutally raped and murdered there by a school custodian in 1917. Fortunately for current students, the fourth floor—where the crime took place—has been closed off for years, but maintenance workers still report seeing bloody footprints appear and then disappear on that floor. Residents elsewhere in the dormitory have heard piano music coming from the vacant floor above, where the murdered coed is said to play her spirited song.

Harvard University (Cambridge, Massachusetts)

Harvard's Thayer Hall—which was once used as a textile mill—is now inhabited by ghosts of years past. Spirits dressed in Victorian apparel have been seen entering and exiting through doors that no longer exist. Perhaps they're seeking the warmth of the building because they are often seen during the winter months.

Huntingdon College (Montgomery, Alabama)

If you visit Pratt Hall at Huntingdon College in Montgomery, Alabama, you might just encounter the ghost of a young lady named Martha. Better known today as the "Red Lady," Martha left her native New York and enrolled at Huntingdon in the early 1900s because it was her grandmother's alma mater. She was known on campus for her love of red: She decorated her room with red drapes and a red rug, and she often wore red dresses. Lonely and taunted by her peers, Martha killed herself in despair.

She now haunts Pratt Hall (which once housed her dorm), where residents occasionally catch a glimpse of a young lady dressed in red. In recent years, she seems to have gotten bolder, as students have reported cold blasts of air surrounding those who are caught picking on their classmates.

Kenyon College (Gambier, Ohio)

Established in 1824, Kenyon is one of Ohio's most haunted colleges. At least three students who committed suicide in different dormitories now haunt them: One rearranges furniture in Manning Hall; one turns off lights, knocks on doors, and flushes toilets in Lewis Hall; and one roams around Norton Hall late at night. And back when Bolton Dance Studio was known as "The Greenhouse" (so named because of the building's glass roof) and housed the college pool, swimmers would occasionally hear a voice calling out to them. More recently, dancers have seen wet footprints in the studio, heard splashing sounds, and observed showers in the locker room turn on and off when no one is present. These strange occurrences are attributed to the "Greenhouse Ghost," which is thought to be the spirit of a male student who died at the pool in a diving accident during the 1940s.

Luther College (Decorah, Iowa)

The ghost of Gertrude—a Decorah high school student who desperately wanted to attend Luther College back in the days before women students were admitted there—is said to make her presence known at Larsen Hall. Students living there have blamed Gertrude for walking the halls at all hours of the night, sounding the fire alarm, and stealing items—especially modern lingerie—and sometimes leaving behind her own old-fashioned garments. She was killed in 1918 when she was hit by a car while riding her bicycle, ending her collegiate dreams before they even started.

St. Joseph's College (Emmitsburg, Maryland)

In 1810, Mother Elizabeth Seton, a Catholic nun, founded St. Joseph's Academy and Free School for Catholic girls. In 1902, the school became St. Joseph's College until it closed entirely in

1973. Mother Seton was buried on campus and was canonized in 1975. Today, her ghost is often seen gliding through the hallways of the school she knew so well. Observers have seen her walking with the ghost of an unidentified doctor who carries a medical bag, both apparently still searching for suffering souls to heal.

University of Notre Dame (South Bend, Indiana)

The hallowed halls of Notre Dame are home to several ghosts, including Father Edward Sorin, the university's founder, who is said to wander all over the campus, including in the Main Building and near the famous golden dome. Native Americans from the Potawatomi tribe are thought to haunt Columba Hall, which is located between the two campus lakes—on land where they once lived and buried their dead. In addition, Washington Hall is rumored to be the home of a few ghosts, among them a steeplejack who fell to his death in 1886 and Brother Canute Lardner, who died peacefully while watching a movie there in 1946. And then, of course, there's the ghost of George Gipp, Notre Dame's famous football star. Gipp died of pneumonia and strep throat, which he may have contracted after spending the night on Washington Hall's front steps because he stayed out after curfew and was locked out of the dorm. On his deathbed, he allegedly told coach Knute Rockne that when his players need a pep talk, he should tell them to "win one for the Gipper." Since Gipp's death in 1920, students have heard unexplained footsteps, doors slamming, and ghostly music in Washington Hall.

San Jose State University (San Jose, California)

San Jose was one of the U.S. cities where Japanese Americans were told to report for assignment to internment camps during World War II. It was in the old campus gymnasium at San Jose State that these people gathered for processing before they were sent to their new "homes." So it's really no surprise that ghostly voices have been heard crying and speaking in a foreign language at the gym. Students there have also heard footsteps and doors closing when no one else is present.

The Ghosts of Gettysburg

The Battle of Gettysburg holds a unique and tragic place in the annals of American history: It was the turning point of the Civil War and its bloodiest battle. From July 1 through July 3, 1863, the Union and Confederate armies suffered a total of more than 50,000 casualties (dead, wounded, and missing) on the battlefields of Gettysburg, Pennsylvania. All that bloodshed and suffering is said to have permanently stained the town and left it brimming with ghosts. In fact, Gettysburg is often cited as one of the most haunted places in America.

First Ghost Sighting

Few people realize that the first sighting of a ghost at Gettysburg allegedly took place *before* the battle was even over. As the story goes, Union reinforcements from the 20th Maine Infantry were nearing Gettysburg but got lost as they traveled in the dark. As the troops reached a fork in the road, they were greeted by a man wearing a tricornered hat, who was sitting atop a horse; both the man and his horse appeared to be glowing. The man, who bore a striking resemblance to George Washington, motioned for the regiment to follow; believing the man to be a Union general, Colonel Joshua Chamberlain ordered his regiment to do so. Just as Chamberlain began to think that something was odd about the helpful fellow, the man simply vanished.

As the soldiers searched for the spectral stranger, they realized that they'd been led to Little Round Top—the very spot where, the following day, they would repel a Confederate advance in one of the turning points of the battle. To his dying day, Chamberlain, as well as the roughly 100 men who saw the ghostly figure that night, believed that they had been led to Little Round Top by the ghost of George Washington himself.

Pickett's Charge

On the final day of the conflict, Confederate General Robert E. Lee felt the battle slipping away from him, so in what many saw as an act of desperation, he ordered 12,000 Confederate soldiers to

attack the Union forces that were firmly entrenched on Cemetery Ridge. During the attack that is now known as Pickett's Charge, the Confederates slowly and methodically marched across open fields toward the heavily fortified Union lines. The attack failed miserably: More than 6,000 Rebel soldiers were killed or wounded before they retreated. The defeat essentially signaled the beginning of the end of the Civil War.

To this day, it is said that if you stand atop Cemetery Ridge and look out across the field, you might catch a glimpse of row after ghostly row of Confederate soldiers slowly marching toward their doom at the hands of Union troops.

Jennie Wade

While the battle raged near Cemetery Ridge, 20-year-old Mary Virginia "Ginnie" Wade (aka Jennie Wade) was at her sister's house baking bread for the Union troops stationed nearby. Without warning, a stray bullet flew through the house, struck the young woman, and killed her instantly, making her the only civilian known to have died during the Battle of Gettysburg. Visitors to the historic Jennie Wade House often report catching whiffs of freshly baked bread. Jennie's spirit is also felt in the basement, where her body was placed until relatives could bury her. When *Ghost Lab* visited the Jennie Wade House in 2010, phantom footsteps were heard and other audio evidence was captured.

Farnsworth House

Though it is next to impossible to determine who fired the shot that killed Jennie Wade, it is believed that it came from the attic of the nearby Farnsworth House. Currently a bed-and-breakfast, the building was taken over by Confederate sharpshooters during the Battle of Gettysburg. One in particular—the one who may have fired the shot that killed Jennie Wade—is said to have holed up in the building's attic. He didn't survive the battle, but judging by the dozens of bullet holes and scars along the sides of the Farnsworth House, he didn't go down without a fight. Perhaps that's why his ghost still lingers—to let us know what really happened in the Farnsworth attic. Passersby often report looking up

at the attic window that faces the Jennie Wade House and seeing a ghostly figure looking down at them.

But the sharpshooter is just one of many spirits that haunt the Farnsworth House. Paranormal experts claim that the home features no less than 14 ghosts—some are friendly, and some are not. Representing the former, "Mary" sits beside the sick and lingers wherever there's cheering up to be done. Many believe that this compassionate phantom—which is dressed in 19th-century apparel—was a nurse or midwife during her mortal years.

Then there's "Walter"—the antithesis of Mary. Believed to be a Confederate soldier who was jilted by his lover before being killed, Walter's ghost seems determined to exact its revenge on women. Reports state that a female guest was once attacked by an invisible presence. Another time, an unseen force hurled a chair at a female visitor; many blame Walter for both incidents.

Pennsylvania Hall at Gettysburg College
Built in 1832, Gettysburg College stands adjacent to the famous battlefield. During the conflict, some of its buildings served as operating rooms and makeshift morgues. Late one night in the early 1980s, two college administrators, who were working on an upper floor, got on an elevator and pushed the button for the first floor. But the elevator descended past the first floor and continued to the basement. Upon reaching the basement, the elevator doors opened. It didn't take long for the workers to realize that they'd somehow traveled back in time: The familiar surroundings of the basement had been replaced by bloody, screaming Confederate soldiers on stretchers. Doctors stood over the men, desperately trying to save their lives. Blood and gore were everywhere.

As the administrators frantically pushed the elevator buttons, one of the spectral doctors began walking toward them. Without a second to spare, the elevator doors closed just as the ghostly figure reached them. This time, the elevator rose to the first floor and opened its doors, revealing modern furnishings. Despite repeated return visits to the basement, nothing out of the ordinary has ever been reported again.

Are There Different Types of Ghosts?

Yes, there are. The general belief is that there are two main categories of ghosts and that the way a ghost behaves can help determine which type you are dealing with.

Residual Hauntings

One type of ghost is known as a residual, which gets its name from the term *residue,* or the idea that something was left behind. Simply put, a residual ghost is believed to be nothing more than energy that is left behind when someone dies. A residual spirit is often explained using the metaphor of an old movie projector that, over time, stores up enough energy that it switches on, plays a short scene, and then shuts back off. For that reason, residuals can be identified by the fact that they always perform the same actions over and over again, never varying what they do. They do not interact with the living.

A residual ghost is believed to be the result of an activity that an individual executed frequently while he or she was alive or the result of a violent, unexpected death—which may explain why so many battlefields are supposedly haunted. In both cases, the release of energy leaves an imprint on the area. A violent death typically results in a sudden release of energy, while a repeated activity results in smaller, more sustained releases. In both cases, it is believed that the released energy is stored in a specific location and somehow replays itself from time to time. For example, the routine of a man who for 50 years would walk from the dining room onto the porch and smoke a pipe every night after dinner might end up causing enough residual energy to linger after the man passes that the action continues to repeat itself. Similarly, a phantom scream that is consistently heard at the same time of day or night could be the result of a residual spirit reenacting its violent death and its last moments among the living.

48

Intelligent Ghosts

Unlike residuals, intelligent ghosts not only interact with the living, they tend to seek them out—hence the term *intelligent*. And whereas a residual haunting repeats the same action in the same place, intelligent ghosts are free to roam wherever they please. So if you sometimes see a particular ghost late at night in the kitchen and at other times in the attic in broad daylight, you are dealing with an intelligent. These are believed to be the spirits of people who, for whatever reason, simply refused to move on after they passed away. In some cases, it's because they want to remain with the people and places they loved while they were alive; other intelligents seem to have unfinished business on this plane. And since intelligents seem to be aware of the living, they are the ghosts that most often make themselves known to us and to mediums. Unlike residuals, intelligents seem to have the ability to communicate from beyond the grave.

The Black Sheep of the Intelligent Family

Two rather intriguing subcategories of intelligents are demonic entities and poltergeists. Exactly who or what demonic entities are varies depending on your religious beliefs, but they are still defined as intelligents because they appear to understand that the living are nearby. In other words, demonic entities have been known to interact with humans, which means that they are intelligents. The same would be true for nonhuman ghosts, such as those of dogs, cats, and other animals. If spirits acknowledge or interact with the living, they are intelligents.

The categorization of poltergeists is a topic that is hotly debated. Some believe that because humans appear to be the targets of poltergeist activity—such as flying plates and glasses—they are intelligents. But others believe that the flying objects are caused by nothing more than violent releases of energy, which would make poltergeists residual. Finally, some even believe that poltergeist activity is the result of irregular brain waves from the living, which would make them non-ghostly. So for now, the jury is still out on poltergeists.

The Ghosts of Seattle's Pike Place Market

Each year, millions of people visit Seattle's Pike Place Market, which is known for the store where employees toss fish at each other at a dizzying pace. As it turns out, however, human visitors aren't the only ones attracted to the market.

Where Shopping Can Be a Spiritual Experience

Pike Place Market, which opened in August 1907, is one of the oldest farmers' markets in the United States. On its first day in business, more than 10,000 shoppers besieged the eight farmers who had brought their wares to Seattle's waterfront. By year's end, the market's first building was open, and it hasn't looked back since. Perhaps that's a good thing, because looking back might well reveal something else besides shoppers: ghosts.

One of the market's most frequent phantom visitors is Princess Angeline, the daughter of Chief Seattle, who was a leader of the tribes that lived in the area before the arrival of white settlers. By the late 1850s, many Native Americans had left the area due to the terms of a treaty between the tribes and the U.S. government. But Angeline stayed in Seattle and was a familiar figure along the waterfront. She became a local celebrity and was frequently photographed later in life.

Angeline died in 1896 at age 85. So when Pike Place Market was built on the site of her former home, it was like sending out an open invitation for her to hang around for a while, and Angeline has apparently accepted the offer. Her apparition has been spotted at many different locations in the market, but she seems particularly fond of a wooden column on the lower level. Abnormally cold air is said to surround this column, and photographs of it reputedly show things that aren't apparent to the naked eye.

With her braided gray hair, slow way of moving, and habit of browsing, Angeline's ghost easily passes for an elderly shopper. She has often fooled people, who react to her as if she's a fellow consumer until she startles them by vanishing right before their eyes.

Sometimes, Angeline even treats folks to a light show, changing from a glowing white figure to blue, lavender, or pink.

You're Never Alone at Pike Place Market

While Angeline does her best to make as many ghostly appearances at the market as possible, she's not the only spectral spectacle at Pike Place. Workers have heard disembodied lullabies drifting through the air late at night after the market is closed; allegedly, they come from the ghost of a large, heavy-set female barber who used to softly sing her customers to sleep and then pick their pockets while they snoozed. Unfortunately, she was not as good at walking as singing, and one day she fell through a weak floor to her death. Nevertheless, her ethereal song continues, which seems to contradict the saying, "It isn't over until the fat lady sings."

Another spirit that calls Pike Place home is Arthur Goodwin, the market's director from 1918 to 1941. Ever the workaholic, Arthur's silhouette can often be seen looking down at the market from his former office on the upper floor, still keeping an eye on the business.

What's more, a small spectral boy is seen in a craft shop that sells beads. He's been known to open and shut the cash register and tug at sleeves to get attention. At one point during renovations to the store, a small cache of beads was discovered in a wall; it's believed that the ghostly boy was stashing beads there to play with later, as kids often do.

A Specter with a Sweet Tooth

Some more temperamental ghosts have been heard arguing inside the walk-in freezer of a Pike Place deli. A few deli employees simply refuse to go into the freezer because they're afraid of being drawn into whatever disagreement these spirits have with each other.

Other ghostly goings-on occur in a bookshop, where employees—who swear that they're the only ones in the store—sometimes hear footsteps echoing through the aisles. And proving that even a ghost can have a sweet tooth, a candy store at the market has its own resident ghost. On several occasions, employees have put the candy scoops away at night, only to find them back out the next morning.

The next time you're in Seattle, be sure to visit Pike Place Market, and remember that the person standing next to you might just be a visitor from the Other Side.

St. Louis Cemetery Is Number One Among Spirits

In one of the most haunted cities in America, you're bound to find ghosts if you know where to look. And even if you don't, keep in mind that old buildings, new buildings, and cemeteries all attract restless spirits. Among the cemeteries in New Orleans, one is known as the most haunted of them all—St. Louis Cemetery No. 1.

Looking Spooky

When European immigrants first settled in New Orleans, they needed a place to bury their dead. Unfortunately in New Orleans, that isn't as easy as it sounds. The city lies below sea level, so anything buried (i.e., a coffin) eventually pops back up to the surface due to the water level. That's why the city is full of aboveground cemeteries where the dead are encased in tombs or vaults. So instead of the tiny tombstones you see in graveyards in other parts of the country, the cemeteries in New Orleans are full of structures that are large enough to hold a coffin (or several). Those cemeteries are known as "cities of the dead."

Near the French Quarter, you'll find St. Louis Cemetery No. 1. Established in 1789, it's a beautiful place that's full of historical significance . . . and ghosts. In fact, many consider it the most haunted cemetery in the United States.

Just the look of St. Louis Cemetery No. 1 is enough to send a shiver down your spine. That's probably why it has been featured in several Hollywood movies, including *Easy Rider* (1969) and *Interview with the Vampire* (1994).

New Orleans is known for its eclectic mix of cultures, and the variety of burial traditions on display at St. Louis Cemetery No. 1 showcase this. French, Irish, and Spanish settlers are among the earliest people who were buried there, and today, their marble tombs mix with crumbling rocks. The graveyard's narrow rows and winding paths lead to dead ends and confusion.

It's no wonder that visitors report hearing eerie sounds surrounding them in this otherworldly place. Is it the wind? Or is it the sound of spirits filling the air with their weeping and moaning?

Ghostly figures and phantom mists hover near the tombs. Some of the spirits are thought to be well-known people; others are anonymous but no less frightening.

Downcast Spirits

One oft-seen spirit is "Henry," who gave the deed to his tomb to a lady friend to have on hand when he died. Unbeknownst to him, she sold the plot while he was still alive, and upon his death some years later, he was buried in a potter's field. To this day, Henry is seen wandering through the cemetery, perhaps searching for a better place to spend his eternal rest. Some say that he has even asked mourners if there would be room for him in their loved one's tomb.

And if you like animals, St. Louis Cemetery No. 1 is a place to meet a few pets that are quite low maintenance. Ghosts of dogs and cats wander along the rows. All are friendly and are thought to be pets that belonged to a 19th-century groundskeeper. They seem to be looking for their beloved master.

Voodoo Resides Here

The most famous spirit at St. Louis Cemetery No. 1, however, is that of Marie Laveau. Considered the Voodoo Priestess of New Orleans, Laveau died in 1881, but her spirit still haunts these grounds. Some say that she comes alive each year on June 23 (St. John's Eve) to lead her Voodoo followers. Between these periods of resurrection, her spirit is often seen wearing a distinctive red-and-white turban with seven knots. And if you don't happen to spot her ghost, you might just hear her mumbling Voodoo curses. She has also been known to appear in feline form as a huge black cat; you'll recognize this specter by its glowing red eyes.

Those brave enough to approach Laveau's tomb will want to heed this ritual: Make three Xs on the tombstone, turn around three times, and then knock three times on the stone, and your wish will be granted. And whatever you do, be sure to leave an offering—you definitely don't want to anger the Voodoo Priestess.

No Ghostly Groupie for This Celeb

Apparently, celebrities don't intimidate ghosts. Actor Charles S. Dutton has been in more than 80 films and TV shows—including *Rudy* (1993), *Roc*, and *The L Word*—but that didn't matter to one ghostly resident of St. Louis Cemetery No. 1. As Dutton recounted in an episode of *Celebrity Ghost Stories*, he was in New Orleans directing a movie in 2006, when he and his girlfriend decided to visit the old cemetery to look for the grave of Marie Laveau.

After much searching, they found the tomb and were admiring the many offerings in front of it when they noticed that a nearby grave—which was marked "Duplessy 1850"—had been broken open. The casket was pulled out and its lid was open about five inches.

Pure curiosity made them look inside, where they saw a skeleton with a colorful scarf around its neck. Dutton decided to close the coffin and shove it back into the tomb so that it wasn't exposed to the elements. It was getting late by then and his girlfriend pleaded with him to leave, but he kept working.

Suddenly, the couple felt a presence behind them. They turned and saw a raggedly dressed man wearing the same scarf around his neck as the skeleton in the coffin. The two men made eye contact, and Dutton described the moment as feeling as though the man was looking straight through his soul. The man eventually turned around and walked away, but when Dutton tried to follow him, he simply turned a corner and vanished. Dutton was convinced that he and his girlfriend had just met Mr. Duplessy, the man into whose casket they had just peered.

Lincoln Still Lingers at the White House

The Colonial-style mansion at 1600 Pennsylvania Avenue may be America's most famous residence, as well as one of the most haunted. Day and night, visitors and staff members have seen the spirits of past presidents, first ladies, and other former occupants. None of them are more celebrated than Abraham Lincoln, whose spirit is almost as powerful today as it was when he led America through the Civil War.

Two Wartime Leaders Meet

During World War II, the Queen's Bedroom was called the Rose Room. While visiting the White House, Winston Churchill strolled into the Rose Room completely naked and smoking a cigar after taking a bath. It was then that he encountered the ghost of Abraham Lincoln standing in front of the fireplace with one hand on the mantle, staring down at the hearth. Always a quick wit, Churchill said, "Good evening, Mr. President. You seem to have me at a disadvantage."

According to Churchill, Lincoln smiled at him and then vanished. Churchill refused to stay in the Rose Room again, but Lincoln wasn't finished surprising guests.

Lincoln Disturbs the Queen

When Queen Wilhelmina of the Netherlands stayed in the Queen's Bedroom in 1945, she was hoping to get a good night's sleep. Instead, she was awakened by noisy footsteps in the corridor outside her room. Annoyed, she waited for whomever it was to return to his or her room, but the individual stopped at her door and knocked loudly several times. When the queen finally opened the door, she found herself face to face with the specter of Abraham Lincoln. She said that he looked a bit pale but very much alive and was dressed in travel clothes, including a stovepipe hat and coat. The queen gasped, and Lincoln vanished.

Lincoln's ghost may be the most solid-looking and "real" spirit at the White House, and hundreds of people have encountered it. Strangely enough, Lincoln seemed to be in touch with the Other Side even before he died: He once claimed that he saw his own apparition and talked about it often.

Honest Abe Sees His Own Ghost

The morning after Abraham Lincoln was first elected president, he had a premonition about his death. He saw two reflections of himself in a mirror: One image showed how he usually appeared, fit and healthy; in the other, his face was pale and ghostly. Lincoln and his wife believed that the vision predicted that he wouldn't complete his second term in office.

Shortly before his assassination, Lincoln saw his own funeral in a dream. He said that he was in the White House, but it was strangely quiet and filled with mourners. Walking through the halls, he entered the East Room, where, to his horror, he saw a body wrapped in funeral vestments and surrounded by soldiers.

Lincoln said that in his dream, he approached one of the soldiers to find out what had happened. "Who is dead in the White House?" he demanded. "The president," the soldier replied. "He was killed by an assassin!"

A few days later—that fateful day when he attended Ford's Theatre for the last time—President Lincoln called a meeting of his cabinet members. He told them that they would have important news the following morning. He also explained that he'd had a strange dream ... one that he'd had twice before. In it, he saw himself alone and adrift in a boat without oars. That was all he said, and the cabinet members left the president's office with a very uneasy feeling. The next day, they received the news that the president had been assassinated.

Lincoln Never Leaves

Hundreds of people have felt Lincoln's presence in the White House, and many have witnessed his apparition as well, including Eleanor Roosevelt's maid, who saw a spectral Abe sitting on a bed removing his boots. Franklin Roosevelt's valet ran out of the White House after encountering Lincoln's spirit, and Calvin Coolidge's wife saw Abe's face in a window in the Yellow Oval Room.

President Lincoln has been seen in many places in the White House, but he appears most frequently in the Lincoln Bedroom. Although the late president's bed is now in this room, during his lifetime, the space served as the cabinet room in which he signed the Emancipation Proclamation.

Abe's Other Haunts

After his death, Lincoln's body was returned to his home state of Illinois to share a tomb with his sons Edward and Willie, who had preceded him in death. It took five years for a more elaborate tomb to be completed, and during that time, unexplainable things began to occur. Visitors reported seeing Lincoln's spirit roaming the area. And after the monument was erected, people heard sobs and footsteps coming from the spot. Cemetery workers had to move Lincoln's body several times to protect it from grave robbers, and to this day, footsteps and whispers can be heard near his final resting place. Perhaps the "Great Emancipator" wonders if his rest will be disturbed yet again.

Considering Lincoln's sensitivity to the supernatural world, it's not surprising that he would haunt Ford's Theatre, where he was fatally shot. Unfortunately, Lincoln's spirit has to share the stage with the ghost of his killer, John Wilkes Booth, who has also been spotted at the theater making his getaway.

Another hot spot for ghostly sightings of Abraham Lincoln is Fort Monroe in Virginia— a Union stronghold that played a prominent role in the Civil War. Lincoln's specter has been seen there conferring with General Ulysses S. Grant over the Union's wartime strategy.

Abraham Lincoln played a huge role in the history of our country, and his powerful spirit will live on at the White House and in the United States forever—literally and figuratively.

Popping His Top: The Seaford Poltergeist

Poltergeists are the publicity hounds of the spirit world. While other ghosts are content to appear in the shadows and then vanish so that nobody's ever exactly sure what they saw, poltergeist activities are always very flashy and conspicuous. Need furniture rearranged or doors opened or slammed shut? How about knickknacks moved around or plates smashed? If so, just call your neighborhood poltergeist; they love to perform such mischief in plain sight. Poltergeists don't care—they aren't part of the ghostly union. They just enjoy annoying (and scaring) the living.

Pop! Pop! Pop!

The science of investigating poltergeist activity has come a long way since the days when people blamed it all on witchcraft. One of the cases that got folks thinking that there might be more to it was the story of the Seaford Poltergeist.

This entity first made itself known to the Herrmann family of Seaford, Long Island, in early February 1958. Mrs. Herrmann had just welcomed her children Lucille and Jimmy home from school when several bottles in various rooms of the house all popped their tops and spewed their contents all over. The family considered various explanations, such as excess humidity or pressure building up in the bottles, but the tops were all of the twist-off variety. Short of a miniature tornado yanking the tops off, there seemed to be no rational explanation.

After the same thing happened several more times, Mr. Herrmann began to suspect that his son Jimmy—who had an interest in science—was somehow pulling a fast one on

the family. However, after carefully watching the child while the incident happened, Herrmann knew that unless his son was a future Einstein, there was no way that the boy could be responsible. With no "ghost busters" to consult, Mr. Herrmann did the next best thing he could in 1958: He called the police.

Dubious at first, the police launched an investigation after witnessing some of the episodes firsthand. But answers were not forthcoming, and the incidents kept occurring. Even having a priest bless the house and sprinkle holy water in each of its rooms didn't help. An exorcism was considered but rejected because the incidents didn't resemble the work of a demon. Rather, they seemed to be the antics of a poltergeist (a noisy spirit).

Explanation Unknown

Word of the events attracted the attention of the media as well as curiosity seekers. All explanations—from the scientifically sound (sonic booms, strong drafts, freakish magnetic waves) to the weird and wacky (Soviet satellite *Sputnik*)—were considered and dismissed. Although this was the Cold War era, it was unclear how tormenting a single American family fit into the Soviets' dastardly scheme of world domination.

What was far more worrisome was that the incidents seemed to be escalating in violence. Instead of just bottles popping open, objects such as a sugar bowl, a record player, and a heavy bookcase were tossed around. Fortunately, help soon arrived in the form of experts from Duke University's Parapsychology Laboratory. Their theory was that someone in the house was unwittingly moving objects via Recurrent Spontaneous Psychokinesis (RSPK). Children seemed to attract such activity, and the Duke team discovered that Jimmy had been at or near the scene of the incidents most of the time.

When one of the researchers spent time with the boy—playing cards, helping him with his homework, or just talking—the unusual activity declined. Two more incidents occurred in early March before the Seaford Poltergeist apparently packed its bags and moved on. After 67 recorded incidents in five weeks, the lives of the Herrmann family returned to normal. To this day, it is still unknown exactly what caused the strange events in the Herrmann household in early 1958.

Alvin Schwartz's Terrifying Tales

Peruse any bookstore's Young Adult section or any school library in North America and you'll probably locate at least one of Alvin Schwartz's Scary Stories to Tell in the Dark *books. But are they too scary for their own good?*

Building a Book of Frights

When Alvin Schwartz was a kid, he liked all kinds of stories, but he had a particular fondness for being spooked. Years later, he began writing to supplement his family's income. The first books he published were lighthearted reads full of folklore, riddles, and poems. But Schwartz knew that all of us—especially kids—love scary stories; as his writing career developed, the first *Scary Stories* book began to take shape.

The yarns Schwartz wrote were aimed at a young-adult audience and were largely based on traditional tales of fear and the unknown. "The Golden Arm" is a classic scary story that even Mark Twain used to tell when he gave public performances. "The Wendigo" is based on a Native American tale. Schwartz also took inspiration from Shakespeare, the Greeks, classic poetry, and folklore from all corners of the world. At the end of each book, Schwartz included pages of notes and source information, though for most of his juvenile readers, this wasn't necessary.

As scary as these early stories were, Schwartz knew that the level of fear could be kicked up a notch, so he went in search of an illustrator.

Author + Illustrator = AAGGGGHHH!

Artist Stephen Gammell began his career doing commercial free-lance work, but by the 1970s, his interest in illustrating children's books had been piqued. His use of watercolor and other media was unique, and it caught Alvin Schwartz's eye. Gammell wasn't the only artist to work on the first *Scary Stories* book—artists Luis Erique

and Daniel Urena contributed as well—but it was Gammell's aesthetic that shaped the truly terrifying images in the *Scary Stories* books that followed.

Haunting, gruesome depictions of oozing ghouls, rotting corpses, and furious witches filled the pages. No one had seen illustrations like these before—certainly not in the Young Adult section of the library. Kids squealed and screamed with a mix of terror and delight when the first *Scary Stories to Tell in the Dark* was published in 1981. But not everyone was happy.

How Scary Is Too Scary?

As more and more kids brought home *Scary Stories to Tell in the Dark,* more and more parents raised an eyebrow. Plenty of people thought that the books were great; after all, kids were reading, talking about what they were reading, and using their imaginations. But some of the tales and accompanying images were causing problems. *The New York Times* said that the stories were "the stuff nightmares are made of," and, sure enough, plenty of kids were having frightening dreams after reading them.

Some parents, teachers, and child advocacy groups demanded that the books be removed from school libraries, stating that occult overtones could be found in the stories. Some went so far as to say that the books were satanic in tone, while others argued that the themes were simply too dark for children. Either way, the books disappeared from library shelves in many areas of the country. However, the popularity of what Schwartz and the artists had created couldn't be denied: *More Scary Stories to Tell in the Dark* was released in 1984 and *Scary Stories 3: More Tales to Chill Your Bones* followed in 1991. Still, the American Library Association reports that for more than 20 years now, Schwartz's *Scary Stories* books have been among the most challenged titles in libraries across the country.

In 2010, a tamer version of *Scary Stories* was released; it featured illustrations by Brett Helquist that were deemed more "kid-friendly." We'll never know how Schwartz feels about this watered-down version of his collection—he passed away in 1992 at age 64.

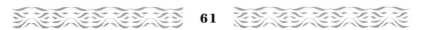

Celebrity Haunts

- *The Oatman Hotel in Oatman, Arizona, hosted newlyweds Clark Gable and Carole Lombard in 1939. Sometimes, in Room 15, guests can hear the happy couple's laughter and conversation, and freshly made beds show the indentations of human forms.*

- *Naturally, John, Lionel, and Ethel Barrymore lived in Beverly Hills. What's more supernatural is that they're still hanging around the Barrymore Estate. Various people have seen and heard their familiar faces and voices.*

- *Entertainer Mitzi Gaynor's Beverly Hills home has a phantom maid, whom Gaynor nicknamed "Mrs. Walker," after the house's former owner. Mrs. Walker is apparently a neat freak that specializes in dusting, especially the chandeliers (two of which the unseen houseguest has knocked down).*

- *Silent-film legend Buster Keaton's spirit still hangs around his old Beverly Hills home. Eternally the prankster, Keaton reportedly likes to switch off lights and disconnect electronic devices. Ironically, in 1921, Keaton starred in a short film titled* The Haunted House.

- *Pickfair—once the Beverly Hills domicile of film stars Mary Pickford and Douglas Fairbanks—was haunted by a phantom woman that carried sheet music up the stairs. And although her beloved home has been demolished, Pickford's spirit wanders around the structure that now occupies the site.*

- *Actress Susan Strasberg became a believer in the paranormal while living in a haunted house in Beverly Hills. She even summoned mediums and clergy in an unsuccessful campaign to identify the female spirit that resided in an upstairs bedroom.*

- *Talented actor and dancer Clifton Webb, whose movie career extended from the silent era to the early 1960s, stuck around his Beverly Hills home for some years after his death in 1966. He often made his presence known when someone was smoking, a habit that Webb despised. After a 1968 séance, Webb stopped haunting the place.*

- On June 20, 1947, at the Beverly Hills home of his girlfriend Virginia Hill, mobster Bugsy Siegel was killed in a volley of gunfire, presumably by his fellow mobsters. Even today, people can feel a terrified presence seeking cover in the house.

- The Brentwood home of actress Joan Crawford was allegedly so haunted that "Mommie Dearest" summoned a minister to exorcise the ghosts, an effort repeated by several subsequent owners. The unwanted presence may have finally taken the hint because by 2000, the haunting seemed to have petered out.

- Robin Givens owned a bungalow that was once leased by John Lennon. According to the actress, Lennon's spirit appeared now and then at his old pad. But she didn't mind—he seemed friendly and she liked to listen to his phantom singing.

- Hollywood Forever Cemetery has a plethora of phantom residents, including actor Clifton Webb, silent film star Virginia Rappe, and the original "Latin Lover," Rudolph Valentino.

- The Hollywood Roosevelt Hotel has been the location of sightings of many spectral stars, including Carole Lombard (who spent time there with Clark Gable), Montgomery Clift, and Marilyn Monroe, who likes to check out her phantom figure in the lobby's mirror.

- In September 1932, actress Peg Entwistle climbed to the top of the Hollywood sign's H and leaped to her death. Since then, a despondent blonde in 1930s-era clothing has been spotted there on numerous occasions.

- The ghost of actor Victor Kilian roams the sidewalk outside Grauman's Chinese Theatre. In 1979, burglars murdered the 88-year-old actor in his apartment near the famed venue.

- For many years, Ozzie and Harriet Nelson lived on Camino Palmero Road in the Hollywood Hills. Ozzie's ghost has been spotted there in recent years and may be responsible for phenomena such as disembodied footsteps, doors opening and closing on their own, and faucets and lights turning on and off by themselves.

The Watseka Wonder: A Tale of Possession

Spiritual possession—in which a person's body is taken over by the spirit of another—is easy to fake, and legitimate cases are incredibly rare. One of the most widely publicized possessions occurred in Watseka, Illinois, in the late 1870s, when the spirit of Mary Roff, a girl who had died 12 years earlier, inhabited the body of 13-year-old Lurancy Vennum. This astounding case became known as the "Watseka Wonder."

A Troubled Life

In 1865, Mary Roff was just 18 years old when she died in an insane asylum following a lifelong illness that tormented her with frequent fits, seizures, and strange voices in her head. She'd also developed an obsession with bloodletting and would apply leeches to her body, poke herself with pins, and cut herself with razors. Doctors thought that Mary was mentally ill, but others—including her own family—came to believe that her problems were supernatural in origin.

At the time of Mary Roff's death, Lurancy Vennum was barely a year old. Born on April 16, 1864, Lurancy moved with her family to Watseka a few years after Mary Roff's death and knew nothing of the girl or her family.

In July 1877, about 12 years after Mary passed away, Lurancy started to exhibit symptoms similar to Mary's, including uncontrollable seizures. Her speech became garbled, and she often spoke in a strange language. She sometimes fell into trances, assumed different personalities, and claimed to see spirits, many of which terrified her.

The townspeople of Watseka didn't know what to make of Lurancy. Many thought that she was insane and should be committed, as Mary had been. But the Roffs, who had become ardent Spiritualists as a result of their daughter's troubles, believed that unseen forces were tormenting Lurancy. They felt that she was not insane but rather was possessed by the spirits of the dead. With the permission of Lurancy's parents, Asa Roff—Mary's father—met with the young girl in the company of Dr. E. Winchester Stevens, who was also a

Spiritualist. During their visit, a friendly spirit spoke to Lurancy and asked to take control of her body to protect her from sinister forces. That spirit was Mary Roff.

Sent to Heaven

After Mary took possession of Lurancy's body, she explained that Lurancy was ill and needed to return to heaven to be cured. Mary said that she would remain in Lurancy's body until sometime in May. Over the next few months, it seemed apparent that Mary's spirit was indeed in control of Lurancy's body. She looked the same, but she knew nothing about the Vennum family or her life as Lurancy. Instead, she had intimate knowledge of the Roffs, and she acted as though *they* were her family. Although she treated the Vennums politely, they were essentially strangers to her.

In February 1878, Lurancy/Mary asked to go live with her parents—the Roffs. The Vennums reluctantly consented. On the way to the Roff home, as they traveled past the house where they'd lived when Mary was alive, Lurancy wanted to know why they weren't stopping. The Roffs explained that they'd moved to a new home a few years back, which was something that Lurancy/Mary would not have known. Lurancy/Mary spent several months living in the Roff home, where she identified objects and people that Lurancy could not have known.

On one occasion, Lurancy sat down at the Roff's family piano and began to play, singing the same songs Mary had sung in her youth. One member of the Roff family commented, "As we stood listening, the familiar [songs] were hers, though emanating from another's lips."

Once word spread of Lurancy's spiritual possession, interested people started to visit. Lurancy/Mary typically met them in the Roffs' front parlor, where she frequently demonstrated knowledge of events that had transpired long before Lurancy was even born.

During one encounter with a Mrs. Sherman, Mary was asked about the people she had met in the afterlife. Immediately, Mary started listing the names of some of Mrs. Sherman's deceased family members, as well as several of Mrs. Sherman's neighbors who had died. Again, this was information that Lurancy could not possibly have known.

Scene at a Séance

In April 1878, during a séance that was held in the Roff home and attended by several people (including Dr. Stevens), one member of the group became possessed by the spirit of another member's dead brother, who addressed the gathering. After the spirit had left the man's body, Mary removed herself from Lurancy's body (which immediately lolled over against the person next to her, as if dead) and possessed the body of a participant named Dr. Steel. Through him, Mary proved to everyone present that it was indeed her. She then abandoned Dr. Steel's body and reentered Lurancy's.

Going Home

Mary permanently left Lurancy's body on May 21, 1878. When Lurancy awoke from her trance, she was no longer afflicted by the numerous problems that had previously plagued her, nor did she have any recollection of being spiritually possessed by Mary. By all accounts, she came away from the experience a healthy young lady. Indeed, Lurancy grew to be a happy woman and exhibited no ill effects from the possession. She went on to marry and have 13 children.

But Mary didn't abandon Lurancy completely. According to some sources, Lurancy kept in touch with the Roff family, with whom she felt a strange closeness, although she had no idea why. She would visit with them once a year and allow Mary's spirit to possess her briefly, just like it did in the late 1870s.

The story of the Watseka Wonder still stands as one of the most authentic cases of spirit possession in history. It has been investigated, dissected, and ridiculed, but to this day, no clear scientific explanation has ever been offered.

"The boundaries which divide life from death are at best shadowy and vague. Who shall say where the one ends and the other begins."
—Edgar Allan Poe, "The Premature Burial"

Will Your Memories Live on Forever?

Suppose that our experiences are recorded and remembered within our ethereal beings, thus influencing our personalities and habits. So if someone receives an organ transplant, is he or she unknowingly influenced—or haunted—by the donor's feelings and memories? Those who support the theory of cellular memory believe so.

The idea that people can gain traits by absorbing the organs of others is nothing new. Ancient warriors regularly ate the hearts of vanquished enemies to capture the essence of their strength, and many cultures have long encouraged the consumption of various organs for increased intelligence (brains) or sexual prowess (bull testicles, anyone?). Is it so odd then that receiving a person's organs would cause the recipient to pick up on certain memories and personality traits as well?

Perhaps it's a stretch to say that a person who receives a cornea transplant from a murderer will begin to see the world through a killer's eyes, but the topic has come up in many films and books. Hollywood even gave the concept a romantic spin in *Return to Me* (2000), in which David Duchovny's character coincidentally falls in love with the woman (Minnie Driver) who received his dead wife's heart.

Some believe that a person may be haunted by new emotions, cravings, and memories after receiving an organ transplant. In 1988, Claire Sylvia received a heart-and-lung transplant from the organs of an 18-year-old man who had died in a motorcycle crash. She attributed her sudden desire for green peppers and beer to his hankerings coming back to life. In her book *A Change of Heart*, Sylvia described her experience and explained the mysterious situation by quoting spiritual medium James Van Praagh, who said, "Donated organs often come from young people…who died quickly…. There may be things that your donor hadn't completed in the physical world, which his spirit still wanted to experience."

Hopefully those desires won't lead to trouble: Juries aren't too keen on, "But the dead serial killer's liver made me do it!" as an excuse for murder.

Haunted Hospitals Have Tales to Tell

*If they could speak, hospitals would have incredible stories
to tell. Within their walls, lives are saved and lives are lost.
People undergo surgeries, heal from injuries, and some simply
never leave. Doctors and nurses have personal dramas and
patients have near-death experiences, so it's not surprising
that hospitals are among the most haunted places you'll find.*

Carrie Tingley Children's Hospital (Albuquerque, New Mexico)

Originally established in the city of Truth or Consequences, New
Mexico, Carrie Tingley Children's Hospital was founded in 1937 to
help kids suffering from polio. It was later moved to Albuquerque,
where it became affiliated with the University of New Mexico
Medical Center. Some unused areas of the hospital are said to have
invisible force fields that sometimes prevent people from moving
through certain doorways or halls. Employees know to listen for a
telltale hissing sound that is heard just before a barrier is encountered. Glowing rooms, disembodied voices, and phantom heart-
beats and sobbing are all elements of the haunting there.

Doctors Hospital (Perry Heights, Ohio)

You'd expect former patients to be the spirits haunting a hospital,
but the ghost of a former nurse's aide also wanders Doctors
Hospital, humming just the way she used to in life. An elderly
woman who died there also reportedly haunts the room in which
she died. After she passed in the late 20th century, patients felt
cold spots in the room and even had their blankets pulled off of
them. The room was eventually sealed off and was no longer in
use when the hospital closed its doors in 2008.

The Ohio Exploration Society, which investigates the
paranormal, visited the hospital in March 2010. They tried to
record electronic voice phenomena (EVPs) in the patient's room
without success, but that doesn't mean all was quiet: The group
did manage to capture an unexplained voice in the hospital lab.

Linda Vista Community Hospital (Los Angeles, California)

A hospital with too many unexplained deaths sounds like the perfect place to find a ghost or two. Linda Vista, which was built in 1904, is now closed and is said to be haunted by both patients and staff. Elevators start and stop by themselves; a green light glows faintly throughout the night and other lights flicker on and off; moans and screams have been heard; the image of a doctor has been observed in an upper window; and on the third floor, unexplained foul odors can often be smelled. Visitors also report seeing a spectral girl playing outside and hearing her laugh.

Apparently Hollywood types don't scare too easily: The building has been used in movies, music videos, and commercials, as well as the pilot episode of NBC's long-running hospital drama *ER* (1994).

Madison Civil War Hospital (Madison, Georgia)

When the Madison Civil War Hospital served as a military medical facility, it certainly saw its share of sick and injured soldiers ... and death. Although it's no longer in use, the building still has some life in it—afterlife, that is. Paranormal investigators have heard phantom footsteps in an empty stairwell and rustling sounds in a seemingly unoccupied basement; they've also seen a ball bouncing down a hallway by itself. In addition, ghost hunters have witnessed a number of strange spirits there, including a man dressed in black who was spotted at the top of the stairs and a woman in a blue gown who lingers in one particular room.

Plymouth County Hospital (Hanson, Massachusetts)

In the early part of the 20th century, the Hanson Tuberculosis Hospital opened to treat terminally ill TB patients from the Boston area. When the tuberculosis epidemic died down, it became Plymouth County Hospital, and in 1992, its doors were closed for good. Since then, ghost stories involving the place have run rampant. A hospital such as this one surely saw its share of death, so it's no surprise that an eerie feeling is associated with the property. People have reported feeling like they are being watched, and odd noises—mostly screams and laughter—have been reported coming from within.

Chicago's Oriental Theatre Is Never Completely Empty

When Chicago's Iroquois Theatre opened for business, one patron is known to have described the place as "a death trap." However, according to records, the building was fully in compliance with the fire code, and advertisements billed it as "absolutely fireproof." Nevertheless, the patron's description would prove prophetic.

False Advertising

When the Iroquois Theatre opened in November 1903, it was easy to feel safe while sitting underneath its ornate, 60-foot-high ceiling and among its white marbled walls and grand staircases. But, unbeknownst to patrons, when the theater was under construction, its owners had cut corners to open in time for the 1903 holiday season.

In retrospect, it's easy to wonder if the owners of the Iroquois were purposely inviting trouble. After all, they had declined to install sprinkler systems, and not all of the fire escapes were completed when the theater opened. In addition, exit signs were either missing or obscured by thick drapes, there were no backstage phones or fire buckets, and no fire alarm system was in place; in fact, the only fire-fighting equipment in the theater was a few canisters of a chemical product called Kilfyre. The owners had even skimped on the stage's safety curtain: Instead of using fireproof asbestos to make it, the owners saved about $50 by having the builders use a blend of asbestos, cotton, and wood pulp. But at the time, it was not uncommon for building inspectors and city officials to accept bribes to look the other way as builders ignored one safety law after another.

"A Death Trap"

On December 30, barely a month after the theater opened, vaudeville star Eddie Foy and his company were onstage performing the musical *Mr. Blue Beard* to a standing-room-only crowd that was estimated to be around 2,000 people—a few hundred more than the theater could safely hold.

At the beginning of the second act, a calcium light arced and sent a spark onto a muslin drape on a wall near the stage. The orchestra stopped playing, but Foy urged the audience to remain calm and stay in their seats. Even after the flames jumped to pieces of scenery that were hanging in the rafters—most of which were painted with highly flammable oil-based paint—Foy stayed onstage and begged the audience to remain calm and exit the theater in an orderly fashion. But Foy was no fool: He knew that when the scenery in the rafters caught fire, the situation was going to get a lot worse.

Above and behind him, the fire spread quickly, and the cast and crew dashed for a backstage exit. Lighting gear jammed the fire curtain after it dropped only a few feet, which left the audience fully exposed to the flames on the stage.

Unbeknownst to the performers who scrambled to open the back door, the owners had ordered the ventilation system nailed shut. This kept the cold December air from getting inside, but it also effectively turned the building into a gigantic chimney. The minute the door was opened, a back draft turned the flames on stage into what audience members described as a "balloon of fire." This massive fireball shot through the auditorium, incinerating some people right where they stood.

Naturally, the crowd panicked and ran for the fire exits, which the owners had locked to keep people from sneaking into the theater without paying. Those who weren't trampled trying to reach the fire exits ran for the front doors, hoping to rush out onto Randolph Street. But the doors opened in toward the lobby, not out toward the street, so rather than escaping through the doors, the people crashed *into* them, and then into each other. More people died from being crushed in the melee than from burns or smoke inhalation.

Meanwhile, the only hallway that led downstairs from the balcony was blocked by a metal accordion gate—which was placed there to keep people from sneaking into better seats—effectively trapping the unfortunate people in the upper reaches of the burning building. Some tried to jump from the balcony to escape; others opened the balcony's fire exit, which was miraculously kept unlocked. However, by the time those who opened the door realized that there *was* no fire escape behind the door, the crowd was pushing too hard for them to turn back: They were shoved out the door and dropped nearly

60 feet into the alley below. By the time the situation had calmed down, more than a hundred people had fallen to their demise in what newspapers called "Death Alley."

In the Wake of Tragedy

The exact number of lives lost in the Iroquois Theatre fire is uncertain. Around 600 people are known to have perished—which is twice as many as died in the Great Chicago Fire—but the actual number is probably much higher because some families picked up their dead before they could be counted. To this day, the fire at the Iroquois Theatre is the deadliest single-building fire in U.S. history. But on the positive side, steel fire curtains, clearly marked exits, and exit doors that swing out toward the street are all provisions that were mandated because of the Iroquois tragedy.

Following the incident, a number of city officials were brought to trial for gross negligence, but they all got off on technicalities. The only people ever successfully prosecuted for crimes surrounding the Iroquois fire were a few of the crooks who broke into the theater to shimmy rings off fingers, yank necklaces from necks, and dig money out of the pockets of the deceased (and the vast majority of these people were never prosecuted, either).

The Building May Be Gone, But the Ghosts Remain

Ghost sightings at the Iroquois Theatre began before the flames had even stopped smoldering: Photographs taken of the ruined auditorium shortly after the fire contain strange blobs of light and mist that some believe are the spirits of the unfortunate victims.

The theater was soon repaired and reopened, and it operated under various names for another 20 years before it was torn down. In its place, a new venue—the Oriental Theatre—was erected in 1926. For years, it was one of Chicago's premier movie theaters until it fell on hard times in the 1970s, when it mainly played kung fu movies. The Oriental Theatre finally shut its doors in 1981, and it seemed as though the Iroquois and its tragic tale had faded into Chicago's history.

But since 1998, when the Oriental Theatre reopened to host touring Broadway shows, employees have found that the ghosts have stuck around. During rehearsals, spectators are frequently seen in

the balcony seats. When staff members are sent to ask them to leave, they find the balcony empty.

Many people who work in the building have reported seeing the specter of a woman in a tutu. This is thought to be the ghost of Nellie Reed, an aerialist who was in position high above the audience when the fire broke out. Although she was rescued from her perch, she suffered severe burns and died a few days later.

Other actors and crew members have encountered the ghost of a young girl who makes her presence known by giggling and flushing one of the toilets backstage. Her happy laugh has been picked up on audio recorders on more than one occasion and can often be heard in the hallways next to the main auditorium.

Staff members who work late at night, after all of the theatergoers have left the building, have reported seeing shadowy blobs that they call "soft shapes." These mysterious forms are seen zipping through the empty auditorium toward the places where the fire exits would have been in 1903.

And the ghosts in the theater may not only be spirits from the fire; female staff members have reportedly been harassed and threatened by a strange male voice in one of the sub-basements located far below the street. Historians suggest that this ghost may be from the 19th century, when the section of Randolph Street where the theater now stands was known as "Hairtrigger Block" and was home to the rowdiest gambling parlors in town.

Sometimes, when a building is torn down, its ghosts seem to go away. But other times, as seems to be the case with the Iroquois Theatre, they only get louder and more active.

"It struck me as I looked out over the crowd during the first act that I had never before seen so many women and children in the audience."
—Actor/comedian Eddie Foy, who witnessed the Iroquois fire firsthand

Hot Springs and Cool Spirits Fill the Banff Springs Hotel

Surrounded by majestic mountains and the healing waters of natural hot springs, the Banff Springs Hotel in Alberta, Canada, attracts many visitors... but not everyone staying at the hotel is among the living.

In the late 19th century, William Van Horne, general manager of the Canadian Pacific Railway, decided to take advantage of the railroads' westward expansion by building a 250-room luxury hotel tucked away in the dense forest of the Canadian Rockies. The inn was a success, but in 1926, it was partially destroyed by a devastating fire. When it was rebuilt, the hotel took on the look of a Scottish castle: The stone walls and grand towers added a touch of class and mystery that was missing from the first building. This time, the hotel became even more successful, and due to its isolated location, it attracted royalty and celebrities who often referred to it as the "Castle of the Rockies."

The Secret Room

During the renovation, construction workers were surprised to discover a secret room that did not appear on any map of the hotel. It resembled a regular guest room, except that it had no windows or doors. This mysterious room is thought to have been an architectural error that was sealed off—and removed from blueprints—to cover up the mistake. Although the room was empty when it was discovered, many people who had experienced unusual phenomena—such as strange noises and apparitions—along a nearby corridor suspected that perhaps something about this odd room could be the cause. Did something sinister happen inside the room? Were spirits using it as a portal to the Other Side?

Regardless of the secret room's purpose, many ghosts call the Banff Springs Hotel home. But that doesn't seem to keep guests away. The hotel now boasts 778 rooms, several restaurants, a spa,

a gift shop, and a golf course. But even with all those amenities, a number of guests still come just to hunt for ghosts.

Sam the Bell-Ghost

One of the Banff Springs Hotel's friendly spirits is that of Sam McCauley, a Scottish immigrant who, for many years, worked there as a bellhop. He so loved the hotel and his job there that he told coworkers he hoped to stay and haunt the place after he died. And it seems that he may have gotten his wish. When Sam was asked to retire in the late 1970s, he became so distraught that he died soon after.

Since then, Sam's spirit has been spotted all around the hotel. Shortly after his death, two female guests were locked out of their room. They asked someone to call the front desk for help, but by the time a hotel employee arrived, the women were already in their room; they said that a friendly bellhop with white hair unlocked their door. After that, "Sam" sightings became commonplace at the Banff Springs Hotel. Some guests have reported seeing him in the hallways, while others have said that he let them into their rooms or carried their luggage. And invariably, when guests reach into their wallets to give him a tip, the kindly bellhop simply vanishes.

The Ghost of Weddings Past

Sam is not the only spirit to inhabit this old hotel. Another ghost that is seen there quite often is that of a bride who was planning to get married at the hotel shortly after it was remodeled. Because it

happened so long ago, records of what happened to the poor bride
no longer exist, and sources vary regarding the details. Some say that
she was descending the grand staircase when her feet became
tangled in the long flowing train of her gown, causing her to trip and
fall down the stairs to her death. Another says that the staircase was
accented with lit candles and her dress caught on fire; in a panic,
she tried to put out the fire and fell down the stairs in the process.
Regardless, guests and staff members have heard strange noises
coming from the bridal suite when it's empty. Many have glimpsed
the bride dancing alone in the ballroom, and others have seen her
descending the staircase; as they watch, her dress catches on fire, and
then she suddenly disappears.

Room 873

Yet another spirit at the Banff Springs Hotel is associated with a
slightly more terrifying tale. Rumors say that a family was murdered
in Room 873. However, a story like this is not so good for business,
so the room was eventually sealed up after guests reported seeing a
child's fingerprints on the mirrors. What's so frightening about that?
Well, after they were cleaned off, they mysteriously—and immediately—reappeared. Visitors have also reported seeing
apparitions of this poor family strolling through the halls.

If these ghosts aren't enough to pique your interest, you might
want to watch out for several other spirits that have been reported on
the property. One is a bagpiper that plays melancholy tunes for the
guests. You'll certainly know him when you see him because he has
no head.

And then there's the helpful bartender in the Rob Roy Dining
Room. Concerned about his customers' safety—and possibly their
potential embarrassment—he's not afraid to tell them when they've
had a bit too much to drink.

Unlike some other hotels that use their ghostly visitors to attract
curious guests, the Banff Springs Hotel does not promote the
possibility of paranormal activity within its walls. But judging by
the tales told by former guests and staff members, it's hard to deny
that something is going on there. You might just have to check it out
for yourself.

The Haunted Toy Store

The ghost at a California Toys"R"Us is just as playful as the customers.

With a cheerful name like Sunnyvale, this mid-sized town in California's Silicon Valley may seem like an odd place for a haunting, but odder still is the location being haunted: a popular Toys"R"Us store. And yet, according to employees, something unseen routinely wreaks havoc there after the staff has left for the night.

Indeed, the actions of the mischievous spirit seem almost like things that a spoiled child would do: Books are tossed on the floor, and roller skates are scattered everywhere, even though everything was put away when employees locked up the night before.

Sometimes the ghost gets more personal. More than one employee has reported being tapped on the shoulder only to find no one there, and several female employees have complained of feeling unseen hands stroke their hair. Then there was the time that a group of employees, including a manager, rolled down a metal door in the store and then heard someone yelling and pounding from the other side. When they rolled the door back up, no one was there.

Psychic Encounter

In 1978, renowned psychic Sylvia Brown visited the store, intent on identifying the silly spook. Brown said that she saw a tall, thin man wearing a coat and that his name was Johnny Johnson. During their chat, Johnny informed Brown that she should move or her feet would get wet. An examination of county records later revealed that there had once been a well where Brown had been standing.

The store has done nothing to get rid of Johnny Johnson's spirit. In fact, most of the employees are fond—even protective—of him, and very few say that they feel scared or threatened. And whether he's just a little clumsy or he simply wants to have fun, it seems that he's in the right place. After all, what better place is there to have some fun than at a toy store?

Haunted Restaurants

Choosing a place to dine is never simple. What type of cuisine? Formal or informal? What type of spirits? And speaking of spirits: Do you want fully apparitional ghosts or invisible entities? In many restaurants across America, the question isn't whether to dine with a ghost or be haunt-free, but rather how many ghosts might join the meal.

Country Tavern (Nashua, New Hampshire)

In 1741, a merchant-ship owner known to history only as Captain Ford built a farmhouse for himself and his young wife Elizabeth. His business often took him away from home for long periods of time; however, after one trip that lasted for about a year, Ford returned home to discover that Elizabeth had recently given birth to a baby girl. Furious, he locked Elizabeth in a closet and killed the infant. After he released Elizabeth from captivity, he stabbed her. Ford buried the baby in the yard and dumped his wife's body in a well.

In the early 1980s, when the Country Tavern opened in the old farmhouse, the ghost of Elizabeth—who had been seen on the grounds of her former abode many times since her death—made herself at home: A blonde woman in a white Colonial-style dress with blue ribbons has been spotted in the quaint establishment's dining rooms, kitchen, and women's restroom. Elizabeth isn't shy, either. Sometimes she moves plates—even while diners are still eating off of them. She also likes to play with female patrons' hair and tinker with small items. Visitors have also noticed Elizabeth peering through a window in an adjacent barn. Elizabeth is the primary ghost at the Country Tavern, but on occasion, people have also heard a baby's faint cry.

Arnaud's (New Orleans, Louisiana)

In 1918, Arnaud Casenave—a French wine salesman—opened a restaurant in the heart of New Orleans; it's been a family-owned center of fine dining in the Crescent City ever since, but it's not without its ghosts. The specter of a man dressed in an old-fashioned

tuxedo is often spotted near the windows of the main dining room; this ghost is believed to be none other than Arnaud himself, still watching over his beloved restaurant. A spectral woman has also been seen walking out of the restroom and moving silently down the hall before disappearing into a wall.

Old Bermuda Inn (Staten Island, New York)

When Martha Mesereau's husband was away fighting in the Civil War, she lit a candle every night and sat by her bedroom window, waiting for his safe return. When she learned that her husband had died in battle, Martha locked herself in her room and died of a broken heart. But she still makes her presence known at her former home, which is now the Old Bermuda Inn—a banquet hall and bed-and-breakfast. Moving cold spots permeate the building, and locked doors open on their own. Staff members have also heard Martha crying. In recent years, when the building was undergoing renovations, a portrait of Martha spontaneously burst into flames in the hallway; perhaps she was showing her disapproval of the changes being made to her house. Diners have seen a woman resembling Martha walk through the dining room, and others have seen her sitting in the window, just like she did in life while waiting for her husband's return.

Poogan's Porch (Charleston, South Carolina)

In 2003, the Travel Channel voted Poogan's Porch the "Third Most Haunted Place in America." Staff members and guests have seen a woman in a long black dress disappear in front of their eyes. The same woman has been sighted waving from a second story window; she is believed to be the ghost of Zoe St. Amand, a former school-teacher who lived in the building until the 1950s. Then there's the ghost of the restaurant's namesake: Poogan was a stray dog that wandered the neighborhood begging for scraps. While the restaurant was being renovated in the 1970s, he liked to hang out on the porch to watch. The lovable mutt died in 1979, but people relaxing on the porch have felt an animal rub against their legs even though no creature was there. Not many restaurants can claim a resident ghost dog.

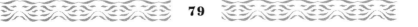

Testimony from the Other Side

*When Zona Heaster Shue of Greenbrier County, West Virginia,
died suddenly at age 23, her doctor attributed her passing
to natural causes. But when Zona's mother encountered
her ghost, a shocking tale of murder was revealed. Would
testimony from the Other Side help to nab Zona's killer?*

Gone Too Soon

On January 23, 1897, a boy who was doing chores at the Shue home
discovered Zona's limp body lying at the bottom of the stairs. He
ran to tell her husband—Edward Stribbling "Trout" Shue—and then
he summoned a doctor. When Dr. George W. Knapp arrived, Shue
escorted him to the bedroom where he'd moved Zona's lifeless body.
Although Shue had already dressed Zona for burial, Knapp examined
her body. As the doctor went about his duties, Shue became notice-
ably distressed, so Knapp cut the examination short. Suspecting
natural causes as the reason for Zona's passing and not wishing to
upset her husband any further, Knapp reported her cause of death
as "everlasting faint" but later changed the finding to "childbirth."
Although Zona hadn't told anyone that she was pregnant, the doctor
surmised that complications from a pregnancy must have been the
culprit because he'd recently treated her for "female trouble." During
his hasty examination, Knapp noticed a few bruises on Zona's neck
but quickly passed them off as unrelated.

Whirlwind Courtship

Little is known about her life, but it is believed that Zona Heaster was
born in Greenbrier County, West Virginia, around 1873. In October
1896, she met Shue, a drifter who had recently moved to the area to
work as a blacksmith.

Only months after they met, Zona Heaster and Edward Shue mar-
ried. But for reasons that she couldn't quite explain, Zona's mother—
Mary Jane Heaster—had taken an instant disliking to her son-in-law.
Despite her concerns, the newlyweds seemed to get along until that

tragic day when Zona was found dead. In an instant, Mary Jane's world was turned upside down. She grieved, as would any mother who must bury a child, but she sharply disagreed with Dr. Knapp's determination of her daughter's cause of death. In her mind, there was only one way that her daughter could have died at such a young age: Shue had killed her and had covered it up.

It All Comes Out in the Wash

At Zona's wake, those who came to pay their respects noticed Shue's erratic behavior: He continued to openly mourn his wife's passing, but something seemed odd about the way he grieved. His mood alternated between extreme sadness and sudden manic energy. He tended to his wife's body like a man possessed, allowing no one to get close to it. He also tied a large scarf around his wife's neck for no apparent reason, and even stranger, he placed a pillow on one side of Zona's head and a rolled-up cloth on the other; he told puzzled onlookers that they would help her "rest easier." And when Zona's body was moved to the cemetery for burial, several people noticed a strange looseness to her neck as they transported her. Not surprisingly, people began to talk.

Mary Jane Heaster did not have to be convinced that Shue was acting suspiciously about Zona's death. She had always hated him and wished that her daughter had never married him. She had a sneaking suspicion that something wasn't right, but she didn't know how to prove it.

After the funeral, Mary Jane Heaster washed the sheet that had lined her daughter's coffin. To her horror, the water inside the basin turned red. Then, even more shockingly, the sheet turned pink and the water again turned clear. Mary Jane was convinced that this was

a sign, so she began praying that her daughter would come to her to reveal the truth. A few weeks later, her prayers were answered.

Ghostly Visions

According to Mary Jane, Zona's apparition came to her over the course of four nights. It described how abusive Shue had been throughout their marriage and stated that he was responsible for her death. The tragedy occurred because Shue thought that Zona hadn't cooked meat for supper; he went into a rage, strangled her, and broke her neck. To demonstrate the brutality of Shue's attack, Zona's ghost rotated her head completely around. This horrified Mary Jane, but it also brought her some relief: Her beloved daughter had returned from the grave to seek the justice that she deserved. Armed with the unbridled power of a mother's love, Mary Jane was determined to avenge her daughter's death.

Please Believe Me!

Mary Jane immediately told local prosecutor John Alfred Preston of her ghostly visit, and begged him to investigate. Whether or not he took Mary Jane at her word is open to debate, but Preston did agree to interview Knapp and others associated with the case.

After learning that Dr. Knapp's examination had been cursory at best, Preston and Knapp agreed that an autopsy would help to clear things up, so Zona's body was exhumed. A local newspaper reported that Edward Shue "vigorously complained" about the exhumation but was forced to witness the proceedings. When Dr. Knapp proclaimed that Zona's neck was indeed broken, Shue was arrested and charged with his wife's murder.

While Shue awaited trial, tales of his unsavory past started coming to light. It was revealed that he'd been married twice before. His first marriage (to Allie Estelline Cutlip) had ended in divorce in 1889, while Shue was incarcerated for horse theft. In their divorce decree, Cutlip claimed that Shue had frequently beaten her. In 1894, Shue married Lucy Ann Tritt; however, the union was short-lived—Tritt died just eight months into their marriage under "mysterious" circumstances. In the autumn of 1896, Shue moved to Greenbrier County, where he met Zona Heaster. Was there a pattern of violence with this lethal lothario?

Trial

Shue's trial began on June 22, 1897. Both the prosecution and the defense did their best to discredit each other: For every witness who spoke of Shue's ill temper, another likened him to an altar boy. After Shue took the stand, many agreed that he handled himself skillfully. Then it was Mary Jane Heaster's turn. When questioned by the prosecution, her ghostly encounter with her daughter was not mentioned. But when she was cross-examined by Shue's attorney, Mary Jane recalled in great detail how Zona's spirit had fingered Shue as her abuser and killer. The defense characterized Mary Jane's "visions" as little more than a grieving mother's ravings, assuming that the jury would agree. They were wrong. When the trial concluded, the jury quickly rendered a guilty verdict. Not only had they believed Mary Jane's supernatural tale, they fell just short of delivering the necessary votes to hang Shue for his evil deeds; instead, he was sentenced to life in prison. And as it turned out, that wouldn't be very long.

Epilogue

In July 1897, Shue was transferred to the West Virginia Penitentiary in Moundsville, where he lived out the rest of his days. The convicted murderer died on March 13, 1900, of an epidemic that was sweeping the prison. But his name lives on, as does the ghostly legend of Zona Heaster Shue. A historical marker located beside Route 60 in Greenbrier County reads:

Greenbrier Ghost
"Interred in nearby cemetery is Zona Heaster Shue.
Her death in 1897 was presumed natural until her spirit
appeared to her mother to describe how she was killed
by her husband Edward. Autopsy on the exhumed body
verified the apparition's account. Edward, found guilty
of murder, was sentenced to the state prison.
Only known case in which testimony from
ghost helped convict a murderer."

Phantoms of Conneaut Lake Park

Would ghosts in an amusement park really be that amusing? It's no joke that guests at Conneaut Lake Park—a vintage entertainment complex and hotel in northwestern Pennsylvania—have reported a host of spirits that seem to be on an everlasting vacation at the historic resort.

It may seem odd that such a fun location would be haunted, but places where large numbers of people congregate naturally seem to accumulate ghosts. Conneaut Lake Park, which is located about 30 miles south of Lake Erie, opened in 1892 as Exposition Park on the western shore of the deep glacial lake that shares its name. The park became so popular that several hotels sprang up nearby to accommodate the crowds. The only one of those inns still operating today, the Hotel Conneaut, is famous for its lively ghosts. In fact, the hotel and park were featured on an episode of *Paranormal State* in 2009.

Conneaut Lake Park still features many quaint, refurbished old rides that evoke the laid-back atmosphere of the lakeside area's past. Its Blue Streak roller coaster is a retro rider's dream, and other attractions at the park bear equally colorful names such as Little Dipper, Witch's Stew, Roll-O-Plane, and Devil's Den. But it was on the wooden-tracked Blue Streak, which opened in 1937, where a rider allegedly died.

Only a few years after the roller coaster thrilled its first riders, legend has it that a tipsy sailor on shore leave made the foolish mistake of standing up just as the coaster made one of its trademark tight turns. The sailor went flying—in the opposite direction of the Blue Streak—and did not survive. The ride has reputedly been haunted ever since...but not by the sailor, by the ghost of a young girl wearing an old-fashioned dress.

The Burning Bride

In 1943, around the same time that the sailor was said to have met his end, a large section of the Hotel Conneaut burned and spawned the park's most famous ghost: "Elizabeth," the phantom bride. According

to local lore, Elizabeth was a hotel guest who perished in the fire after her groom was unable to save her. Although historians have not found evidence that this actually happened, the spirit seems to remain in an eternal holding pattern, waiting to be rescued from the flames. A hint of jasmine-scented perfume is often the first clue that Elizabeth is near.

Many guests have reported seeing the apparition of a young woman wearing a 1940s-era dress gliding silently around the hotel. Sometimes she emerges from a solid wall that at one time was a hallway opening; she seems to be confused regarding her whereabouts. Occasionally, she is spotted waltzing with her groom on the front veranda.

Hotel Horrors

Another ghost at the hotel is the spirit of Angelina, a young girl who was allegedly killed in a fatal tricycle accident on the hotel's balcony or stairs. According to an article in the *Meadville Tribune,* spiritual medium Kitty Osborne saw the tiny trikester pedaling down a hallway just outside her room. Osborne told the *Tribune* that she was "flabbergasted" at the sight.

The *Tribune* also interviewed George Deshner, the park's general manager, who said that he and many other employees have had brushes with unknown forces in the hotel. On several occasions, staff members have checked to make sure that all of the hotel's windows are closed and locked for the night only to discover later that one had mysteriously reopened. Lights turn on and off by themselves, and the manager himself has felt unseen hands shove him against a wall.

Even the hotel restaurant harbors its own spook: a chef dressed in spotless whites with an old-fashioned bow tied around his neck. He is said to move brooms and garbage cans, and guests have reported seeing him staring at them through the restaurant's window after the eatery is locked up for the night. One group of women observed the otherworldly figure writing on a piece of paper. Perhaps he was planning the next day's dessert specials: booberry pie and sheet cake!

Conneaut Lake Park is unlike any other amusement park because it is also a town—its grounds include more than a hundred private residences, and it even had its own post office at one time.

Prison Poltergeists

Old Montana Prison Inmates
Serve Life Sentences... and Then Some

🪦 🪦 🪦 🪦

In 1871, the Old Montana Prison opened its gates in Deer Lodge after citizens of the territory realized that laws needed to be enforced and the wilder elements of the region needed to be punished. Like many other prisons of the day, this facility soon became overcrowded, which led to sickness, poor living conditions, prisoner unrest, and the taut emotions that lead to restless spirits and residual hauntings.

No Escape

The year 1890 marked the beginning of the Conley era—a time when prison warden Frank Conley ruled with an iron fist and put his prisoners to work. But Conley also made significant improvements to both the prison itself and the lives of the inmates. He even established camps that sent the prisoners outside to work in the community.

However, this outside work was a privilege, and in 1908, two prisoners who were not allowed this freedom decided to take matters into their own hands. Their attempted escape resulted in the murder of the deputy prison warden and 103 stitches in the back and neck of Warden Conley. The two would-be escapees were hanged in the prison yard for their crime.

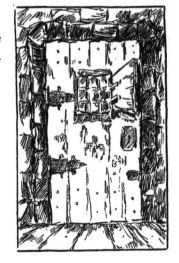

After that, the prison underwent many changes, including the end of prisoners working outside the facility, the addition of a women's prison, and the creation of a license plate manufacturing plant.

In 1959, the Old Montana Prison experienced a riot that lasted for three days and nights. Several inmates attempted to escape by holding the warden hostage and killing the deputy

warden on the spot. After the National Guard was called in to end the melee, the two ringleaders died in a murder/suicide.

The Main Attraction

The Old Montana Prison closed for good in 1979, and a year later, the building opened its doors to the public as a museum. In addition to offering historical tours, the museum also offers tours for those who are interested in things that go bump in the night. In fact, so much paranormal activity has been experienced at the Old Montana Prison that several ghost-hunting television shows have traveled there to investigate and film episodes.

In 2010, a *Ghost Lab* episode titled "No Escape" depicted Brad and Barry Klinge's (founders of Everyday Paranormal) visit to the prison. A wealth of high-tech ghost-hunting equipment helped the investigators uncover supernatural phenomena ranging from mysterious whispers and the sound of footsteps in empty rooms and hallways to objects flying through the air. The investigators also experienced a general feeling of dread and the unshakeable sensation that they were being watched.

See for Yourself

While touring the old prison, one can almost imagine the place as it was in the old days. Many people report hearing the shuffling of cards in the cellblocks, as well as mumbled voices and footsteps. Arguments have even been known to break out between people who aren't visible.

Shadows and ghostly figures are common sights at the museum, and some visitors have reported seeing objects flying through the air in violent, threatening ways. People have also experienced a myriad of emotions and sensations: Some have reported feeling deep sadness or dread overtake them. And even more frightening, others have perceived that someone or something is choking or attacking them.

Living with the Ghosts

Museum Director Julia Brewer is rather matter-of-fact about the hauntings in the old prison. After all, she has smelled burning flesh in her office for the better part of a decade, so you could say that she's a believer.

Brewer leads many of the groups that tour the facility, so she knows most of the prison lore. She also knows how to treat the spirits, and cautions visitors to treat the dead with respect...or else face the consequences.

A place known as the Death Tower produces a high level of otherworldly energy—it's where inmates Jerry Myles and Lee Smart died in a murder/suicide during the 1959 riot. A place called the Steam Hole carries some heavy energy of its own. Prisoners who were deemed unruly were often sent there; at least one prisoner died in the Steam Hole under suspicious circumstances, and another inmate took his own life there by hanging himself from a pipe.

Several ghosts are known to haunt the prison grounds, and many visitors—especially psychics and ghost hunters who are sensitive to the spirit world—have experienced odd and sinister sensations. Some have even reported feeling physically ill.

Playful Spirits

A couple of ghosts are even known to hang around the museum's gift shop. One is the spirit of an inmate named Calvin, who was beaten to death in a corner of the room when it was an industrial area of the prison. Now the site houses a shelf of dolls, perhaps to neutralize the violence. A spirit that the staff refers to as "Stinker" also frequents the gift shop. The jokester of the pair, he likes to play pranks, such as moving merchandise around.

You'd think that ghosts would stick to their old haunts within the prison, but another place on the grounds that definitely seems haunted is the Montana Auto Museum, which is located just outside the gift shop. Staffers and visitors have seen ghostly figures there, and people have heard car doors slam when no one else is around.

And then there's the spirit of a young girl that has been observed by visitors at the auto museum. When a group reached the building on one ghost tour, the leader invited any spirits to show themselves by turning on a flashlight; the playful ghost did. The group also asked her to move a chain that was cordoning off the cars; she did that too.

In a place that's harbored more than its share of violence and despair, the ghost of a little girl seems pretty benign. But as tour guides warn groups about the spirits of the Old Montana Prison: Be careful...they might just follow you home.

The Original Ghost-Hunting Kit

Not only is Harry Price considered by many to be the first ghost hunter, he is also credited with assembling the first ghost-hunting kit—essential items that he took with him on every investigation. And while some of these items are still used by ghost hunters today, you might be surprised by some of the things he took with him to track down the things that go bump in the night—or to expose those who might be trying to pull the wool over his eyes.

Device	Purpose
Still and video cameras	To capture ghostly anomalies
Phone system	To allow investigators to communicate with each other
Tape measure	For checking dimensions to determine if hidden rooms are present
Pencil and paper	For taking notes and making sketches
Flashlights	To see in the dark
Mercury	Price would watch to see if ripples formed in mercury poured into a small bowl, indicating movement in the area (ghostly or otherwise)
Mechanical bell system	For use as a makeshift burglar alarm to alert investigators if someone (or something) had entered an area
Powder or flour	To scatter on a floor to see if anything entered the room, since it would leave footprints behind
String or twine	To set up booby traps in doorways to make sure no one entered the room
Tape	To seal off windows and doors
Powdered graphite	For developing fingerprints to determine if an activity was ghostly or not (i.e., if a person was responsible for moving a lamp instead of a ghost)
Felt shoe covers	To enable investigators to move around without making noise

Hull House:
Chicago's Most Famous Haunted House

*When Charles Hull passed away in 1889, he was a wealthy
man who had helped build Chicago from a mud puddle to
a metropolis. To Helen Culver—his cousin and business
associate—he left an estate worth millions of dollars.*

Helen Culver took her responsibilities as an heir very seriously. One
of her first acts was to allow Jane Addams (a pioneer in the field of
social work) to turn Hull's Halsted Street mansion into a settlement
house—a place where the people in the neighborhood (who were
mostly very poor immigrants) could go to get medical care or a meal,
learn English and other skills, and otherwise work to improve their
chances of success in their new country.

Records are spotty, but two or three members of Charles Hull's
family may have died in the house, after which he abandoned living
in it altogether: His wife died in her bedroom, and his sons Louis
and Charley are thought to have died in the house, as well.

After Hull moved out of the mansion, the area around it became
the worst neighborhood in the city; some said that it was more vile
than Five Points in New York City, which Charles Dickens proclaimed
to be one of the worst places he'd ever seen. Crime, corruption,
drugs, alcoholism, gambling, and prostitution ran rampant, and
most residents were living in overcrowded, unsanitary tenements.

Skeptical of Spooks?

In 1889, when Addams moved into the mansion, the house was
already rumored to be haunted. Addams noticed that the staff placed
buckets of water at the top of the stairs; she came to realize that
they were there to keep ghosts away. After all, at the time, it was
commonly thought that ghosts could not cross over water.

Jane Addams was a bit skeptical about the ghosts, but after moving
into Mrs. Hull's old bedroom, she was often awakened by the sound
of footsteps near her bed. After one of Addams's friends stayed in the

room, the friend reported the same thing. Thereafter, whenever a dignitary visited Hull House, they would half-jokingly be invited to spend a night in "the haunted room." Most accepted the offer; many not only heard footsteps, but some also caught a glimpse of a ghostly woman looking down at them in the middle of the night.

The Devil's Spawn?

The work Addams did for the poor made her famous, and Hull House grew rapidly. To allow the facility to expand, the buildings that flanked the mansion were torn down, along with many crumbling tenements. At its height, Hull House covered an entire city block.

But for all the great works that Jane Addams accomplished at Hull House, it is still best remembered for the rumor that, in 1913, a "devil baby" had been born and was left there.

Stories of how a child with horns, hooves, scaly red skin, and a tail came to exist varied wildly. Among the more common explanations was that a Catholic woman had married an atheist, became pregnant, and placed a picture of the Virgin Mary on the wall. The husband flew into a rage, ripped the picture in two, and said, "I would rather have the devil in this house than a picture of that woman!" Another tale said that a woman had given birth to seven daughters, and upon learning that she was pregnant again, her husband said, "I would rather the next be the devil than another girl!"

All of the stories ended the same way: The child was born looking like a miniature devil, and in some versions, he could speak fluent Latin. Legend has it that when the father brought the baby to Hull House and approached a priest, the infant jumped from the man's arms, stole the priest's cigar, and began to smoke it while cursing the priest and displaying a forked tongue. The story may sound outrageous, but Hull House was mobbed with visitors wanting to see the baby.

Where the story came from is anyone's guess. Some speculate that a neighborhood baby may have been born with *harlequin ichthyosis,* a disease that causes humans to be born with red, scaly skin. Addams suggested that perhaps a deformed baby had been born somewhere on the West Side, but she also noted that the story could have been a thousand years old; in fact, one variation of the origin is identical to the story of the Jersey Devil. If such a child did exist, it was never brought to—and was certainly never exhibited at—Hull House.

 **91**

But that didn't stop hundreds of curious spectators from lining up at Hull House, demanding to see the devil baby, and offering to pay any cost to do so. "To see the way otherwise intelligent people let themselves be carried away by this ridiculous story is simply astonishing," Addams told the *Chicago Examiner.* "If I gave you the names of some of the professional people—including clergymen—who have asked about it, you simply would not believe me!"

Addams eventually came to see the episode as a great sociological phenomenon. Many of the neighborhood immigrants had only recently realized that the stories they'd been taught as facts in their home country were regarded as superstitions everywhere else, so they were looking for something that would help them cling to their old beliefs. Others were women with very little control over their lives who wanted to tell their husbands, "I have seen that devil baby. If you don't start treating me better, the same could happen to us!"

The story eventually died down, and in 1931, Addams became the first American woman to win the Nobel Peace Prize. In the 1960s, Hull House moved its operations elsewhere, and the buildings— except for the dining hall and the original house, which became museums—were torn down to make room for the expansion of the University of Illinois at Chicago.

Hauntings Persist

But the stories of the hauntings that predated Addams persisted, and in the 1970s, Hull House became a popular stop on the first ghost tours in Chicago. While a few people still claim to see the Devil Baby, among the most common sightings are the spirits of Mrs. Hull and a young girl whose identity is not known. Children frequently report seeing a woman in a white bonnet in one of the windows.

Stranger still are the many photos that have been taken of spectral men in hooded robes. No one knows who these ghosts were in life because Hull House was certainly never a monastery.

As with many allegedly haunted houses, dozens of bizarre stories without any basis in fact have circulated about Hull House over the years, causing some ghost hunters to avoid the place altogether. But it is difficult to ignore the fact that even these skeptical investigators continue to report sightings of a spectral older woman and a young girl—the same ghosts that have been spotted there for 150 years.

Haunted Theaters

The Maudlin Spirits of the Mounds Theatre

In 1922, the Mounds Theatre opened on the east side of St. Paul, Minnesota, to showcase silent films. A few dramatic characters from that era are said to remain in the restored Art Deco building, but these entities are not confined to the silver screen.

The most frightening spook at the Mounds is the spectral male figure that lurks in the dusty, antiquated projection room. Building director Raeann Ruth and three paranormal investigators who spent a night in the room all reported hearing a male voice alternately cry and swear up a storm. They also witnessed an angry male ghost staring at them with dark, sunken eyes. It certainly didn't help to alleviate any fears when the group discovered an antique Ouija board lying amid the old projection equipment.

Tragedies Spawn Terrors

A more benign ghost is dressed as an usher and seems to be crying. According to legend, he was a theater worker who found his beloved cuddling with someone else. It is believed that after death, he stayed attached to the scene of his life's greatest tragedy.

Tragic may also be the best way to describe another Mounds Theatre ghost—a young girl who skips around the stage bouncing a ball. During a recent renovation (2001–2003), a small dress and a child's shoe were found hidden in the theater. Some believe that these items could be linked to a possible child assault, which could explain why the girl's spirit still roams the theater.

New Life for Old Spirits

A nonprofit children's theater troupe now owns the building, thanks to the generosity of former owner George Hardenbergh, who bequeathed it to the group, Portage for Youth, in 2001, rather than see the grand old place demolished. Perhaps the influence of these happy young people will eventually banish the sad spirits lingering at the theater and help restore its original festive air.

 **93**

Casper the Friendly Ghost

A friendly ghost so doggone sweet that children run
toward him? What on earth were his creators thinking?
Cha-ching! That's what they were thinking.

He's a Scream!

In 1940, writer Seymour Reit and illustrator Joe Oriolo proposed the idea of Casper the Friendly Ghost as a storybook, but the project was tabled for unknown reasons. A few years later, Paramount Pictures Famous Studios (the studio's animated division) acquired the rights to the dormant project and debuted Casper not as a book but as part of its *Noveltoon* theatrical cartoon series. During this early period, Casper experienced requisite growing pains, found himself mired in existential uncertainty, and survived a brash suicide attempt. Yikes!

Gonzo Genealogy

Believe it or not, lovable Casper's family tree actually has some pretty dark roots. The very fact that Casper is a ghost suggests that he was once alive but died. But did he? While it's true that Casper was seen residing beside gravestones in his earliest cartoon strips, it's also true that later he mysteriously grew very humanlike feet and was often seen in the company of his two ghostly parents. Some say that such clues positively prove his mortality; others disagree, choosing instead to believe that Casper and his family were simply "born" as ghosts or were supernatural beings. While no definitive answer exists (fans debate Casper's origins to this very day), such ambiguity probably sprang from Paramount's concerns over keeping the "Friendly Ghost" friendly—especially to easily startled young viewers. After all, there'd be precious little sense in making Casper the ghost of a dead child if the goal was *not* to scare the wits out of American youngsters. On the other hand, it's difficult to explain Casper's existence any other way. Some things are just better left unknown.

A Suicidal New Yawker?

It may shock some to learn that Casper began his cartoon career at Paramount as a ghost-child from New York, but this was strongly suggested by his accent. It may also be surprising to learn that in "The Friendly Ghost," the very first Casper cartoon short produced by Paramount in 1944, the ghost-boy tried to end his "life" by lying across railroad tracks. Hey, if you were an existentially uncertain, amorphous white blob that scared almost everyone you met, wouldn't you consider the deep sleep? Thankfully, because Casper was already a ghost, the train passed right through him. The outcome pleased fans and spared writers the unenviable task of explaining how a ghost dies again.

Grown-Ups Don't Understand

Perhaps the most memorable part of the Casper experience was the theme song created for the TV cartoon series of the early 1950s. Written by Jerry Livingston and Mack David, the catchy ditty features lyrics that have etched themselves into the minds of baby boomers everywhere:

> *Grown-ups don't understand,*
> *why children love him the most,*
> *but kids all know that he loves them so*
> *Casper, the friendly ghost*

Young Casper fans were eager to jump on the bandwagon. It's no wonder that Casper lunch boxes, board games, Halloween costumes, and stuffed toys sold like hotcakes.

Still Friendly After All These Years

The Casper phenomenon has withstood the test of time. Over the years, the sweet specter has been featured in animated movies and cartoons, comic books, and even a live-action feature film (*Casper,* 1995). It was in this vehicle that Casper's backstory was finally told.... Or was it? Viewers learned that he was really a 12-year-old boy named Casper McFadden, who entered the ghostly realm after dying of pneumonia. But in the follow-up films *Casper: A Spirited Beginning* (1997) and *Casper Meets Wendy* (1998), these ideas are contradicted, clouding the issue once again. With so much conflicting information making the rounds, we may never fully understand Casper. Then again, grown-ups aren't supposed to.

A Murdered Wife's Revenge

Louisa Luetgert tormented her killer from the Other Side. Did she also coax him into an early grave?

In the late 1800s, Adolph Luetgert owned a sausage-manufacturing company in Chicago. Luetgert's business, A. L. Luetgert Sausage & Packing Company, did quite well initially, but then fell on hard times. As a result, his marriage to his second wife, Louisa, began to suffer, and their arguments grew increasingly intense. Then, on May 1, 1897, Louisa simply disappeared. Luetgert told investigators that she had left him, but Louisa's brother didn't buy it, and he pressed the police to continue their investigation.

The Evidence Mounts

When police questioned the Luetgerts' neighbors and relatives, they learned of violent arguments and domestic abuse. Finally, a witness came forward to say that she had seen Luetgert leading Louisa down the alleyway behind the sausage factory on the night she disappeared.

The police also questioned Luetgert's employees. A night watchman told them that at around 3 A.M. on May 2, he saw Luetgert working in the basement. Later that same morning, the watchman saw a sticky, gluelike substance near the vat; he noticed that it seemed to contain bits of bone, but he thought nothing of it. After all, Luetgert used all sorts of waste meats to make his sausage, so the watchman assumed that's what it was.

Detectives eventually uncovered paperwork that proved Luetgert had purchased large amounts of arsenic and potash (a dissolving agent) the day before Louisa disappeared. They also heard rumors that the financially strapped sausage king had been courting a wealthy widow, whom he planned to marry after Louisa was out of the way.

Putting two and two together, investigators concluded that Luetgert had murdered his wife, dissolved her body in potash, and then burned what was left of her remains in the factory's furnace. A few weeks into the investigation, the police searched the factory's

basement, where they found a vat that was two-thirds full of a brownish, brackish liquid. Using gunnysacks as filters, officers drained the greasy slime from the vat and poked through the residue with sticks. Their efforts uncovered several bone fragments and two gold rings—one was engraved with the initials "L. L."

Haunted in the Big House

After two very public trials (the first ended in a hung jury), Luetgert was found guilty of murder and sentenced to life in prison. While behind bars, Luetgert repeatedly told guards that the ghost of his dead wife was haunting him, exacting her revenge for a crime that he still claimed he did not commit. Luetgert died in prison in 1899.

Lingering Louisa

Meanwhile, several witnesses reported that Louisa's ghost had taken up residence in the Luetgerts' former home and was sometimes seen leaning against the fireplace mantel. The home was later rented out, but tenants didn't stay long, complaining that the ghost of Louisa Luetgert—who was apparently still angry about her untimely death—refused to leave them in peace.

Eventually, the home was moved to a different location in the neighborhood and the factory was sold to the Library Bureau Company. And in the late 1990s—around the 100th anniversary of Louisa's death—the former sausage factory was converted into condominiums, and brand-new buildings sprang up to replace the aging relics from the Luetgerts' days. Fashionable brick homes and apartment buildings popped up nearby, and run-down taverns were replaced with trendy coffee shops.

But one thing has not changed: Legend has it that each year on May 1—the anniversary of her death—a ghostly Louisa Luetgert can be seen walking down Hermitage Avenue near the old sausage factory, perhaps reliving her final moments on earth.

"The murdered do haunt their murderers, I believe. I know that ghosts have wandered on earth. Be with me always—take any form—drive me mad!"
—Emily Brontë, *Wuthering Heights*

Haunted Objects:
One Person's Treasure Is Another's Torment

Many people would be frightened to encounter a haunted object. The idea is just a little creepy, whether the object in question is a doll, a painting, or a hairbrush. But some people actually scour estate sales and surf the Web searching for haunted objects. To those people we say, "Let the buyer beware."

What Is a Haunted Object?

A haunted object is an item that seems to give off a certain energy or vibe. Paranormal occurrences accompany the object itself and begin after the object is acquired. Sometimes, human characteristics—such as breathing or tapping sounds—are associated with the item. In other cases, a person can place a haunted object in one place only to find that it mysteriously moves while he or she is absent from the room, is sleeping, or is away from home.

Becoming Haunted

No one knows for sure what causes an object to become haunted. Some people think that the items are possessed. Renowned psychic Sylvia Browne says that oftentimes a spirit has a "lingering fond-ness" for an object and may just stop by to visit it. She stresses that all items are capable of holding imprints, which are not always pleasant.

Another explanation is that certain objects are cursed, but that doesn't seem as likely. Most experts feel that a "haunting" comes from residual energy associated with the people or places connected to the item. For example, a beloved doll or stuffed animal may retain some energy from its human owner. This is especially likely to be the case with an item that was near—or even involved in—a violent event such as a murder, the death of a child, or even a heated argu-ment. The "haunting" occurs when the residual energy plays back or reenacts the traumatic event. Like other residual phenomena, haunted objects can't communicate or interact with humans.

When people experience a paranormal event, they often assume that the building in which the incident occurs is haunted, but sometimes it's just one item. Here's a look at some objects that are reportedly haunted.

An Especially Evil Ouija Board

Many people avoid Ouija boards because they may connect us with the Other Side or evil entities. This certainly seemed to be the case with the board Abner Williams loaned to a group of El Paso "Goths." In mid-2000, after the board was returned to him, Williams complained of scratching noises coming from the board, along with a man's voice addressing him and the sound of children chanting nursery rhymes at his window. When Williams tried to throw the board away, it mysteriously reappeared in his house. A paranormal investigator borrowed the board, and a hooded figure appeared from out of nowhere and growled at his son.

When a paranormal research team investigated the Ouija board, they found spots of blood on the front of it and a coating of blood on the back. They measured several cold spots over areas of the board, and photos revealed a strange ectoplasm rising from it. The board was eventually sent to a new owner, who did not want it cleared of negative energy. That person has remained silent about more recent activity surrounding the board.

Although this is an unusually well-documented haunted Ouija board, it is not an uncommon tale. Many psychics warn that if you ask a spirit to communicate with you through a Ouija board, it's like opening a door between the worlds. You never know what kinds of spirits—good or evil—will use that Ouija board to visit you. Therefore, it's wise to be cautious with "spirit boards" of any kind.

Haunted Painting

Actor John Marley purchased a painting titled *The Hands Resist Him* after he saw it at a Los Angeles art show. Many years later, the piece of art—which Bill Stoneham painted in 1972—was found in a trash bin behind a brewery, and in strict accordance with "finder's keepers" rules, the person who found it took it home.

Unfortunately, it soon became clear why the artwork had been abandoned. The finder's four-year-old daughter claimed that she saw the children in the painting fighting. And sure enough, a webcam that

recorded the painting for several nights confirmed that the figures were indeed moving. The artist didn't have any insight as to why this particular painting might be haunted, but he did remember that both the gallery owner and a Los Angeles art critic died soon after that show. Coincidence? Maybe. Nevertheless, the family listed the painting and its bizarre story on eBay and came away $1,025 richer.

Robert the Doll

When artist Robert Eugene "Gene" Otto was a young boy growing up in Florida in the early 1900s, he owned a doll, which he named Robert. He took this doll with him everywhere and liked to talk to it. The problem was that the doll talked back— and this was long before the days of Chatty Cathy and other "talking" dolls. It wasn't just the young boy's imagination either—servants and other family members also witnessed the phenomenon. Neighbors were surprised to see the doll moving by itself, and when Otto's parents found their son's bedroom trashed, Gene said that Robert the doll did it. Did it? Maybe so, at least according to the daughter of the family that bought the house in 1972: She was terrified when she discovered the doll in the attic. She said that it wanted to kill her. Her parents had no intention of finding out if this was true, so they gave the doll to a museum in Key West. Visitors to the museum are advised to ask permission before they snap a photo of the famous doll. A tilt of his head means yes, but if you don't get the OK, don't even think about taking a picture, or you'll be cursed.

Nathaniel Hawthorne and the Haunted Chair

You may have seen a creepy old chair or two, but when author Nathaniel Hawthorne encountered one that was actually haunted, he wrote a short story about it: "The Ghost of Dr. Harris."

According to Hawthorne, Dr. Harris sat and read the newspaper in the same chair at the Boston Athenaeum each morning. When Harris died, his ghost continued to visit, and Hawthorne, who was researching at the library, saw it daily. The author said that the spirit had a "melancholy look of helplessness" that lingered for several

seconds, and then vanished. So if you visit the Boston Athenaeum, be careful where you sit: Dr. Harris may be in that "empty" chair.

Annabelle and the Haunted Doll

Raggedy Ann and Andy dolls have been popular for decades. But after a young woman named Donna received a Raggedy Ann doll in the 1970s, she didn't have such a warm and fuzzy experience. The doll would often change positions on its own: Once, it was found kneeling—a position that was impossible for Donna and her room-mate Angie to create due to the soft and floppy nature of the doll's body. The girls also found mysterious notes that were written in a childish scrawl. Worried, Donna and Angie called in a medium, who told them that their apartment building was once the home of a young girl named Annabelle. But after the doll attacked Angie's boyfriend, the girls called in demonologists Ed and Lorraine Warren, who determined that "Annabelle" was not the friendly, playful spirit of a young girl, but instead was a demonic entity. The doll went to live with the Warrens, who knew how to handle its antics, and it now resides in a glass case at the Warren Occult Museum in Connecticut.

The Haunted Wedding Dress at the Baker Mansion

In the 19th century, the Baker Mansion in Altoona, Pennsylvania, was home to the Baker family. As the story goes, daughter Anna fell in love with and became secretly engaged to one of her father's employees. But when her father discovered the romance, he sent the suitor away. Poor Anna never got over her lost love, and she never married.

When the Blair County Historical Society took over the building in the 1920s, a beautiful wedding dress that belonged to Anna's rival, Elizabeth Bell, was put on display. Although the dress was showcased under glass in Anna's bedroom, it often moved and swayed of its own accord. Caretakers attributed the movement to a loose floorboard that jarred the case when visitors walked past. But security cameras recorded the dress moving when no one else was around. Eventually, like Anna's suitor, the wedding dress was removed.

Although the haunted dress is no longer displayed at the mansion, some Baker family spirits have apparently remained there. Apparitions have been seen in a mirror and on a staircase, and photos have also shown orbs and misty shadows.

The Haunted Destroyer

Shortly after the Japanese attack on Pearl Harbor, five brothers from Waterloo, Iowa—George, Francis, Joseph, Madison, and Albert Sullivan—enlisted in the U.S. Navy and served together aboard the light cruiser USS Juneau. *Sadly, their inspiring story of family patriotism turned tragic when the* Juneau *was sunk by a Japanese submarine in November 1942, sending all five Sullivan brothers to a watery grave. Their story was immortalized in the movie* The Fighting Sullivans *(1944) and served as an inspiration for Steven Spielberg's* Saving Private Ryan *(1998).*

In 1943, the navy honored the Sullivan brothers by naming a destroyer after them: USS *The Sullivans.* It was a proud ship that served valiantly during the remainder of World War II, in the Korean War, and then in various hot spots around the world as part of the 6th Fleet. But after the vessel was decommissioned in 1965, the navy had a difficult time finding people willing to clean and maintain it. The reason? The spirits of the Sullivan brothers were apparently haunting the ship.

Haunted Happenings Begin

The ghosts were quiet while the ship was on active duty, but they started making themselves known upon its retirement. Those who worked aboard *The Sullivans* after it was decommissioned reported seeing flying objects and hearing weird sounds and terrifying moans. Fleeting glimpses of young men dressed in World War II–era naval uniforms were also common sights.

One of the first acknowledgments that something bizarre was occurring aboard *The Sullivans* came when an electrician's mate refused an order to make a routine check of the ship. It was Friday the 13th he explained, and the last time he had been aboard the ship

on that traditionally superstitious day, an unseen hand had reached out from a bulkhead, grabbed him by the ankle, and tripped him.

More Incidents Revealed

After the sailor's story was made public, others came forward with tales of their own frightening encounters aboard the destroyer. Another electrician's mate reported that something had reached out and snatched away the toolbox he had been carrying, and another sailor claimed that five glowing spheres passed him in a darkened hatchway while he stood paralyzed with fear.

In another account, a sailor assigned to work on the vessel said that he felt a chill and a sense of dread the moment he set foot aboard the ship. Within minutes, he was having trouble breathing, and he experienced an odd buzzing in his ears. "I felt like I had stepped into another world, and it wasn't a world where I wanted to be," said the sailor, who, until that day, had never believed in ghosts. "I knew there and then that I was never going back aboard that ship."

Most of the supernatural phenomena reported aboard *The Sullivans* occurred while the destroyer was docked in Philadelphia. For reasons unknown, removing the ship from active service apparently triggered a tremendous amount of activity from the spirits of the five Sullivan brothers. When the ship was relocated, however, ghost sightings and paranormal activity slowed dramatically.

Now a Museum

In 1977, *The Sullivans* was donated to the Buffalo and Erie County Naval & Military Park in Buffalo, New York, where it was turned into a memorial museum that is open for public tours. In 1986, the fabled vessel was declared a National Historic Landmark.

The story of the five Sullivan brothers and their untimely deaths captured the nation's attention and led to immediate policy changes within the U.S. Navy, which worked to ensure that no American family would ever again suffer such a grave loss. The story of the ship's haunting isn't well known outside of the small fraternity of people who worked aboard the vessel and experienced the brothers' spirited antics firsthand. Why the restless spirits of the brothers manifested when they did, did what they did, and then quieted down remains a mystery.

 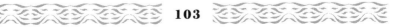

Lily Dale, New York—U.S. Headquarters of the Spiritualism Movement

For centuries, the bereaved have sought ways to speak to their loved ones on the Other Side. In the 1840s, the Spiritualism movement swept across the United States. Spiritualists believe that an afterlife awaits us all, and that in it, ethereal beings retain many of the interests they had during their time on earth. They also believe that with the help of mediums—people who are able to see and communicate with the dead—the living can make contact with their deceased loved ones during formal sessions known as séances.

The Awakening of the Spirits

In the mid-1870s, a group of committed Spiritualists began hosting summer meetings at Cassadaga Lake in southwestern New York. Believing that nothing is preordained or destined, the Spiritualists emphasized free will; they felt that it was up to the living to make choices based on guidance from the spirits.

To practice their religion, the Spiritualists purchased 20 acres of land near Cassadaga Lake and established the community of Lily Dale in 1879. In addition to offering the services of mediums, psychics, and other faith healers, the Lily Daleans also offered summer classes to followers of the Spiritualism movement. Lily Dale became so popular that a hotel was built in the town in 1880, and in 1883, a 1,200-seat auditorium was added.

Over the years, Lily Dale's freethinkers attracted many famous people: Susan B. Anthony spoke there frequently, Mae West visited the assembly, and, in 1916, the cottage of sisters Margaret and Kate Fox was moved to Lily Dale. (In 1848, the Fox sisters claimed that they had communicated with the spirit of a murdered peddler at their home in Hydesville, New York. This incident is often cited as the beginning of the Spiritualist movement.) Unfortunately, the Fox sisters' cottage burned down in a fire in 1955.

Haunting the Spiritualists

Given the presence of so many mediums, it is no surprise that ghosts are often seen in Lily Dale. The full spectrum of spirits—from full-bodied apparitions to shadows and orbs—regularly appear in photos taken around the town. The Maplewood Hotel's lobby is decorated entirely with "spirit precipitated art"—art that was created with the assistance of spirits. Sometimes during a séance, a medium will set out a bowl of paints and a blank canvas; when the session is over, a painting—usually a portrait of the spirit that has just made its presence known—will be complete. One of the paintings in the hotel's lobby depicts a figure with a white beard wearing a white robe; it is unknown who this man was in life, but several guests have seen his apparition in the building's hallways. A blind, mute, quadriplegic woman created a spirit-assisted tapestry over a period of nine years. While the woman was in a trance, the spirits guided her and helped her to embroider the tapestry using only her mouth.

Modern Spiritualist Living

These days, groups often gather around Inspiration Stump (a grove in the Leolyn Woods) during the summertime. At these meetings, a medium gives short messages to the people in attendance from the various spirits present. People sit quietly, barely moving, so as not to disturb the medium's work. Even those who do not receive a message from a spirit feel rejuvenated, and many find themselves more aware of spiritual energies while at Inspiration Stump. Afterward, audience members often book individual sessions with the dozens of certified mediums who live year-round in the Lily Dale community.

People who wish to plan a trip to Lily Dale will find an extensive guide to workshops, lectures, and classes online. Keep in mind that although the Spiritualists practice their religion year-round, Lily Dale's two hotels are closed from late September until June. During the off-season, those wishing to visit a medium or attend a workshop can arrange to stay at a private home through the Lily Dale Spiritualist Church or the Church of the Living Spirit. In order to live amongst the spirits full time, one must become a member of the Lily Dale community and apply to the Lily Dale Assembly Board of Directors to essentially earn the right to call this quaint, yet hauntingly beautiful town home.

The Tormented Souls
of the LaLaurie Mansion

*Marie Delphine LaLaurie was the crème de la crème of
the high society of early 19th-century New Orleans. Rich,
pretty, and intelligent, she entranced nearly everyone she
met. But LaLaurie held a dark and diabolical secret: She
delighted in torturing her slaves in heinous and despicable
ways. Later, the spirits of those who died at LaLaurie's hand
would come back to haunt the socialite's stately manor.*

Social Butterflies

Marie was born in Louisiana around 1775. She was widowed twice
and bore five children before marrying Dr. Leonard Louis LaLaurie
in 1825. In the early 1830s, Marie and her husband moved into the
stunning three-story mansion at 1140 Royal Street in New Orleans.
It was regarded as one of the finest houses in the city and one that
befit their social status, as the family was noted for its wealth and
prominence in the community.

As visible parts of New Orleans society, the LaLauries frequently
hosted grand parties that were attended by the city's most influential
citizens. Like many wealthy people of the time, the LaLauries
owned several slaves who cooked, cleaned, and maintained the
property. Many guests remembered the finely dressed servants, who
catered to their every need. But other LaLaurie slaves—sometimes
glimpsed in passing—were surprisingly thin and hollow-chested.
Rumors began to circulate that Madame LaLaurie was far from kind
to her servants.

One neighbor claimed that he watched in horror as Madame
LaLaurie chased a terrified female slave with a whip. The girl eventually made it to the roof of the mansion, where she chose to jump
to her death rather than face her enraged owner's maniacal abuse.
What happened to the girl's body remains a mystery: Some accounts
say that it was buried on the property, while others report that it was
dumped in an abandoned well.

A Fire Reveals All

The true extent of Marie LaLaurie's revolting cruelty was finally revealed in April 1834, when a fire broke out in the mansion. As the story goes, a cook who simply couldn't handle any more torture at the hands of Madame LaLaurie set the blaze. As the fire swept through the house and smoke filled the rooms, a crowd of onlookers gathered outside. Soon, the volunteer fire department arrived with buckets of water and bystanders offered their assistance. LaLaurie remained calm and directed the volunteers to save expensive paintings and smaller pieces of furniture. But when neighbors tried to enter the slave quarters to ensure that everyone got out safely, Madame LaLaurie refused to give them the key. Enraged, they broke down the door and were horrified to find several slaves tortured and mutilated. Many of the victims said that they'd been held captive for months.

The atrocities committed against the slaves in the LaLaurie home were depraved in the extreme. Some were found chained to the walls, and others were suspended by their necks with their limbs stretched and torn. One female slave was wearing a spiked iron collar that forced her head into an upright position. Some slaves were nearly starved to death, flayed with whips, and bound in painfully restrictive positions. Cruel experiments had been performed on some victims: Eyes were poked out, mouths were sewn shut, limbs were removed, and skulls were left open while they were still alive. The men who found the slaves were overwhelmed by the stench of death and decaying flesh, which permeated the confined chamber. A local newspaper reported that the bodies of tortured slaves were found buried around the grounds of the mansion.

When word of Marie LaLaurie's sadistic and grotesque crimes got out, an angry mob descended upon the mansion, breaking furniture, shattering windows, looting fine china and imported food, and destroying everything that it could find until only the walls remained. But by then, the LaLauries had already fled to France, never to be seen in New Orleans again.

Ghosts Take Up Residence

After the authorities restored order at the LaLaurie Mansion, the property was closed and sealed, and it sat completely empty for years . . . or so it seemed.

The spirits of the dead quickly claimed the house. Passersby often heard agonizing cries coming from the abandoned structure, and several people said that they saw apparitions of the murdered slaves walking on the home's balconies, peering out of windows, and roaming through the property's overgrown gardens. According to legend, vagrants who entered the building were never seen again.

The LaLaurie Mansion was purchased in 1837, but the buyer put it back on the market after only three months, claiming to have been driven out by weird noises and anguished cries in the night.

Hauntings Continue

In the years that followed, the LaLaurie Mansion was converted into a school for girls, abandoned again, and then converted into inexpensive apartments for immigrant laborers. Time and time again, the restless spirits of the tortured slaves made their presence known, much to the horror of the people who lived there. Once, a terrified tenant claimed that the spirit of a naked black man in chains attacked him and then vanished as quickly as it had appeared. Even cheap rent was not enough to convince tenants to stay for very long, and soon the house was vacant again.

The LaLaurie Mansion still stands today. Over the years, it has changed hands several times and has served as a saloon, a furniture store, a refuge for poor and homeless men, and an apartment building. In April 2007, actor Nicolas Cage purchased the property, but two and a half years later, it was back on the market. There have been no reports of ghostly activity there in recent years, but that doesn't mean the spirits of Marie LaLaurie's victims are resting in peace.

During a remodeling of the LaLaurie Mansion some years ago, workers discovered several unmarked graves under the floorboards of the house. This may explain why many of Madame LaLaurie's slaves simply disappeared, never to be seen again.

DIU Ghost-Busting

Something strange in your neighborhood? Something weird and it don't look good? Here's a do-it-yourself guide to ghost-busting. But there are no guarantees, so proceed at your own risk.

We Need to Talk...

First, simply ask your ghost, politely but firmly, to leave. If you think that it is hanging around the physical realm for fear of punishment in the spirit world, let it know that it will be forgiven. Try not to show fear or anger, which may give a negative spirit more power.

Clean and Serene

If tough talking doesn't work, try a spiritual cleansing. Open a window in each room of your home, and then light a bundle of dry sage and walk around (have something handy to catch the ashes), allowing the smoke to circulate while you intone these words: "This sage is cleansing out all negative energies and spirits. All negative energies and spirits must leave now and not return." Do this in each room of the house, and then say, "In the name of God, this home is now cleansed." If that doesn't work, ask a priest or minister to bless your home. There is usually no charge for this, but you might want to make a small donation to the church.

The Last Straw: Exorcism

Using prayers and religious items, clergy members usually perform exorcisms to cast out unwelcome, demonic spirits. Catholic exorcism involves a priest reciting prayers and invocations while displaying a crucifix and sprinkling holy water over the place, person, or object believed to be possessed. Exorcism is no laughing matter: In the past, people who would now be diagnosed as physically or mentally ill have undergone exorcism, sometimes dying in the process.

What Not to Do

Whatever you do, don't use a Ouija board, as it may "open the door" to let in additional unwanted spirits.

Specters on "The Rock"

Located in the chilly, windswept waters of San Francisco Bay, Alcatraz (aka "The Rock") gained fame as a prison that defied escape. Yet one morbid thought comforted the prisoners doomed to spend their lives within its forbidding walls: Death would finally bring them deliverance. Uh ... not necessarily.

Sweet Freedom

Today, Alcatraz is one of the most popular tourist attractions in the Bay Area. But from 1934 to 1963, during its tenure as a federal prison, Alcatraz was touted as escape-proof—a place where hardened criminals and assorted public enemies were sent to serve their time. Sure, there's the dramatic account of inmate Frank Morris (portrayed by Clint Eastwood in the 1979 film *Escape from Alcatraz*), who, on June 11, 1962, managed to flee "The Rock" in an improvised raft along with two other convicts (brothers Clarence and John Anglin). But the success of their escape bid remains questionable due to the ferocious waters of San Francisco Bay. Therefore, the only surefire ways for a prisoner to exit Alcatraz were by serving out his sentence or by leaving in a body bag. But even these certainties now seem dubious, since *deceased* prisoners can still be spotted wandering within the prison walls.

Doing Hard Time

If Alcatraz's wardens leaned toward the boastful, it's with good reason: Never before had the American penal system operated such an impenetrable fortress. Designed to house the very worst of the worst (Al Capone and George "Machine Gun" Kelly were once inmates there), Alcatraz was devised with one staunch principle in mind: Never, *ever* allow the bad guys to escape. The prison's remote island location virtually assured prisoners' compliance (unless they longed to be shark bait), as did its lofty walls, menacing gun turrets, automatic tear-gas canisters, and frequent roll calls. Like other prisons, Alcatraz featured its share of abuses, and in that respect, the

prison's remoteness worked in its favor—"out of sight, out of mind," as the popular saying goes. From sensory deprivation in the dungeon-like solitary confinement (aka "The Hole") to alleged beatings administered by sadistic guards, Alcatraz has scores of skeletons in its closet. It also seems to have more than its share of ghosts.

The Ghost of Cell 14D

One of The Rock's most frightening ghost stories involves a prisoner who was sent to The Hole during the 1940s. Assigned to Cell 14D, the understandably frightened man screamed throughout his first night in solitary confinement. But this prisoner wasn't merely expressing a fear of the dark or the psychological torture of isolation: He begged the guards to save his life before the "creature with glowing eyes" killed him. With the prison's rigid rules being what they were, the man's pleas fell on deaf ears. However, the very next morning, the prisoner was found strangled to death in his cell, which was utterly baffling because, like all cells in The Hole, 14D was a highly fortified, solitary space with no shared doorways. And it had been locked up tight all night.

The following day, something equally puzzling occurred. During a routine roll call, one too many prisoners was counted. Who was the extra man standing in line? According to shocked guards, it was the troubled convict who had met his end in The Hole the previous day. The prisoner was seen only for a brief instant before he vanished, but it was a moment that none of the guards would soon forget.

Hell's Hallway

Opposite the main visitors' room is a metal door that was once welded tightly shut; it is plainly visible to tourists who visit the site today. In 1976, long after Alcatraz had ceased operating as a prison, a night watchman heard a clanging sound emanating from the hallway behind the door. When he unlocked the door and shined his

flashlight onto the jumble of metal conduits lining the spiderweb-covered passage, the sound suddenly stopped. He found nothing out of place, so he shut the door; however, as soon as it closed, the clanging noise returned. Not one to scare easily, the guard opened the door to investigate but again found nothing, so he put the strange incident behind him and continued on his rounds.

Perhaps the guard wasn't aware of the hallway's morbid history. Some 30 years prior, during a bold breakout attempt, six prisoners captured a gun cage and took over a cell house. After two days of trading gunfire with authorities, three of the six men sought refuge in the hallway. Despite this evasive move, inmates Joe Cretzer, Bernard Coy, and Marvin Hubbard were ripped to pieces by bullets and grenades. As the shrapnel sprayed against the pipes, it produced a distinctive clanging sound. Perhaps the guard heard the angry spirits of these prisoners reliving their final moments.

Warden with the Willies

James A. Johnston, the first and most famous warden at Alcatraz, was a no-nonsense sort of guy, so his account of strange happenings at Alcatraz was held in high regard. While leading a tour of the facility one day, Johnston and some VIPs heard the unmistakable sound of a person sobbing. They later recalled that the eerie noise seemed to be coming from "inside the walls" of The Hole. The sobbing quickly ceased, and as it did, an icy cold wind chilled each witness to the bone.

Another time, during a Christmas party at the warden's home on Alcatraz Island, several guards turned ashen when a ghostly man suddenly appeared before them. The apparition wore a gray suit and a brimmed hat, and it sported lamb-chop sideburns, a style that seemed quite out of place for the time period. As the guards continued to stare at the specter, it turned so frightfully cold in the room that the Ben Franklin stove was extinguished. Seconds later, the spirit vanished altogether.

The Musical Mobster

More recently, when a National Park Ranger was going about his duties, he encountered one of Alcatraz's more entertaining ghosts. While standing in a cell house adjacent to the shower room, the ranger heard the distinctive sound of banjo music. After performing

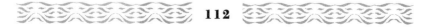

a thorough inspection, he was satisfied that both rooms were unoccupied, yet the melodious sounds persisted.

It should be noted that decades earlier, when Alcatraz's most famous prisoner—gangster Al Capone—was interred on The Rock, he played the banjo in the prison band. In fact, Capone would often stay inside and strum his banjo rather than risk an attack by other inmates in the prison yard. Invariably, Capone liked to play his instrument where the acoustics seemed just right—in the shower room.

We'll never know for sure whether this was the broken spirit of Al Capone creating a mournful melody on his phantom banjo, or if it was another ghostly inmate, still unable to escape—even after death.

Ghost Hunters Surveys the Rock

In 2010, the paranormal possibilities on The Rock snared the attention of television's *Ghost Hunters.* Looking for captivating fodder for their special 100th episode, the team lugged their scientific equipment to the island and got down to business. Viewers were treated to the standard battery of tests and measurements—tried-and-true procedures that the seasoned investigators use. But in this episode, they got something more: While using their audio-recording equipment, the team picked up an EVP (electronic voice phenomenon) of a voice saying "Harry Brunette 374." A rudimentary search of prison records revealed that in 1936, bank robber Harry Walter Brunette was arrested and convicted for the kidnapping and transport of a New Jersey State Trooper; he was issued a life sentence for his crime and shipped off to Alcatraz, where he could commit no more mayhem. Records also showed that Brunette occupied Cell 374. Enough said.

"We are all spirit. When we pass on, we simply get rid of the outer layer and, underneath, there really is a duplicate layer. This inner body—like an inner tube of a tire—is where our personality resides. At death the physical body is worn out and dissolved, so the inner body is where we live."

—Hans Holzer

When the Gray Man Speaks, You'd Better Listen

One of the oldest summer resorts on the East Coast, Pawleys Island is a small barrier island located along the coast of South Carolina. Only a handful of people live there year-round, but one of the perennial residents is the Gray Man. Many say that this restless spirit has no face. However, that seems to be a minor inconvenience; after all, when it comes to warning the living of impending doom, a pretty face—or any face at all—is hardly necessary.

Apparition Identity Crisis

According to legend, before every major hurricane that has hit Pawleys Island since the early 1820s—including Hurricane Hugo in 1989—the Gray Man has appeared to certain folks on the island to warn them to leave before the approaching storm strikes. When they return after the storm, the people who encountered the Gray Man find their homes undamaged, while other buildings nearby have been destroyed.

The identity of the Gray Man is unknown, but there are several candidates. One theory suggests that it's Percival Pawley, the island's first owner and its namesake; others believe that the helpful spirit is Plowden Charles Jennett Weston, a man whose former home is now the island's Pelican Inn.

But the more romantic legends say that the Gray Man is the ghost of a young man who died for love. Stories about how he perished vary: One tale says that on his way to see his beloved, he fell into a bed of quicksand and died. Soon after, while the object of this deceased man's affection was walking along the beach, a figure in gray approached her and told her to leave the island. She did, and that night a hurricane slammed into the area, destroying just about every home—except hers.

Another story concerns a woman who married a man after she thought that her beloved had died at sea. Later, when she met a man who had survived a shipwreck off Pawleys Island, she realized that it

was her lost love, waterlogged but still very much alive. However, he didn't take the news of her marriage too well; he slinked away and died shortly thereafter. But according to legend, ever since then, he's been warning folks to flee when they're in danger from an upcoming storm.

The Ghostly Lifesaver

No matter who this ghost was in life, he has supposedly appeared before hurricanes in 1822, 1893, 1916, 1954, 1955, and 1989. And for decades, local fishermen have told stories of the Gray Man appearing to them hours before a sudden storm roiled up that would have put their lives in jeopardy.

The Gray Man is credited with saving many lives before the advent of contemporary forecasting techniques. In 1954, a couple was spending their honeymoon on the island when they heard a knock on their door at around 5 A.M. When the husband opened the door, he saw a figure in gray whose clothes reeked of salty brine and whose features were obscured by a gray hat. The man in gray said that the Red Cross had sent him to warn people to evacuate because a huge storm was heading for the island. Before the honeymooning husband could question him further, the man in gray vanished. Realizing that this was no ordinary Red Cross worker, the man and his new bride left the island immediately.

Later that evening, ferocious Hurricane Hazel struck the island with the deadly force of a Category 4 storm, with winds gusting as high as 150 miles per hour. In her wake, Hazel left thousands of homes destroyed and 95 people dead. The newlywed couple, however, had been spared by the ghostly grace of the Gray Man.

A Ghost Who Keeps on Giving

The Gray Man apparently doesn't care much for modern technology— he was still on the job as recently as 1989. That year, just before Hurricane Hugo hit, a couple walking along the beach spotted the Gray Man. Although the phantom vanished before the couple could speak to him, his reputation preceded him, and the couple fled the island. When they returned, their home was the only one in the area that had not been devastated by the storm. This incident got the Gray Man a moment in the national spotlight: He was featured on an episode of *Unsolved Mysteries* in 1990.

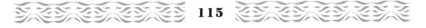

Ghosts of Harpers Ferry

Harpers Ferry, West Virginia, is a picturesque town that has been at the center of a great deal of American history, most notably during the mid-19th century, when abolitionist John Brown staged a raid that proved to be a catalyst for the American Civil War. However, Harpers Ferry is also known for its ghosts. Here are a few of the many spirits that haunt this historic town:

Rachael Harper

In the mid-18th century, Robert Harper founded the town of Harpers Ferry. After he and his wife Rachael lost their first house in a flood, Harper began construction of a much grander home. But this was during the American Revolution, when laborers were hard to find, so the aging Harper did much of the work himself. He was quite concerned about lawlessness during this uncertain time, so legend has it that he instructed Rachael to bury their gold in a secret location and tell no one about it. Harper passed away in 1782, and after Rachael died unexpectedly following a fall from a ladder, the secret location of their gold was buried with her.

For many years, the Harper House has been considered haunted. People who pass it swear that they see a woman in old-fashioned clothes staring out from an upstairs window. Perhaps it's Rachael, remaining watchful and vigilant over the family's gold.

18th-Century Soldiers

In the waning years of the 18th century, an army was sent to Harpers Ferry in preparation for a possible war between the United States and France. The army wound up waiting for a conflict that never happened, so to relieve their boredom, the soldiers paraded to fife and drum music. Unfortunately, a cholera epidemic struck the army while it sat idle, and many men died. Today, the spirits of the men seem to remain. Almost everyone in town has heard the faint sounds of feet marching, drums beating, and fifes playing as an invisible phantom army sweeps through town, doomed to repeat its nightly musical ritual for eternity.

John Brown

John Brown is probably the most noteworthy figure associated
with the town of Harpers Ferry. Many people are familiar with
his tall, gaunt, white-bearded image, so perhaps it's not surprising
that many have seen someone looking exactly like him wandering
around town. The resemblance to Brown is so uncanny that tourists
have taken photos with the spirit; however, when the pictures are
developed, "Brown" is not in them.

John Brown's ghost has also been spotted several miles outside
of town at the Kennedy Farmhouse. It was there that Brown and
his men stayed for several months while planning the raid. Even
today, phantom footsteps, disembodied male voices, and snoring
can be heard coming from the empty attic where the conspirators
once stayed. It's no wonder that particular area of the house is
largely shunned.

Dangerfield Newby

Another ghost seen at Harpers Ferry is that of Dangerfield
Newby, a former slave who joined Brown's raid out of desperation
after a cruel slave owner stymied his attempts to free his wife and
child. Newby was the first of Brown's band to die in the raid; he
was struck in the throat by a jagged spike. Vengeful townspeople
mutilated his body and left it in an alley for wild hogs to devour.

Dressed in old clothes and a slouch hat, Newby's specter
continues to roam the streets of Harpers Ferry, perhaps still
trying to save his family or take revenge on those who treated
his corpse so badly. Across his neck is a horrific scar from the
spike that killed him.

The Hundred Days' Men

Like many other ghosts, the spirits of the Hundred Days' Men
were born out of the violence of war. In 1864, at the height of the
Civil War, the governor of Ohio proposed a plan that called for
several northern states to enlist large numbers of men for a short
period of 100 days. One such group was sent to Harpers Ferry,
where they camped at Maryland Heights. One wet day, the
inexperienced troops sought dry ground on which to build a fire

and cook their dinner. Unfortunately, someone decided to stack some artillery shells to make a dry surface on which to place wood and vegetation. Soon a roaring fire was under way—atop the artillery shells! Inevitably, the shells exploded and many of the Hundred Days' Men were killed.

Mysterious fires are sometimes reported at Maryland Heights, but locals believe that it's just the Hundred Days' Men, still trying to eat a meal that they began more than a century ago.

St. Peter's Catholic Church

During the Civil War, St. Peter's Catholic Church was used as a hospital for wounded soldiers. One day, a wounded young soldier was brought into the churchyard and left lying on the ground as others with more severe injuries were tended to. Hours passed, and the young man's condition worsened as he slowly bled to death. By the time doctors got to him, it was too late. As he was carried into the church, he whispered weakly, "Thank God I'm saved." Then he died.

Over the years, many people have seen a bright light on the church's threshold and heard faint whispers say, "Thank God I'm saved." Some have also watched as an elderly priest emerges from the church's rectory; he turns and walks into the church—right through the wall where the front facade once stood.

Jenny the Vagrant

Another ghost of Harpers Ferry is that of a poor girl named Jenny, who lived in an old storage shed that had been abandoned after the railroad came to Harpers Ferry in the early 1830s. One night, Jenny's dress was set ablaze when she ventured too close to the fire she was using to heat the shed. Jenny bolted out of the shed screaming in a blind panic. Unfortunately, she ran straight onto the railroad tracks and was hit by a train.

Since then, engineers have reported hearing unearthly screams for help and seeing a ball of light careening wildly down the train tracks. Frantically, they blow their whistles, but it's too late: Each engineer feels a bump as if his train has struck something, but when he goes to investigate, he finds nothing.

Myrtles Plantation: A Blast from the Past

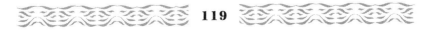

Listed on the National Register of Historic Places and boasting more than 200 years of history, the Myrtles Plantation is a beautiful and sprawling old home in St. Francisville, Louisiana. Now used as a bed-and-breakfast, the mansion has seen its share of drama, including romance, death, and even murder. What better setting for a good old Southern-style haunting? Paranormal experts and amateur ghost hunters all agree that the Myrtles Plantation is one of the most haunted places in America.

Tales to Tell

In 1796, David Bradford built what would eventually become the Myrtles Plantation on 650 acres of land about 30 miles outside of Baton Rouge. At the time, the house—which was originally known as Laurel Grove—was much smaller than it is today. In 1834, Ruffin Stirling purchased and remodeled the plantation, doubling its size and renaming it after the many myrtle trees on the property.

Over the years, many people lived and died at the Myrtles Plantation, so it's not surprising that the place is home to a few restless spirits. Whether it's strange noises, disembodied voices, apparitions, or reflections in a haunted mirror, plenty of paranormal activity can be found at Myrtles Plantation.

In 2005, investigators from the television show *Ghost Hunters* paid a visit to the mansion and documented several strange phenomena. Thermal-imaging video cameras recorded the torso of something not really present, as well as a shadow that appeared to be moving up and down. The team also caught the unexplained movement of a lamp across a table: Over the course of a few minutes, it moved several inches with no help from anyone in the room.

If you visit the Myrtles Plantation, be sure to check out the Myrtles mirror: It is said to reflect the spirit of someone who died in front of it. People have repeatedly seen handprints on the mirror and orbs or apparitions in photos of it. Although many stories say that the images belong to one of the plantation's early owners and

her children—all of whom were poisoned—the mirror was actually brought to the house in the 1970s. If it is indeed haunted, the ghosts may not be from the home originally.

A Spirited Place

Several ghosts are commonly seen inside the house. One is thought to be a French woman who wanders from room to room. Another is a regular at the piano; unfortunately, this spirit only seems to know one chord, which is heard over and over, stopping suddenly when anyone walks into the room. A third is the ghost of a young girl, who only appears right before thunderstorms.

The spirits of two young girls have also been seen playing outside on the veranda, and guests have also felt their presence at night while lying in bed. Sometimes, visitors feel pressure on the bed, as though someone is jumping on it. Soon after, people report seeing the spirit of a maid, who appears to smooth the covers. Another young girl with long curly hair has been seen floating outside the window of the toy room; she appears to be cupping her hands as if she's trying to see inside.

Some visitors report seeing a Confederate soldier on the porch; others have seen the spirit of a man that warns them not to go inside. Many people have glimpsed apparitions of slaves doing their chores inside the mansion. And two other resident ghosts that are certainly entertaining but have little connection to the plantation's rich history are those of a ballet dancer clad in a tutu and a Native American woman who appears naked in the outdoor gazebo.

The ghost of William Winter is also said to haunt the mansion. Winter lived at the Myrtles Plantation from 1860 to 1868 and again from 1870 until his death in 1871, when an unknown assailant shot him as he answered the door. By some accounts, he staggered back

inside and died on the 17th step of the staircase, where his slow dragging footsteps can be heard to this day.

Chloe

Perhaps the best-known ghost at the Myrtles Plantation is that of Chloe, a former slave. Her spirit is thought to walk between the main house and the old slave quarters. People describe her apparition as that of a slender woman wearing a green turban.

As the story goes, David Bradford's daughter Sara married Clark Woodruff, who—it is rumored—had an affair with a beautiful slave girl named Chloe. After enjoying her station in the main house, Chloe was upset when Woodruff ended the affair. When he later caught her eavesdropping, Woodruff became enraged and cut off her ear. (It is said that she wears the green turban to cover the scar.) Two versions of the next part of this story exist: One has Chloe seeking revenge on Woodruff by poisoning his family; the other says that she poisoned them to secure her position as a nursemaid and nanny, so that she would be needed inside to nurse the family back to health, and therefore, she wouldn't be sent to work in the fields.

In either case, Chloe allegedly crushed up oleander petals and added them to a cake she was baking for the oldest daughter's birthday. Clark Woodruff didn't eat any of it, but his wife and two daughters did, and they soon died from poisoning. The other slaves, fearing punishment, dragged Chloe to the yard, where she was hanged. Legend has it that her ghost can be seen in the yard and wandering through the house in her signature headwear.

It's a great story, and it's easy to see why it would be repeated—and possibly twisted a bit each time. But researchers who have dug through old court records have found no evidence that there ever was a Chloe: There is nothing to suggest that a slave by that name (or anything close to it) ever lived at Myrtles Plantation. And although death records show that Sara Woodruff and two of the children did die young, all the deaths were attributed to yellow fever, not poison.

So there you have it. Myrtles Plantation is rife with ghosts, but we may never know exactly who they were in life or why they're still attached to the mansion. Chloe may or may not have existed in the real world, but you never know what you may encounter at one of the most haunted houses in America.

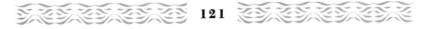

Spirited Celebrities

*By their very nature, celebrities seem larger than life—
but some seem to be larger than death, too. Were the egos
within this group so immense that even death couldn't
contain them? Might they have something important to tell
us? Or are these notables simply performing an afterlife
version of a curtain call? For whatever reason, something
seems to be keeping these celebrity spirits earthbound.*

Marilyn Monroe

As famous in death as she was in life, screen legend Marilyn Monroe
(1926–1962) continues to captivate. Plagued with insecurities from
the start, the blonde bombshell's three marriages ended in
divorce, and she eventually developed a dependency on
substances to counter the overwhelming weight of her celebrity.
Nevertheless, when Monroe exited the mortal world at age 36, the
coroner's pronouncement of "probable suicide" didn't ring true
for many. Since then, countless conspiracy theories concerning
Monroe's death have taken root.

In life, a favorite haunt of the
sexy siren was the Hollywood
Roosevelt Hotel. It was at this
retreat for Tinseltown's elite that
Monroe found peace and could rest,
safe in the knowledge that her private moments would remain private.
Perhaps she is still searching for
such moments in death: That might
explain the sightings of her sashay-
ing across the hotel's ballroom and
lingering near the room that she often occupied. It might also
explain why her haunting image can sometimes be seen in a mirror
that hangs in the hotel's lobby.

In recent years, guests at the Hotel del Coronado in Coronado,
California, have also reported seeing Marilyn Monroe's ghost. She
loved "the Del" when she stayed there while filming *Some Like It*

Hot (1959). She is supposedly seen as a fleeting, translucent apparition near the door to the hotel or on the beach nearby. Those who have seen her specter comment on its windswept blonde hair and its fringed shawl that flutters in the breeze. Others claim to have heard Monroe giggling in the hallways.

Carole Lombard

Another spirit that is said to haunt the Hollywood Roosevelt Hotel is that of actress Carole Lombard (1908–1942). The golden-haired beauty made her mark in notable films such as *My Man Godfrey* (1936) and *Mr. & Mrs. Smith* (1941). Despite her talent, Lombard is perhaps best remembered as the wife of screen legend Clark Gable. The couple married in 1939, but only three years later, on January 16, 1942, fate played its cruel hand when the actress was killed in a plane crash. Lombard's death had a profound effect on Gable: The word *devastated* only begins to describe the depth of the actor's grief. Despite two subsequent marriages, Gable said that with Lombard's passing, he had lost the greatest love of his life. When he died in 1960, he was buried beside his beloved Lombard. But death may not have signaled the end of their romance: Sightings at the Hollywood Roosevelt suggest that this great love carries on. Lombard's apparition has been spotted moving about the hotel's 12th floor. It was there that the famous couple's love first blossomed, and it is there that it apparently continues . . . for eternity.

Lon Chaney Sr.

Known for playing such frightening characters as Quasimodo in *The Hunchback of Notre Dame* (1923) and the title character in *The Phantom of the Opera* (1925), Lon Chaney Sr. (1883–1930), the "Man of a Thousand Faces," scared viewers silly during the silent-film era. With his haunting legacy, it's not surprising that Chaney can still be found wandering the catwalks above Soundstage 28 at Universal Studios. Horror-film buffs know that this is the stage where *Phantom* was shot. Chaney's ghost reportedly moves about in full Phantom garb, flipping lights on and off and opening and closing doors.

Rudolph Valentino

Before "talkies" (movies with sound) came along, silent films ruled the silver screen. In those early days of filmmaking, the strikingly handsome Rudolph Valentino (1895–1926) made women swoon. Moviegoers happily plunked down a quarter to see the "Latin Lover" in films such as *The Sheik* (1921). His immense popularity made Hollywood moguls rich, but the actor's earthly days were sadly limited. Due to complications from a ruptured appendix and gastric ulcers, Valentino left the human realm at age 31. Nevertheless, there are some who say that he never left at all.

Before his former mansion—Falcon Lair—was demolished in the 2000s, Valentino was spotted standing in his bedroom and peering from a second-floor window. He was also seen inside the estate's barn: It was there that a stable worker saw Valentino's ghost petting his favorite horse.

Valentino sightings at Paramount Studios may be even more dramatic. There, the ghost of the eternal ladies' man has been seen wandering around the costume department wearing his costume from *The Sheik*. The handsome apparition has also been spotted looking down from a catwalk high above Soundstage 5. For a brief time, this was his world. Perhaps it still is.

George Reeves

If a post-death appearance suggests unfinished business in the mortal world, the spirit of George Reeves (1914–1959) may be trying to tell us something. Reeves acquired his acting chops long before the popular *Adventures of Superman* TV series (1952–1958) turned him into a household name: Before he was "The Man of Steel," Reeves appeared in several TV shows and movies, including the classic *Gone with the Wind* (1939).

On June 16, 1959, Reeves held a party at his Benedict Canyon home. The get-together suddenly turned tragic when a loud bang was heard in the actor's upstairs bedroom. Upon investigation, Reeves was found dead of an apparently self-inflicted gunshot wound to the head. His death was ruled a suicide, but not everyone was convinced that he killed himself. After all, Reeves had recently launched a career as a TV director and seemed to be

riding a happy wave in life. Some began to wonder if the actor's death was, in fact, a *murder* that was made to look like a suicide. Reeves certainly had his enemies—most notably an insanely jealous ex-lover who resented being jilted for another woman.

Perhaps we'll never know just what occurred in Reeves's bedroom on that sad day, but some believe that his spirit is trying to tell us. Numerous people have claimed that Reeves's ghost inhabits his former residence. Strange noises, moving beds, tossed linens, and a variety of other surreal incidents have kept subsequent owners on their toes. Once, Reeves's ghost was spotted—dressed in Superman garb—lingering in the living room where the ill-fated party had taken place. The apparition hung around until the residents fled in panic. Was the "Man of Steel" trying to relate a message about his untimely trip to the Other Side?

Lucille Ball

After a long and successful career as Hollywood's most beloved comedienne, Lucille Ball died in 1989 at age 77. Although she died during surgery, her spirit apparently returned to her beloved home on Roxbury Drive in Beverly Hills. After Lucy died, her husband Gary Morton sold the home, and the new owners subsequently demolished it. When a friend of Lucy's stopped by the home to assess the destruction, he saw her ghost lingering at the construction site looking bewildered at the rubble.

Elvis Presley

Graceland will never be the same without Elvis Presley. But according to some, Elvis hasn't left the building. Visitors have caught glimpses of his apparition walking through the gates of his beloved estate. One tourist claims to have seen "The King's" face reflected back at her from a glass jewelry case, and it's rumored that his ghost still resides in his old private quarters—an area that is closed to the public. Since his death in 1977, Elvis's spirit has also been spotted near Music Row in Nashville. Workers at a studio there say that whenever Presley's name is brought up, lights flicker, ladders fall down, and unusual noises are heard over the sound system.

Out with the Old, in with the New: The Ghosts of Chicago's Old Town Tatu

🪦 🪦 🪦 🪦

When ghost hunters from the Chicago branch of the American Ghost Society first investigated Old Town Tatu in 2006, their goal was to look for ghosts from the days when the building served as a funeral home. But in later investigations, they turned their attention to communicating with more recent spirits.

Generations of Hauntings

For nearly 75 years, the building that now houses Old Town Tatu on Chicago's north side was the home of the Klemundt Funeral Home. And for years, the Klemundt family had told stories about the building being haunted.

In 2002, the building was purchased for use as a tattoo parlor, and soon after, the new occupants began to experience strange poltergeist activity and other supernatural phenomena: Decorations fell off the walls as though pushed by an unseen force, and small objects—such as ashtrays—flew across the room. One tattoo artist even told of an ashtray that zipped through the air and landed upside down without spilling a single ash.

In the main entryway, several employees encountered the ghost of a young girl. Her presence was usually felt but not seen, so some researchers speculated that the phenomenon was not the ghost of a girl who died in the building but rather residual energy (sometimes known as a "psychic imprint") from a girl who was terrified after being left alone in the building years before.

Employees and customers also reported seeing the shadowy specters of a man in a brown suit, a man in a powder blue suit, and a woman in a white dress. One employee even claimed to hear a disembodied voice in the basement that made a spooky noise like a ghost in a cartoon.

Ghosts Exposed

Prior to the American Ghost Society's first formal investigation of Old Town Tatu (then known as Odin Tatu) in 2006, no one was entirely sure how seriously to take these stories. Veteran ghost hunters are accustomed to people making up tales about women in white and ghosts making scary sounds. But they suspected that the tattoo artists weren't fabricating the stories; after all, the Klemundt family had been telling similar tales for years.

During their investigation, the researchers found a cold spot in the northeastern corner of the basement, and one team member felt something tap him on the shoulder. When one of the investigators called out "What's your name?," the team heard nothing; however, upon reviewing evidence from their audio recorder, they discovered that it had picked up a voice saying the name "Walter."

One theory suggests that this was the ghost of Walter Loeding, whose funeral was held in the building in the 1960s. Klemundt family members recalled that Walter didn't own a suit at the time of his death, so they had to buy one in which to bury him. The suit that they bought was brown, which leads some to believe that Walter is the ghost in a brown suit that some have seen.

"If I Die in This Place..."

None of this activity seemed to surprise Richard "Tapeworm" Herrera, the owner of the tattoo parlor. Not only did Tapeworm work in the building, he also lived there, and over the years, he had seen several ghosts, including the man in the brown suit, whom he sometimes saw watching him while he worked at his tattoo station.

"I stopped what I was doing and tried to motion for other people to look," Tapeworm said during the first investigation. "But I wouldn't take my eye[s] off him for one second, man, 'cause I knew that if I looked away for a second, he'd be gone. And he was! The second I looked away, he vanished."

 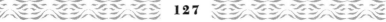

Herrera also claimed that ghosts would mess with the appliances in his apartment above the tattoo parlor and would even open the window while he was in the bathroom. Most of the experiences seemed to amuse Tapeworm more than scare him, but the entity that he encountered on the staircase to his apartment did genuinely frighten him.

Having grown up in the neighborhood, Herrera had always been leery of the old tiled stairway—the only part of the funeral home that could be seen from the front windows. "I remember being a kid in this neighborhood, and you could see those stairs in the window. I was always all superstitious about it because of what the place was, you know. It was where the dead people were. And now…lo and behold, 30 years later, I'm *living* here. And twice, when I've been walking down those stairs, I felt like something was trying to push me! And that freaks me out because everyone knows you can't fight back with these cats! So the first time it happened, I just looked up and shouted, 'Listen! If I die in this place, it is *on!*'"

The investigators and Tapeworm all shared a hearty laugh. Later, when the investigators reviewed their audio, they found that the sound of ghostly laughter had been recorded on the staircase at the exact moment that a psychic, who was assisting with the investigation, claimed that a ghost thought it was very funny that Tapeworm was afraid of being pushed down the stairs. Tragically, barely three weeks after the first investigation, Tapeworm had a heart attack in his apartment. He died at age 37, just steps away from the staircase.

You Can't Keep a Good Ghost Down

After Tapeworm's death, his friends and coworkers came to believe that he was haunting the place, which was renamed Old Town Tatu. The equipment at Tapeworm's old station would frequently malfunction (or not work at all) when anyone who was not a friend of Tapeworm's tried to use it. In addition, motion-activated cameras that had been recently installed recorded unusual orblike blobs that floated up to the camera and hovered in front of it momentarily before drifting away.

Then, on Halloween night, a few months after Tapeworm's untimely death, the tattoo parlor's employees were enjoying their annual Halloween party when one of them checked his cell phone

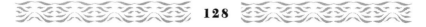

and noticed a missed call—from Tapeworm's old number. He called
the number the next day and found that it belonged to a confused
young woman who had been asleep when the call was made.

One member of the American Ghost Society who was present at
the first investigation said that when he returned to the building, he
felt as though someone was pulling his hair and flicking his ear—
things that a prankster like Tapeworm would do in life.

Current employees also claim that Tapeworm's ghost seems
especially active when they play techno music, which Tapeworm
despised. To make his presence (and his dislike of the music) known,
Tapeworm likes to make equipment malfunction and cause electrical
disturbances. If employees play punk or heavy metal music, which
were Tapeworm's favorites, the parlor is much calmer.

Tapeworm has also been known to announce his presence
verbally: A psychic investigator who toured the building in 2007 was
given no information about the place, yet he said that he sensed the
presence of a particularly foul-mouthed ghost. And in 2009, Brad
and Barry Klinge from *Ghost Lab* noted a 20-degree temperature
drop after calling out, "Hey Richie!" They also picked up an EVP
(electronic voice phenomenon) of a voice that Tapeworm's friends
identified as his. The voice said a few things that cannot be repeated
here (or on television, for that matter).

Whether Tapeworm's spirit is actually engaged in an otherworldly
battle with the funeral parlor ghosts is, of course, unknown. But the
presence of his ghost *has* been reported much more frequently than
those of others in the years since his death, which leads some to wonder if he kicked their butts so far into oblivion that they're afraid to
show up anymore. Those who knew Tapeworm have no doubt about it.

"There are an infinite number of universes existing side by side and through
which our consciousnesses constantly pass. In these universes, all possibilities exist. You are alive in some, long dead in others, and never existed in
still others. Many of our 'ghosts' could indeed be visions of people going
about their business in a parallel universe or another time—or both."
—Paul F. Eno, *Faces at the Window*

West Point's Spirited Residents

The United States Military Academy at West Point has an illustrious history. Since 1802, it has educated young men (and women, beginning in 1976) preparing to serve their country as officers in the U.S. Army; prior to that time, West Point was a military fort. With that much history, it's no surprise that these hallowed halls are home to a ghost or two.

Keeping in line with the pomp and circumstance of the academy, cadets and visitors have reported seeing soldiers from different eras in full-dress uniforms. And back in the 1920s, a spirit inhabiting a house on Professor's Row had to be exorcised. It is unknown whether this was a malevolent ghost or a demonic force, but whatever it was and whatever it did, it frightened two servant girls so terribly that they ran out of the house screaming in the middle of the night.

A cranky Irish cook named Molly is thought to haunt the superintendent's mansion, where she once worked. "Miss Molly"—as she was called when she lived there in the early 19th century—was the maid of Brigadier General Sylvanus Thayer. A hard worker even in death, Molly is often seen kneading bread in the mansion's kitchen.

The Pickpocket Poltergeist

In October 1972, demonologists Ed and Lorraine Warren were invited to give a lecture at West Point. While they were there, they were asked to investigate some paranormal activity that had been occurring at the superintendent's house. It seems that, among other things, personal items and wallets of guests had come up missing... only to be discovered later, neatly arranged on the dresser in the master bedroom.

Lorraine was able to communicate with the "Pickpocket Poltergeist," who identified himself as a man named Greer. In the early 1800s, he had been wrongly accused of murder, and although he was ultimately exonerated, he was anguishing in sorrow and was unable to move on. Lorraine urged him to go into the light.

Room 4714

But it is Room 4714 in the 47th Division Barracks that has caused the most supernatural speculation. Paranormal activity was first reported there shortly after the Warrens' visit, when students Art Victor and James O'Connor shared the room. One day, when O'Connor went to take a shower, he noticed that his bathrobe was swinging back and forth—but nothing was blowing it. Then suddenly, the temperature in the room dropped several degrees.

A couple of days later, O'Connor saw an apparition of a soldier wearing a uniform and carrying a musket. The following evening, both boys felt an extreme drop in temperature and then saw a man's upper body float through the room; it hovered between the floor and ceiling for a few minutes before disappearing.

One night shortly thereafter, two fellow cadets—Keith Bakken and Terry Meehan—volunteered to spend the night in Room 4714. During the night, Meehan awoke and caught a glimpse of a ghostly figure near the ceiling. By the time Bakken woke up, the apparition was gone, but both boys experienced an extreme drop in temperature. After the campus newspaper published an article about the strange activity, several other cadets offered to sleep in the room. A thermocouple was used to scientifically measure any temperature changes. The coldest temperature was always found right next to O'Connor. Oddly, one night when other cadets were in his room waiting for the ghost, O'Connor saw the specter in *another* room while the boys in Room 4714 saw nothing.

Although a significant number of cadets saw the apparition and felt the drastic temperature change in Room 4714, the identity of this spirit remains unknown. The 47th Division barracks are located near the site of a disastrous house fire that killed an officer. The building is also close to a graveyard in which some Revolutionary War–era soldiers are buried. Could the ghost be one of these military men attempting to bond with the new breed of cadet? If so, the spirit eventually gave up—it hasn't been seen or felt since the 1970s.

Unsettled Spirits at the Sanatorium

It was designed to save lives at a time when an epidemic was sweeping the nation. Little did its developers know that they were erecting a building in which scores of people would take their last gasping breaths. Is it any wonder that the halls of the Waverly Hills Sanatorium in Louisville, Kentucky, still echo with the footsteps of those who died there?

Origins

Around 1883, the first building was erected on the site of what is now the Waverly Hills Sanatorium. Major Thomas Hays, the owner of the property, decided that the local schools were too far away for his daughters to attend, so he constructed a small schoolhouse on the land and hired teacher Lizzie Harris to instruct the girls. Because of her love of Walter Scott's *Waverley* novels, Harris named the place Waverly School. Taken by the name, Hays decided to call his property Waverly Hill.

In the early 1900s, an outbreak of tuberculosis spread across the United States. In an effort to confine the highly contagious disease, the construction of TB sanatoriums and hospitals was planned. In 1908, the Board of Tuberculosis Hospitals purchased the Hays property, and in July 1910, a small two-story building was opened; it had the capacity to house nearly 50 patients.

They Just Keep Coming...

Without a cure in existence or any way to slow the disease, little could be done for TB patients at the time. Treatment often consisted of nothing more than fresh air and exposure to heat lamps. More and more patients arrived at the sanatorium; therefore, in the 1920s, expansion of the facility began, and in 1926, the building that stands today opened. This massive five-story structure could house nearly 400 patients. But once again, the rooms quickly filled up. The sad truth was that the sanatorium was only kept from overcrowding due to the fact that, without a cure, many of the patients died. Just how

many people passed away there is the stuff of urban legends—some estimates go as high as 65,000. In truth, the number is probably closer to 8,000, but that's still a staggering number when one realizes that tuberculosis causes patients to slowly and painfully waste away over the course of weeks or even months.

In the 1940s, treatments for TB were introduced, and as a result, the number of patients at Waverly Hills consistently declined until the building was officially shut down in 1961.

The Final Years

A short time later, Waverly Hills was reopened as the Woodhaven Geriatric Center. This chapter of the building's history came to an end around 1980 amid whispers of patient cruelty and abuse. Before long, those whispers became full-blown urban legends involving depravities such as electroshock therapy. Not surprisingly, it wasn't long before people started saying that the abandoned, foreboding structure was haunted.

Meet the Ghosts

So who are the ghosts that are said to haunt Waverly Hills? Sadly, the identities of most of them are unknown, but many of them have been encountered. Almost every floor of the building has experienced paranormal activity, such as disembodied voices and ghostly footsteps. Doors have been known to open and close by themselves, and bits of debris have been thrown at unsuspecting visitors. It is said that all one has to do is wait quietly to spot one of the many shadow people that walk up and down the hallways. Of course, if you're looking for a more interactive ghost encounter, you can always head up to the third floor. There, you might find the spirit of a young girl in the solarium. If she's not there, check the nearby staircases—apparently she likes to run up and down them.

Waverly Hills is also home to the ghost of a young boy who likes to play with a small ball that sometimes appears on the floor. Not wanting to wait to find the ball, some visitors have resorted to bringing their own, which they leave in a certain spot, only to see it roll away or even vanish before it appears on a different floor altogether.

 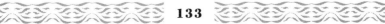

Welcome to Room 502

Of all the allegedly haunted areas at Waverly Hills, none holds a candle to Room 502. Most of the legends associated with the room center on two nurses, both of whom supposedly committed suicide on the premises. One nurse is said to have killed herself in the room in 1928. Apparently, she was a single woman who discovered that she was pregnant. Feeling that she had nowhere to turn, the young woman chose to slip a rope around her neck and hang herself. The other nurse who worked in Room 502 is said to have killed herself in 1932 by jumping from the roof, although the reason why is unclear. Although no documentation substantiating either of these suicides has been unearthed, that has not stopped visitors to Room 502 from experiencing paranormal activity. Upon entering the room, people often report feeling "heavy" or the sensation of being watched. It is quite common for guests to witness shadow figures darting around the room, and occasionally, a lucky visitor catches a glimpse of a spectral nurse standing by the window.

The Body Chute

When expansion of the building began in the 1920s, a rather morbid (though some would say essential) part of the sanatorium was constructed: the Body Chute—a 500-foot-long underground tunnel leading from the main building to a nearby road and set of railroad tracks. Some believe that the tunnel was created simply for convenience, while others think it was designed to prevent patients from seeing the truth—that many of them were dying. Although it was called a chute, bodies were never dumped into it; rather, they were walked through it on gurneys. The tunnel was even equipped with a motorized cable system to help with transportation.

People walking through the Body Chute have reported hearing disembodied voices, whispering, and even painful groans. Sometimes, shadowy figures are seen wandering through the tunnel. But because the only light down there comes from random air vents, the figures vanish almost as quickly as they appear.

Lights, Camera, Ghosts!

After the TV show *Scariest Places on Earth* featured Waverly Hills in a 2001 episode, numerous programs began filming at the

sanatorium. *Ghost Hunters* visited there twice—once in 2006 and again in 2007 as part of its annual live Halloween investigation. *Most Haunted* came all the way from the UK in 2008, and *Ghost Adventures* spent a night locked inside the sanatorium in 2010. But of all the episodes filmed at Waverly Hills, none was more bizarre than that of the short-lived VH1 show *Celebrity Paranormal Project.*

The series' debut episode, which aired in October 2006, was shot at Waverly Hills and featured actor Gary Busey, comedian Hal Sparks, *Survivor* winner Jenna Morasca, model/actress Donna D'Errico, and model Toccara Jones conducting an investigation. The supernatural activity began early in the evening, shortly after Busey and Morasca were sent to Room 418 to investigate. They weren't there long before their thermal-imaging camera picked up shapes moving around the room and even sitting on a bed near them. When Morasca was left in the room alone, she heard all sorts of strange noises and even encountered a small red ball, which wasn't there when the team first entered the room.

When Sparks was in the solarium, he rolled balls across the floor in an attempt to convince the spirits to play with him. The footage shows what appears to be one of the balls rolling back to him. At around the same time, Sparks reported seeing a small black shape, like that of a child, run past the doorway. Later on in the evening, D'Errico reported feeling that someone was following her, an incident that was accompanied by the sound of footsteps. She also heard what sounded like people screaming. She was so frightened that she ran away from the building screaming. Once back in the company of the other investigators, D'Errico said that she actually saw the figure of a man standing in a hallway.

The evening ended with the entire group attempting to contact the spirits in Room 502. As they asked questions, banging noises and footsteps were heard coming from all around them. When they left the building, they were still hearing noises and encountered a child's ball that seemed to appear from out of nowhere.

"Come Join Us"

Waverly Hills Sanatorium is open for tours, both during the day and for overnight ghost hunts. Just be assured that no matter how many ghosts inhabit Waverly Hills, they always have room for more.

Sleepless at the Empire State Building

🪦 🪦 🪦 🪦

*As an international icon, the 102-story Empire State Building
welcomes visitors from all over the world every day. In fact,
it is estimated that 110 million people have made trips to
the top of the revered skyscraper. But some guests never
leave: These are the ghosts of the Empire State Building.*

Located in the center of Manhattan, the Empire State Building
represents financial success as well as architectural beauty, but it wasn't
always that way. The Art Deco building opened in 1931, during the
Great Depression when times were tough. You'd never know that now,
however, as the building bustles with activity. Workers, sweethearts,
families, and tourists are all attracted to the structure, and with all
the activity that has taken place within its walls—especially on the
observation deck—it's no wonder that a few spirits have lingered.

What Makes a Ghost a Ghost?

Throughout the history of the Empire State Building,
numerous people have died there of natural causes.
Others may have passed away elsewhere but returned
to haunt the building because it held a special place
in their hearts in life: Perhaps they worked there or
met their spouse there and wanted to spend a little
more time there—maybe eternity.

The process of building a skyscraper of this
size can also produce a few ghosts. Official records
document only five deaths related to the construction of the Empire State Building, but you can
be sure that some of those workers have
remained to see the finished project.

In addition, on July 28, 1945, a 10-ton B-25 bomber headed for
Newark encountered fog and visibility problems. Just before 10 A.M.,
the plane crashed into the 79th floor of the Empire State Building,
killing 11 office workers and 3 crew members.

Choosing the Afterlife

Over the years, many people who have fallen on hard times have gone to the Empire State Building to end their lives: The structure has been the site of at least 30 suicides. Due to the violent nature of such deaths, suicide victims probably account for most of the unsettled spirits found there. Although several suicide attempts were made from the observation deck in the building's early years, the problem wasn't addressed until a jumper injured a pedestrian upon landing in January 1947. This near miss, coupled with a rash of suicide attempts that year, forced the building's owners to erect a high fence strong enough to deter future jumpers. But that hasn't stopped the spirits of those who succeeded from lingering on the observation deck, usually late at night.

Most of the spirits seen by workers and tourists are of the generic variety—white, filmy, and silent. Who they were and why they stayed behind is unknown, but apparitions do seem to roam the building: In fact, many people have reportedly caught glimpses of a ghostly figure that runs straight through the fence and plunges over the edge.

The Ghost of World War II

More than one person has reported seeing a distraught female spirit on the observation deck. She has been described as a pale, distracted woman wearing red lipstick. She sticks out to all those who tell the story because her clothing appears to be from the 1940s. And unlike many specters, this ghost speaks directly to the living. "My man died in the war," she says, adding that they were childhood sweethearts and were planning to marry when he got home from Germany…but he never returned. She tells of how much she loved her beau and says that she can't live without him. And that is apparently what drove the woman over the edge—literally. One visitor, who encountered the ghostly woman in 1985, actually saw her plunge over the wall, only to return a short time later to tell the same story in the exact same words to another unsuspecting tourist.

Every day, visitors go to the Empire State Building to admire the wonderful Art Deco architecture and take in the spectacular view of New York City and the surrounding area. But if you ever visit the building, keep an eye out for the poor souls that remain there. And if you use your camera, be sure to check your pictures carefully: That white blob may not be a photographic error after all.

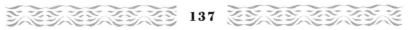

George's Food & Drink:
Serving Food, Wine, and Spirits

You won't find management denying that a ghost resides at George's Food & Drink in Boulder, Colorado; in fact, the place is named after him. Located just south of the Boulder Theater, the restaurant offers fare that it describes as "the next generation in comfort food." That begs the question: Just how much comforting are patrons going to need?

George's Food & Drink, which opened in 2008 near the Boulder Theater, was originally named The Lounge. The ownership's goal was to provide a place where concert- and theatergoers could have a quick meal or relax with an after-show drink. But it turns out that The Lounge attracts more than just patrons of the arts. One frequent visitor is George Paper, who managed the nearby theater in the 1920s, '30s, and '40s. So what's wrong with that? Well, nothing... except that George has been dead for decades.

George's spirit has been haunting the Boulder Theater ever since he suffered a fatal accident there in 1944. As manager, one of George's duties was to fix lighting problems. While performing a routine repair, George slipped and became tangled in the wiring, with tragic results—he accidentally hung himself.

At least George died doing a job that he loved. He loved it so much, in fact, that he stuck around: His friendly presence has been felt in the theater for years. Patrons and employees alike have reported feeling cold spots in the building, and some have even seen a ghostly man dressed in a 1920s-era suit. George's favorite trick is stealing perfectly good lightbulbs.

Owners of The Lounge renamed the establishment George's Food & Drink in his honor after they realized that he was appearing there quite often. Perhaps, like many other patrons, he's simply found a place to relax after taking in a show.

The Black Angel of Death

*The "Black Angel of Death" is unlike other angel statues at Oakland
Cemetery in Iowa City, Iowa. For starters, at eight and a half feet
tall (not including its pedestal), it towers high above the others.
The eyes of the other angel statues gaze up toward heaven, and
their wings are folded on their backs, which signals hope. But
with its wings spread wide and pointing toward the ground,
the Black Angel stares down upon the grave of Eddie Dolezal,
who died in 1891 at age 18. The other angels are made of white
marble; the Black Angel was sculpted out of bronze, which turned
black over the years due to oxidation (or, as some speculate, the
sins of Eddie's mother, who commissioned the statue in 1912).
The Black Angel is different from the other angels in another
important way: According to legend, it likes to take new victims.*

The Black Angel doesn't like to be touched inappropriately or witness
public displays of affection. Locals know that girls should not be kissed
near the statue: The consequence is death within six months. Anyone
who touches the statue on Halloween night has only seven more years
to live. Worse, giving the Angel a kiss can stop a person's heart.

The Black Angel is said to take its ultimate revenge on those who
desecrate it. Legend says that four boys died in a car crash not long
after urinating on the Black Angel. Another story tells of a young man
who removed the thumb of the Angel; soon after, his body was found
hundreds of miles away in the Chicago River, dead from strangulation.
A single thumbprint was imprinted on his neck. Not long after, a
bronze thumb, blackened with age, was reportedly found at the base
of the Black Angel.

Whether or not the Black Angel has actually killed anyone is debat-
able, but photos do often reveal strange lights around it. One couple
found that every one of their pictures featured a red light where the
angel's heart would be. Other snapshots have included orbs, which
signify the presence of spirits. For whatever reason, the Black Angel
does not rest well. Anyone in its presence should beware of its powers.

The Cave of the Murderous Witch

While there have been reports of ghostly encounters in virtually every small town in the world, Adams, Tennessee, stands alone in that it is perhaps the only place where a ghost is said to have been directly responsible for the death of a human being.

Meet the Bell Family

This odd story begins in 1817, when John Bell Sr. was inspecting a field on his farm in Robertson County, Tennessee. He encountered a strange beast that he described as doglike with a rabbitlike head. John allegedly shot at the creature, and it fled into the woods.

Shortly afterward, the Bell family began to experience odd phenomena in their home. What began as soft knocks quickly turned into what sounded like an animal biting or gnawing on the structure of the house. The Bell family scoured the building for rodents, but they found nothing. The activity didn't stop there. What sounded like rocks hitting the house could be heard at all hours of the day and night. Soon, it began to sound like rocks were being thrown from *inside* the house. Once again, the family's searches turned up nothing.

From there, the activity escalated to personal attacks, most of which were centered on John Bell and his youngest daughter, Betsy, who was frequently pushed, grabbed, and slapped by an unseen force.

With nowhere else to turn, John Bell asked his neighbors—Mr. and Mrs. James Johnston—if they had any ideas about what was occurring. After spending some time in the Bell home and witnessing the unusual activity themselves, the Johnstons convinced the Bells that an investigation should be conducted. Reluctantly, John Bell agreed, and several family friends were invited over.

The Investigations Begin

Incredibly, thumping sounds were heard throughout the house when the investigation began. Soon the thumps and groans began to sound like someone growling or clearing his or her throat. And then it

happened: The entity began to speak. It said that it wanted to prevent Betsy Bell from marrying a local boy named Joshua Gardner. It also said that it wanted to kill John Bell.

When asked why it wanted to break up Betsy and Joshua and kill John, the voice remained silent. However, one night, the voice said that it was the spirit of Kate Batts, an eccentric neighbor who had disliked John Bell because of some contentious business dealings between them in the past. Whether or not it was actually the spirit of Kate Batts is unknown, but people began to refer to the entity as "Kate."

Kate would engage in long-winded discussions with those present, and would often quote from Scripture—a rather odd thing for a malevolent spirit to do. She also seemed to know exactly what people were doing at any given time, even if they were miles away. Reports also suggest that Kate sometimes seemed to be drunk, as she would slur her speech and sing bawdy songs.

Soon, word of the "Bell Witch" spread throughout the region and people came from all over to hear her speak. One legend states that when General Andrew Jackson and his men passed through the area, the future president decided that he wanted to hear her for himself. But the witch apparently had other ideas, as she reportedly caused Jackson's wagons to stop right at the Bell property line; more than 30 minutes passed before the entity allowed them to continue. Upon arriving at the Bell residence, the witch cried out that there were two frauds in Jackson's entourage and that she would expose them. However, Jackson and his men left quickly the following morning without Kate ever naming the frauds. Regarding his experience with the entity, Jackson supposedly declared, "I'd rather fight the entire British Army than deal with the Bell Witch."

The Torment Continues

The activity occurred at the Bell house for almost three full years. And while Betsy was certainly under constant attack, John Bell bore the brunt of the witch's anger. From time to time, he would fall deathly ill, his tongue swelling to the point where he could barely speak or swallow, and no medications helped. After some time, John would simply recover and seem fine...until the next time that he would be stricken with a mysterious malady. All the while, the witch would laugh and taunt John, claiming that one day, he would be dead.

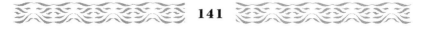

On December 20, 1820, John Bell was found dead in his bed. After hearing Kate's maniacal laughter and shouts that she had finally "done it," the Bell family found a new medicine bottle containing a mysterious substance. John's son placed his finger in the bottle and then got a family cat to lick the substance off. Almost immediately, the cat went into convulsions and died. At that moment, it became clear to everyone that the witch had poisoned John Bell.

When Bell was laid to rest in the family cemetery, some people reported hearing the Bell Witch laugh out loud at the fact that she had succeeded in her mission to kill him.

Unfinished Business

But Kate's work wasn't done. She continued to focus on breaking up Betsy and Joshua Gardner, until finally, in the spring of 1821, Betsy broke off the relationship. After that, the Bell Witch left, but she promised to return in seven years to check up on the family.

According to legend, Kate did return in 1828, this time visiting the home of John Bell Jr. She apparently stayed for several weeks and had many casual conversations with John Jr., but she refused to explain why she needed to kill John Sr. or break up Betsy and Joshua. Before she left again, she promised to return in 107 years. However, 1935 came and went without the Bell Witch making an appearance. Or maybe she never really left the area.

Down into the Cave

Located on the former property of John Bell is a large cave. Many people believe that the Bell Witch fled to this cave when she was not actively haunting the Bell family. Others believe that the cave represents some sort of portal through which she would travel.

The cave, which is open for tours, is still a hotbed of paranormal activity, such as strange sounds, moving shadows, and eerie mists that appear in photographs. So if you're looking for a chance to encounter a murderous entity, stop by the Bell Witch Cave ... but beware if your last name is Bell.

Tormented Spirits at the Lizzie Borden Bed-and-Breakfast

*Lizzie Borden took an ax
And gave her mother 40 whacks,
And when she saw what she had done,
She gave her father 41.*

This poem has been a schoolyard staple for more than a century; however, it contains a few errors. For example, it states that Lizzie Borden whacked her mother with an ax 40 times before turning on her father. In reality, the Bordens were murdered with a hatchet, not an ax. And Mrs. Borden suffered around 20 wounds while her husband suffered 11—still more than enough to kill them both. What's more, Abby Borden was Lizzie's stepmother, not her mother.

But the poem may have yet another inaccuracy: Lizzie Borden may not have been the murderer at all!

"Father's Dead!"

Lizzie Borden grew up in Fall River, Massachusetts. In 1892, when the murders took place, Lizzie was still living at home at age 32, which was old enough to be considered a spinster by the standards of the day.

On August 4, 1892, the family's maid, Bridget Sullivan, was in her upstairs room when she heard Lizzie screaming. "Come down quick!" Lizzie shouted. "Father's dead! Someone's come in and killed him!"

Andrew Borden was lying dead on the couch, the victim of multiple hatchet wounds. By some accounts, he had been rolled over to look like he was merely sleeping, but there was blood everywhere.

While neighbors tended to the shocked Lizzie, she was asked where she had been when all of this happened. She replied that she had gone to the barn to get something.

A little while later, the police found the body of Abby Borden in a guest room. She was even more mutilated than her husband.

Lizzie was the only person who the police ever arrested for the crime. A great deal of tension had existed between Lizzie and her

father, for a variety of reasons. For example, Andrew's decision to divide his property among his relatives, rather than among his children, had caused much strife within the family. Also, he had recently killed Lizzie's pet pigeons,

which he said had become a nuisance; he decapitated them and left the bodies for Lizzie to find.

Not long before the murders, Andrew had suspected that he was being poisoned. However, he didn't know who to accuse; after all, his miserly ways and shrewd business dealings had made him very unpopular in town—the culprit could have been almost anyone. But few people get poisoned simply for being unpopular, and Lizzie had been spotted buying cyanide at a local pharmacy just days before the murders. This made her look fairly suspicious.

In addition, Lizzie's explanation—that she had been in the barn while the murders took place—didn't convince everyone. For one thing, the bodies looked like they'd been moved. And how long could it possibly have taken her to get something out of the barn?

The Verdict

Lizzie was arrested for the murders, although the evidence against her was slim. There were no bloodstains on her dress when the police arrived on the scene, and no bloody clothes were ever found. A broken hatchet was located in the basement, but it could not be connected to the murders. With no solid evidence against Lizzie, the jury deliberated just 90 minutes before acquitting her.

After the trial, Lizzie changed her name to "Lizbeth" and went on with her life. She lived a somewhat lavish lifestyle in her new home, which she called Maplecroft, until her death in 1927.

Today, there are dozens of theories about the identity of the actual killer. Some say that it was Lizzie, while others think that it wasn't her but that she knew very well who it was. Still others believe that Lizzie had nothing to do with it. The sad truth is that we'll probably never know for sure who committed the crime. But the ghosts of Andrew and Abby Borden may want to keep the investigation alive.

Can You Still Hear the Screams?

Years after the crime, the Borden House became a museum/bed-and-breakfast that was made to look almost exactly as it did at the time of the murders. Guests can actually sleep in the very room in which Abby Borden was killed and eat a breakfast of bananas, coffee, and johnnycakes, just like Mr. and Mrs. Borden did on that fateful morning before their brutal deaths.

Ghost sightings in the old green Victorian house are common—MSNBC even listed the house among the top ten most haunted houses in the United States.

The most active ghost there seems to be that of Abby Borden. Many guests have reported hearing the sound of a woman weeping in the bedroom where Abby's body was found. Many others have heard the sound of footsteps, and some have even reported that as they lay in their beds, an older woman in an old-fashioned Victorian-era dress has come into the room to tuck them in for the night.

But Abby is not the only ghost that roams the B & B. Guests have also occasionally spotted Andrew, and he has also manifested during séances that have been held at the house.

Lizzie's spirit has also been seen at the Borden home. From time to time, guests see a ghostly woman carrying a sharp weapon. Could this be Lizzie—or is it the *real* murderer?

Whoever they are, the ghosts at the Lizzie Borden Bed & Breakfast certainly aren't shy. Many guests have captured strange photos, videos, and audio recordings that feature unusual blobs of light, sounds resembling screams, and shadows that simply shouldn't be there. The owner of the house admits to being touched and pushed by unseen hands. And in 2008, a couple visiting on the anniversary of the brutal murders fled the B & B in terror after the door to their room flung open by itself and a lamp moved and lit up on its own. There are many haunted hotels around the world, but few generate as much paranormal activity as the Lizzie Borden Bed & Breakfast.

But allegedly, the Bordens don't just haunt their former home. People have seen mysterious lights at Oak Grove Cemetery, where the family is buried. And a few folks have even heard screams coming from the Borden plot, where Lizzie's body lies right next to the remains of her father and stepmother.

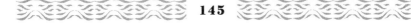

Ghosts Who Take a Bite out of the Big Apple

- Since World War I, a pair of female ghosts has been spotted skating at Central Park's Wollman Ice Rink. Both of these spirits, who wear large Victorian-era bustles, seem to be practicing their figure eights.

- Built in the 1660s, the John Bowne House in Queens is one of the city's oldest buildings. Listed on the National Register of Historic Places, the house now operates as a museum. It is also allegedly haunted by a couple of kind female ghosts dressed in plain Quaker attire.

- The spirit of "Old Moor"—a sailor hanged for mutiny long ago—haunts a former carriage house in Clinton Court, which is located in the Manhattan neighborhood known as Hell's Kitchen. It's said that Old Moor once frightened a woman and a child so terribly that they fell to their deaths.

- Long ago, a ghastly thing happened at a brownstone on the 300 block of Clinton Street in Brooklyn: A doctor botched an abortion that he was performing on his daughter, and she died. Although she was buried in Colorado, her spirit remains at the place where she died, searching longingly for her lover.

- John Lennon lived at The Dakota, an apartment complex across from Central Park. On December 8, 1980, Mark David Chapman murdered him near the building's entrance. Lennon's affable spirit still roams the sidewalk in front of the apartment building.

- The De Geldern House is a large brownstone located on West 87th Street in Manhattan. Since the 1960s, residents have reported seeing the ghost of a teenage girl on the inside staircase. Her identity is unknown, but she wears a blue Victorian-era dress.

- Fire Station No. 2 in Greenwich Village is home to a phantom fireman. A middle-aged man with gray hair and a large mustache, he wears old-school firefighting gear and roams around the firehouse. Legend has it that he hanged himself after learning that his wife had been unfaithful.

- When the Today *show premiered in 1952, its host was Dave Garroway, who lived on East 63rd Street in Manhattan. The Garroways shared their home with the ghost of a mean old man that caused the family members such concern that they called in a medium; however, she was unable to banish the spirit.*

- *Greenwich Village resident Barrie Gaunt lived in a basement apartment on Charles Street during the 1960s. When he tired of being followed around his residence by a strange, foggy mist, he consulted some mediums. They determined that the mist was the spirit of a woman who had died there in 1886, but they were unable to convince her to cross over and leave her beloved home.*

- *The "Gay Street Phantom" is known to reside at 12 Gay Street in Greenwich Village. This sharply dressed entity wears a black suit with old-fashioned tails and a top hat.*

- *In the 1960s, when actress June Havoc lived on 44th Street in Manhattan, she hired well-known medium Sybil Leek to investigate her townhome's resident ghost. Apparently, Havoc's invisible roommate was a Revolutionary War–era rape victim named Lucy.*

- *Harry Houdini had an apartment on West 113th Street in Harlem. A fervent spiritualist, Houdini promised to try to contact his family and friends from the afterlife; he and his wife even had a secret code so she would know that it was really him. Although he was unable to communicate with his loved ones during multiple séances after his death, subsequent residents of his former apartment say that they've seen his apparition there.*

- *The Jan Hus Presbyterian Church and the Jan Hus Playhouse share a building on East 74th Street in Manhattan. They also share the unfriendly "Jan Hus Phantom," which author Marvin Kaye once witnessed.*

- *For many years, the Martha Washington Hotel in Manhattan was a female-only residence, so it's not surprising that the building's resident ghost is a crabby elderly lady. This eternal tenant, who resides on the 12th floor, seems to resent intruders, so she likes to hold pillows over their faces while they sleep.*

The Happiest Haunted Place on Earth?

🪦 🪦 🪦 🪦

According to the proprietors of Disneyland, the Haunted Mansion is home to 999 ghosts ... and there's room for one more. But some people believe that the 1,000th ghost is already there—and that it is no special effect! In fact, many spirits are said to linger at the Magic Kingdom long after the last guest has left for the day.

The Haunted Mansion

The most famous "real" ghost at the Haunted Mansion is that of "Timmy," a young boy who loved the attraction so much that, after he met an unfortunate and untimely death, his mother asked for the park's permission to scatter his ashes on the ride. When the park refused, she was appalled. How could Disneyland, of all places, deny the simple request of a grieving mother?

As the story goes, the poor woman took matters into her own hands. She boarded the ride with her son's ashes in hand and waited until she came to the "Séance Room," where a harp, tambourine, and other instruments float in mid-air while Madame Leota—the face in the crystal ball—calls the spirits to come forth and join the party. Timmy's mother allegedly scattered her son's ashes as her "Doom Buggy" moved through the room. Ever since then, guests have claimed to see the ghost of young Timmy crying in the area where people exit the ride.

Could the story be true? No one has ever been able to verify Timmy's actual identity, but someone could easily scatter ashes while on the ride. In fact, the park is known to intentionally keep the Mansion dusty, so it's certainly conceivable that human ashes could have been hidden somewhere along the dark ride's journey.

During slow periods when they had the ride pretty much to themselves, some guests have reported hearing loud knocks on the backs of their Doom Buggies, even though no one was in the car behind them and no cast members were nearby. Some claim that Buggy No. 55 is the haunted buggy. No one is certain who is

haunting it (perhaps it's Timmy), but having a chance to ride in it is considered the "Holy Grail" among Haunted Mansion enthusiasts.

Uncle Walt's Keeping Watch

While the Haunted Mansion may be the most logical location for ghosts to hang out at Disneyland, it's certainly not the only place they've been sighted. In fact, rumors have long swirled that Walt Disney himself haunts a room that was originally intended to be his apartment. He never actually lived in the space, which is tucked away near the Pirates of the Caribbean ride, but some say that he loved the idea of having his own apartment inside the park so much that he sometimes comes back from beyond the grave to visit it.

The Sad Tale of Disco Debbie

Another ghost that is seen at the park is "Disco Debbie," a former employee that is said to haunt Space Mountain—an indoor roller coaster. According to legend, during the summer of 1979, Debbie's job was to liven up the crowd and encourage guests to dance on the "Space Stage" outside the attraction. After work one day, she was found dead of a brain aneurysm backstage at Space Mountain. She has since been seen on several occasions—often as a pale green apparition that's visible through the ride's windows.

REAL Skeletons!

Other dead bodies have been in the park known as "The Happiest Place on Earth," and people lined up to see them. Believe it or not, when the Pirates of the Caribbean ride first opened in the late 1960s, its designers had not yet created realistic-looking skeletons. Their solution? Use actual cadavers! Scoff if you will, but the tale is reportedly true—every skeleton on the ride was real when it first opened, and the skull and crossbones above the captain's bed still is! The story is hard to believe and the company doesn't like to talk about it, but the "Disney Underground" community insists that it's true.

And as for the rumor that Walt Disney's cryogenically frozen body lies in a secret chamber under the Pirates of the Caribbean attraction? Well, that's a whole other story!

The Haunted Mind of Edgar Allan Poe

Although he died in 1849, Edgar Allan Poe remains one of the world's best-known writers of horror fiction. His stories are continually reprinted and have inspired numerous motion pictures, television shows, and literary works.

Madness Unmasked

Horror wasn't all that Poe wrote. Over the course of his career, the mustachioed wordsmith also invented the modern detective story and penned several well-received works of humor and satire. But it was his work in the horror genre that made him a household name.

A review of Poe's deliciously demented short fiction reveals him to be a master of what we now call the Gothic style of horror, in which characters slowly descend into madness that often leads to horrific consequences. Indeed, his short stories and poems are filled with individuals driven to the brink of insanity—some by their own devices and others by ghosts and spirits in various manifestations.

"The Fall of the House of Usher" is a prime example of this style. First published in 1839, it's the tale of a man named Roderick Usher who suffers from an unknown malady. His sister Madeline is also ill and has a propensity to fall into deathlike trances.

After Madeline dies suddenly, she is interred in the family tomb for two weeks before her final burial. During that time, Roderick experiences all manner of unexplained phenomena, including horrific sounds that echo throughout the house. The manifestations eventually become so unbearable that Roderick falls into hysteria, convinced that his sister—whom he admits he entombed while she was still alive—is responsible. When Madeline arrives at Roderick's bedroom door, she reaches for him and they both fall to the floor dead.

Morella's Curse

Another fine example of Gothic horror from Poe's supernatural canon is "Morella," the story of a woman who dabbles in the black arts.

As Morella's physical body deteriorates, her husband wishes for her to die so that she may find peace. His wish is granted when Morella passes away during childbirth. Unfortunately, because of her experimentation with the black arts, her soul cannot cross over; instead, it is transferred to the baby, who grows up bearing a terrifying resemblance to her mother. Stricken, the father refuses to give the girl a name and restricts her to the house. Eventually, however, he decides to have her baptized. During the ceremony, the priest asks for the child's name, and when the father whispers "Morella," the child turns her head and declares, "I am here!" before dying on the spot. Heartbroken, the father brings the little girl to the family tomb, where he finds no trace at all of his wife's body.

Similar themes can also be found in the short story "Ligeia," in which the title character—a beautiful and intelligent woman—falls ill and eventually dies. Her husband, the story's narrator, marries Lady Rowena, who also becomes ill and dies. Distraught, the grieving husband spends the night with the corpse of Lady Rowena, which slowly comes back to life—as Ligeia.

Genius Revealed

Edgar Allan Poe was an extraordinarily talented writer who had a remarkable gift for establishing a mood of Gothic foreboding. His characters are often insane or drug-addicted (or both), which leaves analysis of their actions and revelations open to interpretation by the reader. Through it all, however, Poe never fails to deliver haunting descriptions of the mind-bendingly grotesque and macabre. As a result, his stories and poems excel at sending shivers down the spines of even the most jaded readers.

Ghosts and bizarre images of the undead in various forms play integral roles in many of Poe's literary works, though readers are occasionally left wondering what is real and what is merely a figment of the protagonist's fevered imagination. In the end, however, it doesn't really matter: A thrill is a thrill, regardless of the cause—a fact that Edgar Allan Poe knew only too well.

 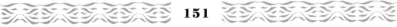

Gearing Up for Ghosts

Back in the old days, the most common tools brought on ghost hunts were guns and swords. Exactly what those people thought these implements would do to the already dead is anyone's guess, but if the "ghost" they found turned out to be a guy in a white sheet, the hunt would've had an awfully unpleasant ending.

By the 1930s, ghost hunts had grown slightly more sophisticated. Organized hunts at England's Borley Rectory involved cameras, tape measures, lengths of string, and other household items. Even today, a very credible ghost hunt can be staged with objects that are commonly found around the house.

In the early 2000s, the popularity of ghost-hunting shows on television introduced many new gadgets to would-be paranormal investigators. Some of these can help eliminate scientific explanations for weird noises, while others simply give an idea of the best area at a location for seeing a ghost. So without further ado, here are some of the most common ghost-hunting tools available today.

EMF (Electromagnetic Field) Detectors

The EMF detector has become the most popular gizmo in the ghost hunter's toolbox. Generally speaking, a ghost is nothing more than a form of energy, which can be measured as it interacts with other forms of energy, such as those with an electric or magnetic charge. An EMF detector allows investigators to measure and track these types of charges in a specific area. Look for unexplainable spikes that could be paranormal in nature.

EMF detectors come in a variety of shapes and sizes; some even have LED screens. Prices range from about $30 for a simple model (which you'll have to calibrate and leave sitting on the ground) to hundreds of dollars for a version that you can carry with you.

Cameras

Get the best camera that you can afford. A camera-phone is better than nothing, but no skeptic is going to be swayed by a photo

taken with a mobile device: Many smartphones tend to produce images that have a lot of digital and visual "noise" that can easily be mistaken for, or presented as, paranormal phenomena.

Whether to go with a traditional film camera or a good digital model is a subject of great debate in the ghost-hunting world. It's true that a lot of problems exist with digital cameras: Older and less expensive models tend to pick up a lot of "orbs" that are actually dust particles or light refraction, but they also eliminate issues that are encountered with film cameras, such as double exposures and overexposures, which have resulted in a lot of false positives over the years. Digital cameras of all sorts can be useful for documenting locations, and modern high-end models are good enough that most investigators think that they're fine to take on ghost hunts. However, some purists will always insist that film cameras are the only way to go.

Audio Gear

Some of the most compelling pieces of evidence that paranormal investigators have captured at haunted places are electronic voice phenomena (EVPs): audio recordings of voices and sounds that aren't audible with the naked ear. It would seem logical that if you want to record voices from the Other Side, you should get a highly sensitive microphone. However, sensitive microphones can pick up voices from *outside* the investigation area, particularly on urban ghost hunts. I was once on a ghost hunt during which we recorded the sound of muffled conversation as we trudged around a sub-basement far below a haunted theater. We got very excited, thinking that we'd picked up an otherworldly chat—and then we realized that the "ghost" was ordering an Extra Value Meal. The voices were coming from a McDonald's restaurant at street level!

This is just one example of the types of false positives that can result from audio recordings; they're also ridiculously easy to fake. Still, some of the most convincing evidence of the paranormal comes from audio recordings. Some investigators insist on using tape instead of digital recorders, but only a very good tape recorder will get better recordings with lower noise levels than a decent digital recorder. Just be sure to set the recording quality

level at the highest setting possible; settling for a "lossy" format (such as MP3 or WMA) that degrades the file's quality in order to reduce its size will result in some digital "artifacts"—garbled sounds that can ruin a recording's credibility.

Thermal-Imaging Cameras

Thermal-imaging cameras (i.e., heat-sensing cameras) have become extremely popular in the ghost-hunting community because they look really cool on television. Of course, good images have been taken with them, and they can be very useful for identifying cold spots. They can also come in handy in some unexpected ways; for example, they can sometimes help you read tombstone inscriptions that have worn away. However, thermal cameras don't seem much more useful for documenting ghosts than other kinds of cameras, and they're extremely expensive (even a halfway decent model will cost thousands) and can be difficult to use. Still, take one of these to a ghost hunt and you'll be the center of attention for sure.

Night-Vision Cameras

Night-vision cameras and glasses pick up near-infrared light that humans can't typically see; they also pick up a different range of usually invisible light than thermal-imaging cameras do. Plus, they're much cheaper than full-color thermal cameras and can keep you from falling over things that you can't see in the dark. Using night vision can also eliminate the need for a flash, which some feel should never be used on a ghost hunt.

Motion Detector

Motion detectors are somewhat useful, but if an entity can walk through walls, it can probably also avoid setting off a motion detector. In ghost hunting, they're most often utilized for security: Set up a motion detector in a room where you've left a camera or an audio recorder running so you'll know if anyone sneaks in to tamper with the equipment. If you can't afford an actual motion detector, you can use a more primitive method: Lay down some string or sprinkle flour on the floor; if anyone comes into the

room, you'll know because your booby trap will be disturbed. It's not foolproof, but it's helpful.

An Internet Connection

Some ghost hunters like to research a haunted location before conducting a formal investigation, but others like to examine a place cold—without hearing any stories that may cloud their objectivity. Either way, questions always come up during a ghost hunt. Doing your homework about the history of a location and its inhabitants can spare you a lot of time and trouble. Membership at Ancestry.com is expensive, but it's totally worth it: You may find that you're scheduled to search for the ghost of someone who never existed or someone who is still alive!

Other online resources can help you determine if a location was ever really a Native American burial ground or a Civil War hospital. The fact that a place's story is wrong doesn't necessarily mean that it isn't haunted—it's common for an owner to be mistaken about the history of his or her building. But if you find out that a client is lying, (i.e., they say, "We've done a ton of research, and we know that Al Capone killed a guy here in 1937," but you find out that Capone was locked up at Alcatraz in 1937 and that the house wasn't built until 1947), that's a major red flag and you're probably wasting your time at the location.

Really, nearly any piece of equipment can be used on a ghost hunt. If you can't afford an EMF meter or motion detector, simply use a compass, a radio, or anything else you have. If it starts acting in an unusual manner or the batteries drain much faster than normal, it might be a clue that you're in the presence of a ghost.

"Ghost hunting is kind of like fishing.... You don't really know if you're going to catch anything or not, and most of the time you're just waiting."
—Rob Thorne, cofounder of the Virigina Paranormal Society

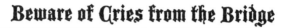

Beware of Cries from the Bridge

Bridges provide us with ways to get from one place to another. But when the destination is the Other Side, a "crybaby bridge" is born. Crybaby bridges are said to mark locations where babies died. According to legend, if you're brave enough to wait patiently on a crybaby bridge, you'll actually hear a baby cry. Here are some of the best-known crybaby bridges in the United States.

Middletown, New Jersey

Cooper Road is a lonely stretch that wanders through the backwoods of Middletown, New Jersey. Stay on it long enough and you'll eventually come to the crybaby bridge under which a baby is said to have drowned. If you want to hear the baby cry, just park your vehicle in the middle of the bridge and wait. But don't turn off your car—you may not be able to start it again.

Monmouth, Illinois

It's a case of "the more the scarier" at this crybaby bridge in western Illinois. According to legend, a bus full of small children once drove off the bridge after the driver lost control of the vehicle. It is said that if you drive to the bridge at night, turn off your engine, and put your car in neutral, you'll hear cries from the dead children. Shortly thereafter, ghostly  youngsters will push your car across the bridge and back onto the road, leaving tiny handprints on the back of the vehicle.

Concord, North Carolina

Just outside of Concord, North Carolina, is a bridge on Poplar Tent Road that locals refer to as Sally's Bridge. According to local lore, a young woman named Sally was driving home with her baby when she lost control of her car, skidded across the bridge, and

crashed. The baby was ejected from the vehicle and fell into the water. Panic-stricken, Sally dove into the water to try to save her child, but sadly, both mother and child drowned.

Legend has it that if you park your car on this bridge, Sally's ghost will bang on the vehicle, desperately trying to find someone to help save her dying child.

Upper Marlboro, Maryland

According to the story associated with the crybaby bridge in Upper Marlboro, Maryland, a young single woman who became pregnant was embarrassed and afraid of being disowned. She somehow managed to conceal her pregnancy from her family and friends, and after the baby was born, the woman waited until nightfall, walked onto the bridge, and then threw the infant into the water below. It is said that if you visit the bridge at night, you'll hear the baby crying.

Cable, Ohio

Far and away, Ohio harbors the most crybaby bridges, each with its own unique story. For example, some say that on a cold November night in the tiny town of Cable, a deeply depressed woman bundled up her newborn baby and walked onto a bridge that crossed over some railroad tracks. She waited patiently until she heard the sound of a distant train whistle. With the baby in her arms, the woman jumped in front of the oncoming train just as it reached the bridge; both were killed instantly.

If you visit this bridge, be forewarned—especially when it's close to midnight: The cars of unlucky travelers crossing the span at that time have reportedly stalled. When they tried to restart their engines, they heard the sound of a distant train whistle, which seemed to signal the start of a bizarre, supernatural flash-back. As the sound of the train came closer, witnesses reported hearing a baby crying. Then, just when it sounded as though the train was right next to the bridge, they heard a woman scream... and then everything went silent. Only then were they able to start their cars again.

The Sad Fate of British Airship *R101*

On October 5, 1930, the British airship R101 *crashed during its maiden flight, killing nearly all aboard. Two days later, a woman with absolutely no knowledge of airships explained the incident in highly technical and freakishly accurate detail. Were the ghosts of the tragedy speaking through her?*

Foretellers or Frauds

Psychics affect people in different ways. Those who believe in concepts such as mental telepathy and extrasensory perception can find validity in a medium's claims. Skeptics, on the other hand, aren't so sure. Psychic researcher Harry Price straddled the fence between the two camps: He deplored fakery but had witnessed enough of the supernatural to believe that there was indeed something to it. At his National Laboratory of Psychical Research, Price worked diligently to separate the wheat from the chaff—the real from the fake.

On October 7, 1930, Price arranged a séance with a promising medium named Eileen J. Garrett. Price's secretary Ethel Beenbarn and reporter Ian D. Coster were enlisted to record the proceedings. Price hoped to contact the recently deceased author Sir Arthur Conan Doyle (of *Sherlock Holmes* fame) and publish an account of the proceedings. Like Price, Doyle held a keen interest in the paranormal. Making contact with him could bring Price the evidence that he sought about the existence of an afterlife.

Strange Contact

Just two days before Price and Garrett met, a horrific tragedy occurred. The British airship *R101* crashed in France, killing 48 of the 55 people on board. Questions about the event arose as quickly as each newspaper went to press. Why had the ship crashed? Who or what was at fault?

Were airships inherently unsafe? A Court of Inquiry was assembled to answer these queries, but not before Price and Garrett had their meeting.

At the séance, Garrett fell into a trance and then began to speak. In a deep, animated voice, she identified herself as Flight Lieutenant H. Carmichael Irwin, commander of the *R101* (not Sir Arthur Conan Doyle, whom Price had hoped to contact), and began to speak words that were as confusing as they were disjointed:

> *"I must do something about it. The whole bulk of the dirigible was entirely and absolutely too much for her engine's capacity. Engines too heavy.... Oil pipe plugged. Flying too low altitude and never could rise.... Severe tension on the fabric, which is chafing.... Never reached cruising altitude—same in trial.... Almost scraped the roofs of Achy!"*

Coster recognized Irwin's name from the recent *R101* tragedy. After the séance, the reporter published highlights from the meeting. Shortly thereafter, a man named Will Charlton contacted Price. Charlton worked as a supply officer at the base where the *R101* was built and was familiar with the airship's construction. He asked the researcher for a transcript of the séance and studied it intently. What he saw amazed him: Garrett—who had no prior knowledge of or interest in airships—had spoken about one in highly technical terms. Moreover, she seemed to be explaining *why* the *R101* had crashed.

Passing Muster

As details of the crash emerged, Garrett's words proved even more insightful. It was revealed that the airship had passed over the village of Achy so low that it almost scraped a church tower, as Garrett had stated during the séance. Garrett also spoke of an "exorbitant scheme of carbon and hydrogen" as being "completely wrong" for the airship. When Charlton and other airship officials heard this, they were stunned. Only a handful of project team members had been privy to this top-secret information. Parlor tricks, no matter how clever, couldn't possibly account for Garrett's knowledge of this information.

The transcript yielded more than 40 highly technical details related to the airship's final flight. Charlton and his colleagues pronounced it an "amazing document." Before launching an official

inquiry, they decided to stage another séance. Major Oliver Villiers of the Ministry of Civil Aviation sat down with Eileen Garrett and observed her as she drifted into a trance. This time, the medium channeled the spirits of others who had perished in the crash. Villiers asked pointed questions regarding the airframe of the *R101*, and the medium responded in startling detail:

Villiers: "What was the trouble? Irwin mentioned the nose."

Garrett: "Yes. Girder trouble and engine."

Villiers: "I must get this right. Can you describe exactly where? We have the long struts labeled from A to G."

Garrett: "The top one is O and then A, B, C, and so on downward. Look at your drawing. It was starboard of 5C. On our second flight, after we had finished, we found the girder had been strained, not cracked, and this caused trouble to the cover…"

Conclusion

When the Court of Inquiry's report was released, Garrett's words matched almost precisely with the findings. The phenomenon so impressed Charlton that he himself became a Spiritualist. After Garrett's death in 1970, Archie Jarman—a psychic researcher and columnist for the *Psychic News*—revealed that the medium had asked him to dig deeper into the *R101* case: She wished to learn just how close her description of the event was to reality. After six months of dogged research, Jarman concluded that the technical terms expressed so vividly by the medium could only have come from the Other Side. In the end, the goal of contacting Sir Arthur Conan Doyle was not achieved; however, this fantastic development had advanced psychical studies immeasurably. Without question, Price had found his "wheat" and the answers to his questions.

"I feel that the period will sooner or later arrive when I must abandon life and reason together, in some struggle with the grim phantasm, FEAR."
—Edgar Allan Poe, "The Fall of the House of Usher"

Prison Poltergeists
The Ghostly Hand of Fate

In 1877, Carbon County Prison inmate Alexander Campbell spent long, agonizing days awaiting sentencing. Campbell, a coal miner from northeastern Pennsylvania, had been convicted of the murder of a mine superintendent. Although Campbell admitted that he'd been present at the murder scene, he swore repeatedly that he was not the killer.

Despite his pleas of innocence, Campbell was sentenced to hang. When his day of reckoning arrived, Campbell rubbed his hand on his sooty cell floor and then slapped it on the wall proclaiming, "I am innocent, and let this be my testimony!" With that, Campbell was unceremoniously dragged from Cell 17 and committed to eternity.

A Condemned Man Leaves His Mark

Today, the Carbon County Prison is not unlike the torture chamber that it was back in Campbell's time. Although it is now a museum, the jail still imparts the horrors of man's inhumanity to man. Visitors move through its claustrophobically small cells and dank rooms with mouths agape. When they reach Cell 17, many guests feel cold chills rise up their spines as they notice that Alexander Campbell's dirty handprint is still there!

"There's no logical explanation for it," says James Starrs, a forensic scientist from George Washington University who investigated the mark. Starrs is not the first person to express disbelief at the handprint's permanence. In 1930, a local sheriff aimed to rid the jail of its ominous mark by tearing down the wall it was on and replacing it with a new one. But the next day, the handprint reappeared on the newly constructed wall. Many years later, Sheriff Charles Neast took his best shot at the handprint—this time with green latex paint. The mark inexplicably returned. Was Campbell truly innocent, as his ghostly handprint seems to suggest? No one can say with certainty. Is the handprint inside Cell 17 the sort of thing that legends are made of? You can bet your life on it.

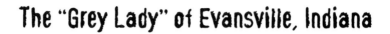

The "Grey Lady" of Evansville, Indiana

🪦　🪦　🪦　🪦

*The Willard Library in Evansville, Indiana, has a long
history of supernatural activity. But while multiple
ghosts typically inhabit many haunted buildings, only
one spirit seems to peruse the stacks at this old Victorian
library—an entity known as "the Lady in Grey."*

Not Shy at All

According to local reports, the Lady in Grey has been haunting the
Willard Library since at least the 1930s. The first known encounter
with her occurred in 1937, when a janitor ran into the lonely ghost
as he entered the library's cellar to stoke its furnace. There, he saw
a mysterious woman dressed all in gray. A veil was draped from her
face to her shoes, and she glowed ethereally in the darkness.

That may have been the first confirmed encounter with the Grey
Lady, but it certainly wasn't the last. In fact, according to library
employees and patrons, this spirit seems to go out of its way to make
its presence known.

On one occasion, the members of a local genealogy group noticed
the distinct odor of perfume in the library's research room. None of
the group members was wearing perfume at the time, and no one
else had entered the room while they were there.

Margaret Maier, who worked at the library for more than four
decades, also smelled the Grey Lady's musky perfume at her own
home. Maier speculated that the spirit briefly followed her home
while the children's room of the library was undergoing renovations.
In addition to the scent of perfume, Maier and her sister reported
feeling an unseen presence in their midst, as well as an inexplicable
chill at Maier's home.

Spooky Shenanigans

She clearly means no harm, but the Lady in Grey isn't above playing
pranks on library staffers. One night, Bettye Elaine Miller, who was
head librarian from 1972 to 1975, was working late when she heard

water running on the second floor. She rushed upstairs to find that a bathroom faucet had been mysteriously turned on. Later, another librarian using the same bathroom watched in horror as a faucet turned on by itself.

Over the years, reports of paranormal activity at the Willard Library have become so commonplace that, with the library's permission, the *Evansville Courier & Press* installed three Internet-connected "ghost cams" in the building so that curious ghost hunters can try to catch a glimpse of the Grey Lady. The cameras have proven quite popular with fans of the paranormal, logging hundreds of thousands of hits since they first went online. Want to check it out for yourself? Visit LibraryGhost.com.

A Ghost Revealed

Of course, everyone wants to know the identity of the mysterious Grey Lady. Local historians believe that she is the ghost of Louise Carpenter, the daughter of Willard Carpenter, who funded the construction of the library and for whom it was named. According to reports, Louise was greatly displeased with the fact that when her father died, he left a great deal of his money for the construction of a public library. She even tried to sue the library's board of trustees, claiming that her father was "of unsound mind and…unduly influenced in establishing the library."

Louise's lawsuit was unsuccessful, and she was unable to stop the library's construction. A theory among many ghost hunters suggests that, upon her death in 1908, Louise's spirit came to reside within the library and will stay there until the property is returned to the Carpenter family, which is quite unlikely.

Libraries are popular haunts for ghosts, but few have logged as many reputable sightings and paranormal occurrences as the Willard Library. It very well may be the most haunted library in the United States, thanks to a gray-clad spirit that still holds a grudge, even from beyond the grave.

Can Dogs See Spirits?

It's late at night and you're lying in bed watching TV with your faithful pooch snoring softly at your feet. Suddenly and without warning, your dog bolts upright and looks into the darkened hallway, growling while the hair on the back of his or her neck stands up. Cautiously you investigate, but you find nothing, which leads you to wonder, "Did my dog just see a ghost?"

What Are You Looking At?

In order to ascertain if dogs can see spirits, we must first determine what a ghost looks like. By most accounts, spirits appear as dark shadows or white, misty shapes, often only briefly visible out of the corner of one's eye. Sometimes, people report ghosts as balls of glowing light that move or dart about. In most cases, they are reported in low-light conditions, which is why many ghost hunters use infrared extenders when they shoot video or take photographs. So to sum up, if dogs are able to see ghosts, they would need to be able to see:

- Dark shadows or white, misty shapes
- Moving balls of light
- In low light

How a Dog Sees

Just like a human's eye, a dog's eye is made up of rods and cones. Rods function well in low light and are also helpful in detecting movement. Cones help to define colors. Unlike a human eye, the center of a dog's eye is made up mainly of rods, so dogs can't see colors very well. But because apparitions are usually described as dark shadows or white shapes, dogs should be able to see them just fine.

The rods in dogs' eyes allow them not only to detect motion but also to see phenomena such as flickering lights better than

humans can. So if ghosts appear as flitting lights that move quickly, dogs should be able to see them.

Finally, the additional rods in the centers of dogs' eyes make it possible for dogs to see much better than humans in low-light situations. So while humans scramble for flashlights and infrared extenders to try to see ghosts, dogs only have to use their eyes.

A Dog's-Eye View

Another factor to consider is from where dogs are seeing. Most adult humans spend the majority of their time viewing the world from a standing position—in general, more than five feet off the ground. Dogs, however, spend most of their lives looking up at things from two feet or so off the ground. That doesn't sound like a big difference, but it is. Just lie on the floor at night and look up at some objects; it really gives you a unique perspective. Perhaps that different vantage point is what's needed to see spirits.

Refusing to Conform

Finally, consider the idea that, despite what most ghost-hunting shows would like you to think, the majority of people do not believe that ghosts exist. Maybe that's exactly why dogs see them: Because modern society cannot force dogs to conform to its beliefs. In other words, dogs don't know that they're not supposed to see ghosts because they allegedly don't exist. Therefore, it would stand to reason that a dog, upon seeing an apparition, simply acknowledges it as being a living, breathing person, unlike many skeptical humans who would immediately try to convince themselves that they did not just have a paranormal encounter.

"A ghost is someone who hasn't made it—in other words, who died, and they don't know they're dead. So they keep walking around and thinking that you're inhabiting their—let's say, their domain. So they're aggravated with you."

—Psychic Sylvia Browne

Meet the Ghosts of Owl's Head Light

Owl's Head Light, which watches over Rockland Harbor on Maine's West Penobscot Bay, has ghostly credentials to hoot about—so much so that in 2006, Coastal Living *magazine named it America's most haunted lighthouse.*

The original Owl's Head Light was commissioned and built in 1825 after a boom in the lime-mining industry in nearby Rockland increased shipping traffic around the bay's rocky shores. A sturdier structure replaced this poorly built lighthouse in 1852, but it wasn't until recent times that ghosts began to visit the promontory where the original 30-foot tower and then its replacement have guarded the bay for nearly two centuries.

No one is sure exactly when the hauntings began, but at some point, caretakers began finding human footprints in the snow on the stairway that leads from the caretaker's house to the tower. The footprints started about halfway up the stairs, as if someone had materialized on the spot. Whoever made the prints had a purpose: The tracks often led to an open lighthouse door, and caretakers would find a fresh shine on the equipment inside.

Over the years, a strange white figure has also appeared in a window of the lighthouse. One caretaker's child reported seeing a mysterious woman sitting on a bedroom chair, and several caretakers claimed that they glimpsed a small spectral woman working in the kitchen. To make her presence known, the ghostly cook likes to jangle tableware and slam cupboard doors.

Bedroom Invader

One strange incident happened around 1985, when lighthouse keeper Andy Germann got up late one night to tend to some chores that he'd forgotten to do outside the house. As he left the bedroom, Andy saw a misty form float over the floor and pass into the room. He shrugged it off—figuring that it was just the bay's formidable fog—and continued with his task.

Andy's wife Denise was trying to get back to sleep when she felt her husband lie down on his side of the bed. But when she turned to ask why he had returned so quickly, all she could see was a body-sized dent on the mattress. The impression could conceivably have been leftover from when Andy exited the bed ... except that it kept changing in depth, as if someone was fidgeting to get comfortable. This continued for several minutes before Denise surmised that it was the work of a ghostly intruder, and she kindly asked it to leave. It did, but other strange phenomena—such as doors opening and closing on their own and the sound of footsteps—continued to occur, especially in a particular upstairs room.

Only a few years later, new residents received a clue about who might have been making tracks in the snow, cleaning the great lighthouse lens, and trying to sleep in the main bedroom. After caretaker Gerard Graham, his wife Debbie, and their young daughter Claire moved into the structure, Claire would often describe a playmate that only she could see. He looked like an old-fashioned sea captain, she said. Claire began to spout technical nautical terms that her parents said she did not know, and she even warned her father when the foghorn needed to be turned on. Incidentally, Claire slept in the bedroom that the Germanns believed was haunted.

The Frozen Couple

Owl's Head Light is also famous as the site of the true story of the "frozen couple." This tale involves no ghosts, but it does include two people who were brought back from the dead.

In 1850, a great storm lashed the bay a few days before Christmas. A small schooner anchored at a neighboring port was having a hard time in the crashing waves, and its captain left the vessel, perhaps to seek help.

Before the captain returned, the schooner's cables snapped and the storm propelled it toward Rockland Harbor. Aboard the schooner were three hapless souls: the first mate, Richard Ingraham;

Ingraham's fiancée, Lydia Dyer; and a sailor, Roger Elliott. It did not take long before the vessel crashed aground near Owl's Head Light. It remained partially intact, but freezing water quickly drenched the three passengers, who were huddled together under blankets that began to collect ice.

Thawed Out

The engaged couple eventually lost consciousness, but Elliott managed to get off the ship and clamber over the rocks to the lighthouse. Fortunately, the caretaker passed by on a horse-drawn sleigh and saw the half-frozen man, who told him of his capsized friends.

The caretaker immediately gathered a rescue party, which found Ingraham and Dyer encased in ice. Both appeared to be dead, but their seemingly lifeless bodies were chipped out and brought back to the caretaker's home, although it took great effort to release the couple from their icy tomb.

The rescuers then managed to thaw the pair out by pouring water on them and rubbing their arms and legs to restore circulation. Much to the surprise and joy of all present, Ingraham and Dyer regained consciousness. They eventually married as planned and raised four children.

Death Takes No Holiday

Elliott was not so lucky; he died, possibly of hypothermia. No one knows for sure what happened to the schooner's captain. Perhaps he never made it ashore to seek help but ultimately found comfort in the caretaker's house, where he visited young Claire Graham more than a hundred years later.

Perhaps the most famous resident of the Owl's Head Light was a springer spaniel named Spot, who belonged to a keeper in the 1930s. Spot learned to use his teeth to sound the foghorn whenever a vessel came into sight. Once, when the foghorn was broken, Spot performed his duty by barking and was credited with preventing a mail boat from crashing into the rocks.

Restless Spirits at the Winchester Mystery House

Every night, in a room at the center of a mansion that was still under construction, an elegant woman with her face covered by a dark veil consulted a planchette board. She summoned good spirits, requesting their assistance with building her house. Only with their help could she continue to design a home that would allow her to outwit evil spirits bent on revenge. Each morning, she passed on new plans to the foreman, whose crews carried out her wishes—seven days a week, 24 hours a day. The woman was Sarah L. Winchester, and her deceased husband had left her a cursed family fortune earned through the invention of the Winchester rifle.

In 1884, construction began on a spacious Victorian mansion in San Jose, California, after Sarah Winchester moved to the West Coast from New Haven, Connecticut, following two personal tragedies. Her infant daughter had died suddenly from a mysterious ailment in 1866, after which Sarah lapsed into a deep depression that plagued her for the rest of her life. Then, 15 years after the death of her daughter, Sarah's husband William died of tuberculosis at age 43.

The loss of her husband was a debilitating blow to the already distraught Sarah. Fearing that she might take her own life, one of her close friends suggested that she should visit a psychic to see if she could contact her husband, her daughter, or both; after all, this was at the height of the Spiritualism movement. The medium told Sarah that William was trying to contact her with a dire message: The Winchester family was cursed as a result of the invention of the repeating rifle. Native Americans, settlers, and soldiers all over the world were dead due to the weapon; those angry spirits were bent on revenge, and Sarah was their next target. The medium told Sarah that the only way to prolong her life was to move out west and build a large house. But here's the kicker: Sarah was told that the key to appeasing the spirits was that construction could never end; otherwise, the spirits would kill her.

Designed by Spirits

Sarah decided that it was not enough to maintain a never-ending construction project: She also needed to *confuse* the spirits that were out to get her. As a result, the house features strange design elements. Doors open into walls (or sheer drops outside). Some stairs end at ceilings or have odd proportions; for example, the steps on the "Switchback Staircase" are each two inches high, allowing a staircase with seven full flights to rise only nine feet. (Odd as this may seem, it may have been necessary for the arthritic Sarah.) Hallways twist and turn, and secret passageways end in bizarre nooks. One stairway goes down 7 steps and then up 11, and one particular linen closet is larger than most three-bedroom apartments. Many of the mansion's architectural elements incorporate the number 13, which was believed to keep unwelcome spirits at bay. Thirteen stairs lead to the 13th bathroom, which has a window with 13 panes.

Another benefit of living in such a large house was that Sarah did not have to sleep in the same bedroom for more than two nights in a row, which she believed made it difficult for ill-intentioned spirits to find her. Unfortunately, this also made it difficult for her staff to find her after a 7.9-magnitude earthquake rocked the Bay Area in 1906. Sarah was trapped in the Daisy Bedroom (one of her favorite rooms) in the front of the house for hours, which led her to conclude that the spirits were sending her a message: She had spent too much money on the front of the building. As a result, the front 30 rooms—including an unused ballroom that cost more than $9,000 to build (when an average house could be built for less than $1,000)—were sealed off.

While Sarah worked desperately to appease the evil spirits, she also tried to make the good ones feel comfortable. She built a special Séance Room that she used nightly to contact friendly spirits and receive their input on how the construction of the house should proceed. Sarah also liked to play her pump organ late at night to entertain her spectral guests (and perhaps to exercise her arthritic hands).

Every Good Project Has an End... Or Does It?

By the time Sarah Winchester died in 1922, construction had been under way for 38 years. The house sprawled over six acres and boasted 160 rooms, 2,000 doors, 10,000 windows, 47 stairways, 47 fireplaces, 13 bathrooms, and 6 kitchens, but it is estimated that

more than 500 rooms were actually built and then sealed over or torn down and refashioned into new spaces.

Over the years, investigators have recorded various paranormal occurrences at the Winchester Mystery House. One group recorded faint sounds of an organ and saw not only moving balls of light but also two apparitions dressed in clothing that was popular in Sarah Winchester's time. Other visitors have felt icy chills in draft-free rooms and observed locked doorknobs turning, and when one guest developed photos that he took in the peculiar mansion, he discovered that he'd captured the ghostly image of a man in coveralls. A caretaker heard footsteps and breathing in otherwise empty rooms. And in 1975, during a midnight séance on Halloween, renowned medium Jeanne Borgen seemed to transform into an elderly Sarah, aging rapidly before the other attendees and falling over in pain.

Many say that the ghost of Sarah Winchester still roams her unusual home, and psychics firmly believe that the house is haunted. This can't be proven, of course, but that doesn't stop the claims—and it didn't stop the lady of the house from undertaking one of the world's most incredible construction projects.

When Sarah Winchester's husband passed away, she inherited a fortune—literally. In the late 1880s, the average family income hovered at around $500 per year; Sarah was pulling in about $1,000 per day!

North Carolina's Train of Terror

North Carolina is rife with haunted houses. In fact, even the Governor's Mansion in Raleigh is said to contain a ghost or two. But one of the Tarheel State's most unusual paranormal events isn't housebound—it takes place on an isolated train trestle known as the Bostian Bridge near the town of Statesville.

On August 27, 1891, a passenger train jumped the tracks while crossing the Bostian Bridge, plunging seven railcars 60 to 75 feet to the ground below. Nearly 30 people perished in the tragic accident.

According to local legend, on the anniversary of the catastrophe, the sounds of screeching wheels, screaming passengers, and a thunderous crash can be heard near the Bostian Bridge. The ghostly specter of a uniformed man carrying a gold pocket watch has also been observed lingering nearby.

Another Victim Claimed

Sadly, on August 27, 2010, Christopher Kaiser, a Charlotte-based amateur ghost hunter, was struck and killed by a real-life train that surprised him on the Bostian Bridge.

According to police reports, Kaiser had brought a small group to the trestle in hopes of experiencing the eerie sounds that are said to occur on the anniversary of the 1891 crash. The group was standing on the span when a Norfolk-Southern train turned a corner and headed toward them. With the train rapidly approaching, Kaiser managed to push the woman in front of him off the tracks. His heroic action saved her life but cost him his own.

Other than witnessing this horrific accident, Kaiser's group saw nothing unusual that night. But many others claim to have seen strange phenomena on the Bostian Bridge. On the 50th anniversary of the 1891 tragedy, for example, one woman reportedly watched the wreck occur all over again. More than 150 people gathered near the trestle on the 100th anniversary of the crash in 1991, but nothing supernatural happened that night.

The Ghosts of the St. Valentine's Day Massacre

🪦 🪦 🪦 🪦

After Chicago gangsters lured their rivals into an ambush,
they thought that they had enjoyed the last laugh. What they
failed to consider was the existence of another syndicate—
one that could reach out from beyond the grave.

Requiem for Racketeers

During the Roaring '20s, Al "Scarface" Capone ruled Chicago. Be it gambling, prostitution, bootleg whiskey, or anything else illegal or immoral, Capone and his gangsters controlled it. Almost no one—including the police—dared to stand up to Capone and his men because resistance certainly meant winding up on the wrong end of a gun. Still, one man was determined to dethrone Capone: George "Bugs" Moran.

Moran and his North Side Gang had been slowly muscling their way into Chicago in an attempt to force Capone and his men out. As 1929 began, rumors indicated that Capone was planning to "take care of" Moran. As the days turned into weeks and nothing happened, Moran and his men began to relax and let their guard down. That would prove to be a fatal mistake.

Gathering for the Slaughter

On February 14, 1929, six members of the North Side Gang gathered inside the SMC Cartage Company at 2122 North Clark Street. With them was mechanic John May, who was not a member of the gang but had been hired to work on a member's car. May had brought along his dog, Highball, and had tied him to the bumper of the car while he worked. At approximately 10:30 A.M., two cars parked in

front of the Clark Street entrance of the building. Four men—two dressed as police officers and two in street clothes—got out and walked into the warehouse.

Murderers in Disguise

Once the men were inside, it is believed they announced that the warehouse was being raided and ordered everyone to line up facing the back wall. Believing that the uniformed men were indeed police officers, all of Moran's men, along with John May, did as they were told. Suddenly, the supposed raiders began shooting, and in a hail of shotgun fire and more than 70 submachine-gun rounds, the seven men were brutally murdered.

After the slaughter was over, the two men in street clothes calmly walked out of the building with their hands up, followed by the two men dressed as police officers. To everyone nearby, it appeared as though a shootout had occurred and that the police had arrived and arrested two men.

"Nobody Shot Me"

Minutes later, neighbors called police after hearing strange howls coming from inside the building. When the real police arrived, they found all seven men mortally wounded. One of the men, Frank Gusenberg, lingered long enough to respond to one question. When authorities asked who shot him, Gusenberg responded, "Nobody shot me." The only survivor of the melee was Highball the dog.

When word of the massacre hit the newswire, everyone suspected that Al Capone had something to do with it. Although Capone swore that he wasn't involved, most people felt that he had orchestrated the whole thing as a way to get rid of Moran and several of his key men. There was only one problem: Bugs Moran wasn't in the warehouse at the time of the shooting. Why he wasn't there is not clear, but one thing is certain: February 14, 1929, was Bugs Moran's lucky day.

Police were unable to pin anything related to the crime on Capone, although they did charge two of his gunmen—John Scalise and Jack "Machine Gun" McGurn—with the murders. Scalise never saw the inside of the courthouse: He was murdered before his trial began. Charges against McGurn were eventually dropped; however,

he was murdered seven years later—on Valentine's Day—in what appeared to be retaliation for the 1929 massacre.

Haunted by the Truth

Publicly, Al Capone may have denied any wrongdoing, but it appears that the truth literally haunted him until his dying day. In May 1929, Capone was incarcerated at Philadelphia's Eastern State Penitentiary, serving a one-year stint for weapons possession. Such a span was considered "easy time" by gangster standards, but Capone's time inside would be anything but. Haunted by the ghost of James Clark—who was killed in the St. Valentine's Day Massacre—Capone was often heard begging "Jimmy" to leave him alone.

The torment continued even after Capone was released. One day, Capone's valet, Hymie Cornish, saw an unfamiliar man in Capone's apartment. When he ordered the man to identify himself, the mysterious figure slipped behind a curtain and vanished. Capone insisted that Cornish, like himself, had seen the ghost of Clark. Some say that Clark didn't rest until Capone passed away on January 25, 1947.

Ghosts Still Linger

Over the years, the warehouse in which the St. Valentine's Day Massacre took place transformed into a morbid tourist attraction, as curiosity seekers felt compelled to see the site for themselves. When the building was demolished in 1967, the wall against which the seven doomed men stood was dismantled brick by brick and sold at auction. An enterprising businessman purchased the bricks and eventually sold each one, but many of them were returned soon after. According to unhappy customers, their luck took a nosedive after they purchased the ghoulish souvenirs. Illness, financial ruin, divorce, and even death caused the frightened owners to believe that the bricks were cursed.

As for the infamous massacre site, nothing much is left there today. A nursing home owns the land and has left the area vacant, save for a parking lot and a few trees. Some people have reported hearing gunfire and screams as they pass by the site; and people walking their dogs near the lot claim that their furry friends pull on their leashes and try to get away from the area. Perhaps they sense the ghostly remnants of the bloody slaughter that took place there so many years ago.

Phantom of the Opera House

Gaston Leroux's The Phantom of the Opera *has scared generations of readers, as well as untold numbers of theatergoers who have watched the many adaptations of the novel on the stage and silver screen. Leroux's story is fiction, but it's said that real-life phantoms haunt the Grand Opera House in Oshkosh, Wisconsin.*

Everyone Has a Story

A regional institution since 1883, the Grand Opera House has served numerous purposes through the years: It was a venue for vaudeville and stage productions and was later used as a movie house. During its heyday, the theater showcased many of the biggest names in show business, including Enrico Caruso, Harry Houdini, and the Marx Brothers. Today, however, it is best known for housing a number of playful poltergeists.

Indeed, almost everyone who has spent time at the Grand Opera House has a tale or two to tell. Once, an actor was rushing from his dressing room to the stage when he turned a corner and almost ran into a spectral man decked out in 19th-century garb. The ghost was holding a playbill, which the actor was able to identify as being for an 1895 production of *The Bohemian Girl.*

Many others who have worked at or visited the theater report equally unusual phenomena, including fire doors opening and closing on their own and unexplained footsteps.

Ironically, in the mid-1970s, a television movie about a haunted theater was filmed at the Grand Opera House. According to producer Bob Jacobs, a variety of inexplicable occurrences took place during the production, but it quickly became evident that whatever was haunting the theater was not trying to scare the cast and crew—it was trying to protect them.

In one especially chilling incident, a young assistant was hoisted above the stage and left hanging there for nearly an hour while a scene was shot. As soon as the assistant was lowered down and his feet touched the stage, the rope that had been holding him suddenly

snapped. Jacobs, who witnessed the incident, became convinced that an unseen force had been acting as the young man's guardian angel, protecting him until he was safely returned to the ground.

Ghosts Aplenty

Others involved in the production of the film reported seeing ghostly figures pass by. Assistant producer Jan Turner witnessed a spectral figure in an underground passage; another time, something grabbed her ankle. Production assistants Dennis Payne and John Jansen reported seeing a man walk out of the orchestra pit and into a room that had no other access point; when the man didn't come out, they checked the room, but it was empty... or so they thought.

Staff members and visitors at the Grand Opera House have long wondered who haunts its halls. The man with the playbill may have been a former actor who performed there, or perhaps he was a deceased audience member. Many ghost hunters believe that another resident spirit is that of Percy R. Keene, who worked as a stage manager at the theater from 1895 until his death in the mid-1960s. Keene was well liked by everyone, and it was evident to all that he loved the Grand Opera House. It makes sense then that after his death, his spirit would return to keep an eye on the place.

An Appreciative Specter

Bob Jacobs had an interesting encounter with a spirit that he believed was Percy Keene. Two days before the premiere of his movie, Jacobs held a private screening at the Grand Opera House for six people who had worked on the film. After the movie ended, Jacobs glanced up at the balcony and saw a figure smiling down at him; it looked just like Keene.

In the 1980s, renowned paranormal investigators Ed and Lorraine Warren visited the Grand Opera House to see what they could uncover. Lorraine reported sensing a male presence and also a dog. Keene's family later confirmed that the much-loved stage manager had once kept a pet dog at the theater.

Ghosts tend to reside at locations that were important to them in life. For Percy Keene and perhaps a few others, the Grand Opera House was a home away from home—and a place that they just couldn't bear to leave.

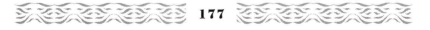

Don't Mess with the Lady in Black

In the opening days of the Civil War—the days of unrealistic expectations, when many thought that the war would be over in a matter of weeks or months—Andrew Lanier was preparing to leave his home in Georgia to serve in the Confederate Army. But before he left, he asked his beloved girlfriend Melanie to marry him. She did, and the two spent just one night together as husband and wife.
The next day, Andrew headed off to war, undoubtedly assuming that he would return home soon. Little did either of them know that they would never again see each other as a free man and woman.

A few months later, Andrew was captured by Union forces and was sent to Fort Warren, a military prison on Georges Island, which is located about seven miles off the coast of Boston. As military prisons go, Fort Warren was not as bad as some others, but to Lanier it was intolerable. He deeply missed Georgia and his wife, and he shared these sentiments with her in a letter.

After Melanie read the letter, she knew that she could not stand by idly while her husband rotted away in prison. So she cut her hair short, disguised herself as a man, and made her way across Union lines to Massachusetts. Finally, during a violent storm, she managed to slip inside the prison, which was not terribly secure. (It was thought that

even if a prisoner escaped from Fort Warren, he would have nowhere to go since he was on an island seven miles from land.) Soon, Melanie was reunited with her husband.

Foiled and Spoiled

The fort's other prisoners were likely pleased to see a Southern woman in their midst. They were certainly happy that she had brought along an old pistol and a short-handled pick. The prisoners hatched a scheme to tunnel underneath the fort's arsenal; once there, they planned to grab guns and seize the fort. Then they would turn the fort's artillery on Boston.

The prisoners worked on the tunnel for the next few weeks. However, they had miscalculated the distance to the arsenal, so when they tried to break through the ground, they were caught. One by one, they came out of the tunnel—except for Melanie. She had planned to wait until all of the others had been accounted for and then pop out of the hole with her pistol and take the guards by surprise.

It was a long shot, but it might have worked. Unfortunately for the Confederate prisoners, after Melanie emerged from the hole and ordered the guards to surrender, they quickly formed a circle around her and closed in. Just as Melanie pulled the trigger on her gun, it was knocked from her hand; the wayward bullet struck her husband and killed him instantly. Melanie was captured and was sentenced to hang as a Rebel spy.

On the day of her execution, Melanie made a final request: She wanted to wear a woman's dress for the hanging instead of the men's clothing that she had been wearing for weeks. She was given an old black dress that had been used for a theatrical performance at the fort. That should have been the end . . . but it was only the beginning.

Un-"fort"-unate Occurrences

A short time later, a soldier named Cassidy was patrolling the area near where Melanie had been executed. Suddenly, he felt two hands grab him around the neck from behind. The hands began to squeeze, trying to strangle him. Struggling for breath, Cassidy managed to twist around so that he could see his attacker: He was staring into the ghostly face of Melanie Lanier.

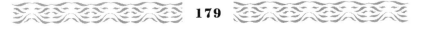

Clad in the black dress in which she had died, Melanie was staring sinisterly at the soldier, her face pale but her eyes ablaze with hatred and revenge. Cassidy screamed, and managed to twist out of her grip. He then ran back to the other guards, crying out in terror. But not only did his story provoke fits of laughter, it also got him locked away in the guardhouse for 30 days for deserting his post. That was just fine with Cassidy, who vowed never to patrol that area after dark again.

The "Lady in Black" has been haunting Fort Warren ever since then. In 1891, female footprints were found in the snow, even though no woman had been on the island. Then, during World War II, an army sentry encountered the ghost of Melanie Lanier near the site where she had died. He was so frightened by the incident that he went insane and spent the next two decades in a mental institution.

A few years after World War II, Captain Charles Norris was stationed alone on the island. He was reading one night when he felt someone tap him on the shoulder. He turned around, but no one was there.

Later, when the telephone began to ring, Norris answered it only to hear the male operator ask, "What number please?"

Norris explained that he was answering a call, not making one. The operator said that Norris's wife had answered the phone previously and had taken a message. All alone on the island, Norris knew that only one female could have answered the phone: The Lady in Black.

The vengeful wraith still roams Fort Warren. Sentries on duty there have been known to shoot at ill-defined forms, and once, a stone rolled all the way across a floor under its own power. It seems that Melanie Lanier is still trying to devise ways to distract the guards stationed there. After all, it was her love for her husband that brought her to the island, and even though they're both long dead, her love—like her spirit—lives on.

🪦 🪦 🪦 🪦

"When people believed the earth was flat, the idea of a round world scared them silly. Then they found out how the round world works. It's the same with the world of the supernatural. Until we know how it works, we'll continue to carry around this unnecessary burden of fear."
—Dr. John Markway, Richard Johnson's character in *The Haunting* (1963)

Chasing Ghosts on the Small Screen

*Unscripted ghost stories and true tales of hauntings have
never been more popular among television viewers.*

Unsolved Mysteries (1987–2002; 2008–????)

Hosted by Robert Stack until 2002 and by Dennis Farina in its
current incarnation, *Unsolved Mysteries* scours the globe looking
for supposedly true stories of the unexplained. Utilizing a docu-
mentary format, the show attempts to reenact these real-life
mysteries using eyewitness accounts. Of course, many such events
involve ghosts, poltergeists, and other paranormal phenomena,
so it's not surprising that many viewers are left believing that our
spirits live on after we die.

Ghost Hunters (2004–????)

Ghost Hunters was one of the first reality TV series to chronicle
the activities of real-life paranormal investigators—in this case
Jason Hawes and Grant Wilson, cofounders of The Atlantic
Paranormal Society (TAPS). Plumbers by trade, Hawes and
Wilson both had ghostly encounters before founding TAPS, but
they prefer not to discuss those incidents. Unlike some of the
other ghost-hunting shows on television, the TAPS team members
seek out reasonable explanations for the supernatural phenomena
that they investigate, such as strange noises and moving objects.
Nevertheless, they have witnessed their share of inexplicable
activity, including shadow figures and objects that have moved
on their own.

Paranormal State (2007–????)

While attending Penn State University in 2001, Ryan Buell
founded the Paranormal Research Society (PRS). By 2006, what
had started as a student club had gained national attention, and
camera crews began following PRS members on their quest to
investigate claims of poltergeists, demons, and other supernatural
entities. The result was *Paranormal State*. Whereas the majority
of ghost-hunting TV shows investigate paranormal activity at

notoriously haunted locations across the United States, *Paranormal State* focuses more on helping average Americans deal with the unseen (and often unwelcome) visitors in their homes, sometimes to the PRS team's own detriment: Buell claims that during an early investigation, he was threatened by a demon that allegedly stalked him for years thereafter. Buell and the PRS members left the show in 2011; however, as of this writing, it is unclear whether or not a new class will pick up where they left off.

Ghost Adventures (2008–????)
Professional ghost hunters Nick Groff, Aaron Goodwin, and the sometimes over-the-top Zak Bagans explore some of the most haunted places in the world. At the beginning of each investigation, the team obtains background information about the location and the alleged haunting. Then they set up stationary cameras in areas where the most activity has been reported. Finally, they are locked inside the building overnight while they conduct their investigation. Bagans has been known to provoke malevolent spirits using aggressive language and trigger objects, including his own tattoos. Both Bagans and Groff claim to have been possessed at least once, and during an investigation at Bobby Mackey's Music World in Wilder, Kentucky, Bagans was scratched by what he believes was a demonic entity.

Psychic Kids (2008–????)
Although some may parody Haley Joel Osment's famous line from *The Sixth Sense* ("I see dead people"), many highly sensitive children in the world not only see spirits but also have the ability to communicate with them. *Psychic Kids* introduces viewers to some of these youngsters as they (and their families) come to terms with their special gift. With the help of renowned psychics/mediums such as Chip Coffey and psychotherapist Edy Nathan, the "Children of the Paranormal" are coached on how to harness their unique abilities and sensitivities so that they can better deal with the spirits they see, quell their fears, and be proud of their gift.

Celebrity Ghost Stories (2009–????)

No, it's not about the ghosts of famous people—this series' title refers to celebrities who describe their supposedly true encounters with the supernatural. Over the years, stars such as Joan Rivers, Carrie Fisher, William Baldwin, Diane Ladd, and Haylie Duff have all shared their terrifying tales on the show. In an episode that originally aired in 2010, Tracy Nelson (daughter of 1950s teen idol Ricky Nelson) recounted some of the paranormal phenomena that she experienced growing up in a home that was reputedly haunted by actor and playboy Errol Flynn. She also shared her belief that a dark force in the house brought about her father's tragic and untimely death in a plane crash in 1985.

Ghost Lab (2009–2011)

In 1990, Brad Klinge witnessed (and videotaped) a group of ghostly soldiers while visiting the historic battlefield in Gettysburg, Pennsylvania. In 2007, Brad and his brother Barry formed Everyday Paranormal—an investigative group that specializes in "using conventional and theoretical mainstream science to prove the existence of the paranormal." And from 2009 to 2011, the Klinge brothers crisscrossed the country examining some of the most haunted locations in America on *Ghost Lab*. The Everyday Paranormal team prides itself on consulting with scientific experts from highly respected institutions such as MIT and UC-Berkeley in order to present the facts and let the viewers decide whether or not they believe that something paranormal occurred.

My Ghost Story (2010–????)

On the show *My Ghost Story*, eyewitnesses discuss their encounters with the paranormal while the incidents are reenacted and supported with personal photos, security-camera footage, and home videos. In one particularly disturbing episode, a couple shared the harrowing experiences they had while living in a home in which a family was brutally killed by an ax murderer in 1912. The restless spirit of a neighbor who may have witnessed the gruesome act haunts the house next door.

New Jersey's Haunted Union Hotel

A New Jersey hotel that witnessed a major event continues to make history of its own—haunted history, that is.

A Shocking Event

In early 1932, in an event that was as sad as it was sensational, Charles Lindbergh—the first man to fly solo across the Atlantic Ocean—again made headlines; however, this time it was for something that would have anything but a happy ending. On the night of March 1, 1932, the famous flyer's 20-month-old son was kidnapped from the family home in Hopewell, New Jersey. Although Lindbergh paid the requested ransom, the boy's body was eventually found half-buried in a roadside thicket not far from his home. Suspect Bruno Richard Hauptmann, a carpenter and small-time crook, was taken into custody on September 19, 1934. A transfixed American public anxiously awaited Hauptmann's trial, which was scheduled to begin on January 3, 1935, at the Hunterdon County courthouse in Flemington, New Jersey.

The Trial of the Century

Due to Lindbergh's fame and the revolting nature of the crime, the five-week proceeding was dubbed the "trial of the century." As such, it drew members of the press like moths to a flame. To keep reporters close to the action, the Union Hotel, which was located just across the street from the Hunterdon County courthouse, was tapped as the press headquarters. The Victorian building was an apt choice: Built in 1877, the four-story hotel was near the site of the trial, and it had a bar on its premises—just the thing to soothe battle-weary correspondents looking to unwind.

On February 13, 1935, the jury handed down a guilty verdict, which carried with it the death penalty. Happy that the villain had received his due, Americans rejoiced. Hauptmann went to the electric chair on April 3, 1936. Since that day, however, speculation

regarding his culpability in the crime has stirred relentlessly. But that's not the only thing that's been stirring.

Harrowing Happenings

After the press departed the Union Hotel, little more was heard about the inn—little more of an *earthly* nature, that is. Staff reports of paranormal occurrences began trickling in, with each story sounding just a tad more terrifying than the one that preceded it. Over the years, several businesses have opened in the building—most recently a restaurant, which closed in 2008. According to witnesses, the ghosts of the Union Hotel have a penchant for vigorously spinning barstools. After this gets the attention of the intended eyewitness, which it unfailingly does, their next trick is to slam doors … loudly.

One night after closing, a bouncer locked the doors to the hotel's foyer and then joined staff members for a drink. Suddenly, the doors flew open—completely unaided—and a cold breeze blew past the group. Dumbfounded by what he had witnessed, the bouncer again closed the doors. As he did, he saw a phantom pair of children's shoes scrambling up the main stairway. Horrified, he turned and fled.

In another incident, a waitress was carrying her cash drawer upstairs after closing. As she reached the top step, she heard a disembodied voice humming a lullaby. Like the bouncer, she fled the scene, never to return again.

Spirits and Other Spirits

At least one ghost at the Union Hotel has its disembodied heart in the right place. While going over her books late one night, a night manager sensed a sudden presence. Startled, she moved back from her desk, and an invisible intruder moved up against her and pressed against her chest. She asked it to move away and the ghost respectfully complied. While some might categorize this turn of events as fortunate, the woman isn't so sure: She regrets telling the entity to back away for fear that she may never have such an encounter again.

Had the manager met the ghost of the condemned man? It's doubtful, since Hauptmann never stayed at the hotel. It's more likely that she brushed up against the spirit of a reporter left over from the days of the Hauptmann trial that was feeling a little frisky after unwinding in the bar.

The Haunted Castle of Mansfield, Ohio

*As you turn onto Reformatory Road in Mansfield, Ohio,
you can't help but gasp as you gaze upon the immense
castlelike structure that looms before you. As we all know,
every good castle needs at least one resident ghost, and the
Mansfield Reformatory doesn't disappoint in that regard.*

From Camp to Castle

During the Civil War, the property on which the Mansfield
Reformatory now stands was the site of Camp Mordecai Bartley.
After the war, the decision was made to construct a reformatory
there that would function as a sort of "middle ground" for first-time
offenders, allowing only hardened criminals and repeat offenders
to be sent to the Ohio Penitentiary in Columbus. But the Mansfield
Reformatory would be no ordinary structure—it would be an imposing
edifice designed to strike fear into the heart of any prisoner forced to
enter its massive gates.

In the 1880s, architect Levi T. Scofield began designing the
reformatory. The entire front portion would house the warden, his
family, and the administrative offices; the rear portion would contain
the massive six-tier cellblock, which would be the tallest freestanding
cellblock in the world.

Incredibly, when the Mansfield Reformatory finally opened in
September 1896, the 150 inmates transferred there entered a building
that still wasn't complete. In fact, the prisoners themselves were
responsible for finishing the construction, a task that included
completing a giant wall surrounding the main building. The structure
would not be fully finished until 1910.

Cramped Quarters and Violence

It doesn't seem possible that such a massive building could become
overcrowded, but that's exactly what happened: By 1930, the
reformatory was already well over capacity. In fact, inmates were
often sleeping three or four to a cell that was designed to fit only two.

The cramped quarters may have been one reason why prisoners at the Mansfield Reformatory were so aggressive. Considering the fact that the facility did not house hardened criminals, the amount of violence that took place there is staggering. A riot in 1957 involved more than 100 inmates. There were also a few instances in which one inmate killed another. Several prisoners couldn't take the living conditions and committed suicide, including one man who set himself on fire. Eventually, word of the horrible conditions reached the public, and in the early 1980s, officials declared the Mansfield Reformatory unfit to continue functioning as a prison; it would be another ten years before the facility was actually shut down.

The building seemed destined for the wrecking ball until Hollywood came calling in the early 1990s, when the majority of *The Shawshank Redemption* (1994) was filmed at the former prison. Not long after, the Mansfield Reformatory Preservation Society was formed. One of the first items on the group's agenda was to open the building for overnight ghost tours. After that, people from all walks of life started to come face-to-face with spirits from the Other Side.

Haunted by the Past

One of the most enduring ghost stories associated with the Mansfield Reformatory centers on Warden Arthur L. Glattke and his wife, Helen. In 1950, Helen was getting ready for Sunday mass when she went into a closet in the warden's quarters to retrieve a box from a high shelf. As she grabbed the box, she bumped a revolver that Arthur had hidden in the closet; the gun went off and wounded her. She was rushed to the hospital, but she died several days later of pneumonia while recovering from her injury.

On February 10, 1959, Arthur was working in his office when he suffered a fatal heart attack. Almost immediately, rumors began to suggest that Helen's death had not been an accident, but rather that Arthur had killed her and made it look like an accident. Further, it was said that Arthur's heart attack was the result of Helen's ghost exacting its revenge. It's a creepy story, but it can't be proven. In fact, by all accounts, the couple truly loved each other. Perhaps that's why when people see the ghosts of the couple, they appear happy as they walk up and down the hallways of the warden's quarters.

Investigating the Reformatory

While the Mansfield Reformatory had been featured on numerous television shows such as *Scariest Places on Earth,* it wasn't until The Atlantic Paranormal Society (TAPS) visited in 2005 for *Ghost Hunters* that people everywhere got a look at a paranormal investigation inside the prison's walls.

During that investigation, TAPS members heard strange footsteps echoing throughout the prison; they also managed to videotape unexplained lights at the far end of the hallway in solitary confinement. But the most intriguing part of the evening came when investigators Dustin Pari and Dave Tango were walking on the second floor of the East Cellblock. The duo heard strange noises coming from one of the cells, but when they were unable to find the source of the sounds, they marked an "X" outside the cell so they could find it later. About an hour later, investigators Jason Hawes and Grant Wilson were in the same area when Hawes thought that he saw something moving inside the cell marked with an "X," and Wilson believed he heard something there. However, upon investigating the cell, it appeared to be empty.

Doing Time with the Ghosts

You don't have to be on a reality TV show to experience the unknown at Mansfield Reformatory. Over the years, paranormal research group The Ghosts of Ohio has spent several nights locked inside the prison. Each time, group members have witnessed strange phenomena, including hearing disembodied footsteps in the hallways, seeing shadowy figures moving in the cellblocks, having equipment malfunction, and experiencing feelings of heaviness while in Solitary Confinement.

The Mansfield Reformatory currently offers tours, so you can see for yourself if anything supernatural is lurking there. But if you're not lucky enough to spot the Glattkes, fear not: Plenty of other ghosts are said to lurk inside the old prison. So if you dare, head to Solitary Confinement, where people report experiencing cold chills, feeling lightheaded, and being touched by unseen hands while sitting in the cells. Or walk either the East or West Cellblock, where you might just hear some ghostly footsteps behind you. Some people have even had small rocks thrown at them from atop the cellblocks. So no matter where you go inside Mansfield Reformatory, keep in mind that you're never more than a stone's throw away from a ghost.

Dream Weaver

As an aeronautical engineer and author of books about paranormal phenomena, John William Dunne (1875–1949) questioned much in life, but nothing more keenly than human dreams and their meanings. His obsession with the twilight world was sparked by an odd event that he couldn't explain. How had Dunne been able to "see" one of the world's greatest tragedies while he was sleeping? And how could this have occurred before the event took place?

J. W. Dunne is best known for the invention of the first practical and stable tailless airplane. But in addition to his aeronautic accomplishments, Dunne offered compelling theories about the very structure of time in his book *An Experiment with Time.* Dunne's interest in this area was prompted by his uncanny knack for forecasting events through his dreams. Of these, one proved particularly mind-boggling.

On the chance that there might be something to his nocturnal visions, Dunne recorded each dream in writing. In early May 1902, while working as an engineer for the British military in South Africa, Dunne had a dream in which he found himself on the island of Martinique. In his vision, the French territory exploded and some 30,000 people perished as a result. Waking up in a cold sweat, Dunne weighed his options. Should he warn the French authorities? Or would his amazing claim fall upon deaf ears? Dunne chose to alert the powers that be, but he was unable to persuade what he later called "incredulous French authorities" to evacuate the island.

A few days after he had his vision, Dunne received a newspaper at his outpost. To his absolute horror, he discovered that his chilling dream had become a reality: Mount Pelée, located on the island of Martinique, had erupted with unbelievable force. In its wake, around 30,000 people lay dead. Had Dunne foreseen the future, or are the past, present, and future simply illusive human perceptions? The question would preoccupy Dunne for the rest of his waking days— and many of his sleep-filled nights, too.

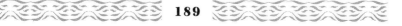

Can Ghosts Hurt People?

One of the most frequent questions that ghost hunters are asked is: "Can ghosts hurt people?" Now that's an intriguing question! We can answer it by observing stories about ghosts.

To answer this question, we have to consider the different kinds of ghosts. Some are no more than shadows or voices, and others are just blips of energy that cause the needle on an EMF detector to twitch. Then there are the translucent apparitions that float down hallways and the forms that are so lifelike that you'd never know that they're ghosts if they didn't vanish before your very eyes. Some spirits, which are known as "intelligents," are thought to be able to communicate with the living. Others, which are known as "residuals," are thought to be far more common and are simply forms of energy reenacting scenes from their life.

Each type of ghost has different abilities. Some are capable of throwing objects across a room, or pressing down on a person's chest while he or she is in bed, or, in rare cases, even possessing people. So if some entities can throw things, it's fair to assume that they can throw things *at* the living.

However, there's some good news behind all of this: If ghosts can hurt people, they very rarely do. Some cases, such as that of the Bell Witch (see page 140), indicate that ghosts have killed people, but such cases are so rare that we're still talking about the Bell Witch haunting nearly two centuries later.

But there's also one slightly frightening thing to consider: Ghosts don't actually have to exist in order to hurt people. A person can be shocked into falling down stairs or even into having a heart attack, merely by *thinking* that he or she has seen a ghost! And being in an allegedly haunted place can certainly play tricks on your mind. It's never safe to let your imagination run wild when you're tromping around a creepy, dark basement.

So don't be concerned about being whisked away to the Other Side by a woman in white, and if you do encounter flatware flying across the room, duck! Chances are, it won't fly directly *at* you, but you can still get hurt if you don't keep your wits about you.

A Voice from Beyond the Grave

After the murder of Teresita Basa in the late 1970s, another woman began to speak in Basa's voice—saying things that only Teresita could have known—to help solve the mystery of her murder.

In February 1977, firemen broke into a burning apartment on North Pine Grove Avenue in Chicago. Beneath a pile of burning clothes, they found the naked body of 47-year-old Teresita Basa, a hospital worker who was said to be a member of the Filipino aristocracy. There were bruises on her neck and a kitchen knife was embedded in her chest. Her body was in a position that caused the police to suspect that she had been raped.

However, an autopsy revealed that she hadn't been raped; in fact, she was a virgin. Police were left without a single lead: They had no suspects and no apparent motive for the brutal murder. The solution would come from the strangest of all possible sources—a voice from beyond the grave.

"I Am Teresita Basa"

In the nearby suburb of Evanston, shortly after Teresita's death, Remibios Chua started going into trances during which she spoke in Tagalog in a slow, clear voice that said, "I am Teresita Basa." Although Remibios had worked at the same hospital as Teresita, they worked different shifts, and the only time they are known to have even crossed paths was during a new-employee orientation. Remibios's husband, Dr. Jose Chua, had never heard of Basa.

While speaking in Teresita's voice, Remibios's accent changed, and when she awoke from the trances, she remembered very little, if anything, about what she had said. However, while speaking in the mysterious voice, she claimed that Teresita's killer was Allan Showery, an employee at the hospital where both women had worked. She also stated that he had killed her while stealing jewelry for rent money.

Through Remibios's lips, the voice pleaded for them to contact the police. The frightened couple initially resisted, fearing that the

authorities would think that *they* should be locked away. But when the voice returned and continued pleading for an investigation, the Chuas finally contacted the Evanston police, who put them in touch with Joe Stachula, a criminal investigator for the Chicago Police Department.

Lacking any other clues, Stachula interviewed the Chuas. During their conversation, Remibios not only named the killer, but she also told Stachula exactly where to find the jewelry that Showery had allegedly stolen from Teresita. Prior to that, the police were not even aware that anything had been taken from the apartment.

Remarkably, when police began investigating Showery, they found his girlfriend in possession of Teresita's jewelry. Although the authorities declined to list the voice from beyond the grave as evidence, Showery was arrested, and he initially confessed to the crime. When his lawyers learned that information leading to his arrest had come from supernatural sources, they advised him to recant his confession.

The Surprise Confession

Not surprisingly, the voice became a focal point of the case when it went to trial in January 1979. The defense called the Chuas to the witness stand in an effort to prove that the entire case against Showery was based on remarks made by a woman who claimed to be possessed—hardly the sort of evidence that would hold up in court.

But the prosecution argued that no matter the origin of the voice, it had turned out to be correct. In his closing remarks, prosecuting attorney Thomas Organ said, "Did Teresita Basa come back from the dead and name Showery? I don't know. I'm a skeptic, but it doesn't matter as to guilt or innocence. What does matter is that the infor-

mation furnished to police checked out. The jewelry was found where the voice said it would be found, and Showery confessed."

Detective Stachula was asked if he believed the

Chuas: "I would not call anyone a liar," he said. "...Dr. and Mrs. Chua are educated, intelligent people.... I listened and acted on what they told me...[and] the case was wrapped up within three hours."

Showery told the jury that he was "just kidding" when he confessed to the crime; he also claimed that the police had coerced him into an admission of guilt. Nevertheless, after 13 hours of deliberation, the jury reported that they were hopelessly deadlocked and a mistrial was declared.

A few weeks later, in a shocking development, Allan Showery changed his plea to "guilty" and was eventually sentenced to 14 years in prison. Some say that Teresita's ghost had visited him and frightened him into confessing.

Obviously shaken by the experience, the Chuas avoided the press as much as possible. In 1980, in her only interview with the press, Remibios noted that during the trial, people were afraid to ride in cars with her, but she said that she was never afraid because the voice said that God would protect her family. Still, she hoped that she would never have to go through such an experience again. "I've done my job," she said. "I don't think I will ever want to go through this same ordeal."

Having attracted national attention, the case quickly became the subject of a best-selling book and countless magazine articles, a TV movie, and a 1990 episode of *Unsolved Mysteries*. The case is often cited as "proof" of psychic phenomena, possession, and ghosts, but it's simply another mystery of the paranormal world. Exactly what it proves is impossible to say; after all, the ghost of Teresita Basa is no longer talking.

"Haunting is information received by the witness who has the experience. Hauntings actually show that we are all psychic receivers (clairvoyant) to some degree."

—Loyd Auerbach, famous paranormal researcher

Ghosts on the Silver Screen

Ghosts and other creepy creatures are cinematic staples that date back to the late 1890s. In fact, the motion-picture industry was just a couple of years old in 1897, when French magician George Méliès embraced the new medium and presented enthusiastic audiences with one of the very first ghost stories on film: The Bewitched Inn.

Méliès's success with movies about the macabre didn't go unnoticed outside of France. In the United States and England, his films were studied and emulated with impressive results. Skeletons came to life and ghosts taunted the living in some of the earliest horror movies, such as *Undressing Extraordinary* (1901) and *The Fairy of the Black Rocks* (1902). By 1910, when Thomas Edison's film company produced what most film historians consider the first cinematic adaptation of Mary Shelley's *Frankenstein*, horror had become an accepted and extremely popular film genre.

As that acceptance grew, haunted houses became the settings for hundreds of movies produced in the United States and abroad. Many have disappeared into obscurity, but film critics and historians still consider a good number of them genuine classics.

From Bookshelves to the Silver Screen

Not surprisingly, many popular haunted house movies are adaptations of literary works. One of the most acclaimed is *The Haunting* (1963), starring Richard Johnson, Claire Bloom, and Julie Harris. Based on Shirley Jackson's 1959 novel *The Haunting of Hill House,* the film concerns a group of paranormal investigators that is psychologically tormented by the spirits residing in the titular abode. A similar theme is explored in *The Legend of Hell House* (1973), an adaptation of the 1971 Richard Matheson novel *Hell House.* Equally notable is the film version of *The Shining* (1980), Stanley Kubrick's excellent reworking of Stephen King's best-selling novel of the same name.

Each decade has seen its share of haunted house flicks, and of course, some are better than others. One of the best from the

1940s is *The Uninvited* (1944), a subtle little terror tale starring Ray Milland and Ruth Hussey as siblings who buy an antiquated old house, unaware that it is haunted.

Best of the '50s, '60s, and '70s

The horror subgenre of ghost/haunted house films really started to hit its stride in the 1950s, a decade that concluded with the popular William Castle thriller *House on Haunted Hill* (1959), in which Vincent Price's character, Fredrick Loren, terrorizes a group of people that spends the night in his supposedly haunted mansion.

Loren seems to be behind most of the mischief that ensues, but the real culprit gets a stiff comeuppance at the end.

The 1960s saw a tremendous resurgence in horror movies in general and ghost stories in particular, including Castle's *13 Ghosts* (1960), a clever little flick with a unique gimmick—audiences had to wear special glasses in order to see the ghosts on the screen. Also worth a view is *The Innocents* (1961), an excellent adaptation of Henry James's 1898 novella *The Turn of the Screw.*

Some of the scariest haunted house films ever made were produced in the 1970s. In addition to *The Legend of Hell House,* Hollywood also gave the world *The Amityville Horror* (1979), which was based on a book by Jay Anson that supposedly chronicled a real-life haunting on Long Island. *The Amityville Horror* proved so successful that it inspired several sequels and a 2005 remake.

Horror Hits of the '80s

The 1980s brought moviegoers several thought-provoking ghost stories, including *The Changeling* (1980)—starring George C. Scott as a man who experiences paranormal activity in a house he rents following the deaths of his wife and daughter—and *The Entity* (1981)—a genuinely disturbing film about a woman who is physically and sexually assaulted by an invisible spirit. The decade also gave us *Poltergeist* (1982), one of the most popular ghost films of all time.

195

Directed by Tobe Hooper—the man behind *The Texas Chainsaw Massacre* (1974)—and an uncredited Steven Spielberg, the film inspired several sequels, a television series, and its own alleged curse.

The Nightmarish '90s

The 1990s were void of many noteworthy paranormal-themed films, with two exceptions: *Ghost* (1990)—a wildly popular supernatural love story starring Patrick Swayze, Demi Moore, and Whoopi Goldberg (see page 450)—and *The Sixth Sense* (1999)—M. Night Shyamalan's film about a young boy (Haley Joel Osment) with the ability to see the spirits of the dead.

Ghosts Make a Comeback

Ghost stories returned with a vengeance in the 21st century, and some of the best that Hollywood has churned out include: *The Others* (2001), starring Nicole Kidman; *1408* (2007), the story of a haunted hotel room that was based on a Stephen King short story; *The Haunting in Connecticut* (2009), which was allegedly based on real-life events; and *Paranormal Activity* (2009), an effective low-budget flick about a young couple that videotapes the terrifying antics of a nasty entity that has invaded their home.

Chilling Chuckles

While most haunted house movies are dramatic thrillers, several cinematic ghost stories have taken more comedic approaches. Don Knotts went up against an organ-playing spirit in *The Ghost and Mr. Chicken* (1966), and *House* (1986)—the story of a writer (William Katt) who is distracted by all kinds of paranormal shenanigans in the weird house that he rents—offers more laughs than chills.

But the king of comedic ghost stories is *Ghostbusters* (1984), starring Bill Murray, Dan Aykroyd, and Harold Ramis as paranormal researchers who start a ghost-removal business in New York City. Directed by Ivan Reitman, it remains one of the funniest paranormal-themed movies ever made.

Though film trends come and go, haunted houses continue to demonstrate extraordinary appeal. And that's good news for movie-goers who love a good scare.

The Philip Phenomenon: Creating a Ghost out of Thin Air

🪦 🪦 🪦 🪦

Which came first: the ghost or the séance? That's the million-dollar question regarding the Philip Phenomenon—an astonishing experiment that successfully conjured up a spirit. The only problem is that this ghost never really lived.... Or did it?

It all began in 1972, when members of the Toronto Society for Psychical Research (TSPR) conducted an experiment to determine if they could "create" a ghost and study how the power of suggestion affected the results. They wanted to know if they could work with a totally fictitious character—a man they invented from scratch—and somehow make contact with its spirit. And they did.

Dr. A.R.G. Owen, the organization's chief parapsychology researcher, gathered a group of eight people who were interested in the paranormal but had no psychic abilities of their own. The Owen Group, as it was called, was made up of people from all walks of life, including Owen's wife, an accountant, an industrial designer, a former MENSA chairwoman, a housewife, a student, and a book-keeper. Dr. Joel Whitton, a psychologist, was also present at many of the meetings as an observer.

The Making of a Ghost

The first order of business was to create the ghost, giving it physical characteristics and a complete background story. According to Dr. Owen, it was important to the study that the spirit be totally made-up, with no strong ties to any historical figure.

The group named the ghost Philip and proceeded to bring him to life—on paper, that is. A sketch artist even drew a picture of Philip as the group imagined him. Here is his story:

Philip Aylesford was an aristocratic Englishman who was born in 1624. As a supporter of the King, he was knighted at age 16 and went on to make a name for himself in the military. He married Dorothea, the beautiful daughter of a nobleman who lived nearby.

197

Unfortunately, Dorothea's appearance was deceiving, as her personality was cold and unyielding. As a Catholic, Philip wouldn't divorce his wife, so he found escape by riding around the grounds of his estate. One day, he came across a gypsy camp. There, he found true love in the arms of the raven-haired Margo, whose dark eyes seemed to look into his soul. He brought her to Diddington Manor, his family home, and hid her in the gatehouse near the stable. But it wasn't meant to be: Dorothea soon discovered her husband's secret affair and retaliated by accusing the gypsy woman of stealing and practicing witchcraft. Afraid of damaging his own reputation, Philip did not step forward in Margo's defense, and she was burned at the stake. After the death of his beloved, Philip was tormented with guilt and loneliness; he killed himself in 1654 at age 30.

Focus, Focus, Focus

In September 1972, after the tale was written, the group began meeting regularly. Reports of these meetings vary. Some accounts describe them as mere gatherings in which group members would discuss Philip and meditate on the details of his life. With no results after about a year, the group moved on to a more traditional method of communing with ghosts: holding séances in a darkened room, sitting around a table with appropriate music and objects that might have been used by Philip or his family. Another version has the group beginning with séances and switching to the more casual setting later.

The setting itself is ultimately secondary to the results: Through the focus and concentration of the group, Philip soon began to make his presence known. He answered questions by tapping on the table for "yes" or "no." Just to be sure, a "yes" tap confirmed that he was, indeed, Philip.

A Physical Presence

After communication was established, the Philip Phenomenon took on a life of its own. Through the tapping, Philip was able to answer questions about the details of his life. He was also able to correctly answer questions about people and places of that historical time period, although these were all facts that were familiar to at least one member of the group. Philip even seemed to develop a personality, exuding emotions that changed the atmosphere of the entire room.

But most amazingly, he was able to exhibit some remarkable physical manifestations, such as making objects move, turning lights on and off at the group's request, and performing incredible feats with the table: It shifted, it danced on one leg, and it even moved across the room.

In order to demonstrate the results of this experiment, the group held a séance in front of an audience of 50 people; the session was also videotaped. Philip rose to the occasion—and so did the table. In addition to tapping on the table and manipulating the lights, Philip made the entire table levitate half an inch off the ground!

The experiment was deemed a success, as there was little doubt that something paranormal was occurring during the sessions. However, the Owen Group never actually realized its original goal of getting the ghost of Philip to materialize. But the TSPR did go on to re-create the experiment successfully on several other occasions with a new group and a new fictional "ghost."

Real, Random, or Re-creation?

So what can be concluded from all this? No one knows for sure, but several schools of thought have developed regarding the matter. Some believe that Philip was a real ghost and that he had once been a living, breathing person. Perhaps he had a few of the characteristics of the fictional Philip and simply responded to the group's summons. Some who believe in the ghost theory say that it may have been a playful spirit (or a demonic one) that just pretended to be Philip as a prank.

A less-popular theory suggests that someone close to the group was aware of the background information as well as the times and places of the meetings. He or she might have planned an elaborate hoax to make it appear as though the ghost was real.

But it is also possible that after creating Philip, the Owen Group put forth enough energy, focus, and concentration to bring him to life, in a manner of speaking. Ghosts may well be products of our imaginations, existing only in our minds, but this study does prove one thing: When people put those minds together, anything is possible—even a visit from the Other Side.

Hospital Haunts

- Over the years, the old Oregon State Hospital in Salem has housed many troubled souls, so it's hardly surprising that many remain. Staff members have reported doors closing on their own, persistent shadows, and disembodied wails of psychological torment.

- La Residencia nursing home in Santa Fe, New Mexico, was once home to St. Vincent Hospital. Years ago, a young boy died there in Room 311 after a car accident, which also claimed the life of his father. The muffled sounds of the boy crying were heard so often that staff members hesitated to assign anyone to that room.

- The new St. Vincent Hospital in Santa Fe is home to a spectral couple that wanders the third floor: The Hispanic man and woman, who are dressed in outdated clothing, seem to be looking for something or someone. Perhaps their son was buried in the former jail cemetery on the premises.

- At the Altru Hospital in Grand Forks, North Dakota, the staff elevator runs on its own, randomly stopping on arbitrary floors. The hospital's security cameras have also recorded ghostly presences in the facility's former mental ward.

- Riverside Manor—a low-income housing complex also located in Grand Forks, North Dakota—was once a hospital and then became a nursing home. Although stories of a nun leaping from the bell tower have no documented basis in fact, a female apparition has been spotted on the premises numerous times over the years.

- The James H. Quillen VA Medical Center in Mountain Home, Tennessee, opened in 1903 to care for veterans of the Civil War and the Spanish-American War. The most visible ghost there is a misty soldier in a Spanish-American War uniform who floats and glides around outside.

The Dark Side of the White House

From the East Wing to the West Wing, our presidential palace is reportedly one of the most haunted government buildings anywhere, which is hardly surprising given the uniquely rich history that has transpired within its walls.

The White House's First Ghost

The ghost of David Burns may be the first spirit that haunted the White House. In life, Burns donated the land on which the structure was built. One day, Franklin Roosevelt heard his name being called, and when he replied, the voice said that it was "Mr. Burns."

FDR's valet, Cesar Carrera, told a similar story: Carrera was in the Yellow Oval Room when he heard a soft, distant voice say, "I'm Mr. Burns." When Carrera looked around, no one was there.

Later, during the Truman years, a guard at the White House also heard a soft voice announce itself as Mr. Burns. The guard expected to see James Byrnes, Truman's secretary of state, but no one appeared. What's more, the guard checked the roster and learned that Byrnes hadn't been in the building at all that day.

William Henry Harrison Feels a Little Blue

William Henry Harrison was the first American president to die in office. While giving his inauguration address in icy, windy weather on March 4, 1841, Harrison caught a cold that quickly turned into pneumonia.

Stories abound about Harrison wandering the corridors of the White House, half-conscious with fever, looking for a quiet room in which to rest. Unfortunately, there was no escape from the doctors whose treatments may have killed him. While Harrison's lungs filled with fluid and fever wracked his body, his doctors bled him and then treated him with mustard, laxatives, ipecac, rhubarb, and mercury. It is speculated that the president died not from the "ordinary winter cold" that he'd contracted, but from the care of his doctors. Harrison passed away on April 4, 1841, just one month after taking office.

Harrison's translucent ghost is seen throughout the White House, but it is most often spotted in the residential areas. His skin is pale blue and his breathing makes an ominous rattling noise. He appears to be looking for something and walks through closed doors. Some believe that he's looking for rest or a cure for his illness; others say he's searching for his office so that he can complete his term as president.

Andrew Jackson Likes the Ladies

If you'd prefer to see a happier ghost, look for the specter of Andrew Jackson; he's often seen in the Queen's Bedroom, where his bed is on display. But Jackson may not necessarily be looking for his old bed; in life, "Old Hickory" was quite the ladies' man, and today, the Queen's Bedroom is reserved for female guests of honor.

Visitors sometimes simply sense Jackson's presence in the Queen's Bedroom or feel a bone-chilling breeze when they're around his bed. Some have reported that Jackson's ghost climbs under the covers, sending guests shrieking out of the room.

Mary Todd Lincoln frequently complained about the ghost of Andrew Jackson cursing and stomping in the corridors of the White House. After she left the presidential estate, Jackson stopped fussing.

Oh Séance Can You See

Séances at the White House have been nearly as numerous as the phantoms that inhabit its hallways. It has been well documented that in the early 1860s, President Lincoln and his wife contacted the spirit of Daniel Webster while attempting to reach their dearly departed son Willie during a séance. According to witnesses, the former secretary of state implored the president to continue his efforts to end slavery. Some years later, relatives of President Ulysses S. Grant held another séance at the White House, during which they reputedly spoke with young Willie Lincoln.

In 1995—with the help of medium Jean Houston—First Lady Hillary Rodham Clinton reportedly established contact with Eleanor Roosevelt and Mahatma Gandhi. It seems some séances yield better results than others. Describing her fascination with White House spirits, Clinton said, "There is something about the house at night that you just feel like you are summoning up the spirits of all the people who have lived there and worked there and walked through the halls there."

Ghosts of Presidents' Families and Foes

Abigail Adams used to hang laundry on clotheslines in the White House's East Room; her ghost appears there regularly in a cap and wrapped in a shawl. She's usually carrying laundry or checking to see if her laundry is dry.

The spirit of Dorothea "Dolley" Madison defends the Rose Garden that she designed and planted. When Woodrow Wilson's wife Edith ordered staff members to dig up the garden to plant new flowers, Dolley's apparition appeared and allegedly insisted that no one was going to touch her roses. The landscaping ceased, and today, Dolley's roses remain exactly as they were when the Madisons lived in the White House in the early 1800s.

After Abraham Lincoln's son Willie died in February 1862 following a brief illness, the president became obsessed with his son's death and had his coffin reopened at least twice, just to look at him. Willie's apparition has been seen at the White House regularly since his death, most often manifesting in the bedrooms on the second floor, where his ghost was once witnessed by Lyndon Johnson's daughter Lynda.

Other spirits also seem to like that room: Harry Truman's mother died there and may have made her presence known afterward. Lynda used to report hearing unexplained footsteps in the bedroom. And sometimes, her phone would ring in the middle of the night; when she answered, no one was on the line.

Also on the second floor, people have heard the ghost of Frances Cleveland crying, perhaps reliving the time when her husband, Grover, was diagnosed with cancer.

One very out-of-place spirit appears to be that of a British soldier from around 1814, when the White House was besieged and burned. The uniformed specter looks lost and holds a torch. When he realizes that he's been spotted, he becomes alarmed and vanishes.

"Now about those ghosts. I'm sure they're here and I'm not half so alarmed at meeting up with any of them as I am at having to meet the live nuts I have to see every day."

—First Lady Bess Truman

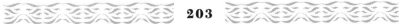

The Feisty Fenton Wraiths

🪦 🪦 🪦 🪦

*The Fenton Hotel Tavern & Grille in Fenton, Michigan, no
longer operates as an inn, but certain spectral guests seem
unaware of that. As a result, the fine restaurant on the main
floor of this historic building may be one of
Michigan's most haunted places.*

Built in 1856 and originally known as the Vermont House, the
Fenton Hotel Tavern & Grille was bought and sold several times
before it received its current name. Over the years, this remarkable
building has been the subject of numerous paranormal investigations
and séances, but the spooks that reside there seem determined to
avoid checking out.

The tin ceilings and original woodwork in the foyer and dining
area of the Fenton add to the illusion of a place that's stuck in time.
Maybe that's why Emery, the old hotel's legendary janitor, still treads
the creaky floorboards of what used to be his room on the building's
decrepit and unused second floor. In life, Emery was a kindly gent
who was a bit of a workaholic. When the last customer leaves in the
evening, it is not uncommon for the staff to hear Emery banging on
the floor of his room as if to say, "Get this place cleaned up!"

The hotel bar is another hot spot for unexplained phenomena.
Bartenders have seen wine glasses scoot right off the stemware racks
and fly across the room. Phantom voices call the staff members by
name, and unseen entities brush up against them. Patrons once saw
a mysterious shadow figure hug a bartender—while the bartender
remained completely unaware of the affectionate display.

The Fenton's most unusual phenomenon—the thirsty ghost—
occurs from time to time at Table 32: It is there that a man sits down
and orders a shot of Jack Daniel's on the rocks, but before the wait
staff can get the drink to the table, the man vanishes.

Table 32 is not the only haunted dining spot at the Fenton. A
waitress and a manager have both seen a top-hat-clad shadow figure
lounging at Table 63; this entity has even been captured in photos.

The dining room is also rumored to house one overly frisky ghost that some waitresses claim has pinched their backsides.

The Fenton's Femme Fatales

Not all of the ghosts at the Fenton Hotel Tavern & Grille are male; supposedly, the spirits of some "working girls" who once lived on the third floor also remain. According to one legend, a young prostitute hung herself in the downstairs restroom and still makes her presence known there by opening and closing stall doors; another version says that the ghostly girl was an unwed, pregnant traveler. Regardless of who she was in life, strange things do happen in the ladies room. Once, a customer seated in a stall watched in disbelief as an unseen force lifted a strand of her long hair and then dropped it back into place. Another time, a workman, who had been sent in to complete some repairs, was unable to open an unlocked stall. After he felt a vaporous mist float through him, he was finally able to open the door. Perhaps this spirit was a modest ghost that just needed some privacy.

The Seal of Disapproval

The second-floor hotel rooms are off-limits to customers, but in the mid-2000s, *Weird Michigan* author Linda Godfrey was given an evening tour of the area. That night, she heard loud, unintelligible whispering directly in her ear while she, a hostess, and another researcher stood quietly in the hallway. Later in the investigation, Godfrey discovered that the viewfinder on her camera was covered with fresh candle wax—however, she had not been near a lit candle all evening. Godfrey felt as though some unseen entity was literally attempting to block her view of that section of the hotel. Perhaps, like all hotel guests, the ghosts of the Fenton simply value their privacy.

In February 1904, the Fenton Hotel's second- and third-story front porches were dragged away by a team of frightened horses. When something at the railroad depot spooked the equines, they took off galloping through town and thundered past the hotel, pulling down support posts as they went. Amazingly, no one was hurt, but the porches were never rebuilt.

Famous Figures in Ghost Research

These days, it seems as though you can't watch an hour of TV without running into people who tout themselves as ghost researchers. And while most of these folks have only been working in the field for a few years, ghost hunters have been chasing after things that go bump in the night for centuries. Here are a few pioneers in the field of paranormal research ... some of the names might surprise you.

The Fox Sisters

Often credited with inadvertently starting the Spiritualism movement, the Fox Sisters—14-year-old Maggie and 11-year-old Kate—spoke to a ghost in their Hydesville, New York, home in 1848. The spirit, whom the girls referred to as Mr. Splitfoot, would communicate by knocking responses to the girls' questions.

By 1850, the sisters were traveling the country giving demonstrations on how to communicate with spirits. According to them, Mr. Splitfoot had revealed that he was the ghost of a man named Charles B. Rosma, a peddler who had been murdered and buried in the basement of the Fox home.

Word about the mysterious gifts of the Fox Sisters quickly spread, and before long, they were conducting séances in crowded theaters nationwide and privately for the wealthy members of society. Fame had its price, however. Skeptics and scientists alike attempted to debunk the sisters' claims by placing the two inside restrictive boxes or asking them to perform their séances in broad daylight. No confirmed sign of trickery was ever detected, and years later, the Fox Sisters retired with their reputations intact.

But in an 1888 interview published in a New York newspaper, Maggie stated that she and her sister had faked the whole enterprise and that the ghostly noises were nothing more than them popping their joints and knuckles. However, a year later, Maggie recanted her story, leaving everyone to wonder what the real truth was when she passed away in 1893. The previous year, Kate had passed away without ever confirming or denying her sister's claims.

A final twist to the story came in 1904, when a group of children who were playing in the abandoned Fox house discovered a false wall. Behind it, they found the skeletal remains of an adult male. Unfortunately, the remains could not be identified, but believers point to this as proof that there had indeed been a peddler murdered and buried in the Fox Sisters' basement.

Harry Houdini

While he will forever be remembered as a magician, Harry Houdini was also a passionate psychic investigator. When his mother died in 1913, he was so devastated that he started going to psychics to attempt to contact her spirit. Upon seeing that many of the psychics he visited were using the same sleight-of-hand tricks that magicians used, Houdini set out on a personal quest to expose those who were trying to deceive the public. He would often travel in disguise, lest the psychics recognize him. He also supposedly developed a series of devices that could restrain psychics from moving, thereby preventing them from faking paranormal activity after lights were extinguished. Forever the optimist, Houdini never abandoned his research or his belief that life continued after death, even promising his wife that if he could reach out to her after he died, he would. He even went so far as to create a secret code that only the two of them knew, so that if his wife was given a message from a psychic, she would know whether or not it was legit. Despite conducting several public séances after Houdini's death, she was unable to contact his spirit.

Harry Price

In 1920, Harry Price joined the Society for Psychical Research and almost immediately began to make a name for himself by exposing hoaxers. He began by showing how certain photographers—who claimed to capture photos of ghosts—were simply performing double exposures. He also found that the "ectoplasm" that a medium was supposedly spewing from her mouth was nothing more than cheesecloth.

In 1929, after spending most of the decade conducting experiments and researching ghosts, Price began the investigation that

 **207**

would make him famous: Borley Rectory, a building in Essex, England, that was long rumored to be haunted. In the late 1930s, after the last residents of the rectory moved out, Price rented the building for an entire year and conducted a series of investigations. Once an avowed skeptic, the enormous amount of activity that Price encountered during his time there—including a psychic contacting two spirits that were inhabiting the building—turned him into a believer. Allegedly, one of the spirits—a ghostly nun who claimed to have been murdered on the property—went so far as to scribble messages to the researchers on the rectory's walls. The other spirit, which identified itself as Sunex Amures, claimed it would burn the rectory down that very evening. It didn't, but the rectory did catch fire and was destroyed a year later, in early 1939. When Price returned to the property after the fire, he excavated the cellar and discovered unidentifiable remains there.

Price's research at Borley Rectory resulted in two books: *The Most Haunted House in England* (1940) and *The End of Borley Rectory* (1946).

Peter Underwood

As a boy, Peter Underwood became fascinated with ghosts and the paranormal because his grandparents lived in a haunted house. Underwood later spent several years compiling interviews with everyone who'd been involved with the original 1929 investigation of Borley Rectory, including Harry Price himself. Along the way, he joined the Society for Psychical Research and was also personally invited by Price to join his Ghost Club, for which he served as president from 1962 until 1993, when he left to serve as president of the Ghost Club Society.

When Price passed away in 1948, Underwood was one of only a handful of people entrusted with the privilege of reviewing all of Price's research. In addition, Underwood has been actively investigating hauntings for decades. His most famous case is his lengthy investigation of Queen's House in Greenwich, England, where perhaps the most famous ghost photograph of all time— a snapshot of a hunched-over figure in white pulling itself up a staircase—was obtained.

Hans Holzer

Perhaps no other individual is more responsible for bringing ghost research to the masses than Hans Holzer. Beginning in the 1960s, Holzer wrote more than 140 books about the paranormal, including many on cases that he investigated firsthand. When not writing books, Holzer taught parapsychology at the New York Institute of Technology and worked with some of the world's most famous psychics, including Sybil Leek and Ethel Johnson-Meyers. It was Johnson-Meyers who, in 1977, accompanied Holzer on his most well-known case: the investigation of the infamous "Amityville Horror" house located at 112 Ocean Avenue in Amityville, New York. The team's work resulted in the claims that the house was built on sacred Native American land (which may have included a burial ground), which caused angry Native American spirits to haunt the property.

Loyd Auerbach

Since receiving his master's degree in parapsychology from John F. Kennedy University in 1981, Loyd Auerbach has been a major player in the ghost-research community. In addition to conducting investigations across the United States, Auerbach also serves as the director of the Office of Paranormal Investigations.

While conducting his research—which has included many famous locations, such as Alcatraz—Auerbach constantly looks for ways to standardize ghost-hunting procedures and protocols. He has written several "how-to" books about investigations, including *A Paranormal Casebook: Ghost Hunting in the New Millennium,* which was published in 2005.

Auerbach believes that one visit to a location does not constitute an investigation. Rather, ghost hunters need to continually visit places and constantly gather data. For that reason, Auerbach has made numerous research trips to historic sites such as the USS *Hornet*—which is currently anchored in Alameda, California—and the Moss Beach Distillery in Moss Beach, California. In fact, Auerbach has been visiting the Distillery since 1991 and has reportedly had several encounters with its resident ghost, "the Blue Lady."

America's Most Haunted Lighthouse

🪦 🪦 🪦 🪦

Built in 1830, the historic Point Lookout Lighthouse is located in St. Mary's County, Maryland, where the Potomac River meets Chesapeake Bay. It's a beautiful setting for hiking, boating, fishing, camping… and ghost hunting.

The Most Ghosts

Point Lookout Lighthouse has been called America's most haunted lighthouse, perhaps because it stands on the site of what was the largest Civil War camp for Confederate prisoners of war. Marshy surroundings, tent housing, and close quarters were a dangerous combination, and because of these conditions, smallpox, scurvy, and dysentery ran rampant. The camp held more than 50,000 soldiers, and between 3,000 and 8,000 men died there.

Park rangers and visitors to the lighthouse report hearing snoring and footsteps, having a sense of being watched, and feeling the floors shake and the air move as crowds of invisible beings pass by. A photograph of a former caretaker features the misty figure of a young soldier leaning against the wall behind her, although no one noticed him when the photo was taken during a séance at the lighthouse. Also, one bedroom there reportedly smelled like rotting flesh at night until the odor was publicly attributed to the spirits of the war prisoners.

The Lost Ghost

On a stormy night in December 1977, Ranger Gerald Sword was sitting in the kitchen of the lighthouse when a young man's face appeared at the back door. The young man was wearing a floppy cap and a long coat as he peered into the bright room. Given the awful weather, Sword opened the door to let him in, but the young man floated backward until he vanished entirely. Later, after a bit

of research, Sword realized that he'd been face-to-face with Joseph Haney, a young officer whose body had washed ashore after the steamboat that he was aboard sank during a similar storm in 1878.

The Host Ghost

One of Point Lookout's most frequently seen spirits is a spectral woman dressed in a long blue skirt and a white blouse. She appears at the top of the stairs and is believed to be the ghost of Ann Davis, the wife of the Point Lookout's caretaker. Although her husband died shortly after he took the post, Ann remained as his successor for the next 30 years. According to inspection reports, she was known for clean and well-kept grounds. Caretakers claim to hear her ghost sighing heavily.

Who Said That?

In 1980, Point Lookout's reputation drew the attention of renowned parapsychologist Hans Holzer, who tried to capture evidence of ghostly activity there. Holzer and his team claimed that they recorded 24 different voices in all (both male and female) talking, laughing, and singing. Among their recordings, male voices could be heard saying, "Fire if they get too close," "Going home," and more than a few obscenities.

Take Care, Caretaker

One former caretaker reported waking in the middle of the night to see a ring of lights dancing above her head. She smelled smoke and raced downstairs to find a space heater on fire. She believes that the lights were trying to protect her and the lighthouse from being consumed by flames.

A Full House

Point Lookout Lighthouse was decommissioned in 1966 after 135 years of service. In 2002, the state of Maryland purchased it, and it is now open for tours and paranormal investigations, so it continues to host a steady stream of visitors—even those who are no longer among the living.

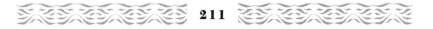

There's Something About Mary

🪦 🪦 🪦 🪦

Most big cities have their share of ghost stories, and Chicago
is no exception. But beyond tales of haunted houses, spirit-
infested graveyards, and phantom-filled theaters, one
Chicago legend stands out among the rest: It's the story of a
beautiful phantom hitchhiker of whom nearly everyone
in the Windy City has heard. Her name is "Resurrection
Mary," and she is Chicago's most famous ghost.

One version of the story says that Resurrection Mary was a young
woman who died on Archer Avenue in Chicago's southwestern suburbs.
On a cold winter's night in the early 1930s, Mary spent the evening
dancing with her boyfriend at the Oh Henry Ballroom (known today
as Willowbrook Ballroom) in Willow Springs, but when the evening
ended with a quarrel between the two lovers, Mary decided to walk
home. Tragically, she was killed when a passing car slid on the ice
and struck her.

Mary's grieving parents buried her in Resurrection Cemetery, just
down the road from the ballroom. She was reportedly wearing a fine
white dress and dancing shoes when she was committed to eternity.

The Girl by the Side of the Road

Since that time, drivers have often witnessed a ghostly young woman
standing on the side of the road near the gates of Resurrection
Cemetery. Time and time again, motorists have reported picking up
a pretty hitchhiker on Archer Avenue, only to see her disappear
before letting her off. These accounts featured eerie similarities: In
most cases, the woman was said to have blonde hair and wear a white
party dress. The encounters almost always occurred near the
ballroom or in the vicinity of Resurrection Cemetery.

Other reports took a more mysterious turn. Many young men
claimed that they'd met a girl at a dance at the ballroom, spent the
evening with her, and then offered her a ride home at closing time.
Her vague directions always led them north along Archer Avenue

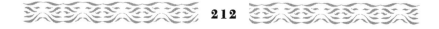

until they reached the gates of Resurrection Cemetery—where the girl would inexplicably vanish from the car.

Although some drivers claimed that the mysterious woman was looking for a ride, others reported that she actually attempted to jump onto the running boards of their automobiles as they drove past. And some even said that they'd accidentally run over her outside the cemetery; when they went to her aid, her body was gone. Others said that their automobiles actually passed through the young woman before she disappeared through the cemetery gates.

Police and local newspapers fielded similar stories from numerous frightened and frazzled drivers who had encountered the ethereal young woman. These accounts created the legend of "Resurrection Mary," as she came to be known.

Jerry's Tale

No Resurrection Mary story is as detailed or as harrowing as that of Jerry Palus. He claimed to have met the apparition at a Chicago dance hall in 1939. According to Palus, the pair shared many spins around the dance floor before the woman asked him for a ride home. She asked him to take Archer Avenue, which he knew was nowhere near the home address she had given him. Nevertheless, he complied. When the car approached Resurrection Cemetery, the woman asked Palus to pull over; he couldn't understand why she'd want to be dropped off in such a remote area. "This is where I have to get out," she explained in a soft voice, "but where I'm going, you can't follow." With that, the mysterious girl hurried toward the cemetery gates and vanished right before Palus's unbelieving eyes.

The next day, Palus visited the home address that the girl had given him. There, an older woman explained to him that he couldn't possibly have been with her daughter because she had been dead for several years. When Palus was shown a photo of the woman's daughter, his face turned ashen as he realized that somehow, the young woman had come back from the grave to dance again.

Will the Real Resurrection Mary Please Stand Up?

This legend has been told countless times over the years, and it may actually have some elements of the truth to it—but there may be more than one Resurrection Mary haunting Archer Avenue.

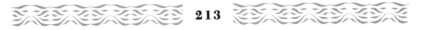

It is possible that in life, Resurrection Mary was a young Polish girl named Mary Bregovy. Mary loved to dance, especially at the Oh Henry Ballroom, and she was killed one night in March 1934 after spending the evening there and then downtown at some of the city's late-night clubs. She died along Wacker Drive in Chicago when the car in which she was riding collided with an elevated train support. Bregovy was buried in Resurrection Cemetery, and a short time later, a caretaker spotted her ghost walking through the graveyard. Stranger still, motorists on Archer Avenue soon began telling stories of her apparition trying to hitch rides as they passed by the cemetery's front gates. For this reason, many believe that the ghost stories about Mary Bregovy may have given birth to the legend of Resurrection Mary.

However, as encounters with Resurrection Mary continued through the years, descriptions of the spectral girl have varied. Mary Bregovy had bobbed, light-brown hair, but most reports describe Resurrection Mary as having long blonde hair. So who could this ghost be?

Perhaps it's Mary Miskowski, who was killed along Archer Avenue in October 1930. According to sources, she also loved to dance at the Oh Henry Ballroom and at some other local nightspots. Many people who knew her in life believed that she might be the ghostly hitchhiker reported in the southwest suburbs.

In the end, we may never know Resurrection Mary's true identity, but there's no denying that sightings of her have been backed up with credible eyewitness accounts. In these reports, witnesses give specific places, dates, and times for their encounters with Mary—encounters that remain unexplained to this day. Mary is also one of the few ghosts that's ever left physical evidence behind.

Burning Desire

Over the years, encounters with Resurrection Mary have been relatively common, but one account stands apart from all others. On August 10, 1976, a man driving past Resurrection Cemetery noticed a woman in a white dress standing inside the gates. She was grasping the metal bars of the gate, looking out toward the road. Thinking that she had been locked in, the driver notified the police. An officer responded to the call, but when he arrived at the

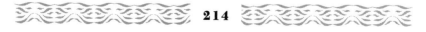

cemetery, the girl was gone. He searched the location but found nothing out of the ordinary—until he glanced at the gate. It looked as though someone had pulled two of the bars with such intensity that small handprints were seared into the metal.

When word about the handprints got out, people from all over the area came to see them. Cemetery officials denied that anything supernatural had occurred, and they later claimed that the marks were created when a workman had tried to heat up the bars and bend them back into shape after a truck accidentally backed into the gate. It was a convenient explanation, but one that failed to explain the indentions that appeared to be left by small fingers and were plainly visible in the metal.

Cemetery officials were disturbed by this new publicity, so in an attempt to dispel the crowds of curiosity seekers, they tried to remove the marks with a blowtorch. However, this process made them even more noticeable, so the officials had the bars cut out and planned to straighten or replace them.

But removing the bars only made things worse, as people wondered what the cemetery was hiding. So the bars were put back into place, straightened, and then left alone so that the burned areas would oxidize and eventually resemble the other bars. However, the blackened areas did not oxidize, and the twisted handprints remained obvious until the late 1990s, when the bars were finally removed. At great expense, Resurrection Cemetery replaced the front gates, and the notorious bars were gone for good.

A Broken Spirit Lingers On

Sightings of Resurrection Mary aren't as frequent now as in years past, but they still persist, and many of them seem to be authentic. Many believe that Mary is on her way to her eternal resting place after one last night of dancing.

Haunted eBay

Many people drive hours to reach haunted destinations, but a new trend might save you some gas money: bringing the ghost into your own home! And all you need is a computer and a PayPal account.

Since the early days of eBay, people have offered all sorts of "haunted" items for sale on the online auction site, and some of the objects have sold for thousands of dollars. These days, eBay even offers a Guide to Buying Haunted Items on its website. So what sorts of haunted objects can be found on eBay? Read on to find out.

Haunted Cane

After Mary Anderson's father passed away in 2004, her five-year-old son was convinced that his ghost was haunting the house. Specifically, the boy felt that it had taken up residence in an old cane. In an effort to convince her son that the spirit was gone, Anderson put the "haunted" cane up for sale on eBay. Following a bidding war that resulted in 132 bids, website GoldenPalace.com shelled out a mind-boggling $65,000 for the haunted cane, making it the most expensive haunted item sold on eBay to date.

Ghost in a Bottle

"Supernatural or novelty? You decide!" That was the tagline for the Ghost in a Bottle when it appeared on eBay in 2008 for $20 a pop. Although the seller wouldn't guarantee what would happen if a customer decided to open one of these bottles and release the ghost inside, that didn't stop people from buying them.

The creator of the "original" Ghost in a Bottle no longer sells them on eBay, but similar items occasionally go up for auction starting at around $29.

Haunted iPhone

In 2008, people lined up for the chance to buy their very own iPhone, and it was at around this same time that someone offered up a haunted iPhone on eBay. Not only did this iPhone act

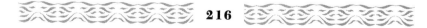

strangely and make odd noises (like laughing out loud), but the ghostly image of what appeared to be (the very much alive) Steve Jobs also seemed to be "burned" onto the iPhone's screen.

With a starting price of more than $8 million, the haunted iPhone seemed unlikely to sell. Several days after it was posted, the auction was taken down without receiving a single bid.

Spooky Dolls A-Plenty

By far, the most popular "haunted" items on eBay are dolls. On any given day, hundreds of listings promise to deliver a haunted doll to your door. While most haunted dolls sell for around $25, some go for $100 or more, especially if they're particularly creepy looking.

Antique Hat Pin

The seller of a haunted antique hat pin claimed to be a paranormal researcher with more than 45 years of experience who was downsizing his personal collection. The pin was supposedly found inside a secret room of a haunted mansion. The seller stated that he'd seen a "blue, glowing streak that swirls" around the item. It also purportedly moved on its own, including "spinning wildly on a table." The auction's sole bidder paid $15 for the pin.

Human Soul

Some people believe that ghosts are the restless souls of the deceased. Perhaps that's why there was so much interest when college student Adam Burtle put his soul up for auction in 2001. Believe it or not, eBay policy dictates that souls fall under the site's "no body parts" policy, so it traditionally shuts down such auctions. However, this one slipped through, possibly because no one was bidding on it. Burtle's ex-girlfriend bid $6.66, and it appeared that she might win the auction, but then a bidding war erupted in the final hour of the sale. When the dust settled, the soul sold for $400 to an anonymous bidder from Des Moines, Iowa. As of this writing, the winner has yet to try and collect her prize. As for Burtle, eBay suspended his account.

San Diego Ghosts
Gather at the Whaley House

*Even if you don't believe in ghosts, you've got to be intrigued by
all the chatter surrounding the Whaley House in San Diego.
According to late ghost hunter Hans Holzer, this old family
homestead might be the most haunted house in America.
The U.S. Department of Commerce lists the building as an
authentic Haunted House (it is one of only two structures in
the country—along with the Winchester Mystery House—to
hold this distinction), and the television show* America's Most
Haunted *called it the Most Haunted House in the United States.*

How It All Began
The first two-story building in San Diego and now the oldest on the
West Coast, the Whaley House needs all of its space to house the
many spirits that reside inside it. Built by prominent Californian
Thomas Whaley in 1856, it began as a one-story granary with an
adjacent two-story residence. By the next year, Whaley had opened
a general store on the premises. Over the years, the building also
served as a county courthouse, a ballroom, a billiards hall, and a
theater, among other things. Now it's a California State Historic
Landmark and a museum.

Squatter's Rights
Hindsight is always 20/20, but perhaps Thomas Whaley should have
thought twice about buying the property on which "Yankee Jim"
Robinson was publicly hanged in 1852. Accused of attempted grand
larceny, Robinson was executed in a particularly unpleasant display.
The gallows were situated on the back of a wagon that was set up
at the site; however, being a tall man, Yankee Jim was able to reach
the wagon with his feet, thus delaying his death for several minutes.
According to newspaper reports, when his legs were finally pulled
out from under him, he "swung back and forth like a pendulum"
until he died. Not a pretty sight.

Although Whaley was actually present at Robinson's execution, he apparently didn't associate the property with the gruesome event that had taken place there. Nevertheless, soon after the house was completed, he and his family began to hear heavy disembodied footsteps, as if a large man was walking through the house. Remembering what had taken place there a few years earlier, the Whaleys believed that the spirit of Yankee Jim himself was sharing their new home. Apparently, Robinson was not a malevolent ghost because the Whaleys' youngest daughter, Lillian, remained in the house with the spirit until 1953. But to this day, visitors to the site still report hearing the heavy-footed phantom.

Family Spirits

After the house became a historic landmark and was opened to the public in 1960, staff, tourists, and ghost hunters alike began to experience paranormal phenomena such as apparitions, noises, and isolated cold spots. Some have even caught glimpses of a small spotted dog running by with its ears flapping, which just might be the spirit of the Whaleys' terrier, Dolly Varden.

Although Thomas and Anna Whaley lived in several different houses, the couple must have dearly loved their original San Diego home because they don't seem quite ready to leave it, even a century after their deaths. They have been seen—and heard—going about their daily business and doing chores in the house. Don't they know there's a cleaning service for that?

The couple has also been captured on film acting as though it was still the 19th century. Thomas was seen wandering through the house and smoking a pipe near an upstairs window, while Anna seems to have kept up her duties as the matron of the house: People have seen her rocking a baby, tucking a child into bed, and folding clothes. Sometimes, the family's rocking chair is seen teetering back and forth all by itself.

Children are especially likely to see the building's former occupants. Employees frequently notice youngsters smiling or waving at people who the adults are unable to see. And the sound of piano music

that sometimes drifts through the air? Most say that it's Anna, still playing the tunes that she loved most in life.

Long before he became one of America's most beloved TV personalities, Regis Philbin worked at a television station in San Diego. In 1964, when he and a companion paid a visit to the Whaley House to investigate the ghostly tales, Philbin was startled to see the wispy figure of Anna Whaley moving along one of the walls. When he turned on a flashlight to get a better look, she disappeared, leaving only her portrait to smile back at him from a frame on the wall.

Wilted Violet

Thomas and Anna's daughter Violet had a particularly sad life and is thought to haunt the old house where she once lived. In 1882, in a double wedding with her sister Anna Amelia, the beautiful Violet was married at the Whaley House to a man that her parents did not trust. Unfortunately, the marriage lasted only two weeks, after which Violet was granted a divorce. Divorce was highly uncommon in those days, and the scandal was humiliating for both Violet and her family. Violet became extremely depressed, and in 1885, she took her own life by shooting herself in the heart.

It is believed that Violet makes her presence known by turning on lights in the upstairs rooms and setting off the burglar alarm. Her spirit is also thought to be responsible for the phantom footsteps that emanate from the second floor and the sudden icy chills often felt by visitors—as though a spirit had just walked right through them.

Ghosts Galore

Most of the spirits at the Whaley House seem to be related to the family or the site. A young girl has been seen in several locations in and around the house. Dressed in 19th-century clothing, she plays with toys in the playroom, sniffs flowers in the garden, and darts in and out of the dining room very quickly. Some say that she was a playmate of the Whaley children and that she died on the property when she got tangled in a clothesline and either broke her neck or was strangled; however, there is no record of such a death occurring at the Whaley House. Others say that although her spirit is real, her story was made up somewhere along the line, which only adds to the intrigue of the place. As if there wasn't enough of that already.

Another female ghost seems to be attached to the part of the house that once served as a courtroom. One visitor said that as she walked into the room, she saw a woman dressed in a calico skirt typical of the 1800s. The spirit didn't seem evil, but it didn't seem to be particularly welcoming either. The visitor captured the spectral woman's shadowy figure in a photo. It seems likely that the ghost is somehow connected to an event that took place in the courtroom.

The ghost of a man dressed in a businesslike frock coat has also appeared in the former courtroom. However, his spirit may not be strongly attached to the building because it fades away more quickly than others that are seen there.

Haunted Happenings

In addition to these apparitions, visitors, volunteers, and employees have reported other odd phenomena inside the house. Unexplained singing, organ music, and whistling have been heard, as has a toddler crying in an upstairs nursery. (This is believed to be the spirit of Thomas and Anna's son, who was also named Thomas; he died of scarlet fever at age 17 months.) Some have witnessed levitating furniture, and others have noticed mysterious scents, such as perfume, cigar smoke, and the scent of holiday baking coming from an empty kitchen.

When visitors first enter the house, they can examine photos taken by previous visitors. These images all have one thing in common: They contain mysterious objects such as shadows, orbs, and misty figures. One visitor reported trying to take photos with an otherwise reliable camera; as soon as she tried to focus, the camera beeped, indicating that she was too close to her subject despite the fact that she was nowhere near the closest (visible) object. Once developed, the photos featured an orb or filmy shadow in nearly every shot.

At least the Whaley House spirits take some responsibility for the place. Once, after an especially long day at the museum, a staff member was getting ready to close up when all the doors and windows on both floors suddenly locked on their own, all at the same time. Sometimes spirits just need a little alone time.

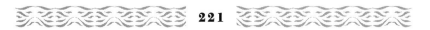

Some Guests Stay Forever at the Chelsea

Since opening in 1884, New York City's famous Chelsea Hotel has been the home of great writers, musicians, artists, and directors, and until 1899, it was the tallest building in the Big Apple. With a rich history and a long list of famous former tenants, it's easy to imagine that the Chelsea may house some notable ghosts. Here are a few of the restless spirits that still call the Chelsea home.

Thomas Wolfe (1900–1938)

Thomas Wolfe was one of the greatest American writers of the early 20th century, and he penned *You Can't Go Home Again* while living in Room 829 at the Chelsea. Although Wolfe didn't die at the Chelsea, it's clear that the author considered the hotel his home, and apparently you *can* go home again…even after death: Wolfe's ghost is said to appear throughout the eighth floor. Many folks who snap photos of mysterious orbs there believe that they are the manifestation of Wolfe, still roaming the halls.

Dylan Thomas (1914–1953)

Welshman Dylan Thomas, who is best known for his poem "Do Not Go Gentle Into That Good Night," died of pneumonia in 1953 while visiting the United States. Before he fell ill, Thomas lived in Room 206 at the Chelsea. Several guests have awoken to see Thomas staring at them intently, deathly pale and with the sunken look of a drunk. One woman claimed that she awoke in the night when her room suddenly grew frigid, and then she heard footsteps. She looked up from her bed and saw a grimacing face staring at her in the mirror, and then the face suddenly vanished. She wasn't familiar with Thomas, but she later identified him from a photograph of famous people who had stayed at the Chelsea.

Eugene O'Neill (1888–1953)

One of America's most famous playwrights, Eugene O'Neill lived at the Chelsea on and off from the 1910s through the 1940s. O'Neill wrote plays such as *The Iceman Cometh,* and he often stayed at the Chelsea (which is only blocks from the theater

district) when his works were in production on Broadway. Even so, his spirit has only been seen at the Chelsea sporadically. Despite the amount of time he spent there, O'Neill actually died at the Sheraton Hotel in Boston, which is now the Shelton Hall dormitory at Boston University; students in Room 401 often claim to see his specter there as well.

Herbert Huncke (1915–1996)

A notable poet from the Beat Generation, Herbert Huncke lived in Room 828 of the Chelsea until his death in 1996. He is credited with coining the term "Beat Generation," and his friends included William S. Burroughs and Jack Kerouac. But while his friends rose to prominence, Huncke had to settle for appearing as characters, such as Elmer Hassel in Kerouac's *On the Road*. In fact, Huncke didn't garner much fame of his own until he published his auto-biography (*Guilty of Everything*) in 1990, just six years before he passed. Current residents claim that Huncke likes to leave the communal bathroom door open on his old floor. They also say that if you listen to the drafts in the air vents, it's his voice that you'll hear wailing on cold nights.

Sid Vicious (1957–1979)

On the morning of October 12, 1978—in one of the most notorious moments in the history of the Chelsea—Sex Pistols' bassist Sid Vicious awoke in Room 100 after a drug binge to find his girlfriend, Nancy Spungen, stabbed to death in the bathroom. The bed was soaked with her blood, and Sid had been so high that he didn't know if he had murdered the love of his life or if they'd been attacked. After being charged with her murder, the punk-rock icon was so distraught that he overdosed on heroin before he went to trial. Since then, numerous people have witnessed Sid's ghost getting on the elevator at the Chelsea; sometimes he's covered in blood and other times he's accompanied by Nancy. Regardless of what happened that night, Sid seems doomed to spend eternity at the Chelsea Hotel.

Celebrities Who've Encountered Ghosts

Who says that ghosts only show themselves to everyday people in out-of-the way locations? The following list just might convince you that when it comes to ghosts, not even the Hollywood elite is safe from a supernatural scare!

Vincent Price

While he was alive, the great Vincent Price frightened the heck out of millions of moviegoers, but Price himself experienced a ghostly shock while he was on an L.A.-to-New York flight on November 15, 1958. Most of the trip was uneventful, but at one point, Price glanced out the window and was shocked to see giant letters that were "lit up with blinding light from within the clouds" spelling out "Tyrone Power is dead."

Price, who was a close friend of Power, was shocked by what he saw, but he was even more perplexed by the fact that no one else on the plane seemed to notice the words, even though some were looking out the windows. Before Price could speak, the words vanished as quickly as they had appeared.

Upon reaching New York, Price dashed to a phone and tried to call Power. That's when he learned that Power had just died of a heart attack in Madrid, Spain. Price originally thought that he'd had a psychic premonition, but as the years passed, he did not experience any similar events, which ultimately led him to believe that he'd been given an otherworldly message for his eyes only.

Paul McCartney

In 1995, Paul McCartney, George Harrison, and Ringo Starr entered a studio to record as The Beatles for the first time in decades. They had chosen to record the song "Free as a Bird," which was written by their dearly departed bandmate John Lennon, who had been gunned down in 1980. While recording the song, McCartney had the

distinct feeling that Lennon's ghost was present for the session. McCartney said that they kept hearing strange noises coming from inside the studio and that the equipment malfunctioned from time to time. "There was just an overall feeling that John was around," McCartney said.

Sugar Ray Leonard

In 1982, after ruling the boxing world for several years, Olympic Gold Medalist and World Champion Sugar Ray Leonard found himself in a bad place. At age 25, he had been forced into an early retirement due to a detached retina. He wasn't happy with himself

or with life. But all that changed when he and his wife were awakened one night by what sounded like children running in the attic above them. Leonard went to investigate, but his search came up empty. The next day, an exterminator was summoned, but he too found nothing.

The following night, Leonard woke up feeling as though he was being watched. Looking across the darkened bedroom, he saw the silhouette of a child, which he initially thought was one of his sons. But as the shape approached the bed, Leonard realized that it was a young girl. He was transfixed for several moments before he decided to reach out to touch the figure. When he did, the girl's image

began to distort, taking on the look of someone who had been horribly burned. It was then that Leonard smelled gas.

Forgetting all about the ghost, Leonard woke his wife. She too smelled the gas, so the couple immediately grabbed their two sleeping children and fled to a relative's house. The following morning, Leonard called a repairman and asked him to check for a gas leak. Several hours later, the repairman called to tell Leonard that not only was there no leak, there weren't even any gas lines in or near the Leonard residence.

Leonard interpreted seeing the ghostly girl as a sign that he needed to recognize the importance of family. And although Leonard never saw the apparition again, he later discovered that a young girl had accidentally burned to death inside the home.

Anson Williams

Years before he would work his way into America's heart as the lovable Potsie Weber on *Happy Days,* Anson Williams had his own guardian angel. Both of Williams's parents told him that on many occasions, they would walk by his room at night and see the ghost of his grandmother standing watch over him as he slept. As he grew older, Williams would take comfort in that, especially since his grandmother had died before he was born and he never had the chance to meet her.

One night in 1971, Williams drove his car into an intersection and was broadsided by a car that had run a red light. Williams states that just as the cars collided, time suddenly began to move in slow motion, and as his head moved toward the windshield, he saw the face of his grandmother in the glass; he also heard her voice telling him, "Everything's fine." And although both cars were smashed beyond recognition, Williams walked away from the accident with only a scratch.

Marilyn Manson

You'd expect shock-rocker Marilyn Manson to have at least one creepy ghost story to tell, but you'd probably never guess that it happened to him at, of all places, a farm in Ohio.

As a teenager in 1986, Manson (then known simply as Brian Warner) befriended a classmate in rural Canton, Ohio. In an attempt to scare Manson, the boy took him to his family's barn, where the boy's older brother had created a sort of makeshift satanic altar, complete with strange symbols and rotting animal carcasses. The boy then picked up a book that was alleged to contain incantations intended to summon evil spirits and ordered Manson to read aloud from it. Before Manson could get very far, the older brother showed up, causing Manson and the other boy to flee into the woods with the book in tow.

After running for a while, the boys came to an old, abandoned house. They made their way to the building's basement, where Manson was once again ordered to read aloud from the book. As he did, Manson became aware of strange symbols written on the cellar walls, along with what looked like handprints. As he continued to read, the boys began to hear people walking just outside the cellar door, followed by voices. Some of the voices were whispering, while others were clearly saying phrases such as, "Do you believe in Satan?" In a panic, Manson dropped the book and the two boys ran home.

The following day, Manson and his friend returned to the abandoned house to retrieve the book only to find no sign that a house was ever there. Manson called it "the most supernatural strange thing" that he ever experienced, which says a lot coming from him.

Michael Imperioli

Actor Michael Imperioli, who gained fame on *The Sopranos,* counts himself among those who have seen the mournful spirit of Mary, which haunts New York's Chelsea Hotel. Mary wasn't a poet or an artist like many of the Chelsea's guests; she was just a woman from Buffalo, New York, who was waiting for her husband's boat to arrive in New York City. Unfortunately, her husband was on the RMS *Titanic,* and when Mary received news of his fate that cold April night in 1912, she hanged herself in her room.

Typically, guests spot Mary on the eighth floor of the Chelsea; she is usually seen crying or staring longingly into the mirrors. While living on the eighth floor in 1996, Imperioli saw a woman weeping at the end of the hall. He approached her and noticed that she was wearing clothes from the early 1900s. When he asked if she needed help, he heard a lightbulb pop behind him and instinctively turned toward it. A second later, when he turned back around, the woman had vanished. Imperioli moved out of the hotel shortly after discovering that the woman he had encountered was Mary…and that she was a ghost.

Haunted Houses=Scary Sums of Cash

*Every October, thousands of haunted attractions spring
up across North America. For the price of admission,
you get thrilled, chilled, and utterly spooked—
and the organizers rake in the profits.*

Will Scare for Donations

Around 2,000 haunted attractions are produced in the United States
every year. Ticket sales, vendors, construction costs, decorations,
and other supplies make this approximately a $500 million industry,
which isn't bad for a business model that offers its product for just
one month a year. The scope of the haunted attraction industry has
become extremely impressive as well: Haunted houses today look
very different than they used to.

Many haunted attractions were originally staged for charitable
causes. Decades ago, nonprofit groups often organized "haunted
houses" to raise money for sick kids or needy folks in the community.
(One Jaycees chapter in Durham, North Carolina, celebrated its
38th haunted house in 2010; in recent years, it has annually raised
more than $10,000 for charity.)

Many groups that create haunted attractions still give at least a
portion of their proceeds to charity, but over time, "scare houses"
have become actual businesses run by companies that focus solely
on entertainment value...and profits. To get people in the door,
haunted houses have gotten scarier and more complex; staging them
takes a lot of creativity, time, and money.

Freak-You-Out Economics

The initial investment needed to launch a successful haunted
attraction can be around $250,000. This may sound like a lot, but
the designers, carpenters, performers, safety teams, cleaning crews,
and Web and marketing professionals needed to create a blockbuster
haunted attraction all cost money. Many of the necessary props and
costumes are specialty items that far exceed most people's budgets,

which is why those who wish to run a successful haunted house typically pursue loans and capital investments.

The good news is that at around $15 (or more) per head, several hundred people lining up to move through your haunted house each night during the month of October makes it likely that you'll turn a hefty profit. To attract enough people, some proprietors enlist the help of metal bands and freak-show-style performers on opening night. For example, Marilyn Manson was once booked by a fright house in New Orleans that wanted to bring in its biggest crowd ever.

Cashing In on the Ghosts

If you're interested in the business of scaring people silly, plenty of Web resources are available. You can also attend the Midwest Haunters Convention, which is held each June. Annually, around 2,000 people attend this event to gather industry information, stay abreast of the latest trends, and make contact with vendors that sell everything from fake bloody limbs to dead-bride costumes.

Consumers are increasingly critical of those who try to earn their spending money, so proprietors of haunted attractions have their work cut out for them. Competition can be fierce: Haunts such as the Haunted Hoochie in Pataskala, Ohio, spans some 40 acres, and in 2010, the Lewisburg Haunted Cave in Lewisburg, Ohio, set a Guinness World Record for "Longest Walk-Through Horror House," boasting 3,564 linear feet of fright. These days, it's typical for haunted attractions to reach 40,000 square feet or more—Canton, Ohio's Factory of Terror spans some 55,000 square feet—so make sure that you've got plenty of space. Those who love the haunted attraction experience are willing to travel to find the cream of the crop, so the scarier and more realistic, the better.

Unless, of course, it's *too* scary: In 2000, a woman filed a lawsuit against Universal Studios in Orlando, Florida, claiming that its annual Halloween Horror Nights attraction was so terrifying that she suffered emotional damage as a result; the outcome of her suit is unknown.

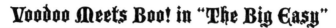

Voodoo Meets Boo! in "The Big Easy"

*Often called America's most haunted city, New Orleans
is well known for its famous Mardi Gras celebration
and endless revelry on Bourbon Street. But the city's origins
give it a supernatural reputation: In 1718, the French founded
the city where swampland meets Native American burial
grounds. Toss in a few major fires, a bunch of murders,
and an epidemic or two, and there are sure to be some
ghosts roaming the city. So whether you plan to visit or
just like a good ghost story, here's a look at some of the
most haunted places that "The Big Easy" has to offer.*

The Andrew Jackson Hotel

Don't stay at the Andrew Jackson Hotel unless you're willing to
share your room with a few uninvited guests. Built on the site of a
boys' boarding school that burned down in the 18th century, the
hotel has welcomed guests who have heard the shouting and laughter of the five boys who perished in the blaze. A courthouse was
later built on the site, and war hero Andrew Jackson was tried there
for obstruction of justice. Perhaps he hung around—some visitors
have reported seeing the specter of "Old Hickory" himself.

The Beauregard-Keyes House

A prime stop on New Orleans ghost tours, the historic Beauregard-
Keyes House boasts a rather intellectual spirit. As ghosts go, a
world-class chess master sounds pretty innocuous—but an *insane*
chess master is an entirely different story. In the late 1870s, Paul
Morphy (the man in question) was living at the Beauregard-Keyes
House when he apparently suffered a breakdown and ran from
the building on Chartres Street to Ursaline Street stark naked and
wielding an ax. In his quieter moments, Morphy enjoyed playing
the piano, so an odd combination of screaming and piano music is
now heard at the historic house at night.

   In addition, a mafia massacre took place on the property in
1908; since then, visitors have smelled gunpowder and heard
gunshots in the garden.

Bourbon Street

A lot of fun can be had on Bourbon Street, but if you're there, look out for rowdy ghosts wielding housewares: Spirits have been seen pounding each other with curtain rods up and down the street. Because of its unique jumble of cultures, religions, and politics, New Orleans has had a volatile history; therefore, it's not clear who the apparitions were in life, or even from what time period they hail. But dodge those curtain rods, just to be safe.

Flanagan's Pub

In the 1920s and '30s, the building that is now home to Flanagan's Pub served as Ruffino's Bakery. Its owners were involved in the Sicilian mob, and it is rumored that members of the Irish labor union were tortured (and sometimes killed) there for information that would allow the Sicilians to take over their organization. Many pub employees and patrons have witnessed a spectral man walk out of the kitchen and through the bar. Several employees have also seen pots and pans fly off their hooks and utensils move on their own. And during a paranormal investigation, a spirit seemed eager to speak to a former employee who had left the area after Hurricane Katrina. Whoever this phantom was in life, it seemed to trust the former employee and desperately wanted her to return.

Le Richelieu Hotel

In 1802, after the French reclaimed Louisiana from Spain, Spanish soldiers were executed for treason on the site where Le Richelieu Hotel now stands. The men who lost their lives there are said to walk the grounds at night. Look for spectral men in Spanish uniforms lingering near the bar or swimming pool.

City Park Golf Course

Golf etiquette dictates that a semblance of quiet be observed when a golfer hits a ball, and ghosts can certainly be silent when they need to be. But at City Park Golf Course, golfers may break the tranquility with screams and gasps when they approach the 18th green of the East Course and encounter an apparition lingering nearby. Even worse is the haunting that many have experienced on the South

 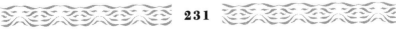

Course, where golfers claim to hear muffled female voices talking and laughing nearby, followed by the sharp crack of a gunshot and a woman shouting, "I'm hit." This seems to be a residual haunting or ghostly reenactment of a death that took place near the course in the early 1960s. No one was ever charged with the shooting.

French Quarter

Numerous spirits are certainly present in New Orleans's historic French Quarter, but one of the most famous specters there is that of the Chicken Man. A voodoo practitioner commonly seen in the 1970s and '80s, the Chicken Man was said to have approached people on the street offering help from the goodies in his mojo bag—which was tied with a dangling chicken claw. He hadn't been seen in the area for quite some time, but after Hurricane Katrina, visitors began seeing him in the French Quarter—in spirit form. One FEMA worker said that a man on the street offered her a bag tied with his signature gnarled chicken claw. It seems that the Chicken Man is back at work.

Lafitte Guest House

You might want to check out Room 21 at the Lafitte Guest House, but you may not want to stay there. Before it became a guesthouse, this bed-and-breakfast was a single-family home, and two girls passed away in that room: The first girl died of yellow fever during the great epidemic of 1853, and many years later, her sister hung herself in the same room. Grief-stricken, their mother lived out the rest of her days in that bedroom, where she died of natural causes. Employees and guests have reported a feeling of complete despair in Room 21, along with the sound of the mother crying.

Le Petit Theatre du Vieux Carre

Before you enter Le Petit Theatre du Vieux Carre, check out the upper part of the building, where it overlooks the courtyard: It is there that many people have seen the ghost of Caroline, a young woman who, in 1924, jumped to her death wearing a wedding dress—her costume for a play. Cold spots chill guests, and many have seen Caroline's reflection in the fountain at night.

The spectral bride may have some company: A ghostly old man dressed in 19th-century formal attire has been reported in the second-story seating area. But when staff members search for him, he mysteriously disappears. Actors and stagehands have also felt cold hands on their shoulders, have had props go missing, and have witnessed a smoke machine turn on by itself.

The Morgue Bar

With a name like the Morgue Bar, you'd expect some paranormal activity to occur at this establishment—and it does. Built as a mortuary in 1849, the Morgue Bar has seen many lifeless bodies pass through its doors. In 1853, more than 10,000 people died in the city due to a yellow fever epidemic; many modern patrons have seen apparitions from that era belly up to the bar. Another ghost that seems ever-present is a former mortician's daughter, who, in life, was known for stealing jewels from the dead bodies that her father worked on. Unfortunately, death hasn't reformed her: She frequently "borrows" items from the bar's female patrons when they visit the restroom, which formerly served as a storage room for bodies. As long as you keep your belongings close at hand, you should be safe from her antics. In the meantime, sit back and relax with the bar's signature drink—a cocktail known as Embalming Fluid.

The Superdome

Many modern ghosts haunt New Orleans, and the Superdome is a popular hangout for old and new spirits alike. After Hurricane Katrina pummeled the city, thousands of people were sent to the Superdome for safety, but it turned out to be a living hell for many. Due to the squalorous conditions, murders, rapes, and two suicides occurred, as well as many deaths from natural causes. Is it any wonder that ghosts roam this stadium?

In addition, the Superdome was allegedly built on the site of an old cemetery, and construction crews supposedly dug up bones and caskets. Today, apparitions both old and new have been spotted during football games played there, especially at night. But are they just the remnants of all that has occurred under this roof?

Hold Me Closer Ghostly Dancer:
The Haunting of the Phoenix Theatre

🪦   🪦   🪦   🪦

Audiences that saw A Chorus Line at the Phoenix Theatre in 2005 got a little more than they bargained for when an unpaid and uncredited dancer twirled her way between the chorus-line performers. Those who saw her may have thought it was odd that a ballerina was prancing around in a show about Broadway dancers. Of course, they may have found it even stranger if they realized that she was just one of the many ghosts that inhabit the theater, which opened in 1951.

Members of Arizona's Phoenix Theatre Company have been entertaining locals and visitors with a variety of productions since 1920. As the oldest arts institution in Arizona, it makes sense that a few of its ghosts want to make one last curtain call.

The aforementioned ghost—which the staff affectionately calls "Tiny Dancer"—is not the only spirit at the Phoenix Theatre with artistic inclinations. "Mr. Electrics" is the spirit of an old man who is sometimes seen sitting on the pipes that hold the lighting instruments. He also appears late at night to help the technicians by manipulating buttons. Another ghost that deals with lighting is referred to as "Light Board Lenny;" he hangs around the lighting booth and has been known to playfully lock out light-board operators and spotlight technicians if they leave their positions in the booth. The spirit known as the "Prop Master" takes a cue from Lenny and sometimes locks people out of the prop room so that it can dig through the props.

Unfortunately, not all the spirits at the Phoenix Theatre are so light-hearted. One of the theater's ghosts is believed to be the angry spirit of Freddy, an actor who was fired from a production and then was killed while riding his bicycle home. Freddy generally likes to make a racket by slamming doors and stomping around in the theater's upstairs rooms.

With all the extra help, it's no wonder that the Phoenix Theatre Company is one of the nation's oldest continuously operating artistic troupes. Hopefully, they will be successful for years to come because ghosts hate auditioning.

Why Are Colleges So Haunted?

Anyone who is familiar with the paranormal can tell you that certain places seem to attract more spirits than others, and colleges and universities are near the top of that list. Are these reports really ghosts? Are they poltergeists? Or are they simply urban legends?

The Poltergeist Profile

A poltergeist is a noisy entity that feeds off human energy and tends to be disruptive, perhaps by throwing objects or moving them around. The reason for this is unclear, but poltergeists tend to manifest close to young people between the ages of 8 and 25; in fact, many reported poltergeist cases involve young women between the ages of 14 and 19. Poltergeists seem to gravitate toward personalities that are outgoing and dramatic, and what better place to find this sort of energy—in ample supply—than at a university?

Ghosts of Students Passed

The college years are some of the best times of many people's lives. But they are also times of growth and change that can be filled with sadness and angst. College students often find—and lose— first loves. They deal with being away from home and struggle to achieve good grades. Due to all this emotion and energy, suicides unfortunately do happen, as do accidents involving alcohol, driving, and domestic violence. Paranormal experts will tell you that it's these types of violent and unexpected deaths that leave spirits rooted to their earthly haunts. They may be seeking a do-over, searching for something (or someone) that they can't bear to leave behind, or haunting someone that they couldn't stand in life.

Uneasiness, eerie feelings, the idea that something is just not right—these are all parts of residual hauntings that result from dynamic, violent, or intensely emotional events that have taken place at a certain site. This type of haunting is not the work of one specific ghost but rather the "imprint" of all the emotion and energy that has been spent there. And with all the youthful energy that's crammed onto college campuses, it's easy to see why they are so haunted.

Prison Poltergeists

Penance for Your Sins

It started out as a unique way to help reform prisoners. It ended up being a literal torture chamber where men often died agonizing deaths. Sadly, many of those tortured souls have been unable to leave the Eastern State Penitentiary—even in death.

The Road to Penance

The remains of the Eastern State Penitentiary—the location of a truly unique experiment in the history of law enforcement—stand on what is now Fairmount Avenue in Philadelphia. Designed by John Haviland, the facility was different from other prisons in that it was meant to stress reform rather than punishment. It was thought that by giving a prisoner plenty of time to reflect on his wrongdoing, he would eventually reform himself by turning to God to make penance—hence the word *penitentiary.*

In October 1829, when the Eastern State Penitentiary officially opened, it was one of the largest public buildings of its kind in the

United States. And after its front gates swung open, its unique features blew prisoners and employees away. For starters, the entire complex resembled a giant wagon wheel, with seven wings of cells emerging from the center like spokes. The hallways themselves looked like the vestibules of a church.

Isolation and Madness

Individual cells were designed to house only

one inmate each. The idea was that prisoners needed time to reflect on what they had done wrong, and giving them cell mates would only distract them from doing that.

The only people with whom inmates were allowed to interact on a regular basis were the warden—who visited every prisoner once a day—and the guards—who served meals and brought inmates to and from their cells. Inmates were permitted to go outside for exercise, but they could only do that alone. When an inmate was removed from his cell for any reason, he was required to wear a hood. Prisoners were to remain silent at all times unless asked a direct question by prison personnel; failure to adhere to this rule meant swift, sadistic punishment.

Torturous Behavior

The facility's initial intent may have been to get inmates to understand that they needed to follow the rules in order to be reformed, but that quickly broke down into brutality by the guards and officials. Minor offenses, including making even the smallest noise, were often enough for authorities to subject inmates to a series of hellish punishments. Restraint devices such as straitjackets and the "mad chair"—a chair equipped with so many restraints that it made even the slightest movement impossible—were often employed. If an inmate was caught talking, he might be forced to wear the "iron gag"—a piece of metal that was clamped to his tongue while the other end was attached to leather gloves that he was forced to wear; movement resulted in excruciating pain. Legend has it that several prisoners accidentally severed their own tongues while wearing the iron gag, and at least one died while wearing the device.

Another method of torture utilized at the Eastern State Pen was the water bath. Inmates were tied to the penitentiary walls and doused with freezing water, even in the middle of winter; under the most extreme conditions, the water would freeze on the inmates' bodies.

Perhaps one of the most heinous means of punishing an inmate was to place him in the "Klondike." While other prisons have "The Hole"—which is essentially solitary confinement—the Klondike at the Eastern State Pen was a group of four subterranean cells without windows or plumbing; inmates were made to live down there—often for several weeks at a time.

Swift Decline and Abandonment

The Eastern State Penitentiary was designed to change the world of
incarceration in a positive way, but it failed miserably. In fact, when
British author Charles Dickens visited the United States in 1842, one
of the places that he wanted to see was the Eastern State Pen. From
across the Atlantic, Dickens had heard about the marvelous and
unique penitentiary and wanted to see it for himself. He was shocked
by what he witnessed there, calling it "hopeless…cruel, and wrong."

Over the years, changes were enacted in an attempt to remedy
the situation, but they didn't help. Finally, in 1971, the penitentiary
was officially closed. In the mid-1990s, after sitting abandoned for
years, the building was reopened for tours.

"Not All Who Walk These Blocks Are Among the Living…"

Looking back at the tortuous history of the Eastern State Pen, it
should come as no surprise that more than a few ghosts can be found
there. In fact, records indicate that inmates reported paranormal
activity on the premises as early as the 1940s, so it seems that ghosts
were in residence there long before the prison closed. Perhaps that
explains what happened to locksmith Gary Johnson while he was
working on a lock during a restoration of the prison in the early
1990s. After Johnson popped the door open, he saw shadowy shapes
moving all around him. It was as if he'd allowed all the ghosts to
once again roam free.

If there's one area of the penitentiary where visitors are most
likely to experience paranormal activity, it is Cellblock 12. Many
people have reported hearing voices echoing throughout the cellblock and even laughter coming from the cells themselves. Shadow
figures are also seen in abundance there.

Another location at the Eastern State Penitentiary that is said
to be haunted is the guard tower that sits high atop the main wall.
People standing outside the prison have seen a shadowy figure walking along the wall; it calmly looks down at them from time to time.

"Dude, Run!"

Over the years, various ghost-hunting television shows have visited
the Eastern State Penitentiary and submitted paranormal evidence
to their viewers. The facility was featured in a 2001 episode of

MTV's *Fear.* In 2009, *Ghost Adventures* filmed an episode at the Eastern State Pen, and the UK-based *Most Haunted* recorded an investigation there in 2007. But if the Eastern State Penitentiary is forever linked to a paranormal research show, it would be *Ghost Hunters,* due to its team's 2004 investigation and the actions of one of its members.

At approximately 3 A.M., investigator Brian Harnois of The Atlantic Paranormal Society (TAPS) entered Cellblock 4 with Dave Hobbs, a member of the show's production crew. As Hobbs snapped a photograph, he and Harnois thought they saw a huge black shape rise up and move in front of them. They both panicked, and Harnois yelled out the now-famous line, "Dude, run!" after which the pair bolted down the hallway, much to the chagrin of their fellow investigators (who quickly deduced that the shape had been caused by the camera flash). The incident overshadowed an intriguing piece of evidence that was captured later that night, when one of the team's video cameras recorded a dark shape—almost human in form—that appeared to be moving quickly along a cellblock. Try as they might, TAPS was unable to come up with a scientific explanation for the shape, leaving who or what it was open to interpretation.

Get Out of Jail Free

If you would like to potentially encounter a ghost and have a firsthand look inside one of the truly unique architectural structures in the United States, the Eastern State Penitentiary is open for tours. You can also take part in a nighttime ghost tour there. Should you choose to embark on one of these adventures, be careful: A lot of the ghosts there are "lifers," and they just might jump at the chance to escape by following you home!

"It is, alas, chiefly the evil emotions that are able to leave their photographs on surrounding scenes and objects, and whoever heard of a place haunted by a noble deed, or of beautiful and lovely ghosts revisiting the glimpses of the moon?"

—British author Algernon H. Blackwood

The Worried Husband

*"You never pay any attention to me!" is a common lament
heard in marriages when a person feels neglected by his or her
partner. But what about the opposite situation—when a person's
concern for his or her spouse extends beyond the grave?*

In the late 1940s, Elaine and her husband lived in an apartment in
Oskaloosa, Iowa. They shared the floor with a single woman named
Patricia, whose husband had died in an industrial accident. The
devastated young woman had moved there to try to regroup.

One evening while her husband was working, Elaine decided to
take a bath. Just as she was about to turn on the bathroom light, she
smelled pipe smoke and then saw a young man with black hair and a
horseshoe-shaped scar on his cheek; he was holding a pipe.

After a moment, Elaine realized that the man was not really looking *at* her, he was sort of looking *through* her. She then deduced that
the man was a ghost. Elaine watched as he began to move through
her apartment. She followed him as he glided down the hall toward
Patricia's apartment. When he got to Patricia's door, he vanished.

Uncertain of what she was doing, Elaine turned the doorknob
to Patricia's apartment; it was unlocked, so Elaine went inside.
There, she found Patricia lying on her bed, barely conscious: She
had slashed her wrists, and her lifeblood was quickly draining away.
Elaine bandaged Patricia as best she could and called her husband.
He raced home with a doctor, who treated Patricia's injuries.

The next day, Patricia thanked Elaine for saving her life. She said
that she had been deeply saddened by her husband's death and had
turned to the bottle as a result. Overcome by grief, the idea of joining
her husband seemed appealing to her, so she had slit her wrists. If it
had not been for Elaine, her plan would have succeeded.

Elaine said nothing about why she had entered Patricia's apartment in the first place. But when Patricia showed Elaine a picture of
her late husband, everything suddenly made sense: The man in the
photo was the same man who Elaine had seen in her apartment.

Unsettling Happenings Aboard *UB-65*

You've probably heard of ghost ships or ghosts that inhabit ships, but how about a submarine that takes such spooky folklore beneath the waves? German sub UB-65 *was one such vessel. From ghostly sightings to freakish tragedies that led many to fear for life and limb, the tale of the "Iron Coffin" is an ominous part of military history.*

Das Boot

During World War I, the German U-boat was feared above all other war machines. It could sink other vessels from great distances without being detected. But the U-boat had its drawbacks. For example, unlike conventional vessels that floated on the water's surface, U-boats were virtually doomed if underwater explosives were detonated near them while they were submerged. But submariners—who are a uniquely brave lot—generally accept such perils as part of their job. This makes the fantastic tale of German submarine *UB-65* all the more interesting.

Commissioned in 1917, *UB-65* seemed cursed from the start. From mysterious mishaps and tragic accidents to ethereal events terrifying enough to scare even the bravest sailors, the events associated with the "Iron Coffin" suggest that it was one wicked vessel.

Devil's Playground

Most warships manage to celebrate their launches before any casualties occur onboard. Not so with *UB-65*. While still under construction at a shipyard in Hamburg, Germany, a structural girder broke free of its chain and fell directly on top of a workman. Pinned by its crushing weight for a full hour, the man shrieked in pain. When the girder was finally lifted off of him, the man died.

Later, just prior to the submarine's launch, another tragedy occurred. This time, a chloride gas leak claimed three lives in the vessel's engine room when dry-cell battery tests went awry. Were such tragedies simply unfortunate coincidences, or was *UB-65*

showing distinct signs of being cursed? No one could say with certainty, but many sailors leaned toward the latter.

Chilling Sea Trials

After launching on June 26, 1917, *UB-65* moved into her sea-trial phase. Designed to debug the vessel before it commenced active duty, *UB-65*'s "shakedown" tests would prove deadly. Macabre events began when *UB-65* surfaced to perform a hatch inspection. Clearly underestimating the ferocity of a storm that was raging outside in the turbulent North Atlantic, the seaman performing the inspection was swept overboard to his death. This event took a heavy toll on the crew's morale, but sadly, even more misfortune was yet to come.

During a test dive, a ballast tank ruptured and seawater began to fill the engine room; noxious vapors that greatly sickened all on board were produced as a result. It took 12 long hours before events were finally brought under control. This time, the seamen had survived and had seemingly beaten the curse, but just barely. The next event would turn the tables once again and grant the Grim Reaper his much-pursued bounty.

Kaboom!

If there were any doubts about *UB-65* being cursed, they were quickly erased by an incident that took place when the vessel was being fitted with armaments for its first patrol. As crew members loaded torpedoes into firing tubes, one of the warheads inexplicably detonated. The blast claimed the life of the second officer, injured many others, and sent shudders through the submarine. Afterward, crew members were given several days off to bury their fallen comrade. It was a somber period and a much-needed time for healing. Unfortunately, ethereal forces were about to wreak further havoc on the submarine and rattle the men's nerves like never before.

Second Life for the Second Officer

After the crew reboarded for *UB-65*'s first mission, a scream was heard coming from the gangplank. It came from an officer who had witnessed something that his mind couldn't quite grasp. Later, when pressed about the incident, the officer swore to the captain that his recently buried comrade had boarded the sub directly in front of him.

Soon after, another crewman reported seeing the dead sailor as well. Believing that his crew was suffering from hysteria, the captain pushed on with the mission. But the situation only got worse when the engine room staff reported seeing the deceased officer's apparition standing where he had perished. Hoping to stave off panic, the captain ordered all talk of ghosts to cease.

Everything went well until January 1918—the pivotal month when the captain himself became a believer. The turnabout took place while *UB-65* was cruising on the surface. A frightened lookout bolted below deck claiming that he'd seen the second officer's ghost topside. Hoping to put an end to spirit-related nonsense, the captain grabbed the lookout and led him back up the ladder. When they reached the deck, the captain's smugness morphed into terror. There, just inches before him, stood the ghost of the dead second officer.

Exorcism

With numerous documented sightings on their hands, the German Navy knew that it had a problem. The sub was temporarily decommissioned, and a Lutheran minister was brought on board to perform an exorcism. Afterward, a new crew was assembled and the vessel was put back into service, but it didn't take long for the fright-fest to start all over again. In May 1918, at least three ghost sightings were reported. One sailor was so frightened to see the second officer's spirit that he jumped overboard and drowned.

That was the last death aboard *UB-65* until mid-July 1918, when the sub mysteriously disappeared  while patrolling in the North Atlantic. Conjecture abounds over what exactly happened aboard *UB-65*: Accidental causes or explosive depth charges head up the list of probable culprits for the vessel's demise. In 2004, an underwater expedition located *UB-65* in the vicinity of Padstow, England, but researchers still couldn't produce a conclusive reason for why the sub was lost.

What is known for sure is that this cursed "Iron Coffin" took 37 souls down with her. The Grim Reaper, determined as always, had received his ill-gotten spoils.

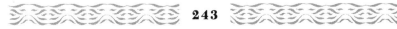

The Ghosts of Wisconsin's Black Point Mansion

Like many spectral beings, some ghost stories evaporate like misty ectoplasm when studied closely. In other words, they don't hold up to scrutiny when examined thoroughly. But the ghosts of the Black Point Mansion on Wisconsin's Geneva Lake boast a solid history to back up the spooky legend of their origin.

In 1888, wealthy Chicagoan Conrad Seipp built a 20-room summer home on the southern shore of Geneva Lake. Known as Black Point Mansion, Seipp's vacation house looks much the same today as it did back then, with an imposing four-story tower that rises above the black oak trees for which it was named. But according to local legend, on stormy nights, the cupola at the tower's peak holds the restless spirits of a priest and nuns who drowned in the lake many years ago.

Unlike many urban legends, this tale has elements of truth to it: On July 7, 1895, Father James Hogan, a beloved Catholic priest from Harvard, Illinois, did indeed drown in Geneva Lake within sight of Black Point Mansion. But the others who died were not Catholic sisters but rather Father Hogan's *actual* sister Mary; his brother Dr. John Hogan; the doctor's wife, Kittie; their two-year-old child; and a steamboat captain.

On that fateful day, the Hogan family had taken a train from Illinois to Williams Bay on the northwestern shore of Geneva Lake. From there, they boarded a small steamboat to visit friends who lived nearby. As the day wore on, storm clouds began to gather, so the family decided to make a fast retreat before the weather worsened. Eyeing the darkening sky, the captain of the steamer *Dispatch* advised the group to postpone their trip until after the storm had passed. But the Hogans persuaded him to make the trip anyway, and the *Dispatch* began what would be its final crossing of Geneva Lake.

The anxious passengers were more than halfway through their journey when a squall kicked up. The storm quickly turned so violent that the small vessel could not make it to the nearest landing—a park

near Black Point Mansion. The captain blew his distress whistle over and over, but no one could get to the steamer before it capsized, tossing all five passengers and the captain into the deep spring-fed lake. The mansion's tower may well have been the last thing any of them saw before succumbing to the cold, dark water. Anguished witnesses on shore saw the baby's white dress fluttering in the harsh wind ... and then the family was gone.

It took some time to recover the bodies, but newspapers said that the doctor was found on the lake bottom with his hands in an attitude of prayer; Mary still wore her ladylike gloves and held her purse; and Father Hogan was lying as if merely at rest. Seventy-five priests and a large crowd of parishioners attended his funeral.

A Lake Monster's Ball

Black Point Mansion's haunted tower is not the area's only supernatural claim to fame. Before European settlers came to Geneva Lake, the Potawatomi people who lived there believed that fierce water spirits fought with thunderbirds in the lake to cause the kind of sudden storm that sank the *Dispatch.* They also thought that the lake was home to an eel-like monster that would pull down canoes during bad weather. And in the mid-to-late 1800s, numerous residents and tourists claimed to have seen a giant creature—which they dubbed "Jenny"—swimming along the lakeshore.

One of the people who spotted Jenny was a minister from nearby Delavan. And in July 1892—just three years before the drowning of the Hogan family—the *Chicago Tribune* reported that three fisher-men saw a 100-foot-long monster in the lake. The sighting occurred in front of the very park that the captain of the *Dispatch* was trying to reach when the steamer went down.

Take an Excursion on the Lake ... If You Dare

Today, Black Point Mansion is owned by the state of Wisconsin; it serves as a museum, and despite the fact that it retains nearly all of its original furniture, the building itself is not believed to harbor any ghosts—just the open cupola. From May through October, tourists can still venture out on the lake by steamboat to get exactly the same view of the mansion and its tower that the ill-fated Hogan family had on that tragic day in 1895.

War Ghosts and Guests
Haunt the Hotel Provincial

The Hotel Provincial is one of the most haunted locations in New Orleans. This inn, which is located in the city's famed French Quarter, is made up of five different buildings. Even though they can't order room service, many of the Hotel Provincial's ghosts have decided to extend their stays ... eternally.

Thought to be the most haunted part of the hotel, the "500 building" dates back to 1722 and was used as a hospital during the War of 1812's Battle of New Orleans (December 1814–January 8, 1815) and during the Civil War. Specters of soldiers from both wars have been seen roaming the halls and imploring guests for help. In one room, guests have glimpsed soldiers moaning in pain, but when the lights are turned on, the room is empty. Bloodstains have appeared—and disappeared—on hotel bedding. And one employee who was riding the elevator was taken by surprise when the doors opened to reveal a hospital ward full of medical staff tending to wounded soldiers. Stunned, the employee remained on the elevator so long that the doors closed; when they opened again, the wartime scene had vanished.

One hotel guest reported being pulled from her bed by an invisible force, and a young girl said that she emerged from a shower to find a pile of bloody bandages on the floor; they quickly disappeared. On the lighter side, a ghost who seems enamored with country music inhabits one room, while another resident spirit likes a specific rock-and-roll radio station; when guests try to change the channel, the tuner mysteriously returns to the one that the unseen visitor prefers.

Throughout the hotel, observers have experienced doors that open and close own their own, whispering when no one else is around, hot spots, cold spots, and phantom figures wandering the property. An older woman even woke up one night to find the upper half of a handsome young soldier in her bed; one can only imagine how she explained that to her husband!

Tombstone Shadows

In its heyday, Tombstone, Arizona, was known as "the town too tough to die." Apparently, its ghosts liked that moniker because there are so many spirits roaming its streets that Tombstone is a strong contender for the title of "Most Haunted Town in America." Here are a few of the most notable phantoms that still call this Wild West town home.

Virgil Earp

A man in a long black frock coat stands on a sidewalk in Tombstone; the people who see him assume that he's a reenactor in this former rough-and-tumble Wild West town. But as he starts across the street, a strange thing happens: He vanishes in mid-stride. Only then do people realize that they've just seen one of the many ghosts that haunt this legendary town.

It is usually assumed that the man in the black coat is the ghost of U.S. Deputy Marshal Virgil Earp, who may be reliving one of his life's darkest moments. On December 28, 1881, he was shot and wounded when outlaws who sought revenge for the infamous Gunfight at the O.K. Corral two months prior ambushed him. Virgil survived the attack, but his left arm was permanently maimed.

Morgan Earp

In March 1882, another group of outlaws—who were also seeking revenge for the Gunfight at the O.K. Corral—gunned down Morgan Earp, the brother of noted lawmen Virgil and Wyatt Earp. Morgan was shot in the back and killed while playing pool. Some say that you can still hear his dying words whispered at the location where he was murdered.

Big Nose Kate

Big Nose Kate was the girlfriend of gunslinger Doc Holliday, a friend of the Earps. Her ghost is reportedly responsible for the footsteps and snatches of whispered conversation that swirl through the Crystal Palace Saloon. Lights there turn on and off by themselves, and gambling wheels sometimes spin for no

reason, causing speculation that, just as in life, Kate prefers the company of rowdy men.

Swamper

Big Nose Kate's Saloon was originally the Grand Hotel, and a man known as Swamper used to work there as a handyman. He lived in the basement, not far from some of the town's silver mines, so when he wasn't working, Swamper dug a tunnel to one of the mines and began supplementing his income with silver nuggets.

After all the effort that he'd put into obtaining the silver, Swamper was not about to let it go easily... not even after he died. He reportedly haunts Big Nose Kate's Saloon; perhaps he's still hanging around to protect his loot, which has never been found. Naturally, he's often spotted in the basement, but he also likes to show up in photos taken by visitors.

The Bird Cage Theatre

Anyplace where 26 people were violently killed is almost certain to be a spectral smorgasbord. Such is the case with Tombstone's infamously bawdy Bird Cage Theatre.

One of the most frequently seen apparitions at the Bird Cage is that of a man who carries a clipboard and wears striped pants and a card-dealer's visor. He's been known to suddenly appear on stage, glide across it, and then walk through a wall. Visitors have raved to the management about how authentic-looking the Wild West costumes look, only to be told that nobody at the Bird Cage dresses in period clothing.

One night, an employee watched on a security monitor as a vaporous woman in white walked slowly through the cellar long after closing time. And although smoking and drinking are now prohibited at the Bird Cage, the scents of cigar smoke and whiskey still linger there. Visitors also hear unexplained sounds, such as a woman singing, a female sighing, glasses clinking, and cards shuffling, as if the ghosts are trying to finish a game that's gone on for far too long.

Nellie Cashman's Restaurant

Nellie Cashman's is another haunted hot spot in Tombstone.
Patrons at the eatery report hearing strange noises and seeing
dishes suddenly crash to the floor. And the ghosts at Nellie
Cashman's have no patience for skeptics: A patron who once noisily
derided all things supernatural found herself suddenly wearing the
contents of a mustard container that inexplicably leaped off a table.

Fred White

Of the many deaths in Tombstone during the days of the Wild
West, one of the most tragic was that of town marshal Fred White.
In October 1880, White was trying to arrest "Curly Bill" Brocius
when Brocius's gun accidentally went off, killing the lawman. White
is rumored to haunt a street near where he was killed, apparently
still angry with the way his life was so abruptly taken from him.

Boothill Graveyard

It would almost defy belief if Tombstone's legendary Boothill
Graveyard wasn't haunted, but not to worry: The final resting place
of so many who were violently taken from this life is said to harbor
many restless spirits, including that of Billy Clanton, one of the
victims of the Gunfight at the O.K. Corral. Clanton's apparition
has been seen rising from his grave and walking toward town.
Strange lights and sounds are also said to come from the cemetery.

George Buford

Violent death came in all forms in Tombstone. One of those
occurred when a man named George Buford shot his lover and
then himself. His aim was better the second time, though: She
lived, but he died. He is said to haunt the building where he once
lived, which is now a bed-and-breakfast. His spirit has been seen
in and around the building; random lights appear there for no
reason, and the doorbell sometimes rings on its own in the middle
of the night. And ghostly George hasn't lost his fondness for the
ladies: Women in the house have felt their hair being stroked and
sensed light pressure on the backs of their necks. Of course, when
they turn around, no one is there.

Griggs Mansion

A notoriously haunted house in St. Paul, Minnesota, changes hands, and then all paranormal activity ceases. Was the house ever haunted? If so, what made the once-frisky ghosts decide to pack up and leave? It's a question that is difficult to answer. A house that's haunted to some seems completely benign to others. Who is right? Let's examine the evidence.

First Frights

Built in 1883 by wholesale grocery tycoon Chauncey W. Griggs, the imposing 24-room Griggs Mansion features high ceilings, a dark interior, and a stone facade that looks decidedly menacing. Although the home bears his name, Griggs lived there for only a scant four years before moving to sunnier climes on the West Coast. After that, the house changed hands quite frequently, which some say is a sure sign that the place was haunted.

The first ghost sightings at the house date back to 1915, when a young maid—who was despondent over a breakup—hanged herself on the mansion's fourth floor. Soon after the woman's burial, her spirit was allegedly seen roaming the building's hallways. According to witnesses, the ghost of Charles Wade arrived next. In life, he was the mansion's gardener and caretaker; in death, he reportedly liked to cruise the building's library.

Unexplained Activity

Strange occurrences are the norm at the Griggs Mansion. Over the years, residents have reported hearing disembodied footsteps traveling up and down the staircases, seeing doors open and close by themselves, hearing voices coming from unoccupied rooms, and experiencing all manner of unexplainable incidents, which suggest that the Griggs Mansion is indeed haunted.

In 1939, the mansion was donated to the St. Paul Gallery and School of Art. During the 1950s, staffer Dr. Delmar Rolb claimed that he saw the apparition of a "tall thin man" in his apartment in the

basement of the building. In 1964, Carl L. Weschcke—a publisher of books relating to the occult—acquired the house. He said that as soon as he would close a particular window, it would mysteriously reopen. Determined to stop this game, Weschcke nailed the window shut; however, when he returned home the next day, it was open once again.

Ghostbusters

In 1969, reporters from a local newspaper spent a night at the Griggs Mansion. The journalists—who were all initially skeptics—became believers after spending a harrowing night on the premises; unexplained footsteps and an unnerving feeling that a presence accompanied them were enough to do the trick. The frightened reporters fled the mansion in the wee hours of the morning and never returned.

More Skeptics

In 1982, Tibor and Olga Zoltai purchased the mansion. "When we first moved in, there were people who would cross to the other side of the street to pass the house," Olga recalled in an interview with a local newspaper. "One even threw a piece of Christ's cross into the yard." However, in nearly three decades of living inside the reputedly haunted house, the couple has never experienced anything out of the ordinary. To show just how silly they found the ghost stories, the playful couple assembled an "emergency kit" that contained a clove of garlic, a bottle of holy water, a crucifix, and a stake. They figured that these items would provide ample protection against any restless spirits in the house.

Yea or Nay

So are there ghosts at the Griggs Mansion or not? Those who claim to have witnessed paranormal activity there stand firmly behind their stories; those who have not offer other possible explanations. "If you go into a situation thinking something is going to happen, it probably will," reasons Chad Lewis, author of *Haunted St. Paul,* in reference to the terrifying night that the reporters spent at the mansion. That said, however, Lewis isn't convinced that the ghost stories surrounding the Griggs Mansion are mere figments of people's imaginations. "I think the stories are true. I don't think people are making them up or hallucinating or suffering from mental illness. I think something happened there, but what happened there, I don't know."

FRIGHTENING FACTS

More Ghosts That Roam the Big Apple

- In 1840, Gertrude Tredwell was born in the building that now serves as the Merchant's House Museum on East 4th Street in Manhattan. She lived there for 93 years and died there in 1933. When a person is so attached to a place, it's understandable that he or she would be reluctant to leave it. Such is the case with Gertrude, whose spirit still keeps a watchful eye over her eternal home, as numerous docents past and present can attest.

- Manhattan's oldest house is the historic Morris-Jumel Mansion in Washington Heights, which was the home of wealthy 19th-century socialite Eliza Jumel, who married noted politician Aaron Burr after her first husband died. Eliza went mad late in life, and several dramatic appearances of her spirit suggest that she hasn't quite left the building. In one case, she tried to hush a group of children; when a medium intervened, Eliza was arrogant, mean, and delusional, just as she was in life.

- Located in Manhattan, St. Mark's Church-in-the-Bowery was built in 1795 on the farm of Peter Stuyvesant, who ruled New Netherland (now New York) for the Dutch during the 17th century. Several ghosts, notably Stuyvesant himself, make frequent appearances at St. Mark's. Stuyvesant's peg leg and cane make him easy to recognize.

- Legendary Civil War photographer Mathew Brady once operated a studio near St. Paul's Chapel at the intersection of Fulton and Broadway in Manhattan. In life, Brady loved the city—so much so that he's been unable to leave it. More than a century has passed since his death, but people continue to see his ghost roaming around the area. He is recognizable by his pointed goatee and the distinctive slouch hat that he wears.

- In 1804, at 27 Jane Street in Greenwich Village, doctors treated Alexander Hamilton for the mortal wound that he received in his infamous duel with Aaron Burr. Hamilton didn't die in the house, but since then, folks there have spotted a man dressed in Colonial attire there. Could it be Hamilton's apparition or that of one of his friends?

- *Legend has it that, on occasion, two phantom Royal Air Force pilots have been spotted walking around Times Square before vanishing at midnight. One witness reportedly spoke with them: They said that they'd always wanted to visit the Big Apple but had died in World War II before they got the chance.*

- *In 1776, the owner of Staten Island's Conference House killed a servant girl in the building. Visitors still hear feminine screams and see a heavyset Colonial aristocrat roaming the building.*

- *The old Crawley Mansion on Staten Island has a weird story— as well as a diminutive specter—attached to it. In the 1800s, dwarfish Estelle Ridley, who had spent her younger days working for the circus, turned to a life of crime by posing as a young girl in order to smuggle jewels in the doll that she carried. Magda Hamilton portrayed Estelle's governess in the scheme. When both women fell for the same man, Magda turned Estelle in to the authorities. Sentenced to life in prison, Estelle vowed revenge. She hung herself in prison, and shortly thereafter, Magda was found asphyxiated in her bed. Some believe that Estelle's ghost suffocated Magda by cramming her doll's porcelain head into her betrayer's mouth. While that seems like a stretch, visitors have reported seeing the pint-sized spirit on the property ever since.*

- *In a series of séances that took place in 1953, mediums made contact with an entity dubbed "the Fifth Avenue Ghost." They learned that it was the spirit of a Confederate general named Samuel McGowan, who had ties to New York City while he was alive; his ghost gave the mediums eerily accurate details about 19th-century Manhattan.*

- *In the 1950s, the residents of 11 Bank Street in Greenwich Village often heard disembodied footsteps and unexplained pounding on the walls. One day, the homeowners found an urn containing human ashes hidden in the ceiling. They consulted a medium and gave the ashes a proper burial; after that, the unexplained noises ceased.*

King's Tavern

Did a love triangle and murder produce a spirit that resides at King's Tavern in Natchez, Mississippi? It seems likely. But the ghost of Madeline isn't the only disembodied soul flitting about at this historic pub.

From Fort to Tavern

The Old Natchez Trace—a 500-mile trail stretching from Natchez, Mississippi, to about 17 miles southwest of Nashville, Tennessee— was cut by Native Americans centuries before Europeans arrived and was used as a crude highway to transport goods and people. It also attracted miscreants in the form of highwaymen, and during Colonial times, robberies and murders were common on the trail. Nevertheless, the path remained popular, and businesses catering to travelers sprouted up along it out of necessity. One such enterprise was King's Tavern. Originally built as a blockhouse for a fort, the building was acquired in 1799 by wealthy New Yorker Richard King, who turned it into a bar and inn. It was a great success, but it would also bring drama into King's life.

Cheating Ways

Despite having a loving wife, King succumbed to the oldest of temptations when he hired a young woman named Madeline as a server and subsequently seduced her. Attractive and industrious, Madeline was only too happy to become the rich man's mistress. Their tryst didn't last long, however: When King's irate wife learned of the affair, she took steps to end it. What occurred next is open to debate: Some believe that Mrs. King hired highwaymen to murder Madeline, while others say that she performed the deed herself. Either way, Madeline vanished without a trace. But without a body, there was officially no murder, so nothing further came of King's wife's permanent solution to her husband's tawdry affair.

Mystery Solved

In 1932, King's Tavern underwent significant renovations. While workers were repairing the fireplace in the pub's main room, they were horrified to find three human skeletons—two male and one female—hidden behind the bricks. The identities of the men were anyone's guess, but many believed that the female was Madeline, the young temptress who'd been done in by the jealous Mrs. King more than a century prior. When a Spanish dagger—a weapon that was quite popular during Colonial times—was discovered nearby, the theory became even more plausible. The bodies were buried in a local cemetery and the remodeling job was completed. A mysterious chapter in the tavern's history had been put to rest ... or had it?

Manifestations

After the renovation, apparitions and other unexplained phenomena arrived like waves on a beach. Shadowy figures were often spotted walking up the staircases or passing directly through them. A spectral man wearing a top hat moved freely about the tavern; sporting a black jacket and tie string, his garb was consistent with that of the era in which the murders occurred. Members of the waitstaff who witnessed the apparition felt that he embodied evil, and many believed that he was involved in the murders somehow—either as a perpetrator or a victim.

But ghosts of grown men aren't the only spirits lingering at the tavern: The unsettling sound of a crying baby has also been reported, and small footprints—presumably left by a woman—appear from out of nowhere on freshly mopped floors. Many believe that Madeline is responsible for the footprints, which usually move across the room directly toward startled employees. Madeline's ghost has also been blamed for spilling pitchers onto the floor, knocking jars from shelves, turning faucets and lights on and off, and opening doors. When her name is called out in protest, she has been known to slam doors.

Someone (or something) more sinister likes to forcefully throw dishes through the air and apply pressure around the necks or on the chests of visitors. And the fireplace where the bodies were discovered occasionally emits heat as if it is burning wood, even though no fire is lit and no firewood is present. Could this be a final plea for justice from a trio cheated out of life?

Party Girl: The Nob Hill Ghost

*If you get an invitation to a party for Flora Sommerton,
you'd best think twice before accepting—especially since
the guest of honor has been dead for nearly a century.*

In 1876, Flora Sommerton was a debutante who was on the verge of
making her grand entrance into San Francisco's high society via a lavish
party. That may have been just fine with her, but what wasn't fine was
the wealthy young man who her parents insisted that she marry. So
the day before her party, Flora packed up her ritzy debutante dress
and took off, leaving behind her parents, her wealth, her fancy party,
the man she disliked, and any semblance of her former life.

Her family searched for her for years, but not even a $250,000
reward could help determine her whereabouts. Then, in 1926,
a housekeeper known as Mrs. Butler was found dead in Butte,
Montana. She was wearing an expensive white ball gown from the
19th century, and her apartment was filled with faded, yellowed
newspaper clippings about the disappearance of Flora Sommerton.
Flora had finally been found.

Perhaps Flora was really a party girl at heart
and always regretted skipping out on what would
have been a smashing shindig. Or maybe all those
years of working for a low wage made her appreciate money all the more. For whatever reason,
a young girl in an elegant white dress haunts
California Street between Powell and Jones in San
Francisco's swanky Nob Hill neighborhood. She
smiles pleasantly at passersby and then suddenly
disappears, leaving both pedestrians and those in
automobiles perplexed and wondering if they've
just seen a ghost.

They have. It's Flora Sommerton, perpetually
young and pretty, still searching for the life that
she gave up so many years ago.

The Glowing Coed

🪦 🪦 🪦 🪦

A tragic kitchen accident spawned a ghost that
continues to haunt…and she's not alone.

In 1908, fun-loving Condie Cunningham—a student at the Alabama Girls Industrial School (now known as the University of Montevallo), which is located south of Birmingham—was cooking fudge with friends in her dormitory's kitchen when flammable cleaning solvent accidentally spilled onto the stove. Condie's clothing caught on fire, burning her severely; she died in a hospital two days later.

More than a century later, Condie's tortured spirit still haunts Main Hall, where the terrible accident occurred. Witnesses report hearing her desperate cries for help, and a few people have even seen her ghost running through the building, glowing brightly as if on fire.

Well, that's the assumption, anyway. In almost every account, witnesses said that they saw a flash of red—like fire—out of the corner of their eye, but when they turned, nothing was there.

College Spirit(s)

Several other spirits are said to haunt the hallowed halls of the University of Montevallo. In Reynolds Hall, one female student was reportedly kicked by an unseen force. Ghosts also haunt both of the school's theaters, where unexplained phenomena include doors swinging open by themselves, windows opening and closing on their own, and odd noises coming from the attic above one of the stages.

According to school historians, one of the theater's ghosts may be that of Henry Clay Reynolds, the college's first president. Another theater-bound specter is believed to be that of Walter H. Trumbauer, a well-respected drama instructor who—according to campus legend—often appears during College Night, an annual competition of student-performed musical theater. Supposedly, Trumbauer makes his presence known by causing a batten above the stage to sway over the performers who will win. After all, once a drama teacher, always a drama teacher—even in the afterlife.

The Phantom Flapper

Nearly every Broadway theater seems to have a resident ghost. For example, the ghost of Samuel "Roxy" Rothafel, the man who opened Radio City Music Hall in 1932, is said to make an appearance at the world-famous venue on the opening night of every new production. But few, if any, Broadway palaces seem to be as notably haunted as the New Amsterdam Theatre—a glamorous Art Nouveau structure located on 42nd Street.

For many years, the New Amsterdam Theatre, which was built in 1903, served as the home of the *Ziegfeld Follies*—an elaborate, highly successful series of theatrical productions and variety shows. The theater was hit hard during the Great Depression, and by the late 1930s, it was turned into a movie house. By the end of the 20th century, the once-lavish venue was crumbling along with many other buildings nearby. But since then, the New Amsterdam has been restored to its original grandeur, and it features at least one ghostly reminder of its past.

The Original Flapper

Born in 1894, Olive Thomas is often referred to as "the original flapper." Born into a working-class family, Olive was married at age 16. In 1914, she won a beauty contest for the "most beautiful girl in New York." This landed her a job as a model, which, in turn, got her portrait featured on the cover of the *Saturday Evening Post*.

After appearing in a bit part in the *Ziegfeld Follies*, Olive was given a juicy role in *Ziegfeld Midnight Frolic*, a racier production that was held after hours at the New Amsterdam's rooftop garden. During her performance, Olive was expected to sing songs with a strict sense of decorum while dressed only in balloons that male patrons could (and did) pop with their cigars. The rooftop stage also featured a glass catwalk that extended over the audience, upon which the girls would "fish for millionaires." It is said that some wore bloomers and some did not.

After putting in her time as a showgirl, Olive made the move to silent films. She appeared in more than a dozen features and shorts, but it was her starring role in *The Flapper* (1920) that would define her career and her generation.

But all the while, Olive kept a secret from the public: In 1915, she had divorced her first husband, and a year later, she married Jack Pickford, whose sister Mary was the most famous actress in the world at the time. Mary Pickford was "America's Sweetheart," and her family didn't approve of Jack marrying a girl like Olive, who had a reputation for scandal.

A Fallen Star

The stress of dealing with Jack's disapproving relatives and the couple's busy careers (which kept them apart for long periods at a time) put great stress on their union. In 1920, they finally found time to take a vacation to Paris, but their trip would end in tragedy. While in the dark bathroom in her hotel room, Olive accidentally drank a large quantity of the poison bichloride of mercury, thinking that it was a different medication (the blue bottle's label was written in French). She died in a hospital three days later amid rumors that she had been murdered or had committed suicide after a wild night of partying. In reality, her death was simply a tragic accident.

Gone but Not Forgotten

Most ghosts tend to haunt the places where they died. But almost immediately after Olive's death, baffled stagehands at the New Amsterdam Theatre reported seeing her apparition backstage. Nearly every witness claimed that the spectral Olive was carrying a blue bottle.

Over the years, the theater fell into disuse and disrepair, and sightings of Olive's ghost tapered off. But in the 1990s, the Walt Disney Company leased the theater and began a massive restoration project.

Early in the process, Dana Amendoula—whom Disney left in charge of the theater—was awakened in the middle of the night by a frantic phone call from a security guard. The guard said that he'd been making his rounds when he encountered a young woman wearing a green dress and a beaded, flapper-style headdress; she was walking across the stage carrying a blue bottle. When he shouted to get her attention, she simply floated off the stage and walked through a wall.

Sightings of Olive continued throughout the theater's four-year renovation. She appeared almost exclusively to men, and, once or twice, she was even heard to say "Hiya, fella!" in a flirty voice. Her presence in the theater became so well known that, to this day, employees have a habit of saying "Good morning, Olive" when they arrive for work and "Good night, Olive" when they leave.

Olive seems to be a friendly spirit, but she has been known to cause disturbances when new shows are performed and on nights when veterans of the original *Ziegfeld Follies* were present. (The theater used to stage *Follies* reunions, but the last surviving cast member, Doris Eaton Travis, died in 2010 at age 106.) Rattling scenery and inexplicable lighting issues are common during these times.

In 2005, Amendoula told *Playbill* (the magazine of the Broadway world) that Olive had also been seen floating around in an empty upstairs room—the room that was once the rooftop garden and the home of the *Ziegfeld Midnight Frolic.* She may have died nearly a century ago, but it appears that Olive Thomas may still be at the New Amsterdam Theatre "fishing for millionaires."

At the Belasco Theatre on 44th Street in New York City, there's at least one person who's no longer in the program but still shows up for every curtain call: the ghost of former owner David Belasco, who built the neo-Georgian playhouse in 1907. (The theater was originally known as the Stuyvesant, but Belasco renamed it after himself three years later.) Once one of the most important men on Broadway, Belasco was so passionate about the theater that he has continued to attend opening night performances since his death in 1931. Sometimes, his spirit is accompanied by that of a woman known simply as "the Blue Lady."

An Eternal Seaside Retreat: Cape May's Ghosts

Located at the very southern tip of New Jersey, Cape May was one of the first resort towns in the United States; it offered visitors exotic thrills long before Atlantic City and Las Vegas. In the second half of the 19th century, Cape May experienced a building boom that saw many opulent summer "cottages" (i.e., lavish mansions) spring up around town; many of these Victorian homes are now lovingly restored B & Bs. Some say that ghosts are attracted to water and old buildings; if that's true, it explains why the following ghosts are so fond of Cape May.

The Haunted Bunker

In Cape May Point State Park, a hulking deserted concrete bunker that was built during World War II looks like a typical haunted structure. It is covered with moss and stains, seemingly just about to collapse into the water, and decay hangs heavy in the quiet air around it. Abandoned for decades, the bunker is now home only to seagulls—and ghosts. Visitors have heard a phantom crew still performing its duties: Commands are shouted and soldiers are heard laughing and yelling to each other. Some say that they've seen crew members running about on top of the bunker, only to find it deserted upon closer inspection.

The Inn at 22 Jackson

Jackson Street is one of the oldest and most haunted streets in Cape May. Rumor has it that up to eight buildings along the street harbor ghosts; perhaps the most notable is the Inn at 22 Jackson, one of the street's charming B & Bs. According to one story, while a man was talking to the inn's owner, he asked if she knew that the place was haunted and if she'd ever encountered Esmerelda. The owner said no and closed the front porch door, as it had suddenly gotten very cold. When she did this, she took her eye off the man for a brief moment, and he disappeared.

The owner later asked a longtime guest if she'd encountered any ghosts; the guest said that she'd seen a woman sitting at the

edge of her bed. Subsequent research revealed that the original owners of the building had a nanny named Esmerelda.

Higbee Beach

Higbee Beach is located on the Delaware Bay side of Cape May Point. Legend has it that Mr. Higbee, who once owned the land, was buried facedown somewhere on the beach so that he could meet Satan face-to-face. Many think it's Higbee's spirit that roams the beach as a glowing, gray apparition that glides toward the water.

A phantom pirate also floats along the beach until he disappears. And the spirit of an elderly African American male—who is thought to have been Higbee's servant—is said to guard his master's grave.

Queen's Hotel

The Queen's Hotel was once home to a pharmacy that served as a brothel and a speakeasy on the side. Even though it's an upstanding establishment today, the building can't seem to put its past totally behind it. The ghost of a former prostitute haunts the third floor, where the faint scent of perfume sometimes lingers in the air and unexplained cold spots come and go. According to legend, this former working girl likes to feel appreciated, so leaving a dollar or two on the nightstand is a good way to stay in her good graces.

Other Haunted Inns

Many inns in town have paranormal tales but don't want them spread for fear that they might hurt business. Such is the case with an inn where a couple in a second-floor room continually heard the sound of a door slamming on the third floor and then children noisily clambering down the wooden stairs right outside their room. Frustrated, the man waited by the door to catch the young perpetrators in the act. The next time he heard the kids running down the stairs, he yanked open the door, ready to confront them, but the hallway was vacant. The man and his wife were so spooked that they left immediately; they wanted nothing more to do with the inn or its resident ghosts.

At another anonymous establishment, a male guest had gone to bed by himself one night. As he was lying on his side, he suddenly

felt the other side of the bed depress, and he knew that he was not alone. The man lay there, wondering what to do. (How do you politely kick a ghost out of bed?) Eventually, he heard the bedsprings creak and felt the mattress rise up, and he knew that the spirit had solved his dilemma for him by leaving of its own accord.

Winterwood Gift & Christmas Gallery

The Winterwood Gift & Christmas Gallery, which was once the site of a dentist's office, is the home of a ghostly man in a white coat who carries something in his hand; he vanishes before anyone can see what he's holding.

While they were alive, the Knerr sisters owned the building, which they operated as a ladies' hat store. Apparently, they still like to keep watch over things, even from the Other Side. After the sisters died, the building became a bookstore. The sisters' spirits could often be heard giggling and knocking books off the shelves until the owner shouted at them to stop. His scolding may have convinced the mischievous sisters to cut it out, but they still like to knock Christmas decorations off the wall from time to time.

The Cape May Lighthouse

The Cape May Lighthouse is yet another haunted spot in town. There, a spectral woman has often been spotted on the first-floor landing. She wears a white dress and holds a child in one hand and a lantern in the other. Another ghost that supposedly resides at the lighthouse is that of a man who fell to his death there in 1995.

More Cape May Ghosts

This list is only a small sampling of the ghosts that reside in Cape May. Many local restaurants report strange occurrences, such as odd odors, chairs and plates that mysteriously move on their own, and misty shapes that manifest from out of nowhere and then suddenly vanish. And a phantom horse-and-carriage clops along like any of the other horse-drawn vehicles in town, only to disappear before unsuspecting visitors' eyes. It seems that the Victorian crown jewel of the Jersey Shore is also a hot spot for paranormal activity.

Paramount and the Paranormal

The studios of Paramount Pictures in Hollywood opened their doors in 1926. Since then, they've hosted everyone from early stars such as Rudolph Valentino and Clara Bow to modern mainstays such as Tom Cruise and Harrison Ford. Certainly, Paramount has been home to some of the greatest performers in Hollywood history—and a few have even stuck around after death.

Location, Location, Location

When you consider the location of Paramount's studios, it's not surprising that they're haunted. After all, the back of the lot shares a border with the famous Hollywood Forever Cemetery. And just as not everyone interred at Hollywood Forever is famous, some of the ghostly residents of Paramount are relatively anonymous. One, a nondescript elderly woman, has been spotted roaming the halls of the Ball Building late at night. Certain that she's lost, several guards have tried to help her, but she always disappears before they can.

A ghost that seems to be afraid of the dark likes to wander around the second floor of the Chevalier Building. Guards say that the floor's lights mysteriously turn on at night after everyone has left the building; but when they investigate, nobody is there. Then there's the woman whose strong, flowery perfume can be smelled on the second floor of the Hart Building. She most often makes her presence known to men by throwing objects from desks onto the floor.

Next-Door Neighbors

Hollywood Forever Cemetery is a prominent neighbor of the studios, and guards working at the Lemon Grove Gate—the entrance closest to the graveyard—tell several spooky stories. One playful yet anonymous spirit seems to revel in getting the Paramount guards to chase it to the gate; then, just as the guards close in, it walks through the wall and into Hollywood Forever Cemetery.

One of Paramount's best-known visitors from next door was also one of its most famous stars. Rudolph Valentino was a heartthrob of

the silent era whose most famous role was as the title character in *The Sheik* (1921). In 1926, when he died unexpectedly at age 31, fans the world over were devastated. A riot broke out at his funeral, and rumors persist that a few women took their own lives rather than live in a world without him. For decades, Paramount guards have reported seeing the original "Latin Lover" hanging out by the soundstages. Others say that he comes in through the Lemon Grove Gate entrance, leaving his tomb to visit the film studio that made him famous. According to some accounts, Valentino even dons his old costume from *The Sheik* from time to time.

She's Heeeeere

One of the youngest ghosts that haunts Paramount made her mark, ironically enough, in a movie about a haunted house. Heather O'Rourke began her film career with a role in *Poltergeist* (1982), and she quickly became a star. Soon after, she was on Stage 19 at Paramount shooting episodes of *Happy Days*. Sadly, in 1988, she died during surgery at age 12. Her friends and costars remembered fondly that she enjoyed running around the catwalks of Stage 19 between takes, filling the air with sweet laughter. In the 1990s, Stage 19 became home to a new sitcom called *Wings,* and the cast and crew of that show reportedly heard a child laughing and playing on those same catwalks. However, no child actors were cast as regulars on *Wings,* and the people who worked on the show were convinced that it was Heather. Paramount is clearly a place where people are dying to get in, and the dead never want to leave.

"Some people believe that when you die there is a wonderful light. As bright as the sun but it doesn't hurt to look into it. All the answers to all the questions you want to know are inside that light. And when you walk to it…you become a part of it forever."
—Dr. Lesh (Beatrice Straight's character in *Poltergeist*)

The Last Run of the *Montreal Express*

🪦 🪦 🪦 🪦

At the site of a major New England train wreck, spirits move about restlessly. Are they searching for answers, looking for deliverance, or trying to prevent the disaster? Perhaps it is all of the above.

Sites of tragedies are hot spots for paranormal phenomena. In fact, such sites seem to feature a perfect amalgamation of the critical elements that are known to attract ghosts. First and foremost, they exemplify the "taken away too soon" factor; haven't we all heard of indignant souls that haunt this world primarily because their mortal stays were cut short? They also feature a distinct "if only I could have warned them" component. Spirits operating with this mindset feel that they could have prevented a particular tragedy if only their actions had been timelier or better orchestrated. Finally, consider the "why did you leave me?" aspect. This is the very sad question that ghosts and survivors alike ask when loved ones suddenly and unexpectedly die. The case of 13-year-old Joe McCabe falls into this category, but others who lost their lives during the ill-fated run of the *Montreal Express* on February 5, 1877, span all of the above.

Vermont's Worst Train Wreck

The accident occurred with the swiftness and brutality typical of such disasters. One moment, the *Montreal Express* was chugging through the night, passing over a wooden trestle at White River Junction, Vermont; the next, it was lying in a heap on solid river ice more than 40 feet below. Overturned gas lamps immediately burst into flames, but the situation went from bad to worse when the huge wooden bridge above the train caught fire. Many would-be rescuers were repelled by intense heat and smoke and could only listen to the plaintive wails of the unfortunate souls trapped in the wreckage. The horrors were

unimaginable: Victims were burned to death, crushed, and, in a cruel twist of fate, slowly drowned as the fiery cars melted through the ice. Despite the valiant efforts of rescuers, 34 people perished.

It was later discovered that the train had passed over a defective piece of railway, which caused four of its cars to derail. But this knowledge hardly consoled survivors and grieving families: Their lives had been irrevocably altered the instant that the train left the tracks. The bridge was eventually rebuilt—this time out of steel— and life continued on as always. But the crash site wasn't quite ready to let go of its tragic past.

Ghosts in Training

The Paine House, which is located beside the 650-foot span, was used as a temporary hospital after the accident; it is one of the few structures in the vicinity that remains from the time of the crash. From a kitchen ceiling stained red with the crash victims' blood (which seeped through the floorboards from the room above, where the injured and dead were placed) to stories of livestock too frightened to enter the barn, the supernatural energy of this place is off the charts. Mysterious noises and loud sobbing have also been heard coming from the long-abandoned house.

While unsettling, these bits of supernatural ephemera pale in comparison to happenings at the crash site itself. A man dressed in a railway uniform has often been spotted patrolling the empty tracks at night. Some suggest that this phantom may be the ghost of the train's conductor, Mr. Sturtevant. As the doomed *Montreal Express* made its way onto the wooden bridge, Sturtevant felt an unfamiliar grinding. Sensing trouble, he instinctively yanked the bell cord to signal the engineer to stop, but it was too late: Even with its brakes fully applied, the train derailed and tumbled onto the icy river below.

Perhaps the saddest tale from this incident involves young Joe McCabe. Just 13 years old at the time of the tragedy, the boy survived the wreck only to suffer the anguish of watching his father burn to death. Today, the spectral boy can sometimes be seen hovering just above the river, praying that his father will somehow survive. But it's an exercise in futility: McCabe's greatest desire shall never come to pass, and it appears that he's doomed to replay the most tragic event of his life over and over again.

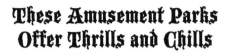

These Amusement Parks Offer Thrills and Chills

Many amusement parks have embraced Halloween. They gear up for this "spooktacular" event by playing special music, presenting Halloween shows, and providing a place for the kiddies to trick-or-treat. But the spirits that hang out at the amusement parks listed below don't limit their appearances to October, and they don't appear at the whim of the public or the management. These ghosts are the real deal. Check them out . . . if you dare.

Kings Island (Mason, Ohio)

For an amusement park that's only been around since 1972, Kings Island is home to a surprising number of ghosts. People have reported seeing a spectral young child walking behind the games and a phantom figure hovering near the International Restaurant at the park's entrance. While no one knows the origins of these two ghostly visitors, three other specters that are seen at the park are more recognizable. The first is thought to be the ghost of a young man who attended a graduation party at the park in 1983. After an evening of imbibing, he climbed the park's replica of the Eiffel Tower and fell to his death. In 1991, another intoxicated visitor unfastened her restraints while she was on the Flight Commander ride; when she stood up to wave to her friends, she too fell to her death. In a less-violent scenario, a security guard is thought to haunt his old workplace. And people have spotted a pair of eyes glowing mysteriously near the park's fountain.

Disneyland (Anaheim, California)

Built in 1955, Disneyland (aka "the happiest place on Earth") was the brainchild of Mickey Mouse creator Walt Disney. But some call it the happiest *haunted* place on Earth. The Haunted Mansion, of course, is rife with legends of real ghosts that supposedly haunt the attraction. Possible spirits include those of an elderly man who died there of a heart attack, the pilot of a plane that crashed at the site before Disneyland was built, a man wearing a tuxedo who lingers where guests disembark from the ride,

a teenage boy who fell through a gap in the walkway, and a small boy who's been seen crying, perhaps because his mother insisted on scattering his ashes in this scary, ghost-inhabited mansion.

Ghosts have also been seen at the Fire Station on Main Street, the Disney Gallery, the Pirates of the Caribbean ride, Space Mountain, Tomorrowland, Tom Sawyer's Island, Splash Mountain, Thunder Mountain, and even on the ever-cheerful "It's a Small World" attraction.

Lake Compounce Theme Park (Bristol, Connecticut)

When it opened in 1895, the Lake Compounce resort featured a restaurant, a casino, and a ballroom. In 1911, a carousel was added, and the amusement park was officially born. The facility is still popular today and has been modernized to enhance its appeal. The site's inauspicious past, however, may have had some lasting effects on it. Native Americans originally occupied the land, and in the mid-1680s, Chief John Compounce sold it to white settlers. A few days after the sale, the chief mysteriously drowned in the middle of the lake. Some thought that it was an accident, but others suspected that he was murdered, and still others believed that he took his own life. Shortly thereafter, John Norton, who had represented the settlers in the sale, met his own demise when he fell off a ladder.

Many years later, when the park was constructed, a workman was decapitated while building a roller coaster. Other workers were killed when they fell from a ride on which people are held in place by centrifugal force. A young child also drowned in the lake. Over the years, park guests have reported strange occurrences, such as hearing distant music, witnessing objects that seem to move by themselves, and watching spirits glide around the Starlight Ballroom.

Disney World (Lake Buena Vista, Florida)

Located just outside Orlando, the Disney World theme park, which opened in 1971, is the largest and most visited theme park in the world. Like Disneyland in California, a ghost is said to haunt the Pirates of the Caribbean ride. When the swashbuckling

crew comes to work each day, they greet the apparition of a former worker who lost his life during the ride's construction. If they forget to do so or attempt to bypass the greeting, the ride often mysteriously breaks down.

Other ghosts at Disney World include those of a young girl with long blonde hair who has been spotted on Epcot's Spaceship Earth ride and a young boy who hovers nearby. The Tower of Terror at Disney's Hollywood Studios is the site of another ghostly presence: Staff members have reported seeing a specter that walks around the ride when the park is closed. A shy spirit, it turns and walks away after being spotted.

Six Flags Great Adventure (Jackson, New Jersey)

One of the largest theme parks in the United States, Six Flags Great Adventure is the home of Kingda Ka, the tallest and fastest steel roller coaster in the world. One couple had an unusual experience while they were taking pictures of the giant coaster. The woman saw a young man out of the corner of her eye; he was about six feet tall with curly reddish hair, and he was wearing a red plaid shirt. When she asked her boyfriend if he had seen him standing there, he replied that he hadn't, but he *had* seen the young man sitting next to him.

The pair agreed that he was wearing vintage 1980s-style clothing. Upon further investigation, the woman discovered the story of Scott Tyler, a 20-year-old park employee who had died in 1981 while performing a routine test of the Rolling Thunder ride without the safety bar fastened. If the ghost wasn't that of Scott Tyler, there is another group of likely suspects: In 1984, eight teenagers were trapped and killed in the Haunted Castle attraction when it caught fire. With so many tragic deaths having occurred at this park, who knows how many spirits wander the grounds?

Ghosts of the *Titanic* Exhibit— Just the Tip of the Haunted Iceberg

🪦 🪦 🪦 🪦

On April 14, 1912, the supposedly unsinkable RMS Titanic *struck an iceberg in the North Atlantic, and by the end of the next day, approximately 1,500 souls lay in a cold, watery grave. Nestled deep in frigid waters, their resting place remained undisturbed until the wreck was discovered on the ocean floor in 1985. Two years later, salvage divers began to recover artifacts from the wreck. Since then, about 5,900 items have been taken from the site. Many of these objects are included in* Titanic: The Artifact Exhibition, *which has traveled the world since the early 1990s—and a few ghosts have gone along for the ride. A permanent* Titanic *museum is also haunted by the past.*

Haunting Atlanta

While taking in the traveling exhibit at the Georgia Aquarium in Atlanta, a visitor initially attributed a sense of being watched and feelings of overwhelming sadness to the items on display. One volunteer who worked at the exhibit said she sensed that lost souls were embedded in the artifacts; she also felt a hand moving over her head and touching her hair. And a four-year-old boy repeatedly asked his mother and grandmother about a lady that he saw in a display case, which—to the adults—held only a dress and a love seat. Another visitor saw a man in a black-and-white suit who seemed out of place amongst the other, more casually dressed people; later, when she felt as if she was being watched, the visitor turned around to see the man in the suit staring at her.

In 2008, when a paranormal investigation team visited the exhibit, its members witnessed shadowy figures and picked up the voices of spirits on audio recordings. The team concluded that at least three ghosts are attached to the exhibit—those of an older gentleman, an elderly woman, and a young crew member.

Jason Hawes and Grant Wilson and their team from The Atlantic Paranormal Society (TAPS) also conducted an investigation of the exhibit; their results aired on a 2009 episode of *Ghost Hunters*.

Their findings were similar to those compiled by other paranormal research groups. In the Iceberg Exhibit (which contains a replica of an iceberg to give visitors a sense of what one feels like), Hawes and Wilson detected a moving cold spot that seemed to be about four to five feet tall and one to two feet wide. Hawes also felt something tug on his shirt. While in the Artifacts Exhibit, both investigators saw a shadowy figure walk into another room, and Hawes felt an unseen hand touch his shoulder. Before they left the room, Hawes asked the spirit to knock on the wall if it wanted them to leave. They heard nothing, but their audio recorder captured an EVP (electronic voice phenomenon) that sounded like a man whispering, "No, please wait," or perhaps even, "Don't leave me." In the end, TAPS concluded that both intelligent and residual hauntings were present at the aquarium, which are likely associated with the exhibit.

Rocking New York City
When the exhibit traveled to New York City, motion-activated security cameras clicked on every night at 3 A.M., even though no living being was present. And one visitor said that as she and her cousin walked through a small hallway, they experienced a rocking sensation, as if they were actually on a ship. They asked an employee if this was some sort of special effect; it was not, but the employee reported that many other people had asked the same question.

Chilling St. Paul
When the artifacts visited St. Paul, Minnesota, one visitor left the Iceberg Exhibit because she suddenly felt dizzy. Then, she felt a hand touching her shoulder, even though no one else was around. Her shoulder felt cold and then hot, as if she had frostbite. A few minutes later, a red mark appeared on her shoulder. Another person reported similar sensations when leaving the Iceberg Exhibit, including dizziness, shoulder taps, and the queasy sensation of being rocked.

Ghosts in Branson
Even a permanent *Titanic* museum seems to be haunted. The *Titanic* museum attraction in Branson, Missouri (and its sister site in Pigeon Forge, Tennessee), is said to be teeming with ghosts. This re-creation of the legendary ship displays approximately 400 artifacts from the

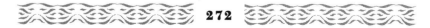

actual *Titanic*—and is thought to be home to at least one ghost-child. Members of the cleaning staff have found child-size fingerprints on the glass separating the Promenade Deck and the Bridge; given that many children visit the museum, this is not unusual. However, the prints reappear after the glass is cleaned when the museum is closed. Even stranger, one museum employee photographed a wet footprint in the shape of a child's bare foot.

Ghosts have also been spotted in other parts of the ship: A man in formal wear has been seen at the top of the Grande Staircase; a gowned figure glides around the First Class Dining Salon and emerges from the area carrying her belongings; and although the museum has a no smoking policy, both staffers and visitors have smelled cigar smoke around the Grande Staircase on numerous occasions.

To determine once and for all if ghosts from the *Titanic* haunt the museum, the owners invited two different teams of paranormal investigators to conduct research overnight. Both teams found high psychic-energy levels that became higher when staff members asked the spirits questions. As museum staffers communicated with two passengers who died on the ship—Robert Douglas Spedden and Mr. Asplund—one staff member became weak and nauseous.

Final Attachments

When the exhibit visited Athens, Greece, employees heard English-speaking voices in the galleries after hours. And in Monterrey, Mexico, several people commented on a man who they described as a "character actor" dressed in a black suit that would have been fashionable in 1912. However, the exhibit did not employ any reenactors.

It makes sense that *Titanic*'s victims would follow the items that they knew in life and rested with in death for many decades. The artifacts will continue to travel the world as long as there is interest in them, but hopefully, the spirits will eventually separate themselves from their earthly belongings and finally rest in peace.

Have a Ghostly Good Time at the Carolina Inn

🪦   🪦   🪦   🪦

*Built in 1924, on the campus of the University of North
Carolina in Chapel Hill, the Carolina Inn was designed
to be a warm and welcoming meeting place for visitors,
students, and area residents alike. A perfect amalgamation of
Colonial and Southern antebellum architectural styles, this
185-room inn is on the National Register of Historic Places—
and it's also one of America's Top Ten Haunted Hotels.*

Some Spirited Fun

Some spirits find it hard to leave the places they called home in life.
Such is the case with Dr. William Jacocks, a well-known physician
who lived at the Carolina Inn for the last 17 years of his life. He was
described as friendly and kind, but he did enjoy a good practical joke.
And it seems that hasn't changed—even though he died in 1965.

Dr. Jacocks lived in Room 252, and he is still quite protective of
the space: He frequently manipulates the locks to keep out potential
guests. On one occasion, a maintenance worker had to climb a ladder
and crawl through a window to gain entry; another time, the door
had to be removed from its hinges.

If Dr. Jacocks decides to let people enter Room 252, he tries to
have his fun in other ways. Two hotel guests reported waking up to
the strong scent of flowers; a quick look around the room revealed
that a bath mat had been rumpled and the curtains had been pulled
back in a jumbled manner. On another occasion, a couple staying in
the room heard a loud whoosh of air that didn't come from the
heating and air-conditioning unit.

The Ghost Hunt

By the early 2000s, the reports of inexplicable occurrences at the
Carolina Inn had piqued the interest of professional ghost hunters.
During one investigation, a team from a local paranormal research
group set up audio recorders, digital cameras, infrared video cameras,

and electromagnetic sensors. They monitored three rooms, including Room 252, for a four-hour period. And they weren't disappointed.

The investigators recorded footsteps, a door slamming, and a loud bang—all in an empty room. During one 20-minute period, they sensed the strong presence of something else in the room and even felt breath on the backs of their necks. Photos taken during this time show orbs of light, as though something was moving through the room. The sound of music playing from a distance was also heard and captured on a recording. Careful listening revealed that the music was coming from a piano, but no piano was in that room or anywhere nearby. A low murmur of voices was also audible.

Bottoms Up!

When the ghost hunters returned to the Carolina Inn in 2009, they heard the sound of ice cubes clinking into a glass and got the distinct feeling that they were in the presence of the spirit of a heavy drinker (which Dr. Jacocks was not). Other team members got the same impression elsewhere in the building that same night.

It seems that the good doctor may have some ghostly company. Some hotel guests have reported seeing the apparition of a large man in a black suit and winter coat wandering the halls and jiggling door-knobs before quickly disappearing.

Just a Little Fun

Several sessions of "Ghost Hunter University"—an event organized by the Carolina Inn to play up its supernatural activity—have taken place at the hotel. These events attract participants who are interested in the paranormal or like ghost stories, and they include tours and seminars about various haunted locations throughout the building.

When Christopher Moon, editor of *Haunted Times* magazine, arrived to host a session of Ghost Hunter University, he, of course, requested to stay in Room 252. And it lived up to its reputation. Photos that he took showed orbs in the room, which are said to indicate a paranormal presence. But the best evidence of ghost play? When he went to use the bathroom sink, both handles fell right off and into the basin, spraying water everywhere. Somewhere, Dr. Jacocks was having a good laugh.

 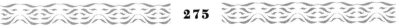

The Ghost of the Gipper

🪦 🪦 🪦 🪦

The University of Notre Dame is rife with history and tradition. Founded in 1842 in South Bend, Indiana, this school is well known for its academics—and its football program. And while the team is busy "winning one for the Gipper," the Gipper himself is busy haunting a few of his old campus hangouts.

The Gipper, of course, was Notre Dame football legend George Gipp. As the school's first All-American, Gipp played a variety of positions—all very well. But like many young men, Gipp also enjoyed a good party and a bit of gambling. Some say that after a night of such revelry, Gipp returned to his dorm—Washington Hall—after curfew and found himself locked out. This was in December 1920, and with no way to call for help, Gipp curled up on the steps and fell asleep. Many believe that this night spent in the elements is what caused Gipp to come down with the dreaded duo of strep throat and pneumonia. Because antibiotics were not yet available, Gipp's condition soon became grave.

On his deathbed, Gipp reportedly had a heartfelt conversation with his coach, Knute Rockne. He told Rockne that someday, when the coach needed to rally his team to victory, he should mention his name and ask that team to go out there and "win one for the Gipper." And in an inspirational and oft-repeated speech to his squad a few years later, Rockne did just that.

Maybe Gipp has been hanging around in case he is needed to help his beloved Fighting Irish on the gridiron, or maybe he is just having a little fun. Whatever the case, before Washington Hall was converted into classrooms in the 1950s, phantom footsteps and doors slamming of their own accord were usually attributed to the ghost of Gipp. Now that the facility houses the theater department, Gipp is thought to haunt the stage and other rooms nearby. Drama students working late at night have heard strange music and other noises in the building. And many students have reported feeling that someone is standing beside them just as they get a fleeting glimpse of a ghost.

Does the Ghost of Aaron Burr Take the Subway?

A particular gentleman has been seen hanging out in a café and at a romantic restaurant in Greenwich Village, wandering the halls of a historic mansion in Washington Heights, and gazing at New York Harbor from Battery Park. He's even been spotted at a historic inn in Pennsylvania and a cemetery in New Jersey. The problem is that he's been dead for nearly 200 years. The spirit of Aaron Burr is a ghost that gets around.

Burr's Long Life Leads to an Even Longer Afterlife

Although Aaron Burr might be most famous for killing Alexander Hamilton in a duel, this incident was not the only part of his life that might have caused his soul to remain earthbound. Born in 1756, Burr was a brilliant lawyer who served under George Washington during the Revolutionary War. He was chosen as a senator from New York in 1791 and was nearly elected President of the United States in 1800; instead, he served as Thomas Jefferson's vice president.

By the summer of 1804, near the end of Burr's term as V.P., it was clear that he would not be on the ballot for reelection. Instead, he decided to run for governor of New York, but much political intrigue ensued, which led to his fateful duel with Hamilton on July 11, 1804. Despite the fact that dueling was illegal in New Jersey (where the fatal encounter took place), Burr never stood trial for murder, and all charges against him were eventually dropped.

After finishing his term as vice president, Burr headed west, where he met up with a friend from the Revolutionary War who turned out to be a spy for Spain. As a result, Burr was accused of plotting to invade Mexico and was tried for treason. He was found not guilty, but to avoid creditors, he traveled to Europe shortly thereafter. In France, Burr attempted to enlist Napoleon in a plot to invade Florida, but the emperor declined to get involved. In 1812, Burr returned to New York to practice law. He died in 1836 in Staten Island—although that is one of the few places his ghost has *not* been

seen—and was buried in Princeton, New Jersey, where his specter has been spotted several times.

A Ghost that Gets Around

In the early 1960s, Burr's apparition was seen in a building in Greenwich Village that, back in his time, would have abutted the stables of his estate, Richmond Hill. In July 1961, the owner of the Café Bizarre entered the building to pick up a package that she'd left behind earlier in the day. Although it was very late at night and the place was closed, she sensed that she was not alone. In a dark corner, she saw a man with piercing black eyes who was wearing a ruffled white shirt. When she demanded to know who he was, he remained silent and seemed to smile. Previously, a waiter had quit immediately after seeing this same spectral figure. In 1962, a psychic confirmed that someone with the initials "A. B." was connected to the site.

A few years later, Burr's ghost spoke to a young girl as she walked by the café; he wanted her to find information that would prove that he was not treasonous. In 1967, a psychic spoke with a spirit that declared that he was not a traitor or a murderer and called out for "Theo," Burr's pet name for his daughter Theodosia.

The psychics who conducted this séance hoped that it would allow Burr's spirit to rest, but unfortunately, it did not. Patrons and staff at the restaurant One If By Land, Two If By Sea on Barrow Street in Manhattan have also experienced Burr-related paranormal activity. They've had chairs pulled out from under them and witnessed dishes thrown by invisible hands. Many women sitting at the bar find their earrings mysteriously removed, and a maître d' quit after being shoved repeatedly by an unseen force. These unexplained acts have been attributed to the restless spirits of Aaron Burr and his beloved daughter, Theodosia Burr Alston, who have apparently been reunited in the afterlife at the site of what was originally part of Richmond Hill. (Theo's ghost has also been spotted near Huntington Beach State Park in Nags Head, North Carolina, where her ship disappeared or was captured by pirates. It is rumored that Theo was forced to walk the plank, which perhaps explains the angry pushing and throwing that takes place at the restaurant.)

Eight miles north of the former Café Bizarre and One If By Land, Two If By Sea, Burr has also been known to greet guests at

the Morris-Jumel Mansion in Washington Heights, where he lived with his second wife, Eliza Jumel. As one might expect given that it is the oldest house in Manhattan, Aaron Burr is not the only spirit that resides there: The specters of a servant girl who committed suicide at the mansion, a Revolutionary War soldier, and Eliza Jumel also wander the property.

Burr has also been seen standing by the American Merchant Marine Memorial at Battery Park, which is located at the southern end of Manhattan. Many have surmised that he waits in perpetuity for Theo to arrive. Only a few blocks away, Alexander Hamilton is buried at Trinity Church. Perhaps Burr seeks another chance to set the record straight about what really happened during their infamous duel.

Breaking Out of the Big Apple

Burr is not content to haunt various neighborhoods in Manhattan, however. After the duel with Hamilton, Burr hid for at least a week at a residence in New Hope, Pennsylvania. Today, his spirit continues to seek refuge there, although the building is now known as the Wedgewood Inn. One woman saw a male figure in Colonial clothing standing behind her as she wiped steam off the bathroom mirror; when she turned to face him, no one was there. Other guests have reported feeling someone staring at them from behind. Known as "Burr's sightless stare," the phenomenon tends to occur on the second floor and in the stairwell leading to the basement, but it has been known to happen throughout the house.

Even before Burr's ghost was reported in Manhattan, the staff at Lindenwald—Martin Van Buren's childhood home in Kinderhook, New York—knew that he was not resting peacefully. After killing Hamilton, Burr spent three years at Lindenwald, and after his death, strange sounds—such as footsteps of a man pacing back and forth—were heard inside the house. Burr—dressed in a burgundy coat with lace cuffs—also presented his spectral self to servants outside the house.

Many historians feel that Aaron Burr was a misunderstood patriot whose enemies destroyed his reputation and career. Whether or not this is the case, his restless wanderings are as extensive in death as they were in life.

Phantom Patients Haunt These Hospitals

Considering how many deaths occur at hospitals, it's not surprising that they're home to many restless spirits. Here are some of the most haunted hospitals in the United States.

Nationwide Children's Hospital (Columbus, Ohio)

At Nationwide Children's Hospital—which is rumored to have been built atop an old cemetery—some rooms are said to be haunted, which has caused some nurses to avoid certain hallways after dark. People have also reported seeing moving shadows and the figure of a ghostly woman gliding through Livingston Park next door. Children—who are often more sensitive to seeing spirits than adults are—have told of watching this "pink lady" from their hospital windows. This misty spirit effortlessly floats through the trees and over the tombstones. The park sits on a piece of land that was part of an old Confederate cemetery, so perhaps she's looking for a husband or relative who died during the Civil War.

Heather Hill Hospital (Chardon, Ohio)

When patients in the C wing at Heather Hill Hospital complain to the nursing staff about a young boy who runs wild in the halls and knocks on the walls of their rooms, they don't get much help with the problem; after all, staff members can hardly discipline a boy they can't see. Although the mischievous boy is a ghost, he tries to converse with patients and staff members. The boy is most likely a former patient, and even though he is dressed in knickers circa the early 1900s, no one seems to know who he was in life or how he came to spend eternity at Heather Hill.

Old Riverside Hospital (Trenton, Michigan)

In 1944, Henry Ford bought the Church family home in Trenton and converted it into a hospital. While the Churches lived there, their daughter owned a horse, which she loved dearly. But when she fell off the horse and broke her arm, her father blamed the animal, so he shot it. The girl was so distraught that from then on, she kept to her room, singing and gazing out the window.

Patients who have stayed in her former bedroom reported hearing phantom footsteps and singing. The building was closed in 2002 and today sits vacant. A newer hospital took its place years ago, but visitors on the grounds who glance up at the girl's bedroom window have seen a young, curly-haired girl looking down at them. She likes to move the blinds up and down, and if you listen closely, you may hear her cries of despair—or perhaps her sweet singing.

North Carolina Orthopedic Hospital (Gastonia, North Carolina)

Closed in 1979, the former North Carolina Orthopedic Hospital kept its supernatural secrets until after it was renovated and repurposed. When the Gaston County Welfare Office moved there in 1982, unusual things started happening. Apparently, the resident ghosts don't know that the building is no longer a hospital: Phantom nurses have been seen moving between the rooms on the second floor. And the Gastonia police have received numerous calls claiming that people are inside the building late at night. But, of course, when officers investigated, they found the place empty... or at least that's how it appeared.

Yorktown Memorial Hospital (Yorktown, Texas)

Yorktown Memorial Hospital, which was built in 1950, has stood empty since it closed in the late 1980s. Caretaker Mike Hanson has reported ghostly experiences there, especially near the nurses' station. He says that the place appears empty while he's making his rounds... until he turns the lights off: In the dark, he's seen shadow figures, phantom patients, and spectral visitors mingling in the hallways. A stairway behind a glass door may also be home to a spirit or two: People have heard unexplained tapping on the glass even though no one is behind the door. In 2009, the Central Texas Ghost Hunters paid a visit to Yorktown Memorial Hospital; although they didn't see any apparitions during their visit, they did capture the sound of organ music coming from the empty chapel. Do these ghosts linger on, still hoping for cures to their ailments?

Riddles of the Riddle House

While functioning as a funeral home, West Palm Beach's Riddle House regularly played host to death. Since then, it's been relocated and repurposed, and now it sees its fair share of life—life after death, that is.

The "Painted Lady"

Built in 1905 as a gatekeeper's cottage, this pretty "Painted Lady" seemed incongruent with the cemetery it was constructed to oversee. Cloaked in grand Victorian finery, the house radiated the brightness of life. Perhaps that's what was intended: A cemetery caretaker's duties can be gloomy, so any bit of spirit lifting would likely be welcomed. Or so its builders thought. In the case of this particular house, however, "spirit lifting" took on a whole new meaning.

The first ghost sighted in the area was that of a former cemetery worker named Buck, who was killed during an argument with a townsperson. Shortly thereafter, Buck's ghost was seen doing chores around the cemetery and inside the cottage. Luckily, he seemed more interested in performing his duties than exacting revenge.

In the 1920s, the house received its current name when city manager Karl Riddle purchased it and took on the duty of overseeing the cemetery. During his tenure, a despondent employee named Joseph hung himself in the attic. This sparked a frenzy of paranormal phenomena inside the house, including the unexplained sounds of rattling chains and disembodied voices.

After Riddle moved out, the reports of paranormal activity slowed down—but such dormancy wouldn't last.

Traveling Spirits

By 1980, the Riddle House had fallen into disrepair and was abandoned. The city planned to demolish the building but instead decided to give it to John Riddle (Karl's nephew). He, in turn, donated it for preservation. The entire structure was moved—lock, stock, and barrel—to Yesteryear Village, a museum devoted to

Florida's early years. There, it was placed on permanent display as an attractive token of days long past. There, too, its dark side would return—with a vengeance.

When workers began to reassemble the Riddle House, freshly awakened spirits kicked their antics into high gear. Ladders were tipped over, windows were smashed, and tools were thrown to the ground from the building's third floor. Workers were shocked when an unseen force threw a wooden board across a room, striking a carpenter in the head. The attacks were blamed on the spirit of Joseph, and the situation became so dangerous that work on the structure was halted for six months. After that, however, the Riddle House was restored to its previous glory.

Ghostly Unveiling

During the dedication of the Riddle House in the early 1980s, two unexpected guests showed up for the ceremony. Resplendent in Victorian garb, the couple added authenticity to the time period being celebrated. Many assumed that they were actors who were hired for the occasion; they were not. In fact, no one knew *who* they were. A few weeks later, century-old photos from the Riddle House were put on display. There, in sepia tones, stood the very same couple that guests had encountered during the dedication!

When the *Ghost Adventures* team spent a night locked inside the Riddle House in 2008, a medium warned the investigators that the spirit of Joseph is an evil entity that did not want them there. But that didn't stop investigator Zak Bagans from provoking the spirit. Bagans left a board at the top of the stairs and asked the entity to move it if it didn't want them there. Later, after the team heard footsteps in the room above them, the board fell down several stairs on its own. Throughout the course of the night, the team experienced unexplained noises and objects moving and falling by themselves. In the end, the researchers concluded that the Riddle House is definitely haunted and that whatever resides in the attic does not like men in particular, just as the medium had cautioned.

Ethereal stirrings at the Riddle House continue to this day. Unexplained sightings of a torso hanging in the attic window represent only part of the horror. And if history is any indicator, more supernatural sightings and activity are certainly to come.

Stephen Decatur's Ghost

In Washington, D.C., a sullen figure stands at a window, looking at the world outside—even though he is a visitor from the Great Beyond. The figure is the ghost of Stephen Decatur, one of the country's greatest military heroes—long dead but condemned to prowl the halls of his former home.

Rising Star

In 1807, Stephen Decatur was already a war hero for the young United States. He garnered accommodations for his bravery against the Barbary Pirates and for serving as a member of a naval commission that investigated the actions of Commodore James Barron. Barron was the commander of the U.S. frigate *Chesapeake;* after the British ship *Leopold* fired a shot across the *Chesapeake*'s bow, Barron boarded the *Leopold* and took four of its sailors into custody. At the time, tensions between Britain and America were running high, so the commission on which Decatur served was organized to investigate Barron's actions. It found that Barron had not received permission for his actions, so he was court-martialed and suspended for five years. Decatur spoke against Barron at the hearing, and Barron was not a man to forgive and forget.

When the War of 1812 broke out between the United States and England, Decatur took command of the *Chesapeake* and built up his reputation while Barron seethed on the sidelines. Then, in 1818, Decatur and his wife, Susan, became power players on the Washington, D.C. social scene after they built a house on fashionable Lafayette Square. However, Decatur's past would come back to haunt him. Over the years, Barron had unleashed a series of personal attacks on him. The whole affair culminated in early 1820 when Barron challenged Decatur to a duel.

Fallen Star

The night before the duel, Decatur stared glumly from his bedroom window, looking at his estate and the neighborhood. The next day,

at a field in Maryland, Decatur—apparently channeling his inner Alexander Hamilton—attempted only to wound Barron (even though Decatur was an expert marksman). However, Barron—taking a page from Aaron Burr's playbook—shot to kill and mortally wounded his enemy. Decatur was carried home, where he died an agonizing death on March 22, 1820. While he lay dying, the heartbroken Susan could barely look at him because she was so upset.

Eternal Star

Soon after his death, people began seeing a figure staring sadly out of the window where Decatur himself had stood on the night before the duel. The ghost was seen so often that eventually the window was sealed up. But bricks and mortar can't keep a good ghost down—Decatur's apparition continued to manifest throughout the house and at other windows.

Today, the former Decatur home is a museum of White House history. However, that has not stopped the ghost of Stephen Decatur from roaming its halls and appearing in various rooms, always with an expression of infinite sadness on his face.

Sometimes, in the early morning hours, a figure is spotted leaving the building through the back door. It carries a black box—perhaps containing a dueling pistol—just as Decatur did on the last day of his life. Inside the house, people have felt unbelievable sadness and emptiness in the first-floor room where Decatur died.

However, Stephen Decatur is not the only restless spirit that haunts the Lafayette Square property. Disembodied sobbing and wailing have been heard throughout the house; some speculate that it's the ghost of Susan Decatur reliving her life's greatest sorrow.

A Host of Ghosts Haunt the White Eagle Saloon

The building housing the White Eagle Saloon in Portland, Oregon, has been many things since it was constructed in the early 1900s: a hotel, a brothel, a rooming house, and, most recently, a tavern that features live music. For much of its history, it has also been haunted.

Over the years, a great deal of paranormal activity has been reported at the White Eagle Saloon. Most of it has been harmless—but not all of it. For example, many years ago, a waitress was walking to the basement after closing to tabulate the day's receipts when something unseen shoved her down the stairs. The woman's hysterical screams got the attention of the bartender and doorman, who had a bucket hurled at them by an invisible force. Not surprisingly, the waitress quit the next day.

To date, this is the most violent outburst from the spirits at the White Eagle Saloon; however, many other, more innocuous events that simply defy explanation have occurred there.

Weirdness in the Bathroom

One of the White Eagle's ghosts seems to enjoy flushing the toilet in the men's room. Many people have observed this unusual activity, usually after closing. A faulty toilet? No way, says owner Chuck Hughes—the flushing has occurred with two different commodes, and it is sometimes accompanied by the sound of footsteps in the hallway outside the restroom.

Hughes has experienced quite a bit of unexplained phenomena over the years. For example, one day he was removing a lock from a door on the second floor when he heard what sounded like a woman crying at the other end of the hallway. But as he walked toward the source of the noise, the crying ceased. Hughes checked all of the rooms on the second floor but found nothing. When he returned to his work on the door, the crying began again. Hughes again tried to find the source of the sound, and this time he felt an overwhelming chill.

Frightened, Hughes rushed downstairs and exited the tavern. Looking back at the building, he saw what he later described as a ghostly shape in one of the second-floor windows. After moving to the back of the building, Hughes saw the same specter at another window. Shaken, he refused to go upstairs again for nearly a year.

A Ghost Named Sam

It is believed that one of the ghosts haunting the White Eagle Saloon is a former employee named Sam, who some say was adopted at a young age by one of the building's early owners. A burly guy, Sam lived and worked at the White Eagle until his death in the 1930s.

After Sam died in his room at the White Eagle, his boss had his body removed and then locked the room and left it pretty much the way it was for a long time. Is Sam still hanging around the tavern? Many believe so. Hughes recalled that after he bought the White Eagle, the door to Sam's room would not stay open. Time after time, the door was left open, only to be found shut—and locked—a couple of days later. Apparently, Sam likes his privacy.

Hughes says that he's experienced enough unexplained phenomena at the White Eagle to fill a book. For example, he used to keep a bed in the basement to use when he worked late; one night, he awoke to find himself being nudged by invisible hands. Understandably disconcerted, he got dressed and went home.

While working in the basement after hours, Hughes often heard voices and footsteps above him; sometimes the voices even called his name. But every time he went to investigate, no one was there.

Suspected Spooks

The White Eagle Saloon has hosted its share of wild times and even wilder characters over the years, so it's no surprise that it's haunted. Sam is believed to be the spook that flushes the men's room toilet, and the crying woman may be the spirit of one of the many prostitutes who worked there when the building housed a brothel.

But who pushed the waitress down the cellar stairs? Some suspect that it was the ghost of a Chinese bouncer known for harshly treating the African American prostitutes who worked in the basement. One day, the guy simply disappeared. Was he murdered? If so, it may explain why his angry spirit is still attached to the White Eagle.

The Curse of Griffith Park

Griffith Park in Los Angeles, California, is one of the largest urban parks in America. Many who visit it snap photos of the Hollywood sign, take in the view of the city, gaze at the heavens at the Griffith Observatory, and marvel at the animals at the Los Angeles Zoo. Others, however, come away from their visits to Griffith Park with bone-chilling tales of paranormal encounters.

Where There's a Will . . .

The dark history of Griffith Park began in 1863, when it was called Rancho Los Feliz. That year, owner Don Antonio Feliz passed from this world, and many expected that his blind niece, Doña Petranilla, would inherit his fortune. Unbeknownst to Petranilla, however, local lawyer Don Antonio Coronel had visited Feliz to help him rewrite his will. When Feliz succumbed to smallpox, most of his wealth went to Coronel. Petranilla was outraged, and from the family adobe, she laid a curse upon the land that is still felt to this day.

A Curse Fit for a Colonel

Following Petranilla's curse, the Coronels and other subsequent owners were all plagued with misfortune and disease until Colonel Griffith J. Griffith, a wealthy industrialist, purchased the property. When Griffith acquired the land in 1882, opening a park was the last thing on his mind: His first order of business was to build housing developments on the land, but that venture soon failed. Griffith also allowed a small ostrich farm to open on the property, and surprisingly, it was quite successful. However, in 1884, storms plagued the area and the ostriches stampeded every night. Ranch hands claimed that the cause of the ruckus was a phantom rider that appeared in the rain. Some said that it was the ghost of Don Feliz, but others believed that it was Doña Petranilla, back from the dead to fulfill the curse that she imposed on the land. Regardless of who it was, Griffith refused to visit the property

except at midday, and in 1896, to rid himself of the ghost once and for all, he donated 3,015 acres of his land to the city of Los Angeles.

However, that didn't stop the spirit from making appearances from time to time. In 1898, when the city's wealthy and influential residents gathered for a fiesta at Griffith Park, an ethereal horseback rider chased them out. Over the years, many visitors to the park have reported seeing this spirit sitting atop a horse and roaming the park's trails, or riding through the park at night.

Unfortunately, Griffith's mind deteriorated after that, and in 1903, he tried to kill his wife because he thought that she was conspiring against him with the Pope; he spent nearly two years in San Quentin for the crime. When he died in 1919, Colonel Griffith bequeathed his remaining fortune to the city of Los Angeles. If he relieved himself of the cursed property in an attempt to appease its restless spirits, the maneuver seems to have failed.

To Live and Die in Hollywood

In the 1930s, Griffith Park claimed another victim. Like so many others, Peg Entwistle had come to Hollywood to realize her dream of seeing her visage on the silver screen. However, after receiving poor reviews for her performance in her first motion picture, Entwistle concluded that her career was a failure. And so, on the night of September 16, 1932, she climbed to the top of the Hollywood sign's "H" and leaped to her death in the ravine below. A suicide note was found in her purse, and within days, she had achieved the fame that had eluded her in life.

Over the years, several hikers and park rangers have reported seeing a woman dressed in 1930s-era attire near the sign. And from time to time, a spectral blonde woman has been known to set off motion sensors located near the sign. When the rangers investigate, they notice the scent of gardenias.

The City of Angels' Lady in White

Park rangers spend more time in Griffith Park than anyone else, and they know that they're not alone. In their headquarters in the old Feliz adobe, the rangers have reportedly caught glimpses of a ghostly Hispanic woman who is dressed all in white. Most people seem to think that this is the tormented spirit of Doña Petranilla, the woman who originally cursed the land back in 1863. She died soon after placing the curse, and she is one of the property's oldest lost souls. In 1884, the worst of the storms that ripped through the area stripped most of the vegetation from the land. Around that time, Griffith's ranch hands witnessed the Lady in White cursing the land and all who lived on it, just as she had done in life. Some have reported hearing her wailing near the Los Angeles Zoo and the golf course, but her favorite haunt seems to be her former home. Although the park is closed overnight, Petranilla seems to prefer to make nocturnal appearances, and like her uncle and Colonel Griffith, she is sometimes seen on horseback going for a midnight ride.

Reversing the Curse

Those who might avoid one of the nation's most beautiful public parks for fear of its ghosts probably shouldn't: Most of the spirits that are said to haunt the grounds of Griffith Park seem to visit at night, often after the park is closed. Also, many movies and television shows have been filmed there over the years, all without a single apparition having been captured on film. In the years since the land passed from Colonel Griffith to the city of Los Angeles, no mysterious tragedies have befallen visitors to the park, but if you find yourself on the property at night—perhaps hiking in view of the Hollywood sign or the historic Feliz home—know that there's a good chance you're not alone.

"Then away out in the woods I heard that kind of a sound that a ghost makes when it wants to tell about something that's on its mind and can't make itself understood, and so can't rest easy in its grave, and has to go about that way every night grieving."

—Mark Twain, *The Adventures of Huckleberry Finn*

Spend the Night with a Ghost at One of These Hotels

By their very nature, hotels would have a lot to say if their walls could talk. So many travelers passing through, so many stories— and so many ghosts left behind. Hotels provide their guests with soft beds and hearty breakfasts, but if your hotel happens to be haunted, you may get a little more with your room than you expected.

The Heathman Hotel (Portland, Oregon)

Choose your room at the Heathman Hotel carefully because there's a certain column of rooms that reportedly sees quite a bit of paranormal action: You should pick rooms ending in 03 (between 303 and 1003) only if you don't mind spending the night with a ghostly companion. George Heathman built the hotel in 1927 for lumber and railroad tycoons who sought luxurious lodging in the West. No one knows what actually caused the hauntings, but ghost hunters speculate that someone fell or jumped out of a window and now haunts the rooms that he or she passed on the way down. Today, guests in those rooms experience odd occurrences, such as towels being used and glasses and chairs being moved when no one else has been in the room. Visitors have also felt a strange presence in some rooms; one guest even awoke to find himself wrapped up tightly in his sheets.

Hotel Vendome (Prescott, Arizona)

As a quaint and welcoming community in the Arizona mountains, Prescott holds a lot of history. Former manager Abby Byr and her cat, Noble, are said to haunt this hotel, which was built in 1917. At around that same time, Abby, who suffered from tuberculosis, moved to Arizona for health reasons. There, she met and married her husband, and the couple bought the Hotel Vendome. They soon lost the place due to unpaid taxes, but the next owners hired them to run it. One night in 1921, Abby sent her husband out for medicine; he never returned. She died a short time later, and employees, guests, and ghost hunters have all felt her presence lingering at the hotel. Some have even seen her apparition in Room 16, where she and her husband lived. Is it Abby who makes noise by moving

hangers around in the closet? Guests have also reported having their possessions inexplicably moved around the room, and some report getting sudden whiffs of strong perfume.

Fairmont Hotel Vancouver (Vancouver, British Columbia)

Opened in 1939, the Fairmont Hotel is still going strong today. Adding to the hotel's distinguished architecture and fabulous ambiance are a few ghostly spirits. Over the years, guests and employees alike have reported seeing a spectral Lady in Red that roams the hallways of the 14th floor and sometimes appears to walk along an invisible ledge. Also, elevators have been known to make unscheduled stops on the 14th floor, even though the button was not pressed and no one is there when the door opens.

Jerome Grand Hotel (Jerome, Arizona)

Jerome, Arizona, got its start as a mining town in the late 1800s. In the late 1920s, the United Verde Copper Company built a hospital there to treat sick and injured miners. In addition to the many deaths that are typically associated with a hospital, several violent ends occurred in the building as well. In 1935, an orderly was found crushed beneath the elevator, and another fell from a fifth-floor balcony; both deaths are thought to have been murders. A suicide also took place at the hospital when a patient rolled his wheelchair over a balcony and onto the street below.

The hospital closed its doors in 1950 and the building sat vacant for nearly half a century until two brothers opened the Jerome Grand Hotel there in 1997. The third floor has seen the most paranormal activity, but disembodied voices and coughing, a dusty smell, and apparitions have been reported throughout the building; they're most likely the antics of spirits left over from the days when the sick and injured lived and died there.

Fairmont Château Laurier (Ottawa, Ontario)

The spirits of this hotel are evidence that ghosts from the *Titanic* do not just haunt the ship and its artifacts. In 1912, Charles Melville Hays journeyed to Europe to choose dining-room furniture for the Château Laurier. Unfortunately, he and his men went down

with the *Titanic* just days before the hotel was scheduled to open. However, Hays's spirit is believed to have returned to the Château Laurier, where guests report objects that have moved by themselves and walls that shake and rattle—just like on a topsy-turvy ship.

Landmark Inn (Marquette, Michigan)

A certain romance surrounds sailors and their lives on the water. In the 1930s—shortly after the Landmark Inn first opened its doors—a local librarian fell in love with a sailor on leave from his ship on Lake Superior. He planned one last trip before returning to marry her, but neither the sailor nor his ship ever returned. It is said that the librarian died of a broken heart shortly thereafter; she is thought to haunt the Landmark Inn's Lilac Room, where her apparition looks out over the lake, awaiting the return of her lost love. Men who have stayed in this room have reported having tricks played on them: Their keys don't always work in the lock, objects are moved around the room, and they receive phone calls in the middle of the night—with no one on the other end. The hotel's front desk has also received phone calls *from* the Lilac Room when the room was vacant.

Pfister Hotel (Milwaukee, Wisconsin)

Professional sports teams like to psych out their opponents, but putting them up in a haunted hotel might be a bit extreme! Actually, the elegant Pfister Hotel in downtown Milwaukee has all the amenities that professional baseball and basketball players appreciate; the ghosts are just incidental.

The specter of hotel founder Charles Pfister is thought to look out over the grand staircase to make sure that guests are well cared for. Other spirits have been noted near the ballroom, and odd noises are heard in several of the guest rooms. Longtime MLB manager Tony La Russa says that guests get first-class service at the Pfister, and if there happen to be a few ghosts, "they're good friends." But just to be safe, some baseball players always request to share rooms when they're in Milwaukee, and one sleeps with his bat when his team stays at the Pfister.

Ontario School Hosts Ghostly Visitors

Ghosts probably don't care about the architecture of their earthly domains, but the Collegiate Gothic style of the three-story Dundas District Public School in Dundas, Ontario, does set the scene for a haunting quite nicely. Built in the late 1920s, the edifice was originally a high school that later became part of the Hamilton School District. It was closed in 1982 when two newer high schools were built. Over the years, the school often housed younger students, but it closed for good in 2007. A developer plans to turn the structure into condos, but a few residents are already calling the place home—they're just a bit invisible.

Ghost Train

Some say that ghosts are likely to inhabit the sites of terrible tragedies. If that's the case, the Dundas District Public School is certainly a place that calls out to the spirit world. The story is both picturesque and sad: On Christmas night in 1934, two trains collided outside of the Dundas train station, which is near the school building. Fifteen people were killed and many more were injured. The local hospital was unable to handle so many victims on such short notice, so the school's basement was used as a makeshift morgue. Are some passengers still looking for their loved ones? Or are they trying to find the way to their final destination?

The Janitors' Pact

Whether it's urban legend or the gospel truth, one story states that a group of five custodians who worked at the old school were curious about the Other Side. They made a pact that whichever of them died first would come back and make his presence known.

The idea originally came from Russell, the janitor in charge of the third floor. Ever the perfectionist, Russell took care of the rooms on his floor as if they were home to royalty. Coincidentally, Russell was the first of the group to pass away—and some say that he was the first to return.

Housekeeping High Jinks

Veronika Lessard was one of the custodians that experienced this helpful ghost firsthand. She said she sometimes felt that she was being watched while she worked. That might make a person feel a bit uncomfortable, but if the ghost pitched in to help, who could complain?

Veronika was assigned to the third floor, just as Russell had been. One night, she left her bucket in Room 306 while she went to eat with her coworkers. When she returned, her bucket had been moved, and Room 306 had been cleaned from top to bottom. Was it Russell?

On another occasion, Veronika was working in Room 305 when she heard the jingling of keys and assumed that it was one of her coworkers. Tony, another custodian, entered the room and heard the sound too. When Veronika challenged the ghost to show itself, she saw the shadow of a tall, lanky man stroll by the door jangling his keys.

Another night, Tony observed five shadow people walking down the back stairs. He and Veronika both heard whistling, and one evening, both swore that they heard someone call out, "Help me."

Former principal Peter Greenberg laughed at the tales until he experienced something strange himself. One Saturday morning, Greenberg entered the building by himself after a security guard told him that the school's alarm had gone off, but no footprints were found in the dew. That's when locker doors began to bang. Greenberg called the police, who arrived just in time to hear glass breaking and other noises coming from the third floor. When they reached the top of the stairs, the racket suddenly stopped, and no one was found.

From a Dog's-Eye View

A Dundas resident named Kay liked to walk her dog in the vicinity of the old school. One evening, she sat down under a tree to rest. Feeling as though someone was watching her, Kay looked around but couldn't see anyone nearby. That's when she noticed her dog staring up at the third floor of the abandoned school. The school's lights started to flicker, and her dog began to bark. Kay is certain that it was Russell, but what he was trying to tell her is still a mystery.

Was this the ghost of Russell? Or was it the spirit of a train passenger who met an untimely demise so many years ago? Many think that Russell and the other ghosts have made the old building their eternal home.

Fort Delaware Prison
Hosts Ghosts Through the Ages

Pea Patch Island. Sounds quaint, doesn't it? Hardly the name of a place that you'd imagine would host a military prison ... or the ghosts of former inmates who still can't seem to escape, even in death. But then, the hardships and horrors that were experienced there might just trump the loveliness that the name suggests.

Shaped like a pentagon, Fort Delaware Prison was completed in 1859, just prior to the Civil War. With a moat surrounding its 32-foot-high walls, it was a very secure place to hold Confederate POWs.

With no extra blankets or clothing, Fort Delaware's inmates struggled to keep warm and suffered through the cold, harsh winters that are typical in the Mid-Atlantic region. Malaria, smallpox, and yellow fever were commonplace, and they traveled quickly through the facility; estimates suggest that between 2,500 and 3,000 people may have died there—and many tormented souls seem to remain.

Now Appearing...

One ghost that has been seen by many workers at the Fort Delaware Prison—which is now a living-history museum—is not the spirit of a prisoner at all: It's that of a former cook who now spends her time hiding ingredients from the current staff. Visitors have reported hearing a harmonica in the laundry area, where a ghost has been spotted threading buttons in a long string.

In the officer's quarters, a spectral child is known to tug on people's clothes and a ghostly woman taps visitors on the shoulder. Books fall from shelves, and chandelier crystals swing back and forth by themselves.

And then there are the darker, more sinister spirits—the ones that suffered in life and found no relief in death. Moans, muffled voices, and rattling chains fill the basement with spooky sounds

of prisoners past. The halls echo with noises that resemble the sounds of someone trying to break free from chains. Apparitions of Confederate soldiers have been seen running through the prison, and sailors have witnessed lights on shore where there were none. Screams and desperate voices plead for help, but so far, no one has been able to calm these restless souls.

Ghost Hunter Endorsed

If you're searching for proof that these ghosts are the real deal, check out a 2008 episode of *Ghost Hunters* that was shot at Fort Delaware. Jason Hawes, Grant Wilson, and their team of investigators found quite a bit of paranormal activity when they visited the old prison. In the basement's tunnels, they heard unexplained footsteps and voices, as well as something crashing to the ground. A thermal-imaging camera picked up the apparition of a man who appeared to be running away from the group. And in the kitchen, the investigators heard a very loud banging sound that seemingly came from nowhere.

In the Spirit of Things

It's not *all* terror at the old prison. Today, Fort Delaware is part of a state park that's open to tourists and offers many special programs. One event that appeals to athletes and history buffs alike is the "Escape from Fort Delaware" triathlon: Each year when the starting musket blasts, participants reenact the escape route of 52 inmates who broke out of Fort Delaware Prison during the Civil War.

During the Civil War, so much misery was experienced at Camp Sumter—a prison for captured Union soldiers near Andersonville, Georgia—that the absence of a haunting there would be remarkable. It only served as a POW camp for a little more than a year, but during that time, 13,000 Union soldiers died there. Captain Henry Wirz, who was in charge of the prison, was hanged after the war for conspiracy and murder. His angry spirit still wanders the compound, and many visitors have smelled a vile odor that they attribute to his ghost.

Atchison, Kansas: A True Ghost Town

*According to census records, approximately 10,000 people
call Atchison, Kansas, home. While this is a good indication
of how many people live in the town, it doesn't measure
another important piece of data: how many ghosts reside there.
Considering the ratio of ghosts to living residents, Atchison could
quite possibly be the most haunted town in the United States.*

Madam of the Missouri River

One of Atchison's oldest ghost stories traces its origin back more than
a hundred years, when what is currently Atchison Street was called
Ferry Street. This road travels down the side of a steep hill and
ends at the Missouri River. In years past, the riverside site was used
to board ferries, and legend has it that a woman lost control of her
buggy and crashed into the water, where she drowned. Her lonely
spirit supposedly tries to lure men into her watery grave.

Mournful Molly of Jackson Park

Jackson Park is the site of a purported haunting by a female spirit
named Molly. One story suggests that Molly was a black woman who
was lynched by a mob for having an affair with a white man. Another
version indicates that Molly was a high school girl who fought with her
date on prom night, leaving his car in disgust and entering the park; the
next morning, her body was supposedly found hanging from a tree with
her dress torn and tattered. Other stories contend that after Molly's
boyfriend broke up with her, she jumped to her death from a high
ledge in the park. Whoever the female spirit is, she often moans and
unleashes shrill screams in the park around midnight, and some
claim that they have seen her ghostly figure hanging from a tree.

The Abandoned Baby of Benedictine College

Two dorms at Benedictine College—a Catholic university founded in
Atchison in 1858—are haunted: one by a baby and the other by one
of the school's founding monks. The monks protect the school, and

one has often been sighted at Ferrell Hall. The ghost-baby resides in Memorial Hall; legend has it that a female student once gave birth in the closet of her dorm room, but the newborn died. Several residents of Memorial Hall have reported feeling a phantom baby in their beds at night. Even more terrifying, one woman was trapped in her closet when a dresser mysteriously moved in front of the door while she was inside. Her roommate was not there, so she had to scream for help. Another student reported that her desk chair suddenly began to rock back and forth. And yet another woman awoke around 3 A.M. to see a shadowy figure going to and from her closet; in the morning, she discovered that her possessions had been tossed onto the floor.

The Phantom Fryer

There truly is no rest for the weary at Muchnic House on North Fourth Street in Atchison. Legend has it that a maid died in the building when she fell down the back stairs one Sunday morning. Her spirit has been known to turn lights on and off, and residents have also experienced the inexplicable scent of bacon frying. In 2005, a visitor who was taking a tour of the house—which is now an art gallery—saw a young woman dressed in a maid's uniform peering at the group from the top of the stairs. However, when the group arrived upstairs, no one was there.

Deal with the Devil

The Gargoyle Home on North Fourth Street is named for the menacing gargoyles that decorate the facade of the house, which is rumored to be cursed. The gargoyles were supposedly built to honor the original owner's pact with the devil; when a subsequent owner tried to remove the gargoyles in an attempt to make the house more pleasant, he fell to his death. In 2005, when the Travel Channel sent a paranormal investigation team to Atchison, the researchers equipment detected the presence of ghosts in the building.

A Really Friendly Ghost Can Be So Helpful

A beautiful two-story home on the corner of Fifth and Kearny Streets offers a great living space—as well as a helpful, friendly ghost. Once, a gentleman who lived in the house received help putting on his coat; he assumed that it was his wife, but when he turned around, nobody was there. Another time, while driving home from an event, the

man's wife commented that she would love a cup of tea. The kindly spirit must have heard her because when the couple arrived at home, they discovered that hot water was in the kettle, and a cup, spoon, and tea bag were waiting for them. The couple also heard sounds coming from the attic when it was empty and experienced the mysterious scented of clover wafting through the house.

When Ghosts Don't Get Their Way...Watch Out!

Although every ghost story is unsettling in its own way, a restless spirit at Sallie's House might just be the most disturbing specter in a town full of them. This building on North Second Street once served as a doctor's office; the physician lived with his family upstairs and ran his practice on the ground floor. One night in the early 1900s, a girl named Sallie was brought to the office. It is unclear whether she had a severe respiratory infection or her appendix burst, but in any event, she died.

Sallie's spirit seems to have been reawakened in 1993, when a couple moved into the house with their young child. Sallie liked to rearrange the child's toys while the family was out, turn appliances on and off, and move pictures so that they hung upside down.

But Sallie was not the only spirit in the house: Allegedly, another ghost physically attacked the husband. A psychic told the couple that this spirit was in her thirties and that she had fallen in love with the husband. (Sallie told the medium that she did not like this other ghost.) The malevolent spirit tried to turn the man against his wife, but when that didn't work, the entity became violent. Just before the jealous spirit attacked the man of the house, the room grew very cold. Then, suddenly, scratches and welts appeared on his arms, back, and stomach. After the ghost tried to push the man down the stairs, the couple moved out. The malevolent haunting stopped, but in 2005, audio recordings picked up the sounds of children playing while the house was empty.

Take the Trolley and See Them All

These sites—and others—are all part of the popular Haunted Atchison Trolley Tour. The company that conducts this tour says the town has enough haunted sites to fill an itinerary of three full days, so it rotates its routes frequently.

FRIGHTENING FACTS

Prison Phantoms

- In 1878, Henry Wells of Carrollton, Alabama, stared out of the window of his jail cell, nervously watching the mob that had gathered to lynch him. The curiosity seekers got their man, but Henry's fearful face still appears on the window's glass, no matter how often the jail replaces it.

- A housing development in Citrus Heights, California, stands on the site of a former holding camp for Japanese nationals and Japanese Americans who were awaiting internment during World War II. From time to time, residents still see the ghosts of Japanese couples wandering about, looking as forlorn as one might expect people awaiting imprisonment to appear.

- For underdressed Confederate POWs, the prison camp on Lake Erie's Johnson's Island was a frozen hell. Over the years, visitors have seen the haggard figures of phantom Rebel soldiers and have even heard them singing the song "Dixie," which was the de facto anthem of the Confederacy.

- The majority of the paranormal activity at Alcatraz—America's most notorious prison—takes place in Cells 11D through 14D, which is where visitors often hear unexplained, disembodied voices and experience a profound sense of sorrow and extremely low temperatures.

- In Tolland, Connecticut, several spirits haunt the Benton Homestead, which has a long history that dates back to 1720. During the Revolutionary War, some German mercenaries who were in British service were confined to the building's cellar. One particular ghost seems reluctant to leave: He appears dressed in full Hessian uniform.

- In 1784, when the Spanish colonel in charge of Castillo de San Marcos—a fort in modern-day St. Augustine, Florida—found out that his wife had been unfaithful, he chained her and her lover up and then walled them in. Her spirit still prowls the fort in a white dress.

Dead Men Tell Tales

In recent years, American moviegoers have gone gaga over pirates. Perhaps the most famous buccaneer of all was Edward Teach, better known as Blackbeard. His career was built on fear and intimidation, and apparently he hasn't changed—even in death.

The Devil of the Deep Blue Sea

Blackbeard's reign of terror on the high seas lasted for more than two years. During that time, he commanded a fleet of captured vessels and ambushed any ship he pleased. He pillaged and murdered up and down the East Coast until he turned himself in and was pardoned in July 1718.

After receiving his pardon, it didn't take long for Blackbeard to return to a life of piracy. In November 1718, Virginia Governor Alexander Spotswood ordered Lieutenant Robert Maynard to capture Blackbeard. On November 22, Maynard and his men finally caught up with the famed pirate and his crew just off Ocracoke Island. A battle ensued, during which Blackbeard and Maynard exchanged gunfire. The men then drew their swords, and Blackbeard managed to break Maynard's blade, but before he could kill the officer, a member of Maynard's party slit Blackbeard's throat. It took a total of 5 gunshot wounds and 20 sword strokes to bring down the notorious pirate, and to ensure that he was dead, he was decapitated; his head was suspended from the bowsprit of Maynard's vessel.

Home Is Where the Head Is

Since that fateful day, Blackbeard's bloody specter has been seen on Ocracoke Island carrying a lantern, apparently searching for his missing head. The island is known locally as "Teach's Hole," and visitors and residents alike have reported seeing his phantom swimming along the shore at night; some have even watched him rise up from his watery grave and continue his search along the shore. Fishermen in Pamlico Sound have dubbed any strange lights viewed on North Carolina's Outer Banks "Teach's Lights." The few souls brave enough

to follow the unearthly glow of Blackbeard's lantern ashore never find footprints or other signs of life when they investigate. Try as he might to find his missing head, some local legends suggest that Blackbeard is looking for his noggin in the wrong place.

Death to Spotswood!

In the 1930s, North Carolina judge Charles Whedbee claimed to have seen Blackbeard's skull. According to the judge, when he was in law school at the University of North Carolina, he was invited to join a secret society. His induction into the group involved a large silver chalice and the chanting of the mysterious phrase, "Death to Spotswood." Whedbee was told that a silversmith had made the cup from Blackbeard's skull after stealing it from atop a pole at the mouth of the Hampton River more than two centuries prior. The macabre chalice seems to have been lost to time, but it isn't the only treasure that Blackbeard is said to have left behind.

Blackbeard's Lady

Another legend suggests that Blackbeard left two treasures on Lunging Island—which is located off the coast of New Hampshire—during his reign of terror. One was a large amount of silver; the other was his 13th wife. Over the years, several expeditions have undertaken quests to find the missing treasure, but always to no avail. However, many people have encountered the wispy figure of a woman wandering along the beach at night. Legend has it that she was Blackbeard's wife and that she was left behind to guard his loot.

When Teach returned to North Carolina, he was offered a pardon and was also granted Mary Ormond's hand in marriage. The pirate decided to settle down with Ormond—the daughter of a wealthy plantation owner—but clearly, domestic life was not for him: The excitement of pillaging on the high seas got the best of him, and it was there that he met his doom shortly thereafter.

Blackbeard never returned to Lunging Island—at least not while he was alive. Although the ghostly woman is said to whisper, "He will return," she apparently doesn't recognize the headless specter that also reportedly wanders the island. Whether he's come back for his treasure or is searching for his missing head, Blackbeard's ghost still roams the Atlantic coast.

"Lotz" of Ghosts Gather at Carter House

Franklin, Tennessee, which is located about 20 miles south of Nashville, has a population of 62,000—unless you count its ghosts. The site of what some historians consider the bloodiest one-day battle of the Civil War, Franklin is rich with history—and restless spirits. It seems that many of the soldiers who lost their lives in that famous battle are still hanging around the city.

Before the Blood

In 1830, Fountain Branch Carter built a beautiful home in the heart of Franklin. In 1858, Johann Lotz constructed his own house across the street on land that he'd purchased from Carter. Both were blissfully unaware of what would occur there just a few years later.

After the fall of Nashville in 1862, Franklin became a Union military post. In 1864, in an attempt to "take the bull by the horns," the Confederate army decided to attack the enemy head-on in Franklin, hoping to drive General Sherman's army north. It didn't quite work out that way; instead, during the Battle of Franklin on November 30, 1864, more than 4,000 lives were lost, and because the battlefield was small, the concentration of bloodshed was very high. And most of it took place right in front of the Lotz and Carter homes.

The Battle Begins

When the Confederate troops arrived in town, Union General Jacob Cox commandeered the Carter House as his base of operations. Fearing for their lives, the Carter family took refuge in the basement during the five long hours of the battle. In all, 23 people—including the Lotz family—crowded into the cellar. They all survived, and when the fighting was over, both houses were converted into field hospitals. Surgeries, amputations, and death filled the days and weeks that followed. Between the violence and the chaos, it's no wonder that some of the dead never found peace.

One of the men who was killed during the battle was Tod Carter, Fountain's son and a Confederate soldier who was thrilled to be

heading home. He was wounded just 300 feet from his front door and was taken to his sister's bedroom, where he later died. Some say that his spirit remains there today.

History Comes to Life

In 1953, the Carter House was opened to the public. Today, it's a museum and a National Historic Landmark; its eight acres stand as a tribute to the battle that took place there so long ago. If you look closely, more than a thousand bullet holes can be found on the property. The Lotz House—which was added to the National Historic Register in 1976 and opened to the public in 2008—bears its share of scars as well: Bloodstains are evident throughout, and a round indentation in the wood floor is a reminder of a cannonball that crashed through the roof and flew through a second-floor bedroom before landing in the parlor on the first floor, leaving a charred path in its wake.

In the Spirit of Things

Visitors to the Carter House have reported seeing the specter of Tod Carter sitting on a bed or standing in the hallway. His sister Annie has also been spotted in the hallways and on the stairs. She's blamed for playful pranks such as rolling a ball along the floor and causing objects to appear and disappear. But then again, the mischief-maker might be the spirit of one of the children who took refuge in the cellar during the battle. After all, staff members and visitors have reported feeling the sensation of a child tugging at their sleeves, and one worker even saw a spectral child walking down the staircase.

The ghosts of soldiers and other family members may be responsible for some of the other unusual phenomena experienced in the house, such as furniture moving on its own, doors slamming, and apparitions peering through the windows.

Not to be outdone, the ghosts at the Lotz House manifest as phantom voices and household items that move on their own or come up missing. While they haven't been identified, they seem to be civilian spirits rather than military ones. It's tough sharing space with so many ghosts, but the staff members are used to it, and they're happy to share the history—and the spirits—with visitors who stop by on the Franklin on Foot Ghost Tour. And don't worry: These lively spirits have never followed anyone home—at least not yet.

These Haunted Libraries Contain More Than Just Spooky Stories

In the blockbuster film Ghostbusters *(1984), a team of paranormal investigators encounters the ghost of an elderly woman reading a book while floating amongst the stacks at the New York Public Library. When they speak to her, she shushes them; after all, libraries are supposed to be quiet places—even ghosts respect that rule! However, the team persists, which causes the sweet specter to transform into an evil entity. Think it can only happen in the movies? The ghosts at the following libraries will make nonbelievers think again.*

Amelia Gayle Gorgas Library, University of Alabama (Tuscaloosa, Alabama)

From 1883 to 1907, Amelia Gayle Gorgas served as the first female librarian at the University of Alabama. She is believed to haunt this facility, which was built in 1939 and named in her honor. She makes her presence known by stopping the elevator on the floor that holds the special collections—even when the elevator bank is locked down. When the doors open, the errant elevator is always empty.

A. B. Safford Memorial Library (Cairo, Illinois)

Resident spirit "Toby" likes to hang out on the second floor of the A. B. Safford Memorial Library. Staff members have heard his footsteps at night, and he's been blamed for the creaking noises that a rocking chair makes even when no one is in it and it's not moving. Toby has also been known to switch lights on and off. And library employees once witnessed a "ghostly light" emerge from behind a desk and travel down a hall before vanishing in the stacks.

Lee County Library (Tupelo, Mississippi)

The Lee County Library was constructed in 1971, on the site of the former home of Congressman John Mills Allen. Although the house was torn down, some of its original features were used in the library, including the glass panels and doors in the Mississippi Room. Apparently, Allen's spirit remains as well. Whenever staff

members find books removed from shelves and spread across the floor, the congressman is deemed responsible. His ghost is also blamed for removing items from the book drop.

Hutchinson Public Library (Hutchinson, Kansas)

After librarian Ida Day Holzapfel died in 1954, she began to hang around her former place of employment, the Hutchinson Public Library. One day in 1975, a librarian saw a strange woman hovering below the stairs, and after describing what she had seen to a coworker, her colleague identified the visitor as Holzapfel. Footsteps and disembodied voices have been heard in the basement, and some witnesses have glimpsed Holzapfel's apparition in the stacks.

Millicent Library (Fairhaven, Massachusetts)

In 1893, Henry Huttleston Rogers founded the Millicent Library, which he named for his daughter, who had died at age 17. Bathed in blue light, Millicent walks the halls during the day and stands in the turret window at night. But apparently, she's not alone: Witnesses have also seen a woman dressed in black running her fingers along the books. And a man wearing a purple bow tie, a tweed jacket, and small round glasses has been spotted mopping the basement floor.

Detroit Public Library—Skillman Branch (Detroit, Michigan)

The Skillman Branch of the Detroit Public Library occupies the site of a former jailhouse where, in the early 1800s, prisoners were routinely executed. These tormented souls make their presence known by moaning and mumbling. They can be so disruptive that the stacks sometimes reverberate with the unsettling sounds.

The Carnegie Library Branch of the St. Joseph Public Library (St. Joseph, Missouri)

After hours, the ghostly footsteps of "Rose," who is thought to be a former librarian, are heard traipsing across the second floor. Although Rose is also blamed for phantom whispers and giggles, she takes her job very seriously and has been known to shush patrons. Rose also likes to reshelve books, but she often puts them in the wrong place.

Capitol Ghosts in Raleigh, North Carolina

Ghosts abound in North Carolina, but Raleigh—the state's capital since 1792—seems to be home to more than its share of playful poltergeists. The ghost of former governor Daniel Fowle haunts the North Carolina Executive Mansion, which has been the official residence of the state's governor since 1891. But whereas the governor's mansion holds just one ghost, the State Capitol is practically overflowing with spooks, almost all of whom prefer to make their presence known late at night.

Weird Sounds

Longtime security guard Owen Jackson reported numerous encounters with the ghosts of the Capitol building. On several occasions, he heard the sound of books falling in the authentically restored state library on the third floor. But when he investigated the noises, no books were missing from the shelves or found on the floor.

Once in 1981, Jackson heard the sound of glass breaking on an upper floor; he fetched a broom to clean it up, but he found all of the windows intact and nothing else was broken. And on several occasions, Jackson heard mysterious footsteps and the sound of the building's elevator moving from floor to floor, as if transporting unseen visitors.

Another time, Jackson was sitting at the receptionist's desk preparing to make his rounds when he felt a hand rest on his shoulder. He quickly whirled around, but no one was there.

Watchful Wraiths

Jackson isn't the only person who has encountered the Capitol's ghosts. Late one evening, curator Raymond Beck felt the eerie sensation that someone was looking over his shoulder as he shelved some books in the building's library. After it happened a second time, Beck didn't wait around for it to happen again—he finished his chore and left as quickly as possible.

Later, Beck told Sam Townsend Sr., an administrator at the Capitol building, about his bizarre experiences. Townsend admitted

that he, too, had heard and felt things there that he couldn't explain. One evening in 1976, for example, Townsend was finishing up some paperwork when he heard a key rattling in the lock of the Capitol's north entrance. He assumed that it was Secretary of State Thad Eure returning to his office to catch up on some work (as was his habit), but when Townsend went to say hello, Eure was nowhere to be found. As Townsend stood near the north entrance, he suddenly heard keys rattling at the south entrance. He searched the building from top to bottom but found no logical explanation for the mysterious noises.

On another occasion, Townsend was again working late when he heard footsteps approaching from elsewhere on the same floor. Thinking that it was Beck, Townsend went to Beck's office to let him know that he was there too, but the room was empty. Townsend heard the same phantom footsteps on several occasions and always at the same time—8:30 P.M.

Seen and Heard

Townsend is one of the few people to see the Capitol ghosts as well as hear them. Once, Townsend walked by the Senate chamber on his way to his office and was startled to see someone standing just inside the chamber's doorway. But when he checked to make sure that his eyes weren't deceiving him, the figure had vanished.

Another time, Townsend almost bumped into a ghost that floated by him in the rotunda. Recalling the incident, Townsend said that he stepped aside quickly so as to "avoid a collision."

Owen Jackson also caught a glimpse of one of the spirits that dwells within the Capitol building. One night after he finished his rounds, he turned off all but the security lights, checked all the doors, and then exited the building and walked to his car. As he waited for his vehicle to warm up, Jackson glanced up and saw a man walk past an illuminated window on the second floor. According to Jackson, the figure was wearing the uniform of a Confederate soldier.

Rather than investigate, Jackson simply went home. As he later told a reporter, "I figured anybody [that's] been dead that long, I didn't want to tangle with him."

These Lighthouses Harbor Spirits

There's something beautiful about the simplicity of lighthouses:
They stand high above the water and shine their beacons
to guide weary sailors home. But there's also something
about lighthouses that seems to attract spirits. Ghosts of
sailors and lighthouse keepers alike seem to find it hard
to leave this earthly plane. Here are a few lighthouses
that harbor phenomena that are a bit otherworldly.

St. Augustine Light (St. Augustine, Florida)

Visitors to the St. Augustine Light—one of the most haunted
places in a very haunted city—have heard phantom footsteps on
the tower stairs and observed a tall man who haunts the basement.
Some have reportedly heard the laughter of two girls who
drowned in 1873 while their father was working on the property.
There's also a prankster ghost that likes to play tricks on staff
members by relocating merchandise in the gift shop. And several
times a week, someone reports the smell of cigar smoke wafting
from the tower—even though no one else is around.

Gibraltar Point Lighthouse (Toronto, Ontario)

Toronto's Gibraltar Point Lighthouse doesn't hide its ghostly
secrets—it announces them outright: A plaque on the property
warns visitors that the site is thought to be haunted. According
to legend, in the early 1800s, two drunken soldiers killed the
lighthouse's first caretaker, John Paul Rademuller, but his body
was never found. (In the late 19th century, another caretaker
unearthed some human bones, which gave credibility to the tale.)
Today, unexplained lights appear in the windows, bloodstains have
reportedly been found on the stairway, moaning can be heard, and
the ghostly figure of a man is seen walking on the beach nearby.

White River Light Station (Whitehall, Michigan)

Listen for the tap-tap-tapping of Captain William Robinson's cane
as he continues to tend to his former home—the White River
Light Station—even though he died in 1919, just two weeks after

he was forced to retire at age 87. No scandal or tragedy occurred at this lighthouse; Robinson and his wife simply loved their home of 47 years so much that they've apparently found it impossible to leave. Mrs. Robinson has been known to help out by doing some light housekeeping, leaving display cases cleaner than they were without the help of human hands.

St. Simons Lighthouse (St. Simons, Georgia)

In 1880, an argument between lighthouse keeper Frederick Osborne and his assistant John Stevens ended with a fatal gunshot that killed Osborne. Stevens was arrested, but he was acquitted of the murder, and he subsequently took over tending the lighthouse. He later said that he could hear strange footfalls on the spiral staircase to the tower. Subsequent caretakers, their families, and visitors have also heard the same slow tread on the tower's 129 steps.

Boston Light (Boston, Massachusetts)

The ghost that resides at the Boston Light is thought to be that of a sailor who was once guided by the beacon. Cold spots, phantom footsteps, empty rocking chairs that move back and forth on their own, and something eerie that makes cats hiss are all hallmarks of this haunted lighthouse. These are all typical behaviors for a ghost, but this one does have its quirks: Coast Guard members on the premises report that whenever they turn on a rock-and-roll radio station, the receiver suddenly switches to a classical music channel further down the dial.

Heceta Head Lighthouse (Yachats, Oregon)

Home of Rue (aka "the Gray Lady"), this former lighthouse is now a bed-and-breakfast. It is believed that Rue was the mother of a baby who was found buried on the grounds. Perhaps she feels the need to stay and protect her child, but if that's the case, she finds plenty of other ways to stay busy: Objects are moved, cupboard doors open and close by themselves, and a fire alarm was once mysteriously set off. Although Rue doesn't seem to mean any harm, she once frightened a workman so terribly that he accidentally broke a window and fled, leaving broken glass all over the floor. That night, workers

heard a scraping noise coming from upstairs; in the morning, they found that the broken glass had been swept into a nice, neat pile.

Barnegat Lighthouse (Barnegat, New Jersey)

If you travel with children, you may draw the attention of the ghosts at the Barnegat Lighthouse. According to legend, a couple was on a ship off the New Jersey coast when a severe storm struck. Feeling that the ship was safe, the man decided to stay aboard, and his wife stayed by his side. They did, however, send their baby ashore with one of the ship's mates. Although the ship survived the storm, the couple was not so lucky: They froze to death that winter night. Now, on cold, clear nights in January and February, their spirits approach other parents who are out for a stroll with their own infants. The friendly ghosts typically compliment the parents on their beautiful baby, and then they quickly disappear.

Seguin Island Lighthouse (Seguin Island, Maine)

Lighthouses can often be lonely places; this was the case for the wife of one of the Seguin Island Lighthouse's early caretakers. At great expense, her husband had a piano brought to the lighthouse for her. But she had only one piece of music, which she played over and over, until one day, her husband went insane. He took an ax to the piano and then to his wife and then killed himself. Death may not be the escape he hoped for, however: People still report hearing faint strains of the tune that his wife played incessantly.

Fairport Harbor Light (Fairport Harbor, Ohio)

Lake Erie's Fairport Harbor Light is home to an unusual spirit: a ghost cat. This old lighthouse was abandoned in 1925 and later became a museum; its curator was the first person to see the spectral kitty with golden eyes and gray fur. They became friendly, and the curator even threw socks for the cat to chase. In life, the animal most likely belonged to the last family who tended the lighthouse; when the caretaker's wife became ill, she was comforted by a small kitten that loved to chase a ball down the hall. In 2001, workers found a mummified cat in a crawl space; the little guy must have gotten trapped and was unable to get out.

Haunted Hotels

Full Moons Are for Werewolves, but Ghosts Gather at the Crescent

While werewolves must lead boring lives waiting for the next full moon, the ghosts at the Crescent Hotel in Eureka Springs, Arkansas, keep themselves busy all the time. Some say that the fresh spring water that runs beneath the hotel might attract spirits. Or perhaps it's the building's rich history that draws them there.

The Early Years

Built in 1886 to cater to the many visitors who flocked to the curative elements of the hot springs located nearby, the Crescent Hotel was billed as the grandest inn west of the Mississippi when it opened. And many folks wanted to stay at this elegant resort.

But perhaps it was *too* grand: The upkeep became unmanageable, and the hotel began to fall into disrepair. Financial difficulties forced the resort to close its doors in 1907. A year later, the building reopened as the Crescent College and Conservatory for Young Women; it served as a junior college from 1930 to 1934.

Then, in 1937, Norman Baker bought the property and converted it into a hospital and "health resort." Although he had no medical degree, Baker *considered* himself a doctor. However, the state of Iowa, where he had been living, didn't agree and kicked him out for practicing without a license. So Baker moved—with his patients in tow—to Eureka Springs, where he declared that he had found a cure for cancer: drinking the area's natural spring water. After he was hauled off to jail for fraud, the hospital sat empty for many years before it was opened as a hotel once again.

A Gathering of Ghosts

Hospitals, colleges, and hotels are typically hot spots for ghosts, so it's no surprise that this building is filled with them. Today, at least four spirits are known to haunt the Crescent Hotel. One is the ghost of a young woman who most likely attended college there in the 1920s or '30s. She is thought to have committed suicide by jumping from

the roof—or perhaps she was pushed. Either way, the trauma of the event was more than enough to keep the poor girl's spirit earthbound.

And if you see a nurse wearing clothes from the 1930s or '40s, don't be alarmed: It's just the ghost of a woman who likely worked there when the hotel was used as a hospital. She's often seen pushing a gurney down a corridor.

More in keeping with the hotel's image as the "grand lady of the Ozarks," the apparition of a man in a top hat and tails has been seen in the lobby on several occasions. It's believed to be the ghost of Dr. John Freemont Ellis, a frequent visitor to the resort during its glory days in the late 1800s. Near the elevators, visitors often smell smoke from his pipe.

Not Camera Shy

After hearing the tantalizing tales about the resort, Jason Hawes and Grant Wilson of the television show *Ghost Hunters* visited the Crescent Hotel in 2005. They hit the paranormal jackpot when their thermal-imaging camera caught the "Holy Grail" of the ghost-hunting world: a full-bodied apparition. The form seemed to be that of a man wearing a hat and nodding his head. Hawes and Wilson said that in 20 years of paranormal research, they'd only captured a full-bodied apparition on camera a handful of times.

Most Talked-About

The most famous ghost at the Crescent is "Michael," a spirit that haunts Room 218. In 1886, during the building's construction, an Irish stonemason was working on the property when he fell from the roof and landed in what is now Room 218; he was killed instantly. Guests have heard pounding noises coming from inside the walls and other strange sounds in this room. Some visitors have reported

hearing Michael cry out in terror, as if reliving his fatal fall. Ever the prankster, Michael has been known to manipulate the room's doors, lights, and television set. Some terrified guests have even witnessed hands that seem to come out of the bathroom mirror. Incidentally, Room 218 is the most requested room at the Crescent Hotel. Go figure.

Other rooms at the Crescent that are popular with ghosts and ghost hunters alike include Room 202 (in which a wispy apparition was photographed in a closet) and Room 424 (in which numerous ghosts have appeared). Guests have also reported seeing the spirit of a waiter carrying a tray and walking down the hallway past Room 424.

Apparitions have also been observed sitting around a table in the lobby, and a ghostly bearded gentleman wearing Victorian clothing and a top hat has been seen loitering in the lobby and sitting at the bar, where he stares straight ahead. Former bartenders have told stories about glasses and whiskey bottles that suddenly rose from the shelves and then crashed back down. Apparently, someone thinks that he or she is not being served quickly enough.

Today, the Crescent Hotel offers the best of both worlds: the modern amenities that guests expect while providing the romantic ambiance of yesteryear. And if you happen to see a few spirits lingering, just smile and realize that for some people, things never change.

In downtown Austin, Texas, across the street from the state capitol, the governor's mansion has been the site of drama, victory, tragedy, and hauntings. Former governor Sam Houston is said to haunt the mansion. Legend has it that he's hiding from his third wife, who, in life, tried to reform him into a sober, churchgoing man. Apparently, he'd rather spend his afterlife without her.

The Sisters of Kemper Hall

Kemper Hall—which is situated on the shore of Lake Michigan in Kenosha, Wisconsin—is one of the Dairy State's oldest buildings. The structure originally served as the home of Wisconsin's first congressman, Charles Durkee. When he became governor of the Utah Territory in 1865, Durkee donated the estate to the Kenosha Female Seminary. In 1878, the Sisters of Saint Mary took over the property, renamed it Kemper Hall, and turned it into a preparatory school for girls—and that's when many of its ghostly stories began.

The Spectral Sister Superior

Perhaps the most famous of the ghost stories involving Kemper Hall revolves around Sister Margaret Clare, the school's first Sister Superior and the embodiment of the stereotypical stern parochial-school nun. Sister Margaret Clare was well liked in her order, but students knew her for her demanding nature and unrelenting temper. One legend says that the nun met her end when an angry student pushed her down the spiral staircase that led to the school's observatory; other rumors suggest that she fell down the stairs after tripping on her own habit. Not surprisingly, the observatory and staircase still attract visitors. Many who have peered down the stairwell at night claim that they have glimpsed her shattered body staring back at them from the bottom. The problem with these tales is that Sister Margaret Clare actually died of natural causes in 1921. Still, the reports of the fallen nun persist; perhaps it's a different nun.

A Mysterious Disappearance

Sister Margaret Clare may have gone to her grave harboring a sinister secret about the mysterious disappearance of another nun: Sister Augusta. In 1899, Sister Augusta arrived at Kemper Hall for an annual retreat; but shortly thereafter—on January 2, 1900—she vanished without a trace. Some said that she'd been driven to the edge of madness by the amount of work she'd been given and was granted a time-off request. But her disappearance seemed suspect to

316

authorities, who undertook a search that stretched all the way back to Sister Augusta's hometown of St. Louis, Missouri. Then, on January 5, Kemper Hall sent word to the nun's family and the authorities that Sister Augusta had been found, safe and sound, in Springfield, Missouri. However, the school failed to offer an explanation for why she had left behind her handbag, her crucifix, and her insignia of the holy Sisterhood. Just three days later, Sister Augusta's body

washed up on the shore of Lake Michigan. Her death was ruled a suicide, and to this day, locals still report seeing a spectral nun in tears walking along the beach. Many maintenance workers and watchmen have also reported hearing a woman sobbing in Kemper Hall late at night, but when they investigate, they find no one. Sister Augusta may well be the crying nun that so many hear, but she does not cry alone.

Picture of the Paranormal

Kemper Center, Inc., has not allowed paranormal investigators to access Kemper Hall since it took control of the building shortly after the school closed in 1975. But much of the property is now a public park, and on several occasions, nighttime visitors have seen a nun— perhaps Sister Augusta or Sister Margaret Clare—peering at them from the windows of the former school. People visiting Kemper Hall for wedding receptions have also reported hearing crying and footsteps in hallways that are clearly unoccupied by the living.

In 1997, a television crew from WTMJ in Milwaukee filmed a story at the original Durkee Mansion. The shoot went off without issue, but when the crew was editing the footage, they found that the picture turned to static every time a portrait of Charles Durkee entered the frame. It seems that the Sisters of Kemper Hall have maintained an ethereal presence in the building, but perhaps they're not the only spirits who still consider the place home.

Anguished Spirits Haunt Abandoned Mental Hospitals

The setting alone is enough to raise goose bumps: Mental hospitals—especially those that operated during times when medicine and treatments were ineffective or tortuous—are synonymous with loneliness, pain, and despair. And moans, groans, and screams can still be heard at the following facilities... even though most of them are long abandoned.

Athens Mental Health Center (Athens, Ohio)

After the Athens Mental Health Center closed in 1993, the state of Ohio purchased the property, and today, much of it is used by Ohio University. In December 1978, patient Margaret Schilling went missing and was found dead a month later on the top floor. Her body left such an imprint on the floor that the wrinkles in her clothing and the details of her hairstyle can still be seen to this day; the area has been cleaned countless times, but the outline remains. Employees say that at night, Margaret's ghost walks the halls of the old building—which is now known as Lin Hall—along with the spirits of other people who once lived there.

Bartonville State Hospital (Bartonville, Illinois)

At the Bartonville State Hospital (also known as the Illinois Hospital for the Incurable Insane), four on-site cemeteries served as burial grounds for the many unfortunate souls who died there. The best-known ghost there is that of a patient called "Old Book," who dug graves until his own death. Hundreds of people attended his burial, and they all saw the same thing—the spectral figure of Old Book standing next to a tree crying; that tree is now known as the Graveyard Elm or the Crying Tree. The hospital closed in 1973, but the building and the grounds are listed on the National Register of Historic Places.

Ghost researcher Rob Conover has visited the abandoned site numerous times and feels certain that it is haunted. He tells of an unexplained force that once prevented him from opening unlocked doors. He also videotaped an apparition in a corridor of the building.

Other visitors have also seen ghosts there and describe residual hauntings—replays of events that took place in the hospital when mentally ill patients lived there many years ago.

Byberry Mental Hospital (Philadelphia, Pennsylvania)

Byberry Mental Hospital closed in 1990 due to the alleged mistreatment of the people in its care, so it's not surprising that it's home to an angry ghost that is thought to be the spirit of a former patient. This unhappy spirit likes to chase visitors who dare to venture into the property's underground tunnels and catacombs. Did we mention that this phantom figure carries a machete?

Lakeshore Psychiatric Hospital (Etobicoke, Ontario)

The Toronto Ghosts and Hauntings Research Society calls the Lakeshore Psychiatric Hospital (also known as the Mimico Hospital for the Insane and the Mimico Insane Asylum) one of the "busiest" haunts in the city, based on the number of ghost sightings that it receives. Once one of the nicest mental hospitals of its day, the facility boasted beautiful grounds, a caring staff, and even planned activities for the patients. But anyplace where more than 1,500 deaths occurred is bound to be haunted—and the Lakeshore Psychiatric Hospital doesn't disappoint in that regard. Phantom whistling, loud sighs, and cold gusts of air are just some of the ghostly phenomena that take place there.

Rolling Hills Asylum (Bethany, New York)

Often cited as one of the most haunted places in America, the Rolling Hills Asylum certainly has a few stories to tell. At least 1,750 people died on the property, although the actual number is probably much higher. Needless to say, a sad energy lingers in the halls of this facility, which closed in 1974. Since then, paranormal investigators have captured voices, images, and videos of the spirits that remain there. At least two particular apparitions have been witnessed there, and people on the second floor have heard footsteps coming from above; this might not seem all that unusual until you realize that the building has no third floor! (Read more about this haunting on page 456.)

Northern State Mental Hospital (Sedro-Woolley, Washington)

Built in 1912, the Northern State Mental Hospital was intended to treat nonviolent but mentally unstable patients. Because it was a humane facility with beautiful grounds and educational and vocational opportunities for the patients, it quickly became known as *the* place to send the mentally ill. But all that changed in 1950, when Dr. Charles Jones took over the hospital. He began performing a new, innovative, and highly experimental procedure known as the trans-orbital lobotomy, which involved slicing into the brain to disable certain functions. The exact number of deaths that occurred at this hospital is unknown, but it is estimated to be around a thousand. One ghost, which is known simply as "Fred," enjoys tossing pans and other objects through the air. Witnesses have also spotted the apparitions of a young girl playing with a red ball and her father chasing after her.

Friends Hospital (Philadelphia, Pennsylvania)

Founded in 1813, this hospital once served as the home of the building's superintendent and his wife. Doors open and shut on their own, and random laughter has been reported coming from empty rooms. Third-shift employees have often witnessed these odd events; some have even seen the ghostly figure of a woman—thought to be the superintendent's wife—roaming the halls at night.

Trans-Allegheny Lunatic Asylum (Weston, West Virginia)

As if being in a mental hospital wasn't tough enough, the patients who lived at the Trans-Allegheny Lunatic Asylum (which operated from 1864 to 1994) faced harsh conditions due to limited funds: The heating, cooling, and lighting systems all had problems; the facility did not have enough furniture to go around; sanitation was poor; and the meals were far from appetizing. It's no wonder that the ghosts that remain there are anguished. Visitors to the abandoned building have caught glimpses of spirits roaming the halls and have heard phantom crying, screaming, and whispered conversations.

Weston's Tea Room Dishes Up a Healthy Serving of Ghosts

Old buildings with rich histories tend to have an abundance of ghosts. People who lived and died in these places sometimes feel an earthly pull that keeps them from crossing over into the afterlife. Such is the case with the Tea Room in Weston, Missouri.

Founded in 1836, Weston's population reached 5,000 people by 1850, but then tragedy struck: Two major floods, two fires, and the Civil War all devastated the city, and by 1870, its population had dwindled to just 900 residents. In 1881, flooding of the Missouri River shifted it two miles away from the town—forever.

Thanks to all of those disasters, the area is ripe for paranormal activity. And this tiny town of about 1,600 (living) residents doesn't disappoint in that regard. A great deal of ghostly phenomena occurs at the Tea Room of the Main Street Galleria. For more than 50 years beginning in the early 1900s, the ground floor of this building—which is located at 501 Main Street—housed a pharmacy that was run by Beno and Creola Hillix; the couple lived in the upstairs apartment that the Tea Room now occupies. Because they were childless, the couple may have felt the need to remain in this world a while longer. (Beno got his nickname from his trademark phrase, "When we're gone, there will be no more.")

Some of the older residents of Weston still remember Beno smoking his Lucky Strike cigarettes downstairs, and even though the building is now smoke-free, guests often smell the unmistakable odor of cigarette smoke there today. The ghostly pair also loves to play tricks, often moving objects around and hiding them. In addition, diners and staff have heard Beno and Creola speaking from far away.

The pies at the Galleria Tea Room are delicious at any time of year, but if it's spirits you're looking for, stop by for Weston's Ghost Tales celebration in October or settle in for a chat with the café's owner any day; she's always happy to serve up a little slice of ghostly lore.

Making Fun of Fear:
The *Scary Movie* Franchise

When the Wayans Brothers released Scary Movie *in 2000,
they likely didn't expect that the film—or its sequels—would
become a cultural sensation. Read on for some background
information on the flicks that make fun of freaking out.*

Scary Funny

The original *Scary Movie* film was the brainchild of Marlon and
Shawn Wayans, two members of the prolific Wayans family. While
watching horror movies one summer, the brothers decided that it was
high time for a parody of fright flicks—and they had plenty of material
to spoof. Huge horror hits such as *Scream* (1996), *I Know What You
Did Last Summer* (1997), *The Blair Witch Project* (1999), *The Sixth
Sense* (1999), as well as others that had recently been released,
seemed to offer endless opportunities for jokes.

Of course, Marlon and Shawn had plenty of classic films to mine,
too: With their predictable and formulaic plots, *Halloween* (1978),
Friday the 13th (1980), and their numerous sequels, as well as other
horror movies like them, were also ripe for the spoofing. Nobody had
ever made such a film before, and the Wayans team was determined
to get it right. Keenan Ivory Wayans—the older brother of Marlon
and Shawn—was tapped to direct the film, and, in 1999, production
began on *Scary Movie,* which had a budget of just $19 million.

The Original *Scary Movie*

Scary Movie (2000)—the original (and most successful) film of the
series—is a spoof that can hang with the best of the lampoon genre:
It's rife with sight gags and sexual innuendos similar to those found in
movies such as *Airplane!* (1980) and *The Naked Gun* (1988).

The film featured mostly relative unknowns, including a young
Anna Faris, who portrayed protagonist Cindy Campbell. The Wayans
team initially wanted an African American lead, but they realized
that if they wanted to spoof the genre, they had to play by its rules,

which dictate that a Caucasian high-school girl with more beauty than brains should lead her clueless friends to their doom.

Audiences came out in droves to watch the movie: It earned a whopping $42 million in U.S. box-office sales over its opening weekend, knocking out the previous week's champion, the hotly anticipated George Clooney/Mark Wahlberg film *The Perfect Storm* (2000). In just two weeks, the Wayans Brothers' silly movie raked in $110 million. The film was more successful than anyone had ever imagined it would be; a sequel was inevitable.

More, More ... More?

Just as some classic horror flicks seem to spawn endless sequels, *Scary Movie* became a bona fide franchise: In July 2001, *Scary Movie 2* was released in U.S. theaters. It was widely panned by critics, who said that its creators were relying on the success of the first movie and didn't offer anything new. The gross-outs were grosser and the sexual content was more provocative, but audiences were less excited by the concept. Still, the film opened with $20 million in box-office sales, which was enough for its producers. A third *Scary Movie* was scheduled to begin shooting shortly thereafter.

In *Scary Movie 3* (2003), moviegoers continued to follow Cindy Campbell, who by then was out of college and investigating strange phenomena in her town. The movie spoofed popular films that had been released around that time—such as *Signs* (2002) and *The Ring* (2002)—but the public was tiring of the *Scary Movie* series. *Entertainment Weekly* even went so far as to say that the *Scary Movie* series was "a franchise that needs to stop." Audience interest dwindled, and box-office numbers were lukewarm. But was the *Scary Movie* franchise dead? No way!

Three years later, *Scary Movie 4* (2006) hit theaters and surprised naysayers by bringing in $40 million during its opening weekend. Sure, it had a budget of $45 million, but in movie terms, those are good numbers. Who knows if the frighteningly popular series will have another installment: Like one of the brain-eating zombies that the films make fun of, the Wayans Brothers' creation may continue to live on.

 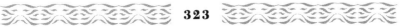

The Haunting of the Holly Hotel

The Holly Hotel in Holly, Michigan, is more than just a historical landmark—it's allegedly a hotbed of paranormal activity. But are the stories surrounding the place fact or fiction?

A Hotel with a Future

In the 1860s, America's railway systems were enjoying epic expansion. As tracks were laid, more people and more products than ever before were crisscrossing the nation. Major midwestern cities such as Detroit and Chicago were bustling, and the need for hotels near stations was growing because they served locals and travelers alike.

Built in 1863, the Holly Hotel (originally called the Hirst Hotel after its first proprietor, John Hirst) and the surrounding area certainly looked different in that era than they do today. Back then, the building was larger than it is now, and Martha Street—on which the Holly stands—was lined with taverns that hosted brawls so often that it was dubbed "Battle Alley" (a nickname that persists to this day). It might've been rough-and-tumble outside the hotel, but inside, the Holly boasted hot water, elegant rooms, fine dining, and a large staff, which set a tone for luxury that continues to this day, even though the establishment is only a restaurant now.

In 1912, Hirst sold the hotel to Joseph P. Allen, who renamed it "the Holly Inn." But in 1913, a massive fire completely destroyed the building's second and third floors. Hirst, once a cigar-smoking, boisterous host, was crushed by the loss of the beautiful hotel that he'd built; when he passed away seven years later, the townspeople said that he never overcame the grief that he suffered following the devastating fire. Enter the Holly Hotel's first ghost.

Employees have long said that John Hirst haunts the Holly. The smell of cigar smoke is often perceived at the bar, even when no one is smoking. And over the years, numerous visitors have spotted the figure of a man wearing a frock coat and a top hat, and disembodied laughter is frequently heard traveling from the stairs down to what was once the hotel's lower-level parlor.

A Fiery Déjà Vu and More Ghostly Figures

Even if you don't believe in spooks, it's hard not to be freaked out by the fact that in 1978—exactly 65 years to the day *and hour* of the first disastrous fire—the Holly Hotel burned again. Although no one was killed, the fire caused more than a half million dollars of damage. The building was repaired, and once again, stories about ghosts roaming the halls came pouring in.

The spirit of Nora Kane—a frequent visitor to the hotel in her days among the living—still lingers at the Holly. When photographers are contracted to shoot weddings at the restaurant—a popular place for receptions due to its lush Victorian decor and fine food—they're warned that apparitions or strange shadows may obscure some of their photos. On the websites of paranormal investigators who have visited the Holly, wispy, cloudlike strands can be seen in images of the stairwell. Is it a trick of photography, or is Nora Kane walking into the shot? Guests and employees have also claimed to hear her singing near the piano when things get too quiet.

One of the most active spirits at the Holly Hotel is that of a fiery red-haired girl who likes to play with a meat cleaver in the kitchen. Disembodied giggles and footsteps have been reported there, and during a séance in the 1990s, the girl allegedly manifested. It is believed that, in life, she was either the daughter of Nora Kane or a young girl who died tragically after sustaining injuries at the livery stable that once stood adjacent to the hotel.

Other unexplainable phenomena at the hotel include sudden drops in temperature, floating orbs, phantom barking and the sound of a dog running down the halls, and appearances of a Native American figure that vanishes as quickly as it arrives.

Not Just a Ghost Motel

The legacy of the Holly Hotel is worth studying, regardless of potential spirit activity, and the proprietors tend to focus on promoting it as a historical landmark and fine-dining establishment. High tea is held there weekly, and the grounds are often used for private events.

But for those who believe in ghosts, it remains a popular destination. Often cited as one of the most haunted places in America, the Holly Hotel may hold secrets that none of us can unlock—at least not on this plane of existence.

Married to the Mob...Even in Death

When people hear the phrase "mob haunts," they generally think of places where members of the Mafia or other gangs congregate. But the following locations are literally haunted by their connections to organized crime. Whether they are spreading cautionary tales or committing acts of revenge, these restless spirits are trying to ensure that no one ever forgets what happens when you tangle with the mob.

Never Leaving Las Vegas

The ghost of Benjamin "Bugsy" Siegel is a very active spirit, which is not surprising considering that he was one of the most famous mobsters in history. By the time he was a teenager, Brooklyn-born Siegel had started a gang with friend Meyer Lansky on New York's Lower East Side. In the 1920s, Siegel's activities in gambling, bootlegging alcohol, and stealing cars caught the attention of the New York underworld. He was sent to California to watch over the mob's gambling operations and to arrange the murders of its enemies, which he often carried out himself; he also became obsessed with Las Vegas.

Siegel's dream—which he convinced the mob to finance—was to turn this little oasis in the desert into the most glamorous gambling destination in the United States. This dream became a reality in December 1946, when he opened the Flamingo casino and hotel. The Flamingo got off to a slow start, so mob bosses demanded that Siegel turn business around—or else. By 1947, he believed that the enterprise had become successful, but what he didn't know was that the bosses had already condemned him to death. On June 20, 1947, Siegel was killed in a hail of gunfire at the Beverly Hills home of his mistress Virginia Hill.

Siegel died instantly, but his spirit never really left the scene of the crime. Since then, witnesses have watched in awe as a spectral male figure suddenly appears, runs across the mansion's living room, ducks for cover, and then disappears. A psychic verified that the man was none other than Bugsy Siegel, who seems to be condemned to spend eternity trying to evade his killers.

However, just as in life, Siegel is also drawn to Las Vegas. His spirit was seen hanging out in the Flamingo's Presidential Suite (which was his home in life) by the pool table and in the two bathrooms, and guests reported moving cold spots and objects in the suite that inexplicably changed locations or disappeared entirely.

Even after the Flamingo was demolished in 1993, Siegel's ghost continued its residency. He's been observed in the new hotel's wedding chapel and in the rose garden near a monument dedicated to him. It seems fitting that the spirit of a man who took so many lives is doomed to prowl his old stomping grounds for all eternity.

Dark Spirits Torment La Palazza

Given that the mob essentially built Las Vegas, it is not surprising that many gangster ghosts call the town their eternal home. Some of Sin City's darkest spirits seem to congregate at a mansion known as "La Palazza." For years, rumors suggested that the house contained a room that was used exclusively for murders, and a former owner found guns hidden under the floorboards there.

Previous residents experienced multiple disturbing incidents while living in the house. For example, a former owner's dog would tremble and follow an invisible entity with its eyes. This man later saw what had disturbed his dog: a spectral older woman wearing a wide-brimmed hat and large sunglasses.

The same man and his girlfriend once watched as wineglasses moved by themselves and then crashed down onto the tabletop. The girlfriend also claimed that disembodied male voices repeatedly harassed her, especially while she showered. In addition, she heard voices coming from the attic and saw the ghostly figure of a tall man. When a medium asked this spirit what his business was, he replied that he "did whatever needed to be done" when he was alive.

Another former owner—a self-proclaimed skeptic—admitted that he heard mysterious voices coming from the attic, even though it was unoccupied.

The spirits of the house seemed to negatively influence its male residents. One man had the sensation that unseen hands were choking him and felt that the dark energy of the house was possessing him. After uncovering bloodstains in what might have been the room that was used for executions, he became prone to fits of rage and began

carrying a gun. He decided to sell the house before it caused him to do something that would ruin his life.

In 2010, the team from the TV show *Ghost Adventures* visited the mansion to investigate. Interviews with the former homeowners left the team members so concerned that they were dealing with a demonic entity that they brought a crucifix and holy water with them when they were locked inside the house overnight. While they were there, fully charged batteries were instantly drained, cameras blacked out when ghosts were asked to show themselves, and the readings on the team's EMF detector spiked. And just as one of the previous owners had experienced, the physical features and temperament of investigator Zak Bagans seemed to transform throughout the session. The team concluded that the place is full of dark energy, perhaps due to the heinous deeds committed at the site and the spirits of those who remain.

Is that Really John Dillinger?

Phantom mobsters also continue to spook the city of Chicago. Less than a mile from the site of the St. Valentine's Day Massacre (see page 173), another gangster ghost supposedly roams an alley near the Biograph Theater, which is located at 2433 N. Lincoln Avenue. On July 22, 1934, notorious bank robber and Public Enemy No. 1 John Dillinger was supposedly shot and killed by FBI agents after watching a movie at the Biograph. His death was widely reported in the media, although some said that the corpse was not that of Dillinger but rather a low-level gangster who had been set up to impersonate him.

Regardless of who died there, people have since observed the hazy figure of a man fleeing, only to fall and then disappear. Others have reported feeling cold spots and inexplicable chilly breezes.

No Escape from Their Actions

Some mobsters meted out violent deaths and met brutal ends; others were caught by the law and imprisoned for their crimes. And a fortunate few lived long lives, during which they were never held accountable for their dastardly deeds. Wherever they are, in life or death, mobsters and gangsters leave their marks. No matter how they finished out their lives on earth, it seems that some members of the mob remain eternally restless.

McRaven House:
The Most Haunted House in Dixie?

Located near Vicksburg, Mississippi, the McRaven House was haunted even before it became a Civil War hospital.

The oldest parts of the estate known as McRaven House were built in 1797. Over the next 40 years, its owners gradually added to the property until it became a classic southern mansion, standing proudly among the magnolia blossoms and dogwood trees of the Old South.

And like nearly all such mansions, it has its share of resident ghosts. Today, McRaven House is often referred to as "the most haunted house in Mississippi." Some researchers believe that environmental conditions on the property make it particularly susceptible to hauntings: Ghosts that may not be noticeable in drier, less humid climates seem to be more perceptible in the dews of the delta. Of course, it helps that the McRaven House has seen more than its share of tragedy and death during its 200-year history.

The Ghost of Poor Mary

In the early 1860s, the house's supernatural activity seemed to center on an upstairs bedroom in which Mary Elizabeth Howard had died during childbirth in 1836 at age 15. Mary's brown-haired apparition is still seen descending the mansion's grand staircase. Her ghost is blamed for the poltergeist activity—such as pictures falling from the wall—that is often reported in the bedroom where she died. And her wedding shawl, which is occasionally put on display for tourists, is said to emit heat.

Ghosts of the Civil War

Mary Elizabeth's ghost alone would qualify McRaven House as a notably haunted reminder of Mississippi's antebellum past, but she is far from the only spirit residing there, thanks in part to the bloody atrocities of the Civil War.

The Siege of Vicksburg, which took place in 1863, was one of the longest, bloodiest battles of the entire conflict. When General Ulysses S. Grant and his Union forces crossed the Tennessee River into Mississippi, Confederate forces retreated into Vicksburg, which was so well guarded that it was known as a "fortress city." But as more and more Union forces gathered in the forests and swamps around Vicksburg, Confederate General John C. Pemberton was advised to evacuate. Fearing the wrath of the local population if he abandoned them, Pemberton refused.

By the time the siege began in earnest, the Confederate troops were greatly outnumbered. Rebel forces surrendered the city of Vicksburg on July 4, 1863, after more than a month of fighting. Nearly all of the Confederate soldiers involved in the battle—around 33,000 in all—were captured, wounded, or killed. The Union victory put the entire Mississippi River in northern hands, and combined with the victory at Gettysburg that same week, it marked the beginning of the end for the Confederacy.

Captain McPherson's Last Report

In the middle of the action stood McRaven House. In the early days of the siege, it served as a Confederate hospital, and, at that time, it was full of the screams of anguished and dying men. Cannons from both armies shot at the mansion, destroying large portions of it.

Later, after Union forces captured the house, it served as the headquarters for General Grant and the Union army. One of the officers put in charge of the house was Captain McPherson, a Vicksburg native who had fled to the North to fight for the Union. Sometime during the siege, he disappeared. Soon after, according to legend, McPherson's commanding officer awoke to find the

 captain in his room. He was furious at the intrusion until he noticed McPherson's mangled, bloody face and torn uniform. The commanding officer then realized that this was not McPherson himself— it was his ghost, which had returned to deliver the message that Rebels, who couldn't forgive him for abandoning the South, had murdered him. McPherson's

ghost reputedly still wanders the grounds dressed in Union blue with blood oozing from a bullet wound in his forehead.

Other Civil War Ghosts

Nearly a year after the siege ended, John Bobb—the owner of McRaven House at the time—spotted six Union soldiers picking flowers in his garden. Outraged by the trespassers, Bobb threw a brick at them and hit one of the Yankees in the head. After going to the local field commander to report the intruders, Bobb returned home to find 25 Union soldiers waiting for him; they marched him into the nearby bayou and shot him to death. His ghost has been seen roaming the property ever since.

The War Ended, But the Ghosts Kept Coming

Mary Elizabeth and the Civil War–era ghosts aren't the only spirits that haunt McRaven House. In 1882, William Murray purchased the home, and over the next 78 years, five members of his family died on the premises. The most recent death there was that of his daughter Ella, who spent her last years as a recluse in the house, where she reportedly burned furniture to stay warm. After her death in 1960, the mansion was restored, refurbished, and opened for tours and battle reenactments. In the early morning hours, tour groups and staffers have often spotted the ghosts of Ella and the other Murrays who died in the house.

The Most Haunted House in the South?

Today, visitors can tour the McRaven House in all of its antebellum glory. Extensive collections of 19th-century furnishings, artwork, jewelry, and other artifacts are displayed at the mansion, and several ghosts from both sides of the Civil War are believed to share the house with Mary Elizabeth and the other spirits from the mansion's past. Ghost hunters have been conducting investigations at the house since at least the 1980s, and they've frequently photographed mysterious forms outside the building, often around the portion of the property that served as a burial ground for soldiers; some are simply odd blobs of light, but others appear to be human-shaped forms.

Few argue with the claim that McRaven House is "the most haunted house in Mississippi." In fact, some even call it "the most haunted house in Dixie."

The Residents of Lourdes Hall

In 1990, Lourdes Hall opened its doors on the campus of Winona State University in southeastern Minnesota. Since then, students have learned that they are not the dorm's only residents.

The College of St. Teresa

Lourdes Hall was originally part of the College of St. Teresa, an all-women's Catholic school that was known for its nursing program. When St. Teresa's closed in 1989, the building was sold to Winona State; after all, with its heated swimming pool and large cafeteria, Lourdes Hall made for an attractive addition to the university—even if it was rumored to be haunted.

Priestly Indiscretions

Many of the stories about the building center on the tragic tale of a young woman named Ruth, who lived and died in Lourdes Hall during the 1920s. According to legend, Ruth was a nursing student at St. Teresa's, who became pregnant by a young Franciscan priest named Father William. For the duration of her pregnancy, Ruth hid herself in the infirmary on the fourth floor of Lourdes Hall. After giving birth, she tried to keep her baby, but fearing that his indiscretion would be exposed, Father William threw the infant down an elevator shaft. Unable to deal with the shame and heartbreak of this experience, Ruth committed suicide by throwing herself down the third-floor stairwell. Then, likely realizing that he had made every wrong choice that a person in his situation could make, Father William hanged himself in the vicinity of where the swimming pool is now located. Because the school was located in a mostly Catholic small town, the deaths were covered up, and most people hoped that the controversy would fade with time. But you can't forget something that refuses to be forgotten.

Shared Housing

Most students at WSU don't know about Ruth or Father William when they move into Lourdes Hall, but they soon learn their sad

story. On the first floor, students wandering the halls toward the building's only elevator hear footsteps behind them, but when they turn around, they find that they are alone. The elevator leads to the laundry facilities in the basement, and more than one student has decided to wait out the spin cycle in his or her dorm room after the elevator doors open multiple times for no reason. At night, students wonder if the high-pitched noises that they hear are coming from a squeaky dryer—or if they're the unanswered cries of Ruth and William's murdered baby. It might seem that there's a reasonable explanation for these phenomena, but how do you explain Ruth's continued presence in her old room?

Room 4450

As is the case at many universities, on-campus housing is a valuable commodity at Winona State, and very few can afford to turn down a room—even if it's haunted. For years, residents on the fourth floor of Lourdes Hall have reported hearing strange sounds at night. A knock at the door may turn out to be no one at all, and footsteps heard echoing through the hall at night might come from an unseen source. But the students residing in Room 4450—Ruth's old room—always leave with stories. Oftentimes, posters and other decorations will fall off the walls; beds will be overturned when residents are away; and, no matter how many blankets Mom sends from home, it's impossible to stay warm in Room 4450. Ruth makes her presence known in her room and perhaps elsewhere in the building, but there is one place that she seems to avoid.

Night Swimming

It would seem that a pool in a college dorm would be very busy, but at Lourdes Hall, swimmers report feeling as if they're being watched, and rumor has it that if a student dares go for a nighttime swim alone, he or she is guaranteed to see the specter of Father William hanging from the rafters. The disgraced priest—condemned by his own actions—hates being alone, and many students have felt clammy hands tugging on their ankles while they swim at night.

Living with the ghosts of Lourdes Hall may not be easy, but the students who reside there know that one day they move out. For Ruth and Father William, however, Lourdes Hall is their eternal home.

The USS *Hornet:*
The Spirits of World War II Live On

The USS Hornet *is a floating piece of history. This World War II–era aircraft carrier is as long as three football fields, and in her heyday, she housed a hospital, a tailor shop, a cobbler shop, three barbershops, and seven galleys. The recipient of nine battle stars for military service, the* Hornet *could carry 3,500 sailors. During World War II, her pilots destroyed 1,410 Japanese aircrafts and almost 1.3 tons of enemy cargo. But in her 27 years of service, the* Hornet *saw 300 deaths from battles, accidents, and suicides; in fact, this ship is believed to hold the Navy record for the most suicides. If that isn't enough to produce a ghost or two, what is?*

It's a Strange, Strange World

Considered one of the most haunted ships in history, the USS *Hornet* now sits docked at the Alameda Naval Air Station in California. Since completing a storied military career, the ship has become a naval museum—which happens to be full of ghosts.

Since the *Hornet*'s arrival in Alameda, tourists and staff members have noticed some very strange phenomena aboard the old ship. In fact, several websites are devoted to reporting strange happenings on the *Hornet,* all of which are noted by regular people who just happen to experience them. Many witnesses were self-proclaimed skeptics who are now believers.

The paranormal activity on the USS *Hornet* includes unusual noises, items that come up missing, and apparitions. Psychics and ghost hunters who have investigated the abnormal occurrences there agree that the ship's spirits are probably the souls of departed sailors who died abruptly. Perhaps they're still trying to carry out their final orders.

Many people report feeling that someone touched or grabbed them when no one else was in sight. There's no need to be afraid, though, because almost all accounts describe friendly spirits. In fact, many of the ghosts—which are primarily men—are quite

the pranksters. And oddly, not all of them seem to be naval men: Members of other branches of the military—dressed in their respective uniforms—have also been spotted onboard.

No place is off limits to these free spirits. Those who have seen the ghostly figures on the ship say they are so real-looking that they blend in with the living. They appear dressed in uniform, patrolling the hallways and performing their shipboard duties. They've also been spotted on decks, climbing ladders, in bathrooms, and in the Combat Information Center. Toilets mysteriously flush by themselves, lights turn on and off on their own, and men are heard talking in areas where no one else appears to be present.

The Spirits of World War II

The steam room is one of the most haunted sections of the USS *Hornet,* probably because it was one of the most dangerous areas of the ship. One sailor who died in the steam room is thought to remain there. Some say that because he died so quickly, he doesn't realize that he's dead.

Not all the ghosts on the USS *Hornet* are American. One spirit that has appeared to many visitors is that of a Japanese pilot who was a prisoner of war on board the ship during World War II; he allegedly went mad in the small cell in which he was kept. He still inhabits that room—and he's still trying to get out.

Another ghost that has been seen on the ship quite often is that of Admiral Joseph "Jocko" Clark, who served as the vessel's commander during World War II. After calling the *Hornet* home for so many years, it seems that his spirit may have sought out the place where he felt most at home. Even decades after his passing, he's still married to the sea.

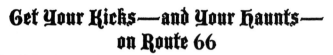

Get Your Kicks—and Your Haunts— on Route 66

Route 66 was the historic two-lane highway that guided travelers from Chicago to Santa Monica, California, by way of small rural towns. Although it may no longer appear on maps, portions of the windy road that passed through eight states can still be traveled today. And as befits a ride through the past, plenty of ghosts can be found along the way.

The Mill (Lincoln, Illinois)

Designed to look like a Dutch windmill, The Mill originally opened in 1929 as a quaint restaurant known as The Blue Mill. Travelers on Route 66 could stop in at any time, day or night, to enjoy a tasty grilled sandwich served by a waitress dressed in a blue dress with a white apron. The restaurant was famous for its fried schnitzel, but rumors suggested that notorious Chicago gangster Al Capone had buried at least one body near the building.

Unfortunately, as interstate highways replaced Route 66, drivers bypassed small towns such as Lincoln, and The Mill fell on hard times. In the mid-1980s, the restaurant was replaced by a museum that displayed oddities such as a mechanical leg that emerged from the ceiling. The museum closed in 1996, but Illinois Route 66 enthusiasts launched a campaign to save The Mill. During a paranormal investigation at the building in 2009, no apparitions were seen, but the researchers sensed their presence. A few investigators felt as if their hair, shoulders, and arms were being touched, even though no one else was nearby. Others experienced cold sensations on their necks, and photos revealed orbs and inexplicable beams of light. Worst of all, several members of the team were overwhelmed by a sense of dread, the words "Help me," and symptoms of drunkenness, including dizziness and headaches.

Tri-County Truck Stop (Villa Ridge, Missouri)

Like The Mill, the Tri-County Truck Stop was a restaurant that Route 66's drivers appreciated for its grub. It is now closed, but former employees and customers shared many stories about

strange things that occurred there. Several of these reports centered on the basement, where a misty figure was seen pacing back and forth and hot and cold spots would suddenly pop up despite a lack of ventilation. A paranormal research team investigating the basement had a lightbulb thrown at them from some 50 feet away, even though they were the only living beings there at the time. A former employee said that she'd also had objects thrown at her when she was the only person in the building.

All over the building, doors open and shut by themselves. At least two people witnessed a spectral man stab a ghostly woman on the stairs that used to lead to apartments and an office on the top floor; the next day, a red stain appeared on the wall. Another person saw chairs moving themselves into a circle on the top floor. One former patron said that he hated going there because he felt as though he was being watched all the time, even when he was in the bathroom.

Oklahoma's Spook Light
The Tri-State Spook Light (aka the Hornet Spook Light) is an orb that appears almost nightly near Quapaw, Oklahoma. While many claim that it's merely the headlights from cars on Route 66, the phenomenon was witnessed in the area long before cars were even invented; in fact, local Native American tribes knew of it centuries ago. The orb maintains a careful distance from those who gather to see it; it pulses and varies in intensity and then disappears when cars on the road approach it. Many theories speculate as to what (or who) the orb is: Some believe that it's the ghost of a miner carrying a lantern; others believe that it is two Native American lovers who killed themselves because their romance was forbidden; and still others speculate that it is a solitary Native American, or even a portal to another world.

The Nat (Amarillo, Texas)
The old Amarillo Natatorium—affectionately known as The Nat— has had a long life with many identities, and those who enjoyed it most are reluctant to leave. The structure was initially used as a natatorium—a building housing an indoor pool—but in 1926, when the pool was covered with a wood floor, it became a dance

hall. During its heyday, The Nat played host to legendary acts such as Benny Goodman, Louis Armstrong, and Buddy Holly; oddly, a sign advertising "Monty McGee and His Orchestra" has reappeared through every coat of paint administered to the structure's exterior since 1942. In the 1990s, when the building housed an antique mall, several people commented on strange cold spots in some of the stores. Often, storeowners would arrive in the morning to find that the furniture in their shops had been rearranged overnight. People also witnessed a female ghost with red wine stains on her white dress, and a spectral couple was spotted dancing in the former ballroom. When a paranormal research team spent a night in the building in 1996, cameras mysteriously shut themselves off, but a tape recorder captured a woman singing and a phantom drummer playing a tune. The past was obviously too much fun for these playful spirits to let go.

KiMo Theatre (Albuquerque, New Mexico)
In 1951, Bobby Darnall was just six years old when the boiler at the KiMo Theatre exploded and killed him. The boiler was located in the lobby behind the concession stand in the 1927 Pueblo Deco–style building; Bobby had been watching a film with his friends but decided to get a snack. Just as he approached the concession stand, the boiler blew; the force of the explosion demolished part of the lobby. These days, employees appease Bobby's hungry spirit by leaving doughnuts on a pipe that runs along the back wall of the theater, behind the stage. If any doughnuts remain the next morning, they sometimes contain child-sized bite marks. Bobby has also been seen playing by the stairs wearing jeans and a striped T-shirt, but he is not the only ghost in the theater: A woman in a bonnet has also been seen roaming the building, but she generally keeps to herself. The KiMo Theatre closed in 1968, but it was restored and reopened in 2000, just in time for Route 66's 75th anniversary celebration.

Hotel Brunswick (Kingman, Arizona)
For the most part, the ghosts at the Hotel Brunswick seem to be friendly, and some are downright playful. A spectral young girl has been seen in the dining room, and elsewhere in the hotel, several

guests have seen a small ghost-child, who seems to be seeking a playmate. Others have reported that something tugged on their legs or feet while they were sleeping. One family woke up in the morning to discover that their necks had yellow marks on them. (Fortunately, the marks washed off easily with soap and water.) Old coins were found in stacks lined up in hallways and near the bar, which a former owner interpreted as the spirits letting him know that prosperous times were ahead. Another owner saw a ghostly man walking up the stairs when he opened the cellar door; he got chills as the figure passed right through him. Guests have experienced similar shadow phenomena in the second-floor hallway. It is not known who most of these ghosts were in life, but some believe that one of the spirits is W. D. McKnight, a wealthy gentleman who died in his room at the Hotel Brunswick in 1915. Although it can be a bit unsettling to bunk with a ghost, no one has reported any harmful encounters with the hotel's resident spirits.

Colorado Street Bridge (Pasadena, California)

When the Colorado Street Bridge opened in Pasadena, California, in 1913, it was one of the many impressive bridges that Route 66 crossed before it terminated in Santa Monica. But these days, it is commonly referred to as "Suicide Bridge" because it is believed that 100 to 200 people have ended their lives by jumping off this high span; many of these deaths took place during the Great Depression. But the high suicide rate can't be blamed entirely on economic circumstances because the first one occurred there only six years after construction was finished. It is also believed that a construction worker died there six months before the bridge was complete, when he fell off the structure into a concrete pit supporting a pillar; his body was never recovered, but legend has it that his ghost lures people to follow him.

Many people have witnessed a spectral woman in a flowing robe throwing herself off the bridge. She may be the ghost of a mother who flung her baby and then herself from the span in 1937. (The baby actually landed on some treetops and survived.) People have also heard strange cries coming from the canyon 150 feet below the bridge.

Bachelor's Grove:
America's Most Haunted Cemetery?

🪦 🪦 🪦 🪦

*Hidden inside the Rubio Woods Forest Preserve near Midlothian,
Illinois, lies Bachelor's Grove Cemetery, which is thought to
be one of the most haunted cemeteries in the United States.
Haunted or not, this site certainly has an intriguing past
that raises many questions but provides few answers.*

Abandoned and Vandalized

Like almost everything associated with the cemetery, the very origins
of Bachelor's Grove are cloaked in mystery. Some claim that the
location got its name in the early 1800s when several unmarried men
built homes there, which led locals to nickname the area "Bachelor's
Grove." Others, however, believe the name was actually "Batchelder's
Grove," after a family that lived in the area.

Despite its small size (about an acre), the cemetery became
popular because of its convenient location right off the Midlothian
Turnpike. The quaint pond at the rear of the site added to its allure,
and as a result, about 200 individuals made Bachelor's Grove their
final resting place.

All that changed during the 1960s, when the branch of the
Midlothian Turnpike that ran past the cemetery closed, cutting the
graveyard off from traffic. With the road to it essentially abandoned,
people stopped coming to the cemetery. The last burial at Bachelor's
Grove took place in 1965, although an interment of ashes did occur
in 1989.

Without a proper road leading to it, Bachelor's Grove fell into a
state of disrepair. Due to the cover of the Rubio Woods, the cemetery
became an attractive location for late-night parties, vandalism, and
senseless desecration. Today, of the nearly 200 graves at the site, only
20 or so still have tombstones; the rest have been broken or stolen.
This—combined with rumors that some graves have been dug up—
is why many believe that the spirits of Bachelor's Grove do not
rest in peace.

Glow in the Dark

Who haunts Bachelor's Grove? For starters, the ghost of a woman dressed in white has been spotted late at night walking among the tombstones and sitting on top of them. Because she seems oblivious to those around her, it is thought that this is a residual haunting—a replaying of a sad time in her life when she would visit the grave of her child. So many people have seen her throughout the years that she is commonly known as "the Madonna of Bachelor's Grove." In the early 1990s, a paranormal research group claimed to snap a photo of her.

People have also reported seeing strange floating orbs of light darting around the cemetery, especially near the algae-covered pond. Some believe that the pond was used as a makeshift burial ground for Chicago-area gangsters and that the lights are the spirits of their victims; others think that the ghostly lights are related to the legend that, many years ago, a man plowing a nearby field died when

his horse became spooked and ran into the pond, drowning both itself and the man. The spectral farmer and his horse have also been witnessed from time to time.

Probably the most fascinating paranormal activity reported at Bachelor's Grove is the phantom house. On certain nights, a spectral building is said to appear along the abandoned road leading to the cemetery. Those who have witnessed this strange apparition say that the two-story house slowly fades away until it disappears without a trace. Similarly, some have spotted a ghostly car barreling down the road, complete with glowing headlights.

Should you wish to visit Bachelor's Grove in the hopes of encountering some of these spirits, the cemetery is open every day but only during daylight hours. The abandoned road now serves as a well-worn path through the woods to the graveyard. Just remember that you are visiting hallowed ground—the final resting place of men, women, and children; be sure to treat it as such.

Sunset Boulevard: Where the Ghosts Come Out at Night

Hollywood is not all glitz and glamour: For every success, there are countless failures; for every Rodeo Drive, there are numerous back alleys filled with debauchery, drugs, and depression. Hollywood is a city of extremes, and wherever you find such heightened emotions, you're bound to find a few ghosts. Here are a few restless spirits that prowl Sunset Boulevard.

Beverly Hills Hotel (9641 Sunset Boulevard)
In 1977, actor Peter Finch died of a heart attack in the lobby of the Beverly Hills Hotel, but several other Hollywood ghosts haunt its guest bungalows as well. Built in 1912, the hotel has a rich history, which includes ghostly visits by composer Sergei Rachmaninoff and actor/comedian Harpo Marx.

Chateau Marmont (8221 Sunset Boulevard)
Best known as the place where actor John Belushi died of a drug overdose in 1982, the Chateau Marmont has been the site of so much paranormal activity that it's considered one of the most haunted hotels in the United States. Guests there tell of mysterious sounds, the feeling that someone (or something) is touching them, and inexplicable pockets of cold air. One woman felt that someone climbed into bed with her, although no one was there.

The Comedy Store (8433 W. Sunset Boulevard)
Once known as Ciro's, this nightclub was a hangout for the Who's Who of the Hollywood set during the 1940s and '50s; mobsters were also known to frequent the joint back then. In 1972, the building became The Comedy Store, and since then, it has served as a launching pad for the careers of big-name comedians such as Jim Carrey and Robin Williams. The club is thought to harbor the ghost of gangster Mickey Cohen, and an unexplained negative energy is said to reside in the basement.

Former employee Blake Clark said that many of the building's ghosts are active in the early morning hours. He saw chairs move

across the stage by themselves and heard the loud banging of an unmanned piano. He also caught a glimpse of a man wearing a World War II–era uniform, but he quickly disappeared.

Late comic Sam Kinison said that ghosts at The Comedy Store toyed with him by causing the lights to flicker and the sound system to emit a buzzing noise while he was on stage.

El Compadre Restaurant (7408 W. Sunset Boulevard)

Originally called Don Pepe, this restaurant was the site of a holdup in the 1950s. Two employees were killed during the robbery, and their spirits are said to roam the building at night. After closing, shadowy figures are sometimes seen by the piano, which leads some to speculate that they hid there during the burglary. Today, the victims are said to turn the lights on and off, move items around the room, and produce heavy footsteps. A large mirror in the restaurant is also thought to be haunted, as the reflection frequently displays a little more than what is right in front of it. When patrons look at the glass, they often see a strange male figure looking back at them and feel an unexplained presence standing nearby.

The Pink Palace (10100 Sunset Boulevard)

Unfortunately for ghost hunters and fans of old Hollywood, this sprawling 40-room mansion—the former home of actress Jayne Mansfield—was torn down in 2002. In 1957, Mansfield moved in and redecorated it with liberal use of her favorite color—thus the house's descriptive moniker "the Pink Palace." After Mansfield's tragic death in a car accident in 1967, the mansion's subsequent owners encountered ghosts and other strange phenomena. One female occupant who found some of Mansfield's old clothes heard the actress warn her to "Get out"; she did. After former Beatle Ringo Starr purchased the house, he tried to paint over the ubiquitous pink, but the rosy tint kept emerging. Singer Englebert Humperdinck was the last owner of the Pink Palace; he felt that fate had brought him there. He said that he was able to smell Mansfield's perfume and that he even saw her spirit clad in a black dress. Humperdinck said she appeared so real that he almost said hello … until he realized that she was a ghost.

Fond du Lac Ghosts Haunt Their Old Stomping Grounds

Listed on the National Register of Historic places, the Ramada Plaza Hotel in Fond du Lac, Wisconsin, is also on more than one "most haunted" list. Built in the 1920s, this structure was originally known as the Hotel Retlaw, after owner Walter Schroeder. ("Retlaw" is "Walter" spelled backward.) And even though Walter is no longer alive, he appears to have remained at his namesake hotel.

In its heyday, this eight-story building was one of the premier hotels in Wisconsin along with several others that were owned by Schroeder. Located at the junction of four major Wisconsin highways, the inn attracted some prominent guests, such as John F. Kennedy, Eleanor Roosevelt, Hubert Humphrey, and numerous Wisconsin politicians.

Over the years, there have been so many stories of ghosts at the hotel that employees started keeping a log to record the activity. Some say that Walter Schroeder was murdered there and that it's his ghost that haunts the property. But it seems that he's not alone.

The most haunted area of the hotel is Room 717, where visitors and staff have heard screams and other noises—all while the room is empty. Faucets and lights turn themselves on and off, and the TV changes stations on its own—this ghost seems to favor C-SPAN.

Other paranormal activity has been observed throughout the hotel. Strange humming when no one is around, a ghostly figure walking into walls, and an odd glow in the banquet room are all part of the fun. One frequently seen apparition is a redheaded woman in a white bathrobe; she disappears into the wall when startled.

In addition, the chandelier in the ballroom sometimes sways for no reason, and an employee spotted a couple dancing there. He thought it was rather sweet...until the pair vanished before his eyes.

On a side note, it was believed that the ghost of Walter Schroeder also haunted the Retlaw Theater, which was located just a block away from the hotel. Coincidence? Probably not.

If These Walls Could Talk…
Oh, Wait, They Do Talk!

There are few haunted places featured in more publications and on more television shows than the Whispers Estate, which is considered one of the most haunted places in Indiana. This 3,700-square-foot Victorian mansion in the town of Mitchell has attracted tourists, ghost hunters, psychics, the media, and of course, ghosts galore.

When Dr. John Gibbons and his wife, Jessie, moved into their dream house in 1899, they had no idea that it would one day become famous for incredibly unusual reasons. The childless couple adopted three orphans, but tragedy surrounded the family. Their oldest daughter, Rachael, set a fire in the building's parlor, severely burning herself in the process. She died in an upstairs bedroom two days later, and soon after, her spirit began showing itself to the living. Her apparition is often seen roaming around the estate, and burn marks are still visible in the parlor.

The Gibbons family suffered another tragedy when adopted daughter Elizabeth died of unknown causes at age 10 months. She passed away in the master bedroom, and many guests who have stayed in this room have reportedly smelled baby powder lingering in the air. Some have also heard the soft sound of a baby crying.

Due to yet another misfortune that befell this family, the master bedroom has been the site of other paranormal activity as well. After the deaths of her two children, Mrs. Gibbons contracted pneumonia. Already run-down, she developed respiratory complications and succumbed to her illness two weeks later—in the master bedroom. In addition to the sound of a baby nearby, visitors to this room have heard noises that resemble ragged breathing and coughing. Some have even noticed the distinct feeling of pressure on their chests. Other odd occurrences have been observed there as well, including a closet door that opens suddenly and doorknobs that jiggle by themselves.

A Gathering of Ghosts

Old houses often have rich histories, but the Whispers Estate has witnessed more sadness than most. In 1966, a man died in the house of a heart attack. In 1974, his nine-year-old son—who suffered from hydrocephalus (water on the brain)—fell down a flight of stairs and passed away before help could arrive. In the estate's early years, Dr. Gibbons ran his practice on the main level of the house, and it is quite likely that several of his patients died there as well.

In addition to the house, which seems to have produced quite a few ghosts of its own, four graves and an area called the "pit grave" are on the property. In the pit grave, the doctor disposed of the by-products of his medical practice, such as miscarried or aborted fetuses, amputated limbs, and organs that he removed.

While there is no evidence of illegal or immoral activity on the property, psychics who have investigated the Whispers Estate without knowing its history sensed that sinister things happened there. They all felt that the doctor may have been involved in unethical practices, including performing abortions and unnecessary surgeries, taking liberties with his female patients, and keeping several mistresses at a time. There's nothing like a little dark energy to contribute to the paranormal activity at a house.

It's Hard to Sleep with All That Whispering

In 2006, the building was turned into a bed-and-breakfast, but apparently, the spirits of those who once lived there objected to the idea, so they came out in full force. Guests at the B & B have reported hearing whispering throughout the entire mansion. It is difficult to pinpoint the source of these voices, but those hearing them—and there are many—all describe the same type of muffled noises. Thus, the place became known as the Whispers Estate; unfortunately, the building's reputation proved to be bad for business.

However, word about the house spread among those interested in the paranormal, and the Whispers Estate has since become a

popular destination for ghost hunters and reporters who come to document the terrifying tales.

One paranormal phenomenon at the inn that does not seem directly related to any one person or event is an apparition or shadow figure that has been dubbed "Big Black," which investigators agree is "not of this world." Big Black has been viewed most often in the doctor's quarters, but it has occasionally been seen in other areas of the building as well.

In addition, guests who've stayed at the bed-and-breakfast have reported feeling intense tremors while in the doctor's bathroom. And in the master bedroom, many have seen the beds shake violently. Women, especially, have felt the sensation that Dr. Gibbons is whispering in their ears, and some have reported feeling that his ghost actually touched or groped them.

Sensory Scent-sations

Unexplained smells commonly occur in haunted places, and the Whispers Estate is no exception. In addition to the smell of baby powder—which is strongest in the master bedroom but has been detected throughout the house—many visitors have caught whiffs of cologne, cigars, and the rancid odor of discarded bandages.

Paranormal investigators who have studied the Whispers Estate have experienced many unusual phenomena, but one that has been noted over and over is associated with the door in the servants' quarters. When investigators leave that area, the heavy wooden door often mysteriously slams shut behind them with tremendous force. This may be the ghostly version of the phrase, "Here's your hat; what's your hurry?" After all, the ghostly whispers never seem to say, "Please stay."

The legend of a ghost deer echoes through the canyons of Mt. Eddy in northern California. Hunters describe a giant buck with 12 points on one antler and 10 on the other. Those who have shot at it say that bullets pass right through it, and its tracks are said to disappear at natural barriers such as great ridges or bodies of water.

The Ghosts of Antietam

🪦 🪦 🪦 🪦

*With nearly 23,000 total casualties, the Battle of Antietam was one
of the bloodiest single-day skirmishes of the American Civil War.
More than 3,600 of these men died suddenly and violently that
day—ripped out of this existence and sent reeling into the next.
It's no wonder that the ghosts of some of these soldiers still haunt
the Antietam battlefield in western Maryland. Perhaps they're still
trying to understand what happened to them on that terrible day.*

Gaelic Ghosts

Bloody Lane at Antietam National Battlefield is a sunken road that's
so named because of the incredible slaughter that took place there
on September 17, 1862. One of the notable battalions that fought at
Bloody Lane was the Union's Irish Brigade, which lost more than
60 percent of its soldiers that day. The brigade's Gaelic war cry was
"faugh-a-ballaugh" (pronounced "fah-ah-bah-LAH"), which means
"clear the way."

Several years ago, a group of schoolchildren took a class trip to
Antietam. After touring the battlefield, several boys walked down
Bloody Lane toward an observation tower that had been built where
the Irish Brigade had charged into the battle. Later, back at the
school, the boys wrote that they heard odd noises coming from a
nearby field. Some said that it sounded like a chant; others, however,
likened the sounds to the "fa-la-la-la-la" portion of the Christmas
carol "Deck the Halls." Did they boys hear the ghostly battle cry
of the Irish Brigade?

On another occasion, some battle reenactors were lying on the
ground near the sunken road when they suddenly began hearing a
noise that they were very familiar with—the sound of a regiment
marching in full battle gear. Their experience as reenactors allowed
them to pick out specific sounds, such as knapsacks, canteens, and
cartridge boxes rattling and scraping. However, no matter how
hard they looked, the men could find no marching regiment. They
concluded that the sounds were made by an otherworldly entity.

Prying Eyes

Because of its strategic location on the battlefield, the Phillip Pry House was pressed into service as a makeshift hospital during the battle. Much misery took place there, including the death of Union General Israel B. Richardson, despite the loving care of his wife Frances. In 1976, the house was damaged by fire, and one day during the restoration, the wife of a park ranger met a woman dressed in Civil War–era attire coming down the stairs. She asked her husband who the woman was, but he had no knowledge of a woman in period clothes at the park.

Later, a woman was seen staring out of an upstairs window in the room where General Richardson died. Nothing was particularly unusual about this . . . except that the room was being renovated at the time and didn't have a floor. Was it the ghost of Frances Richardson, still trying to take care of her dying husband?

Members of the construction crew that was working at the house decided that this was not the project for them and abandoned it immediately after sighting this female phantom. Disembodied footsteps have also been reported going up and down the home's stairs.

Screaming Specters

The spirits of Antietam are not just confined to the battlefield. Injured Confederate soldiers were brought to St. Paul Episcopal Church in Sharpsburg, and sometimes, the sounds of the wounded screaming in agony can still be heard there. Mysterious lights have also been seen in the church tower.

A Bridge Between Two Worlds

Burnside Bridge was another scene of massive slaughter at Antietam, as Union troops repeatedly tried to take the tiny stone span only to be driven back by intense Confederate fire. Many of the soldiers who died there were quickly buried in unmarked graves near the bridge, and now it seems as if that arrangement wasn't to their liking. Many credible witnesses, including park rangers, have reported seeing blue balls of light floating near the bridge at night. The faint sound of a phantom drumbeat has also been heard in the vicinity.

Although the Battle of Antietam took place around 150 years ago, it seems that in some places, the battle rages on—and for some, it always will.

Was *The Exorcist* Really Based on a True Story?

Almost everyone is familiar with the movie The Exorcist. *The 1973 film stars Ellen Burstyn, Jason Miller, and—most memorably—Linda Blair as a young girl who is possessed by a demon. Naturally, everyone wants to know if the story— which was based on a best-selling novel by William Peter Blatty—is true. The answer to that question is . . . maybe.*

In January 1949, a 13-year-old boy named Roland (some sources say that his name was Robbie) and his family—who lived in Mount Rainier, Maryland—began hearing scratching sounds from behind the walls and inside the ceiling of their house. Believing that their home was infested with mice, Roland's parents called an exterminator. However, the exterminator found no evidence of rodents in the house. After that, the family's problem got worse: They began to hear unexplained footsteps in the home, and objects such as dishes and furniture seemed to relocate on their own.

But these incidents would seem minor compared to what came next: Roland claimed that an invisible entity attacked him and that his bed shook so violently that he couldn't sleep. The sheets and blankets were repeatedly ripped from his bed and tossed onto the floor. One time, Roland tried to grab them, but he was yanked onto the floor with the bedcovers still clenched in his fists.

Roland liked board games, and his aunt "Tillie"—a woman who had a strong interest in the supernatural—had taught him how to use a Ouija board before she died. Some blamed the Ouija board for causing the trouble, claiming that it had allowed a demonic being to come into the home and target Roland.

Not Such Good Vibrations

By this time, the family was convinced that an evil entity was afoot, so they appealed to a Lutheran minister named Schulze for help. Reverend Schulze prayed for Roland and had his congregation do

so as well. He even took Roland to his own home so the boy could get some sleep. However, both the bed and an armchair that Roland tried to sleep in there vibrated and moved, allowing the boy no rest. Schulze noted that Roland seemed to be in a trance while these incidents occurred.

If Schulze had any doubt that it was time to call in the cavalry, he was certainly convinced when scratches mysteriously materialized on Roland's body. These marks were then replaced by words that appeared to be made by claws. The word *Louis* was clearly visible, which was interpreted as St. Louis—Roland's mother's hometown. With all signs pointing to the need for an exorcism, Father Edward Albert Hughes of St. James Catholic Church was summoned.

Truth or Fiction?

At this point, accounts of the story begin to splinter, as no two versions are alike. According to the version that has been more or less accepted as fact, Father Hughes went to see Roland and was disturbed when the boy addressed him in Latin—a language that was unknown to the youth. Hughes decided to perform an exorcism, during which a loose bedspring slashed him. The priest was supposedly so shaken by the ordeal that he was never the same again. (However, according to some sources, this part of the story never happened; they say that Hughes only saw Roland once at St. James, Roland never spoke in Latin, and Hughes never performed an exorcism on the boy, nor was he physically or emotionally affected by it. It is unclear why someone felt that dramatic license needed to be taken here, because the actual events are strange enough.)

During Roland's visit to Hughes, the priest suggested using blessed candles and special prayers to help the boy. But when Roland's mother did this, a comb flew across the room, hitting the candles and snuffing them out. Other objects also flew around the room, and at one point, a Bible was thrown at the boy's feet. Supposedly, Roland had to stop attending school because his desk shook so badly.

It seems that an attempt was made to baptize Roland into the Catholic faith as a way of helping him. However, this didn't work out so well: As his uncle drove him to the ceremony, the boy grabbed him by the throat and screamed that the baptism wouldn't work.

The Battle of St. Louis

Finally, at their wits' end, the family decided to stay with relatives in the St. Louis area. Unfortunately, the distance between Maryland and Missouri proved to be no deterrent to the invisible entity, and the assaults on Roland continued. In St. Louis, a relative introduced the boy and his family to Jesuit priest Father William Bowdern, who, in turn, employed Father Raymond J. Bishop, a pastor at St. Francis Xavier Church in St. Louis, in his efforts to help the family.

Father Bishop made several attempts to stop the attacks on the boy but to no avail. After Bishop sprinkled the boy's mattress with holy water in the shape of a cross, the attacks ceased. However, after Bishop left the room, the boy suddenly cried out in pain; when his pajama top was pulled up, Roland had numerous scratches across his abdomen. He could not have done it to himself, as he was in the presence of several witnesses at all times.

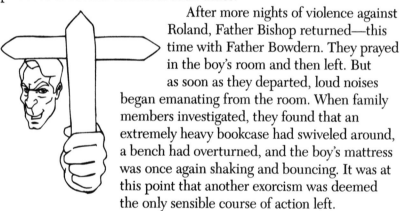

After more nights of violence against Roland, Father Bishop returned—this time with Father Bowdern. They prayed in the boy's room and then left. But as soon as they departed, loud noises began emanating from the room. When family members investigated, they found that an extremely heavy bookcase had swiveled around, a bench had overturned, and the boy's mattress was once again shaking and bouncing. It was at this point that another exorcism was deemed the only sensible course of action left.

The exorcism was a desperate battle that was waged over the course of several months. Some of it took place in the rectory at St. Francis Xavier Church, some of it at a hospital, and some of it at Roland's home; one source says that the boy was exorcised no less than 20 times. During this time, practically everything and anything typically associated with an exorcism occurred: Roland's body jerked in uncontrollable spasms, he experienced projectile vomiting, and he spit and cursed at the priests; he also conveyed information that he couldn't possibly have known. However, his head didn't spin completely around like Linda Blair's did in *The Exorcist*.

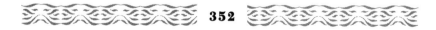

Gone, but Certainly Not Forgotten

Eventually, Bowdern's persistence paid off. He repeatedly practiced the ritual and ignored the torrent of physical and verbal abuse hurled at him by the entity that was residing inside the boy. Finally, in mid-April 1949, Roland spoke with a voice that identified itself as St. Michael. He ordered Satan and all demons to leave the boy alone. For the next few minutes, Roland went into a titanic rage, as if all the furies of the world were battling inside of him. Suddenly, he became quiet, turned to the priests, and simply said, "He's gone."

The entity *was* gone, and fortunately, Roland remembered little about the ordeal. Some months later, a 20-year-old Georgetown University student named William Peter Blatty spotted an article in *The Washington Post* about Roland's experience. He let the idea of demonic possession percolate in his brain for years before finally writing his book, which became a best seller. Out of privacy concerns, Blatty changed so many details from the actual case that the source was virtually unrecognizable—until the intense publicity surrounding the movie forced the "real" story out.

Over the years, numerous theories regarding the incident have been suggested: Some say that it was an elaborate hoax gone too far, while others claim that it was the result of poltergeist activity or an actual possession. Regardless, this case continues to resonate in American culture.

On July 24, 1915, hundreds of people died in the Chicago River when the *Eastland,* a steamer that was overloaded with passengers who were on their way to a company picnic, capsized just a few feet from the dock.

There are many stories of hauntings related to the *Eastland* disaster, but none are more famous than the phenomena experienced at Oprah Winfrey's Harpo Studios. At the time of the *Eastland* disaster, the building served as the Second Regiment Armory and was used as a temporary morgue for the victims. Some Harpo employees have heard odd sounds, such as children's laughter, old-time music, clinking glasses, whispering voices, footsteps, slamming doors, sobbing, and muffled screams. Others have seen a spectral woman in a long gray dress who walks the corridors and then mysteriously vanishes into the wall.

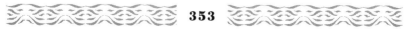

FRIGHTENING FACTS

Prison Phantoms

- *Point Lookout State Park in Maryland was the site of a Union prison camp that housed Confederate POWs during the Civil War. Thousands of soldiers died there of disease and exposure. To this day, many visitors see gaunt, ragged phantoms trudging around the park.*

- *The old Jackson County Jail in Independence, Missouri, is now a museum. It's been the site of many reported ghost sightings, but the most commonly seen apparitions there are two town marshals, who were both murdered by inmates in the 1860s.*

- *On May 18, 1906, behind the Silver Bow County Jail in Butte, Montana, prospector Miles Fuller was hanged for murder. The jail has since been demolished, but Fuller's spirit still seems to be searching for something where it once stood.*

- *Old prisons seem to make great museums; they also seem to be gathering places for ghosts. Such is the case with the former Burlington County Prison in Mount Holly, New Jersey. In 1833, inmate Joel Clough was hanged there for murder. Visitors to the museum have heard his anguished moans and the rattling of the chains that secured him to the floor of his cell.*

- *In 1955, several girls murdered a matron while escaping from the Summit County Juvenile Detention Center in Akron, Ohio. The building is now used as a rehab center, but residents have witnessed the matron's spirit confiscating cigarettes.*

- *California's Folsom Prison has seen so much sorrow and violence that it would be surprising if it wasn't haunted. The most prominent of the prison's many spirits is the "Folsom Phantom"—a ghostly guard who was killed during a riot in 1927.*

- *Before Mary Surratt was hanged for her part in the conspiracy surrounding the death of Abraham Lincoln, she was jailed at the Federal Penitentiary, which is now Fort McNair in Washington, D.C. Perhaps the sorrowful sobs that modern residents hear are Mary's laments over what she believes was a miscarriage of justice that led to her untimely death.*

Yale's Spirited Organist

You know that an institution is rich with history when it is old enough to have celebrated its 300th anniversary in 2001. That's the case with Yale University, which opened its doors in New Haven, Connecticut, in 1701. While ghosts of students, professors, and even early colonists surely remain on these storied grounds, one particular area of Yale has quite a reputation for being haunted: Woolsey Hall.

Built in 1901—in recognition of the university's 200th anniversary—Woolsey Hall is the institution's main auditorium. It seats more than 2,500 people and has hosted performances by several symphonies, as well as rock concerts; but its ghosts aren't quite so fond of the latter.

The haunting of the building centers on the 1902 construction of the Newberry Memorial Organ—one of the largest and most renowned organs in the world. It is named for the Newberry family, which made a large donation to fund the instrument's upkeep. Harry B. Jepson, the school's first organist, played and maintained the pipe organ, but it periodically became outdated. The Newberry family stepped up to fund improvements to the organ in 1915 and 1928 to keep it state-of-the-art.

But in the 1940s, Yale forced Jepson to retire, and he never again played the Newberry Organ. While unhappy with this turn of events, the organist seemingly made peace with his situation—at least until the hall began hosting rock concerts. Some say that the last straw was when Jimi Hendrix played at Woolsey Hall on November 17, 1968. When Jepson's ghost saw this beautiful concert hall used for rock-and-roll music, he became angry.

Since that time, workers and visitors have reported feeling a menacing presence and a sense of evil in the hall, especially near the organ chambers and in the basement. People have heard the organ playing when the auditorium is locked and no one is sitting at the bench. One thing is certain: Jepson won't be playing any rock-and-roll music.

Ghosts of Shiloh

The Battle of Shiloh was a major conflict in the American Civil War. After the smoke cleared, tales of resurrected soldiers flowed almost as freely as the blood that precipitated their rise.

Taking place on April 6 and 7, 1862, in southwestern Tennessee, the Battle of Shiloh proved sobering. It resulted in more than 23,000 casualties and made Union and Confederate soldiers realize that they were in for a protracted, bloody war. After the battle, tales of ghostly uprisings became commonplace. One of the most frequently told stories centered on the "Bloody Pond," where the injured cleaned their wounds during the battle, their blood staining the water a crimson shade. Since then, eyewitness accounts have claimed that every so often, the haunted pond turns blood red. Other reports told of ghostly shadow figures dressed as soldiers that continued to fight the battle, usually after sundown. Sounds of gunfire, screams, and Rebel yells were said to accompany these otherworldly skirmishes.

After the battle, slave owners and southern protectionists grew increasingly worried that their way of life was coming to an end, and when the Civil War came to a close in 1865, their fears were realized as hundreds of thousands of newly released slaves roamed the countryside in the South. However, six white supremacists in Pulaski, Tennessee (which is approximately 90 miles east of the battle site), stumbled upon a tactic that they hoped would help frighten the newly freed slaves back into passivity.

During a night of raucous behavior, the bumbling group dressed in sheets and rode drunk through the streets of Pulaski. They soon learned that frightened former slaves who had seen them that night believed them to be the legendary spirits of Shiloh. Realizing the possibilities, the group—which called itself the KyKlos Klan—posed as "ghosts" and staged countless raids during the Reconstruction period. Eventually, their fledgling organization would come to be known by a more familiar name: the Ku Klux Klan. Real or imagined, the Confederate ghosts of Shiloh had made their presence felt.

Literary Ghosts

The ghost story is undeniably one of the most popular types of literary fiction, and tales featuring specters and spooks date back eons. Hundreds of supernatural thrillers have been penned through the years, some of them by literature's most influential writers, including Edgar Allan Poe, Ambrose Bierce, Charles Dickens, Henry James, and Edith Wharton. Read on for a more detailed look at how the ghost story has shaped literature.

Haunting Homer

In Homer's epic poem *The Odyssey,* the hero Odysseus encounters three noteworthy ghosts after digging a special pit to honor Greek gods Hades and Persephone. The specters include the apparition of Odysseus's mother, who died while he was away, and the spirit of a shipmate whose body had been left unburied on Circe's Island. The third ghost is that of the blind prophet Tiresias, who warns Odysseus about what lies ahead during his journey home.

Shocking Shakespeare

Spirits are also common characters in the works of William Shakespeare. In fact, two of Shakespeare's most popular plays—*Hamlet* and *Macbeth*—feature ghosts in pivotal roles.

As anyone who has read the works of "The Bard" knows, the ghost of Hamlet's father appears several times over the course the play, providing the title character with information about his demise. Similarly, *Macbeth* is rife with all manner of supernatural characters, including the spirit of Banquo and several apparitions conjured up by the witches who give Macbeth a sneak peek at his future.

Dickensian Spooks

Charles Dickens is best known for his non-supernatural works of fiction, including *Oliver Twist, David Copperfield, Great Expectations*, and *A Tale of Two Cities.* But like Shakespeare, he wasn't afraid of ghosts. In fact, Dickens was fascinated by the paranormal, and he wrote 20 short

stories starring ghosts over the course of his career, including "The Signalman," which is considered a classic of the genre.

Of course, short stories weren't Dickens's only foray into literary hauntings. His novella *A Christmas Carol* features four extremely famous apparitions: Ebenezer Scrooge's deceased business partner Jacob Marley and the ghosts of Christmas Past, Present, and Future, all of whom conspire to make the heartless, penny-pinching Scrooge a better person.

Henry James's Haunted Heroine

In 1898, Henry James—another Victorian-era literary superstar—penned one of his best-known works, *The Turn of the Screw.* This seminal ghost story concerns a governess who's in charge of caring for two children, Flora and Miles, at their isolated country home. Shortly after starting her job, the governess sees a strange man glaring at her, first from a tower attached to the house and then through a window. A maid identifies the specter as that of Peter Quint, a deceased valet.

Convinced that the spirit of Quint and the ghost of the governess who came before her (which she also sees) are after them, the governess becomes increasingly protective of the children in her charge. The specters make their presence known throughout the story, which concludes with Miles dying in the governess's arms. James's story leaves the reader wondering whether the apparitions were real or merely a figment of the governess's imagination.

Ghosts in the Comics

In the 1950s, ghost stories became very popular in American comic books. With sales of titles starring superheroes on the wane, publishers jumped on horror and science fiction in an attempt to retain readers; the results were remarkable. Titles such as *Tales from the Crypt, Weird Mysteries,* and *Menace* filled the racks, and kids couldn't get enough. In fact, during the heyday of the horror-inspired comic book (1950–1955), between 50 and 100 terrifying tales were released monthly, many containing variations on the traditional ghost story. The comic-book industry saw a resurgence of supernatural stories in the early 1970s after the easing of the Comics Code, which earlier had banned words such as *horror* and *terror* from comic-book covers.

Hill House Meets Hell House

In 1959, Shirley Jackson published a landmark ghost story: *The Haunting of Hill House.* It's about a group of paranormal investigators, led by Dr. John Montague, that stays in the titular dwelling in an attempt to determine what is behind the supernatural occurrences reported there. It quickly becomes apparent that the house contains an otherworldly entity and that it has a thing for one member of the investigative team—a troubled young woman named Eleanor.

The *Haunting of Hill House* has twice been adapted for the silver screen—once in 1963 and again in 1999; both versions were titled *The Haunting.* It's a remarkable book that inspired another classic of the genre: *Hell House* (1971), which was penned by acclaimed fantasy writer Richard Matheson.

Hell House also concerns a group of paranormal investigators; however, in this tale, they are hired by a terminally ill millionaire to investigate whether there is life after death. The researchers do this by moving into the notorious Belasco House, which, according to the story, is considered to be the most haunted house in the world. This building also contains a very malevolent spirit, but unlike the ghost in *The Haunting of Hill House,* which mostly played mind games, the specter haunting Belasco House is physically violent toward its unwanted guests.

Three Men and an Angry Ghost

Twenty years after Shirley Jackson published *The Haunting of Hill House,* novelist Peter Straub upped the ante with his best seller *Ghost Story.* A rather complex tale, it's essentially about three elderly men who share a horrible secret from their youth: the accidental death of a woman whom they all knew. Many decades later, the spirit of the woman returns to exact revenge upon her killer and those who helped cover up her death. In 1981, *Ghost Story* was made into a movie starring Fred Astaire, Melvyn Douglas, and Douglas Fairbanks Jr.

Ghosts have long been—and remain—a popular topic in literature for one main reason: Readers love to be scared. What's the most terrifying tale ever written? That's a matter of opinion. But in the eyes of most, the best ghost stories turn the reader's knuckles as white as the things that go bump in the night.

FRIGHTENING FACTS

Ghostly Prostitutes

- In 1898, a brothel opened in the building that now houses the Red Onion Saloon in Skagway, Alaska. Little is known about its resident ghost, "Lydia," who probably worked there. Today, people see her upstairs watering plants (even though the saloon has none); they also smell her strong, cheap perfume.

- From the late 1880s through the mid-1930s, Jerome, Arizona, was a mining boomtown. And like most boomtowns, it had a red-light district. In the late 1800s, while two miners were fighting over a woman, they accidentally stabbed her to death; now her spirit (among others) haunts the nearly deserted town.

- Jerome was also the home of Miss Jennie Banters, a wealthy madam in the early 1900s whose former brothel is now the Mile High Grill and Inn. The establishment has little choice but to remember Jennie because she and her spectral cat have stuck around their former residence. The feline walks on freshly made beds and noisily sharpens its claws, while the spirit of Miss Jennie turns off radios and knocks down items that are not properly put away in the kitchen.

- Las Cruces Adobe—an old stagecoach stop in Gaviota State Park, California—was built on a Native American burial ground, which is never a good idea. At least three prostitutes died violently there in the late 1800s, and although the building no longer exists, the restless souls of these unfortunate women still prowl the area.

- In 1867, famed prostitute Julia Bulette was murdered in her home. A cemetery in Virginia City, Nevada, is her final resting place . . . or is it? Legend has it that the undertaker in charge of preparing Julia's body wanted to keep her near him, so he buried her in his basement and filled her coffin with sand and rocks. Since then, her ghost has been spotted at the former funeral parlor, which is now a gift shop. The spectral seductress has also been seen near the site where her home once stood and at the cemetery in which her body may or may not be interred.

- In 1947, in Ventura, California, a disturbed "working girl" named Sylvia Michaels allegedly hung herself at the Bella Maggiore Inn. Sylvia's ghost likes to make her presence known by flickering lights, moving objects around, and overwhelming guests with the scent of perfume. Her shadowy figure has spooked visitors so frequently that management hired ghost hunters to calm the sorrowful spirit. Although the amount of paranormal activity decreased after that, some still lingers.

- In 1880, "Timber Kate"—a Carson City, Nevada, prostitute—was murdered by a miner at the Bee Hive Whorehouse. The building is gone, but Kate's spirit still roams the area.

- With a name like Deadwood, it's not surprising that this legendarily lawless South Dakota town hosts its share of ghosts. At the former Green Door Brothel, disembodied voices and footsteps are often heard. They may belong to the restless spirits of former prostitutes—or their clients.

- In June 1879, during a brawl over a client, prostitute Susan Kennedy murdered colleague Mary Gallagher with an ax at an apartment in the Griffintown section of Montreal. Kennedy went to prison, but every seven years, Mary's headless specter is said to manifest in the vicinity of William and Murray streets.

- In 1929, Club Arrowhead of the Pines—which was a private gambling resort and brothel in Lake Arrowhead, California—opened under the management of the infamous Bugsy Siegel. Violet, a resident prostitute, killed herself after organized-crime figures murdered her lover. More recently, the building became home to Bracken Fern Manor Bed-and-Breakfast, and apparently Violet has made it her eternal home too; she makes her presence known with whiffs of violet-scented perfume.

- The building that now houses Old Town Pizza in Portland, Oregon, is the setting of many stories from the days of Shanghai Tunnels and white slavery. When Nina—an involuntary prostitute from the late-1800s—informed on the criminals who took her hostage, she was thrown down an elevator shaft. Folks often see her ghost around the pizzeria wearing a black dress.

Going on a Ghost Hunt

*So you're getting ready to go on your very first ghost hunt.
How exciting! But what exactly are you getting yourself
into? And what's going to happen? Will you encounter
shadowy shapes moving around you, hear phantom
footsteps, or even see a full-bodied apparition? Read on
to find out what to expect—straight from our experts.*

"Do I Need to Do Anything to Prepare for the Hunt?"

Try not to overexert yourself on the day of the investigation, and
try to sleep well the night before. Don't eat a huge meal right
before the hunt, as that may make you sleepy. Be sure to bring
along some water and snacks; being tired, hungry, or dehydrated
can impact your senses, possibly making you see, feel, or hear
things that doesn't really exist. Your mood could also impact the
investigation, so try to be as relaxed as possible.

"What's the First Thing I Should Do When I Get There?"

Familiarize yourself with your surroundings. I like to spend a
few minutes sitting quietly and absorbing as many of the sights,
sounds, and even smells of the location as possible. As the night
progresses, you'll find this extremely helpful in determining
whether or not the phenomena you're experiencing is of a
paranormal nature.

Also, because you'll probably be spending a lot of time in the
dark, it helps to know your way around the location. That way, you
won't be so concerned with groping your way through the darkness
that you inadvertently miss any paranormal activity around you.

"What Sort of Things Will I Do During a Ghost Hunt?"

Unlike ghost hunts on television shows, which condense entire
investigations into 30- or 60-minute segments, a full ghost hunt
lasts several hours. Be prepared to spend a lot of time sitting
around in the dark waiting for something to happen.

Some paranormal investigation groups like to separate the
participants into smaller groups and assign them to specific areas

of the haunted site. After about an hour, the groups rotate so that everyone gets ample time in each area.

While at a location, you may be asked to take photos and note any temperature changes or spikes in electromagnetic field readings, which may indicate paranormal activity. You might also take part in EVP (electronic voice phenomenon) sessions, during which you can ask any spirits present questions in the hope of recording otherworldly responses.

Even if you don't have access to some of the sophisticated ghost-hunting gear that's on the market these days, you can always rely on your senses to "feel" the room and see if you notice anything out of the ordinary.

"What Can I Expect to See?"

If you're lucky, you just might see a ghost! But once again, it's important to get used to your surroundings. You're most likely going to be spending a lot of time in the dark, so make sure that your eyes adjust to the lack of light. "Shadow people"—moving shadows that are seen out of the corner of one's eye—are among the most commonly spotted paranormal phenomena. Should you see a shadow person, take a look around to make sure that what you saw was not caused by something playing tricks on your eyes. For example, nearby streetlights can often cause tree branches blowing in the wind to cast odd shadows.

If you get really lucky, you might see what many consider the "Holy Grail" of the ghost-hunting world: a full-bodied apparition. Should this happen, try to remain calm and observe as much as possible, such as the specter's attire, its actions, and whether or not it seems to know that you're there. This information might help you to determine who the ghost was in life and, more importantly, why it's still hanging around.

"Will I Hear Ghosts Talking and All Sorts of Weird Noises?"

Yes, you'll probably hear lots of weird noises. Every site has its own unique set of normal noises (houses settling, animals wandering through, etc.), but because the location is new to you, everything is going to sound a bit spooky. It will be up to you to decide which

noises are normal and which might be *para*normal in nature. Typically, when I hear a strange noise during an investigation, I call out, "If that was you, could you please make that noise again?" If the noise repeats, it will help you figure out where it came from, which will, in turn, allow you to determine if there is a natural explanation for it.

Of course, you are likely to hear voices at some point in the evening. Even if all of your fellow ghost hunters are accounted for, consider that sounds can carry quite far, especially if you're in an empty building. If you hear a "disembodied voice," make note of how it sounded and what it said; perhaps ask it to repeat itself or talk louder.

"What Will I Learn?"

First and foremost, you'll learn that ghost-hunting TV shows tend to overdramatize situations. You probably won't encounter any ghosts that pick you up and toss you around the room; instead, you'll likely spend most of the investigation sitting quietly in the dark, waiting for something to happen. And if and when something *does* happen, the event will be so fleeting that you might not even notice it until you review your video and audio recordings from the hunt.

But above all, you will learn that ghost hunts are truly unique opportunities to explore the Other Side in an attempt to unravel the age-old mystery of what happens to us after we die. Have fun!

Scooby-Doo: The Original Ghostbuster

*One of animation's top dogs has been hunting
ghosts for more than 40 years.*

The team of Bill Hanna and Joe Barbera created some of history's
most memorable cartoon characters, including the Flintstones and
Tom and Jerry. The duo also struck creative gold with a crime-
fighting pooch named Scooby-Doo.

In 1969, *Scooby-Doo, Where Are You?* premiered as part of
CBS's Saturday morning lineup. Viewers couldn't get enough of
the perpetually frightened Great Dane and his human pals Shaggy,
Velma, Fred, and Daphne, who traveled the country in their van
chasing criminals, hunting ghosts, and solving mysteries.

Bad Guys Revealed

Scooby-Doo, Where Are You? featured an array of ghosts and other
paranormal creatures, the majority of whom inevitably turned out to
be criminals in costumes or masks. More often than not, after the big
reveal, the bad guy would mutter, "...and I would have gotten away
with it if it hadn't been for you meddling kids!"

Scooby-Doo and the gang have been on TV almost nonstop since
their debut. In 1972, the show was retitled *The New Scooby-Doo
Movies,* and it featured the voices of popular entertainers such as
Phyllis Diller, Jonathan Winters, and Tim Conway. In one episode,
the gang worked as housekeepers in a spooky mansion owned by the
Addams Family, who had their own live-action series in the mid-1960s.

A New Network

The series moved to ABC in 1976, and a new character—Scooby's
feisty, pint-sized nephew Scrappy-Doo—was introduced in 1979. Two
live-action Scooby-Doo movies have been produced (Scooby was
computer-generated), and several animated films have been released
on DVD. The show remains a TV staple, with a fan following as
strong today as when Scooby and crew went on their first ghost hunt.

Haunted or Just Hollywood?

We see the words "Based on a True Story" all the time, but how often is that really the case with movies? Sometimes films address well-documented ghost stories, and other times their legitimacy is little more than media hype. This list of well-known films reveals which are merely inventions of screenwriters and which owe their origins to something supernatural.

The Shining (1980)

Based on a novel by Stephen King, *The Shining* initially seems to be pure fabrication. However, King based his story on his stay at the Stanley Hotel in Estes Park, Colorado. Guests there have reported music coming from an empty ballroom, and spirits are often spotted in rooms on the fourth floor. King hadn't actually heard any of these stories until *after* he reported to the staff that he had seen a young boy on the second floor who was calling for his nanny. Of course, the staff at the Stanley was familiar with the boy, as his spirit had appeared to many of them over the years. (Read more about the Stanley Hotel on page 406.)

Poltergeist (1982)

Horror director Tobe Hooper teamed up with writer, producer, and uncredited co-director Steven Spielberg to create *Poltergeist*—one of the most successful haunted house movies ever. The film was based entirely on a story written by Spielberg; but despite its roots in fiction, the film is famously rumored to be cursed. According to legend, the *"Poltergeist* Curse" took the lives of four cast members within six years of the film's release, including child star Heather O'Rourke, who died tragically at age 12, and Dominique Dunne, who was murdered by her boyfriend at age 22.

The Blair Witch Project (1999)

Perhaps one of the shortest-lived film hoaxes in history, *The Blair Witch Project* became a hit thanks to clever marketing and amateurish cinematography. Although the truth about the film's authenticity was quickly revealed through interviews with the

filmmakers and actors, many people still filled theaters based on the belief that it was composed of actual footage shot by three hikers who went missing in the woods in Maryland.

The Ring (2002)

Although the story sounds more like an urban legend, *The Ring* is actually based on a novel by Japanese horror writer Koji Suzuki. His best seller has inspired films in America, Japan, and Korea, as well as a comic book, a TV series, and even a video game. While not rooted in fact, Suzuki's story seems to have universal appeal.

An American Haunting (2006)

An American Haunting is based on the case of the Bell Witch (see page 140), an entity that tortured a Tennessee family in the early 1800s and is said to have caused the death of its patriarch—the only known case of a spirit killing a human.

The Haunting in Connecticut (2009)

The Haunting in Connecticut is based on the experiences of the Snedeker family of Southington, Connecticut. When Carmen Snedeker moved her family into a former funeral home, she had no idea that they would deal with moving dishes or buckets in which water turned blood red. Though the film offers clever explanations for the haunting and a clear conclusion, the Snedekers didn't discover bodies or burn the house down: Eventually, like many haunting victims, they simply moved out of the house. Regardless of the embellished Hollywood ending, it seems that everything else that is portrayed in the film actually happened to the Snedekers.

Paranormal Activity (2009)

Made on a shoestring budget (estimated to be only $15,000), Oren Peli's *Paranormal Activity* looks authentic, but it's little more than a compelling work of film fiction. Peli channeled his own fear of ghosts to create a flick that feels like a true haunting, and worldwide, audiences bought into it to the tune of nearly $200 million. Though not based on a true story, the film conveys the fear felt by anyone living in a home that truly is haunted.

Dinner & Drinks with a Ghost

Catfish Plantation

Fort Worth Paranormal once deemed the Catfish Plantation in Waxahachie, Texas, "one of the most haunted restaurants in the entire country," and with several earthbound spirits in residence there, this quaint Victorian building lives up to that designation.

As is the case at many haunted places, this restaurant has cold spots, doors that lock and unlock by themselves, water faucets and lights that turn on and off without human intervention, and refrigerator doors that open and close on their own. In addition, a number of dinner knives mysteriously come up missing every night. Perhaps some of this is the doing of the restaurant's three resident ghosts.

The quietest spirit is that of Will, a farmer who died of pneumonia when he lived in the building in the 1930s; he's been seen loitering on the front porch. It is believed that he is responsible for some of the cold spots. He's typically very shy, but he has been known to touch women's legs while they're eating.

A more active ghost is that of Elizabeth Anderson, a young woman who lived in the building until the early 1920s, when a former boyfriend murdered her on the day that she was supposed to marry another man. Her appearances are preceded by the scent of roses. Elizabeth is sometimes seen in the bay window in the front room. Once, she even followed a customer home and presented her with an antique powder box as a gift.

A third spirit that resides at the Catfish Plantation is believed to be that of a woman named Caroline, who died in the building in the 1970s at age 80. Although no one has actually seen her ghost, her presence is deeply felt, and she wants to remind everyone that the building is still her home. When the restaurant opened in 1984, Caroline greeted the new owner with a pot of freshly brewed coffee. Another time, the owner was surprised to discover a large tea urn positioned in the middle of the kitchen floor; all the cups were stacked neatly inside it. Caroline has also been known to throw coffee cups, wineglasses, spices, and food.

Ghosts in the Witch City

One of the darkest chapters in American history, the Salem Witch Trials have haunted our country for more than 300 years. Numerous plays and movies have recounted the tale of two young girls from Massachusetts who, in 1692, wrongfully accused people in their town of witchcraft. This sparked a mass hysteria that led to charges against hundreds and the executions of 20 innocent people. The lessons learned from this miscarriage of justice have stuck with the people of the United States, but so have the restless spirits of the victims of this tragedy.

The Last House

Today, the people of Salem, Massachusetts, acknowledge the crimes of the past, and the town recognizes its history in many ways, from witch logos on its police cars to a number of kitschy attractions erected solely to attract tourists. Among the gift shops and New Age bookstores, only one building with a connection to the trials remains: Known locally as "The Witch House," Judge Jonathan Corwin's former home still hosts visitors on Essex Street. Some of those visiting the historic site are overcome with feelings of anxiety, fear, and anger—all emotions likely experienced by those Corwin sentenced to death. Some have seen the apparition of a woman lingering in the bedrooms on the second floor, and others have witnessed a couple that vanishes into thin air while walking the grounds. Some employees report strange noises after hours, including what sounds like the shuffling of feet on the floorboards and the dragging of furniture from one room to another. The spirits of The Witch House have even been captured on film, although most appear to be little more than manifestations of light or swirling mists.

The Gallows

Judge Corwin's former home is not the only place in Salem where the spirits of those he condemned make their presence known. Photographs of orbs and mists that are similar to those snapped at The Witch House have been taken in the area once known as

Gallows Hill. Though precise records of where the accused were hanged no longer exist, many believe that a playground and basketball court now reside where the town's gallows once stood. This would explain the eerie photographs of apparitions, as well as other strange phenomena that occur at the site. Electronics frequently malfunction there, and it isn't uncommon for people to hear otherworldly crying at the location at night. Some visitors have reported feeling an invisible presence brush up against them, while others have had their hair pulled by an unseen force.

Harbinger at Howard Street

Of course, a town as old as Salem inevitably has several cemeteries, and one of the most haunted is Howard Street Cemetery, which sits across from where the old jail once stood. Photographers at the graveyard have captured images of the same unexplainable mists, orbs, and lights that are found at other locations, and reports of physical contact with an invisible entity abound as well. For more than a hundred years now, passersby have witnessed apparitions wandering among the old tombstones. Although most of the graves at the Howard Street Cemetery don't date back further than the 1800s, the site itself is inextricably tied to the witch trials: The graveyard was built on the location where Sheriff George Corwin tried to crush a confession out of Giles Corey—and when Corey's ghost is seen, the entire town of Salem trembles.

More Weight...

When Anne Putnam accused Giles Corey of appearing to her as a spirit and trying to entice her with his satanic ways, Corey—who was over 80 years old at the time—didn't give the charge much credence. He even briefly supported accusations against his wife until he realized how seriously the charges were being taken. Sheriff Corwin, the son of Judge Jonathan Corwin, was getting rather wealthy off

the prosecution of so-called witches in Salem because anyone found guilty of witchcraft was subject to having his or her property seized and redistributed. That placed Giles Corey in a tough situation: If he pleaded guilty to the accusations against him, he would lose everything; at the same time, no one who had pleaded not guilty had been found to be innocent. Either outcome would mean that Corey's sons would not inherit his estate; instead, it would fall into the hands of the sheriff and the other town leaders. Corey did the only thing he could do: He refused to play their game.

Corey's Curse

Sheriff Corwin attempted to press a plea out of the old man—literally—by placing more and more weight on his chest every time he refused to confess, instead demanding, "More weight!" The act preserved his sons' inheritance but cost Giles Corey his life. Before he died, however, Corey spat at Corwin and sneered, "Damn you, Sheriff! I curse you and Salem!" Since then, sightings of Corey's ghost have meant disaster for the town. The last time he was spotted was in 1914, just before a fire that nearly wiped Salem off the map. The curse doesn't only target the town itself, though: The very position that George Corwin once held is said to be cursed as well. Every sheriff of Salem since Corwin has either died in office or retired due to heart problems. Between the curse of Giles Corey and all the other restless spirits, one wonders why Salem hasn't changed its nickname from "The Witch City" to "The Haunted City."

For years, Cleveland's Drury Mansion served as a halfway house for parolees. The building had boasted a long history of hauntings, but when the ex-cons moved in, it got much worse. The two most commonly seen ghosts were female. One was described as a woman with long, dark hair who liked to whisper and then scream—and then vanish in a burst of flames; she may have been the spirit of a victim of a 1929 fire at the nearby Cleveland Clinic. The other specter was that of a matronly lady who wore her hair in a bun. Witnesses claim that the mansion's doors and windows sometimes opened and closed on their own, and residents often felt as if someone was staring at them.

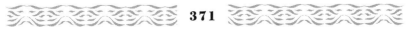

The Haunted Bunk Beds of Horicon

Haunted houses are supposed to sport broken windows, gothic architecture, and perhaps looming towers. However, a modest, well-kept ranch house in Wisconsin shattered that stereotype when it became one of the most famously haunted homes in America.

The small town of Horicon, Wisconsin, is best known for its proximity to a large marsh where thousands of Canada geese stop on their migratory route. But in the late 1980s, a small home on Larrabee Street stole the spotlight from the marsh when the young family living there claimed that it was sharing its home with a horrific entity.

Nightmare in the Nursery

In June 1987, Deborah and Allen (whose names have been changed to protect their privacy) and their children (Kenny, Maryann, and Sarah) began to experience frightening and inexplicable events after purchasing a secondhand set of bunk beds for Kenny.

The unusual activity began in Kenny's room. First, a radio would change stations by itself. Then, a babysitter reported that an unoccupied chair teetered back and forth, and a suitcase that was stored under the bottom bunk shot out as if someone under the bed had shoved it. Kenny also told his parents that he often saw a glowing old lady with long black hair standing in his doorway.

Fog, Flames, and Fear

As events escalated during the fall and winter, Allen tried to verbally confront the spirit that he and Deborah were sure had somehow moved in with them. When he told the unseen presence to leave his children alone, he was shocked to receive a response from a loud voice that told him to "Come here." This was followed by the appearance of a glowing flamelike specter in the garage. The fiery entity glared at Allen with two large green eyes.

In early January 1988, Allen saw a "foggy" spirit with large green eyes rise out of the floor, and he again heard the loud voice. This

time, the voice told Allen that he was dead, and then the apparition vanished in a streak of faux flames. Allen and Deborah asked their minister to try to bless the spirit away, but that didn't help. Rumors about the house being haunted quickly spread around town, and on January 11, the family moved out and trashed the bunk beds at a distant landfill.

By January 21, an onslaught of people who hoped to see some paranormal action had besieged Larrabee Street; in fact, the Horicon police had to patrol the area because of greatly increased traffic and trespassers. At the same time, the gossip grew wilder: Area newspapers reported that people were claiming that the house had blood dripping from the ceiling, strange graffiti had materialized on the walls, the family's snowblower was seen racing around the yard by itself, and the home's basement had a large hole in the floor that served as a gateway to hell. In short, the reaction from the populace was almost scarier than the family's actual experience.

Fame but No Fortune

Milwaukee Sentinel reporter James Nelson, who tracked down the family at a relative's house, wrote an extended series of articles based on exclusive interviews with Allen and Deborah, who agreed to participate on the condition that he withhold their identities. The Associated Press then spread the story far and wide. The *National Enquirer* offered the couple $5,000 for their story, but they declined, even though they had lost about $3,000 by returning the house's deed to their mortgage lender.

Later in 1988, the TV show *Unsolved Mysteries* filmed an episode about the haunted ranch house in Horicon, even though new owners had moved in and had reported nothing unusual. Actors played the roles of Allen and his son, whose chilling encounters ceased after the family moved and the bunk beds were discarded.

Skeptics claim that the family made up the story, but because the couple shunned publicity and offers of money—and even suffered considerable financial loss—that seems unlikely. The Horicon chief of police, the family's minister, and the *Sentinel* reporter all stated their belief in Allen and Deborah's sincerity.

Hopefully, the couple buried those bunk beds very deep in that landfill.

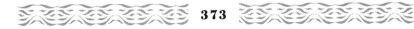

Specters on "The Strip"

According to the popular slogan, "What happens in Vegas stays in Vegas." As it turns out, some celebrities never leave Las Vegas—even after they're dead.

Benjamin "Bugsy" Siegel (1906–1947)

When gangster Benjamin "Bugsy" Siegel first arrived in Las Vegas in the 1930s, the town was still a sleepy backwater in the Nevada desert. But soon, Siegel had Vegas on its way to becoming the world's premier gambling mecca. However, on June 20, 1947, Siegel's associates rewarded him for his hard work by blasting him into oblivion at his girlfriend's Beverly Hills home. Since then, his ghost has been seen there running and ducking as if trying to avoid being struck by a hail of bullets. Siegel's specter is also often spotted at his Flamingo Hotel, where he's seen dressed in a smoking jacket and sporting a wide grin. He usually hangs out in the hotel's Presidential Suite, which is where he spent much of his mortal time. And later in the evening, when the pool area isn't particularly crowded, Siegel often shows up there. (Read more about the ghost of Bugsy Siegel on page 326.)

Elvis Presley (1935–1977)

Clad in the famous white-sequined jumpsuit that he often wore in his later years, the spirit of Elvis is reportedly seen at the same Hilton hotel in Las Vegas where he used to perform. The spectral "King" has been glimpsed wandering around backstage and sometimes even taking a final bow.

Redd Foxx (1922–1991)

Redd Foxx's ghost supposedly still resides at his former home in Las Vegas, playing pranks on the house's current occupants. He likes to make himself known by opening and closing doors and randomly turning computers on and off. But considering that Foxx was a comedian and a prankster in life, this doesn't seem all that unusual for the former star of *Sanford and Son*.

St. Augustine: Where Past and Present Meet

Founded in 1565, St. Augustine, Florida, has more than 400 years of history under its belt. As "The Nation's Oldest City," its beautiful old cemeteries are full of people who called St. Augustine home—but some of them don't seem to realize that they're dead.

Our Lady of La Leche Church

America's very first Catholic mass was held at Our Lady of La Leche Church on September 8, 1565, and the church, grounds, and cemetery are still called "America's Most Sacred Acre." The holy site is now the final resting place of many nuns and priests, and it is believed that some of them still visit the church on a regular basis. The spirit of one particular nun is often seen wandering the mission grounds dressed in a black habit; she is frequently spotted kneeling in prayer in front of the chapel. A bit shy, she disappears if anyone gets too close.

The Apopinax Tree

Just outside Tolomato Cemetery, a ghost lingers near the famous Apopinax Tree. According to local lore, Colonel Joseph Smith met and fell in love with a married woman in 1823. After she became ill and died, her husband made plans to bury her according to the custom of the times, which included carrying her to Tolomato Cemetery in a seated position. But when the thorny branches of the Apopinax Tree scratched her face as she passed beneath, she began to bleed! Her husband tried to bury her anyway, but the Colonel insisted that she be removed from her grave. She went on to live another six years, and after her actual death, her husband commanded pallbearers to avoid the tree so that the same thing wouldn't happen again. Dressed in black, the woman still wanders throughout Tolomato Cemetery, apparently looking for someone. Is it her husband ... or her admirer?

Harry's Seafood Bar and Grille

Beware the restrooms on the second floor at Harry's Seafood Bar and Grille: They may contain an uninvited visitor. The de Porras

family once owned the building, and their daughter Catalina loved it very much. Her family moved away from St. Augustine in the 1760s, but Catalina eventually returned, and she and her husband purchased the house in 1789. Unfortunately, she died soon after.

A fire destroyed the original building in 1887, but Catalina's spirit is thought to haunt the replica of her beloved home, which was built in 1888. A spectral woman wearing a white dress or nightgown is often seen near the ladies room, but no one knows for sure if it's Catalina or a female guest who perished in the fire.

Spanish Military Hospital

Many spirits are thought to haunt the former Spanish Military Hospital, which is now a museum. The reconstructed building showcases rooms of the past, such as a mourning room with priests' tools for administering Last Rites; a surgeon's room with medical instruments from the 18th century; a ward, where a typical patient would have slept; and an apothecary, which stocked common medicines of the day. A host of ghosts from the old hospital are also present. Doors in the building open and close on their own, and on numerous occasions, the front door has mysteriously been

unlocked with no human help. Unseen hands have touched visitors, and some people have even been scratched or bitten by malevolent entities. Footsteps are commonly heard when no one is around, strange smells linger, and objects move all by themselves—and

have even been thrown at unsuspecting guests. Full-bodied apparitions of former patients have also been reported both inside and outside of the building.

St. Francis Inn

Ghost hunters will want to visit Lily's Room at the St. Francis Inn—one of the oldest continuously operating hotels in the United States. Built in 1791 as a single-family home, it was converted to an inn in 1845. In those times, social classes were strictly maintained, so when the homeowner's nephew fell in love with a

servant girl from Barbados, the relationship was doomed from the start. The two met secretly until the young man's uncle discovered the affair. After that, the servant girl was fired and the lovers were forbidden to see each other again. Distraught, the young man hung himself in the attic, which is now known as Lily's Room. Guests who have stayed in the room have seen the ghost of a young woman carrying sheets or towels and searching for her lover. She has also made her presence known by moving toiletries and turning lights and faucets on and off.

The Old Jail

You'd think that anyone in the clink would be thrilled to escape, but that doesn't seem to be the case at St. Augustine's Old Jail—several ghosts still call it home. In the late 1800s, conditions were harsh for prisoners there. Sheriff Charles Perry was cruel, and he carried out death sentences with a vengeance. Many people lost their lives there—either as punishment (for crimes that they may or may not have committed) or due to sickness or poor sanitary conditions. Now listed on the National Register of Historic Places, the Old Jail tells its tales of the past with the spirits that linger there. Visitors hear footsteps and the sound of dragging chains mixed with the soft strains of "Swing Low, Sweet Chariot." Disembodied barking is heard quite often; it is believed to come from the phantom hounds of Sheriff Perry. Shouts and wails also pervade the corridors. And try as they might, employees can't get rid of the sweet smell of molasses that fills the air.

After Liberace's death on February 4, 1987, at least two psychics claimed that his spirit remained at his restaurant, Carluccio's in Las Vegas. Staff members reported seeing floating capes, doors opening and closing on their own, and unexplained electrical disturbances. In February 2005, a magazine reporter, who accompanied investigators on a ghost hunt at Carluccio's, wrote in an article that the researchers snapped a photo of a restaurant employee that revealed a ghostly form standing next to her.

Walker House:
Keeping the Miner Spirit Alive

Mineral Point, Wisconsin, was a prime lead-mining town in the early 19th century. The mineral-rich bluffs attracted miners to the area, and a railroad line that ended there made the southern part of town the perfect place to build an inn. Established in 1836, the Walker House served many visitors over the years. Some lived there while they worked the mines; many were just passing through; and a few others decided to stay ... forever.

In the Beginning

After the Walker House opened, it quickly gained a reputation as an upscale inn. The first floor featured a pub, a kitchen, and a large area that was used for food storage; the second floor included two rooms that offered fine dining; and the third floor consisted of guest rooms for the many miners, gamblers, travelers, and railroad workers who decided to stop in for a bit of shut-eye.

The inn was open for more than a century before it closed its doors in 1957. Since then, the building has been in a state of flux, and it has been placed on the market several times. Numerous pubs and inns have occupied the space, but they never seemed to flourish. At the start of the 21st century, the building was listed as one of the ten most endangered historical structures in Wisconsin. Then, in 2005, it was brought back to life as an inn, complete with a restaurant, a pub, and, naturally, a few ghosts. But the building's new life would be short lived: As of this writing, the Walker House is once again closed and for sale.

A Hauntingly Good Time

The most famous spirit at the Walker House is that of William Caffee, who was hanged on the premises in November 1842. Caffee apparently got into an argument with another man and shot him. While the shooting may have been self-defense or even an accident, Caffee's trial was quick—and, some say, rigged—and he was

sentenced to a public hanging. More than 4,000 people turned out to watch the spectacle, which included the condemned man riding to the gallows in his own coffin. With two beer bottles in hand, he played a funeral dirge on the sides of the casket. Apparently, he had a good sense of humor—even at the end.

Although Caffee was not able to prevent his own death, no one can force him to leave the Walker House, as his spirit has remained there for more than 150 years. His specter has been seen walking the halls, and he may be responsible for doorknobs mysteriously turning on their own on the second floor. Staff members and guests both say that they have experienced his pranks; he especially likes to pull employees' hair. In 1981, the inn's owner watched Caffee's headless ghost sit on a bench on the back porch for quite some time. A few weeks later, another employee saw Caffee—with his head intact—walking down the hallway on the second floor. Both times, Caffee was dressed in a rumpled gray outfit that was typical of miners of his day.

While he is certainly the building's most prolific ghost, Caffee doesn't seem to be the only spirit hanging out at the Walker House; in fact, one psychic claimed that 22 ghosts were on the property. One was quite devoted to the most recent owners and would tell anyone who filled in for them to "Get out of here! You're not the owner." Employees have seen an apparition watching from the top of the staircase, clearly not happy with how things are run. Many think that it is the spirit of a past owner who feels that he needs to keep a close watch over things. One can only imagine how he's filling his spare time now that the inn has closed.

"I have never yet heard of a murderer who was not afraid of a ghost."
—John Philpot Curran, Irish orator and politician

Prison Poltergeists

Yuma Territorial Prison Holds Inmates for Life—and Some Even in Death

🪦   🪦   🪦   🪦

*What could be worse than being locked in a prison cell for life?
How about being locked in a prison that you were forced to help
build? That's what happened to the first seven inmates at the Yuma
Territorial Prison back in 1876. Is it any wonder that the place
is considered one of the most haunted locations in Arizona?*

There were no minimum- or maximum-security prisons in the 1800s,
so inmates at the Yuma Prison ranged from petty thieves to murderers.
By the time the prison closed in 1909, more than 3,000 convicts had
been held within its walls. Compared to today's standards, prison
life back then was hard. Each cell measured only nine feet by nine
feet, and it was not uncommon for the indoor temperature to reach
110 degrees in the summer. A punishment known as the "Dark Cell"
was similar to what we now call solitary confinement. And a ball and
chain were used to punish prisoners who tried to escape. It must
have worked because plenty of souls never left this place.

The Good, the Bad, and the Ghostly

Despite the brutal conditions, a library and educational programs
were available to inmates, and a prison clinic even gave them access
to medical care. But the jail soon became overcrowded, and in such
close quarters, tuberculosis ran rampant. During its 33-year history,
111 prisoners died there, many from TB; eight were gunned down in
unsuccessful escape attempts.

From 1910 to 1914, the former prison building housed Yuma High
School. Considering the restless souls that were left over from the
structure's days as a prison, it probably did not make for the best
educational experience. During the Great Depression, homeless
families sought shelter within its walls. And later, local residents who
wanted to have a little piece of Arizona history "borrowed" stones
from the building's walls for their personal construction projects.

Solitary Spirits

Today, all that remains of the former Yuma Territorial Prison are some cells, the main gate, a guard tower, the prison cemetery—and the ghosts. A museum is located on the site, and visitors and employees report that spirits have settled there as well. Lights turn on and off randomly; objects are moved from one place to another; and once, the coins from the gift shop's cash register leaped into the air and then fell back into place.

The Dark Cell is also a focal point for ghostly activity: The restless spirits of prisoners who were sent there for disobeying rules are thought to linger. At least two inmates were transferred directly from that cell to an insane asylum, but whether anyone actually died there is unknown. It makes for a few unsettled spirits, though, doesn't it?

Linda Offeney, an employee at the prison site, once reported feeling an unseen presence in the Dark Cell. And a tourist who visited the prison in the 1930s had her photo taken near the Dark Cell; the picture looked perfectly normal—except for the ghostly figure of a man standing behind her within the cell.

Offeney also tells the story of a writer for *Arizona Highways* magazine who witnessed the hauntings: The journalist wanted to spend two days and two nights in the cell just as prisoners would have—in the dark, with only bread and water. She only made it a few hours before she called for assistance, explaining that she couldn't shake the feeling that something was in the cell with her.

In June 2005, Arizona Desert Ghost Hunters spent the night at the Yuma Territorial Prison and gathered enough evidence to convince them that the place is indeed haunted. Photos taken of the guard tower and in Cell 14 both show suspicious activity: An orb can be seen near the tower and a misty figure is clearly visible in Cell 14, where inmate John Ryan hung himself in 1903. The investigators also captured EVPs (electronic voice phenomena) in Cell 14, where a voice said, "Get away," and in the Dark Cell, where a male spirit told the group to "Get out of here."

Although the Yuma Territorial Prison only operated for 33 years, it certainly spawned its fair share of paranormal activity. This begs the questions: Was the prison built so soundly that for many, there was no escape, even in death? Or did the inmates just give up and choose to stay there forever?

Out of Body, Out of Mind?

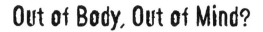

Does having an out-of-body experience (OBE) mean that you're out of your mind? Absolutely not. In fact, statistics show that between 5 and 35 percent of the population has had at least one OBE. And many of the people who have had them don't even know it.

So What the Heck Is an OBE Anyway?

Definitions in scientific journals can get pretty technical, but the simple explanation of an out-of-body experience is that it's the feeling that you've left your physical body and can see yourself and the world from outside of your earthly vessel. Some people describe the OBE as a state in which a person's consciousness separates from his or her body, usually for a very short period of time. Sometimes those who experience an OBE report hearing or seeing something that they couldn't have seen or heard from within their own body.

People seem to find out-of-body experiences fascinating, but we don't really know much about what causes them at this point. What *is* clear is that an OBE can happen to anyone at any time. It can happen just as easily to a paranormal skeptic as it can to a believer. And although an OBE can occur during a near-death experience (NDE), the two are not one and the same. An OBE occurs when the mind separates from the physical body, but the spirit remains in the physical world. During a near-death experience, the person may or may not experience an OBE. The person may look down at her body lying on a hospital bed or see herself in a wrecked car, which would be considered an OBE, but the rest of the NDE involves *leaving* the physical world and traveling to "the Other Side." Most people who experience an NDE report seeing a bright light, traveling down a tunnel, and seeing deceased relatives; those components are not part of the simple OBE, during which the person remains in this realm.

One survey asked people who'd had an OBE to describe the circumstances surrounding it. More than 85 percent of respondents said that they'd had their OBEs while they were resting, sleeping, or dreaming. Others reported being sick in bed or even medicated. But

still other people—especially those moving at fast speeds like in an airplane or on a motorcycle—have reported feeling as if they were floating above themselves.

Do It Yourself... or Not

While many OBEs simply occur, researchers have confirmed that some people are able to create their own out-of-body experiences. Using relaxation techniques and isolating sensory input, subjects have succeeded in making OBEs happen. Those who can do this at will report a greater feeling of control, as if they are out of their regular body but remain empowered in the situation; many even describe a "silver cord" that attaches their corporeal body to their ethereal form. The silver cord and the feeling of empowerment are much less pronounced among those whose OBEs are spontaneous. Many subjects reported a sense of great energy. They saw bright colors and heard loud noises. Everything was vivid and vibrant, yet more like being awake (except that the person observed it from above) than like the hallucinatory quality of a dream. OBEs seem to be more grounded and feel more "real" than dreams.

Tell Me More

We could analyze OBEs and NDEs all day, but it's more fun to read about actual experiences rather than the science behind them. Here are some reports from people who have actually experienced them.

No Fear of Flying

Eileen T. said that she had an out-of-body experience when she was nine, so she wasn't afraid when she had another one more recently. When it happened to her as a child, she simply rose to the ceiling and hovered above her body; during her adult experience, Eileen was lying near her grandson, who was very ill. Suddenly, she felt herself leave her body through the bottoms of her feet. She reported feeling as though she was flying feet-first for a hundred miles. After a short time, her ethereal form—which seemed as though it was still attached—reentered her physical body. Initially, reconnecting was uncomfortable, but she eventually settled back in. When she awoke, her body was lying calmly with its feet crossed, as though she hadn't a care in the world.

Scared Back to Reality

Although it happened in 1980, Paul R. said that he remembers his OBE like it occurred yesterday. He had gone to bed with his wife and was drifting off to sleep when, suddenly, he awoke to hear a loud humming noise and felt his entire body vibrating. The next thing he knew, he was looking down at himself and his wife in the bed. He decided to visit an aunt who lived nearby, but as he left the apartment, he encountered a strange man who tried to hand him a small scroll. Something about the man or the paper must have frightened Paul because he swiftly returned to the bedroom, where he "slammed" back into his body. He said that it was like nothing he had ever experienced before, but he's certain that he wasn't dreaming, and he hadn't been under the influence of any mind-altering substances.

A Campfire Story

A nine-year-old boy had an out-of-body experience while camping and told his mother about it when he returned home. His parents were divorced, and the boy was vacationing with his father and his father's girlfriend in early 2004. While the youngster was drifting off to sleep, he felt a huge burst of energy. Suddenly, he found himself back at the campfire, where he could see and hear the adults quite clearly. However, glancing back at the tent, he was surprised to see that his body was still inside—fast asleep.

A Spiritual OBE...

Kevin G. of Toronto described his out-of-body experience as being something of a religious experience. It occurred one night in 1990, when he was feeling especially tired and went to bed a bit earlier than he normally would. He thought that he fell asleep right away, but the sensation that he experienced was not at all like a dream: He "woke up" and realized that he was about six feet above the bed, where his body was still lying. Kevin said that he felt an incredible peace and happiness. He was raised in a religious home and has always been interested in spiritual matters. He felt his personal OBE was a message to him that each person's spiritual journey is just a part of life; he remembers that message each and every day.

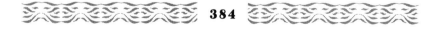

...And a Spiritual NDE

When Baptist minister Don Piper was on his way home from an out-of-town conference in the early 2000s, his vehicle was hit head-on by an 18-wheeler. Pronounced dead at the scene, his spirit was immediately transported to the Great Beyond. According to his book *90 Minutes in Heaven,* Piper experienced an out-of-body experience like nothing he had ever imagined. He had no memory of the crash or of hovering above his body; instead, he went directly to heaven and was reunited with deceased friends and relatives. He knew that he was no longer on earth because he was in a place that was more beautiful than anything he had ever seen. All of his senses were heightened, and he recognized people who were no longer living. After 90 minutes, he was sent back to earth, where he found himself awake and in pain, with heaven nothing more than a memory.

Escaping Earthly Illness for a While

Linda S. had been ill for some time when she made the decision not to fight her disease anymore. No more doctors, no more medication; she was going to be free. And free she was. Shortly thereafter, Linda had a near-death experience during which she felt supreme quiet followed by a detachment from her body. In fact, she watched her spirit leave her physical body: She could see her diseased body lying there, but she no longer had a connection to it. Suddenly, she felt no pain. Gone was her struggle to breathe. As her weightless spirit lifted, so did her depression. Linda felt a profound sense of calm. When she made a conscious decision to let go of her lifeless body, she felt a powerful force lift her upward. Linda described the rest of her experience as a peaceful and loving journey to heaven, which ended when God told her that she must return to earth. She could

not recall her trip back to this world, but she has since recovered from her illness.

The Weeping Woman in Gray

If you ever find yourself at Camp Chase Confederate Cemetery in Columbus, Ohio, find the grave of Benjamin F. Allen and listen very closely. If you hear the faint sound of a woman weeping, you're in the presence of the cemetery's Lady in Gray.

Established in May 1861, Camp Chase served as a prison for Confederate officers during the Civil War. However, as the number of Confederate POWs grew, the prison could not be quite so selective. As 1863 dawned, Camp Chase held approximately 8,000 men of every rank.

The sheer number of prisoners soon overwhelmed Camp Chase. Men were forced to share bunks, and shortages of food, clothing, medicine, and other necessities were common. Under those conditions, the prisoners were vulnerable to disease and malnutrition, which led to many deaths—500 in one particular month alone, due to an outbreak of smallpox. Eventually, a cemetery was established at the camp to handle the large number of bodies.

Although Camp Chase was closed shortly after the war, the cemetery remains. Today, it contains the graves of more than 2,100 Confederate soldiers. Although restless spirits are commonly found where miserable deaths occurred, just one ghost is known to call Camp Chase its "home haunt": the famous Lady in Gray. Dressed in a flowing gray dress with a veil hiding her face, she is often seen standing and sobbing over Allen's grave. At other times, she can be found weeping at the grave of an unidentified soldier. Occasionally, she leaves flowers on the tombstones.

The Lady in Gray has also been spotted walking among the many gravestones in the cemetery; she's even been observed passing right through the locked cemetery gates. No one knows who she was in life, but some speculate that she was Allen's wife. However, her attention to the grave of the unknown soldier baffles researchers. One thing seems certain, though: As long as the Camp Chase Confederate Cemetery exists, the Lady in Gray will watch over it.

Celebrities Who've Encountered Ghosts

Celebrities are only human, so it's not surprising that many of them have had run-ins with ghosts. Here are a few terrifying tales of stars who have collided with the spirit world.

Telly Savalas

As television's Kojak, actor Telly Savalas was able to solve almost any crime. But long before he became famous, Savalas had an encounter that would have left even the famous detective scratching his bald head.

On a cold night in February 1957, Savalas ran out of gas while returning from a relative's house on Long Island. As he was walking along the road in search of a service station, he was picked up by a Good Samaritan in a black Cadillac. The man drove Savalas to a gas station and even gave him a dollar for fuel because Savalas had forgotten his wallet. Savalas asked the man to write down his name and address so that he could repay him; the man did so, and the following day, Savalas went to the address with a dollar in hand. He spoke to the man's wife, who told him that her husband had passed away three years prior. When Savalas showed the woman the piece of paper that the man had written on, she confirmed that it was indeed her husband's handwriting.

Richard Dreyfuss

It takes a lot of support to kick a drug habit. For actor Richard Dreyfuss, it took help from beyond the grave.

In the late 1970s, Dreyfuss developed a nasty cocaine habit, which led him to cause a car crash. No one was seriously injured in the accident, but immediately afterward, Dreyfuss began to see the ghostly image of a girl. She would appear to him every night, no matter where he was. Try as he might, Dreyfuss was unable to recognize who the girl was. He eventually concluded that the girl represented "either the child I didn't kill the night I smashed up my car, or it was the daughter that I didn't have yet." Regardless of who she was, she convinced Dreyfuss to clean up his act, and, after he did, he never saw the spectral girl again.

Daryl Hannah

As a young girl, actress Daryl Hannah had issues interacting and communicating with others, so much so that doctors thought she should be institutionalized. Drastic times call for drastic measures, so Hannah's mother decided to move to Jamaica with her daughter and live in a small, secluded seaside cabin.

With no neighbors nearby, Hannah was permitted to walk along the beach and dunes as she pleased. On one such excursion, she found a well-worn path that led to a little house that had the most amazing garden Hannah had ever seen. An older Jamaican woman was out front; upon seeing Hannah, she motioned for the girl to enter the garden. Taking Hannah by the hand, the woman walked the young girl around the property, teaching her about the different flowers and plants that grew there.

Hannah so enjoyed herself that she returned to the house on several occasions. The kind woman was always more than willing to show the girl the wonders of her garden.

One day, Hannah told her mother about the old woman. Hannah's mother naturally wanted to meet this lady for herself, and Hannah was more than happy to take her. However, after walking down the path that she had trod so many times before, Hannah was shocked to find a vacant lot. Even the garden was gone.

At first, Hannah's mother was skeptical of her daughter's story, but after hearing her talk in detail about plants and flowers, she was convinced that there was no way the girl could have known that information otherwise. Hannah credits her ghostly companion with helping her overcome her debilitating shyness.

Ernie Hudson

Actor Ernie Hudson should have known that his role in *Ghostbusters* (1984) would require him to make some rather strange public appearances to promote the film. To that end, he was asked to spend the night at the allegedly haunted Amberian Peaks Lodge in Greer, Arizona. Hudson accepted the invitation and brought his wife and son with him.

Upon their arrival, Hudson and his family were told about the inn's resident ghost, "Zeke," who was said to have murdered his

wife in the building, and as a result, was condemned to haunt it. Unfazed, the Hudson family retired to their suite for the evening.

At around 3 A.M., Hudson awoke to find what looked like a bright ball of light floating over his son's bed. He woke his wife, and they both stared at the orb for several minutes until it slowly moved away from the bed and toward the door, changing into a dark shadow in the process. When Hudson's son awoke and saw the shadow near the door, he screamed because he thought that an intruder was in the room. At that point, Hudson turned on the light, which revealed nothing out of the ordinary.

Terribly shaken, the family began searching to see if anyone else at the hotel was awake. When they came to the room in which Zeke reportedly committed his dastardly deed, they found the door slightly ajar. To their horror, the trio watched as the door swung open on its own, at which point the family was hit with a blast of icy cold air. The Hudsons fled the hotel, but they eventually returned and waited impatiently in their room until the light of day; they made a hasty exit shortly thereafter.

Sammy Hagar

When rocker Sammy Hagar was 20 years old, he moved his wife and their newborn son to San Francisco, leaving the rest of his family back in southern California. Hagar was estranged from his father, who was known as the town drunk and had taken to sleeping in local parks. Perhaps that's why, when there was a knock on Hagar's door in the middle of the night, he was surprised to see his father standing in the doorway. Hagar said that his father was clearly intoxicated and was being quite boisterous, laughing and talking loudly. Enraged, Hagar refused to allow his father inside and told him that if he wanted to come by and visit, he would have to be sober. Then he shut the door in his father's face.

Hagar had barely gotten back into bed when he heard another knock on his door. This time, it was his manager, who told him that his sister was calling to say that their father had just been found dead in a city park—more than 400 miles away.

To this day, Hagar is convinced that his father's ghost stopped by the apartment to say goodbye, and he regrets not letting him inside.

Phantom Hitchhikers

The tale of the vanishing hitchhiker is what's known as an urban legend—an account of something that usually happened to a "friend of a friend of a friend" (almost never to the person telling the story) that typically contains some kind of moral or surprise ending. According to Jan Harold Brunvand, who has written numerous books about urban legends, the story of the vanishing hitchhiker is one that has been reported in newspapers and elsewhere since at least the 1930s, and possibly earlier. Are any of these anecdotes true? That's for you to decide.

The Hitchhiker's Tale

The basic story goes like this: A motorist driving down a country road sees a young lady hitchhiking, so he stops to offer her a ride. The girl tells him that she lives in a house a few miles down the road, but she is otherwise uncommunicative, spending most of the drive staring out the window. When they arrive at the house, the driver turns to his passenger, only to find that she has disappeared. Curious, he knocks on the door of the house and tells the person who answers about his experience. The homeowner says that he or she had a daughter who fit the description of the hitchhiker, but that she disappeared (or died) several years earlier while hitchhiking on the road on which the driver found the girl. The parent tells the driver that, coincidentally, it's the daughter's birthday.

The specifics of this tale often vary. For example, sometimes a married couple picks up the ghostly hitchhiker, and sometimes the hitchhiker is a young man. However, the story's shocking ending is almost always the same.

In the Early Days

The legend of Chicago's Resurrection Mary is perhaps the earliest "phantom hitchhiker" story. (Read more about Resurrection Mary on page 212.) Another early account of a vanishing hitchhiker was first told sometime between 1935 and 1941. A traveling salesman from

Spartanburg, South Carolina, stopped for a woman who was walking along the side of a road. The woman told the man that she was going to her brother's house, which was about three miles up the road. The man offered to give her a ride and encouraged her to sit next to him, but the woman would only sit in the backseat. They talked briefly, but soon the woman grew quiet. Upon arriving at the home of the woman's brother, the driver turned to the backseat, only to find it empty. The driver told the woman's brother his story, but the brother didn't seem surprised: He said that the woman was his sister and that she had died two years earlier. Several drivers had picked her up on that road, but she had yet to reach the house.

Like all good stories, the tale of the vanishing hitchhiker often acquires some unique details with each retelling. In one example collected by Brunvand, the female hitchhiker suddenly pulled the car's emergency brake at a particular intersection, preventing a deadly collision; the driver was momentarily shaken, but when he finally remembered his passenger, she was gone—though she had left a book in the back-seat. (In other accounts, the object is a purse, a sweater, or a scarf.) The driver assumed that she simply got out so that she could walk the rest of the way. Regardless, he drove to the intended destination, where the homeowner told him that the girl the driver had picked up was his daughter, who had died in a car accident at the same intersection where the collision had been averted. Taking the book from the driver, the father went to his library, where he found an empty space where the book should have been.

The story of the vanishing hitchhiker may only be an urban legend—a story designed to shock the listener—but when dealing with the paranormal, who can be sure? Keep that in mind the next time you spot a young lady hitchhiking along the side of the road.

The Canadian Haunters Convention Offers Tricks and Treats for All

Although the notion is certainly intriguing, most people haven't actually seen a ghost; in fact, many wouldn't even want to see one if they could. But most people will admit to enjoying a good old-fashioned haunted house. The Canadian Haunters Convention is the place to learn how to make your very own haunted attraction.

Humble Beginnings

First held in May 2010, the Canadian Haunters Convention actually evolved from a private event. When Halloween enthusiast Matthew Flagler created his own haunted house many years ago, it was a nonprofit attraction that raised money for local charities, such as the Little Lake Musicfest and Habitat for Humanity. Located in Ennismore, Ontario, the fright-fest was called C'ooks Lane Haunted Hallow. Supposedly, a house of ill repute was once located on the site; the madam was murdered, and her restless spirit is rumored to haunt the property. What better place to stage a haunted house than a location with its very own starter ghost?

"If You Build It, They Will Come"

Hoping to make his attraction even better, Flagler attended the Midwest Haunters Convention in Ohio a few years back. Armed with some great ideas and a batch of new acquaintances, he left wondering why Canada didn't have a similar event, so he organized one himself. About 200 people attended the inaugural Canadian Haunters Convention, which was held in St. Catharines (Canada's "capital of the paranormal").

So who attends a haunters convention? The event is open to anyone who has an interest in ghosts and all things supernatural. Attendees range from Halloween enthusiasts to people who own haunted attractions to those who are fascinated by the paranormal. Speakers include experts in a variety of fields, ranging from the

founder of *Haunted Attraction* magazine to operators of well-known attractions to paranormal investigators. Although plenty of hands-on workshops are presented, there are also fun activities, including a ghost tour, screenings of horror films, and a magic show. Children can watch a few "scary" movies—such as *Coraline* (2009) and *The Nightmare Before Christmas* (1993)—so the convention truly has something for everyone.

Tricks of the Trade

One focus of the Canadian Haunters Convention is making haunted houses and other frightful attractions the best that they can be. It's an opportunity for vendors and exhibitors to buy and sell products related to the building and maintenance of haunted attractions. The event also provides educational and networking opportunities for folks in the industry.

Much more goes into the creation of a haunted attraction than most realize. In addition to the obvious topics (makeup, special effects, and using liquid latex), attendees discuss more mundane but equally important issues, including finances, fire safety, liability, and attracting enough volunteers to make the attraction a success.

But keep in mind that this isn't your ordinary tradeshow. At the Canadian Haunters Convention, vendors sell an assortment of ghoulish props, including wigs, masks, fog machines, theatrical blood, lighting, and realistic-looking corpses. The 2010 convention featured a fully restored hearse, and, in 2011, guests toured a mock medieval torture exhibit.

A New Haunt

In 2011, the convention was held in London, Ontario, to better accommodate increased attendance. As part of the weekend's activities, guests were invited to tour the site of one of Canada's most brutal murders: In 1880, the Donnelly family was murdered at its homestead, and then the house was set on fire, undoubtedly releasing a few restless spirits. What better way to set the stage for a haunters convention than to visit a place that's said to harbor a host of real ghosts?

The Ghosts of Bradford College

What came to be known as Bradford College started as a preparatory school in 1803 in Haverhill, Massachusetts. In 1932, it became a junior college for women, and in 1971, it became a four-year coed institution. When the school closed its doors for good in 2000, it left behind a host of ghosts. Two scandalous stories of romance resulted in less-than-fairytale endings for two young women who are said to haunt the campus to this day. And they're not alone: Ghost hunters have detected several other spirits on this old campus.

A Holy Ghost

One rumor that has circulated around the campus for several years suggests that a young female student named Amy had an affair with a priest. She became pregnant, and soon after, she died. Whether she took her own life or was killed by the priest is not known, but her ghost is said to haunt the Academy Building, which has served as both a dormitory and the home of the school's administrative offices.

When a team of ghost hunters investigated the college in 2000, they found that the Academy Building did indeed give off negative energy. They experienced cold spots and caught glimpses of two spirits that fit the descriptions of Amy and the priest. Inside, they saw a young blonde woman dressed in a school uniform; she appeared to be frightened. And in the alley just outside the building, they spotted an angry man dressed entirely in black.

Room 457

Students and investigators alike have experienced unusual phenomena in many of the former dorm rooms in the Academy Building, but Room 457 has proven to be especially disturbing. Some people felt like the room was closing in on them, and others sensed that very bad things had occurred there. Some reported feeling a sensation of falling, and one of the investigators said that she felt the room had once been full of children and had been used for discipline.

Some ghost hunters use pendulums to measure paranormal activity. While one group was in this eerie room, their pendulum suddenly broke; no one could fix it until it was off the property. Oddly, a camera also malfunctioned at the same time, in the same place.

The Denworth Ghost

In a tale that's similar to the one that allegedly took place in the Academy Building, a female student had an affair with a professor. When she found out that she was pregnant, she told her lover that she was going to tell administrators what had occurred. But she never got the chance: He killed her, and her ghost reportedly still haunts the Denworth Hall Theatre. Some people have heard her singing "Hush Little Baby," and others have been the subjects of her pranks.

This makes for a good story, but some paranormal investigators were skeptical. Many theaters have ghosts, and let's face it, actors can be dramatic. So they didn't have high hopes of finding any ghosts in the theater—until they came face-to-face with one.

While some of the researchers were waiting in a stairwell, the shadow of a girl with long hair appeared on the wall for everyone to see, yet no human body was there to create such a shadow. As the onlookers watched intently, the shape began to take form. It floated down the stairs singing "Hush Little Baby" to a doll in a clear, melodic female voice. The team sensed that the spirit had been through a terrible tragedy; it seemed to long for company and began to cry softly. As the group left the building, the specter could be heard imploring them, "Wait! Wait! Don't leave!"

Other stories of the Denworth ghost say that she's usually much more playful. But she's also rumored to be highly sensitive to gossip: She doesn't like to be discussed around campus, so her distress may have manifested itself in the sad, negative cloud of energy that surrounded her. Apparently, you need to mind your manners, even when dealing with a ghost.

The Spirit Who Likes Spirits

Even ghosts enjoy the occasional nightcap—just ask the spirits that reside in "Woodburn," Delaware's governor's mansion.

Located in Dover, Delaware, Woodburn was constructed in the late 1700s and is a classic example of Colonial-style architecture. Before it became the official governor's mansion in 1965, it had several owners, as well as several ghosts—including one with a fondness for alcohol spirits.

According to legend, early owners of the house frequently left wine-filled decanters out for the thirsty entity, only to find them completely empty the next morning. One staff member claimed to have actually seen the ghost enjoying its beverage; he described the specter as an older man who was wearing Colonial-era attire, including a powdered wig. Former owner Dr. Frank Hall told friends that he occasionally found mysteriously empty wine bottles in the pantry.

A Host of Ghosts

The spirit-loving spirit may be the most active ghost in the house, but it isn't the only one that resides there. In 1805, an apparition nicknamed "the Colonel" made an appearance before evangelist Lorenzo Dow, who was in town for a series of revival meetings. Dow mentioned to his hosts that he had passed a gentleman in the upstairs hall; the hosts were surprised because Dow was their only guest at the time.

Other ghosts that have been witnessed at Woodburn include a young girl wearing a checkered gingham dress and a man who, in life, was rumored to have been involved in slave kidnapping and is known for rattling chains on the grounds of the estate.

The slave kidnapper was part of a pro-slavery mob that attacked the mansion, which was a stop on the Underground Railroad at the time; however, the mob was rebuked by a group of Quakers. According to legend, the kidnapper hid in an old tree, where he hanged himself. Whether his death was an accident or a suicide remains a mystery; either way, the incident seems to have kept his spirit earthbound.

Pets That Have Passed ... and Returned

Many of us have had pets that will live on forever in our hearts. Some people keep their pets' ashes, and a few go so far as to have their former companions stuffed. But is there any other way to keep them around? Some pet owners have found that their furry friends continue to linger around the house after they pass away...just in a slightly less furry, more spectral form.

Shep the Dog

Is it love that brings back a beloved pet? Affection was probably a factor in the case of Joe and his beloved dog Shep. One night, Joe was walking home after returning from serving in World War II; his dog Shep met him along the way. As Joe was about to cross a bridge, Shep began to bark and pull on his master's pant leg, until Joe finally relented and took a different route home. When Joe arrived at home, he told his family that Shep made him go another way. Everyone looked at him oddly, and then Joe's father gave him the sad news: Shep had died the previous winter. Joe also learned that the middle section of the bridge he was going to take had been washed away by heavy rains.

Big Black Dog

When Harry Potter sees a big black dog, he's comforted to know that it's his godfather Sirius, but when most of us see a similar apparition, it's a bit scary. Children are often more susceptible to seeing spirits; such was the case with a particular person who

reported seeing a spectral black dog as a child. One night, the individual woke up suddenly to find a large black dog sitting on its haunches in the doorway of the bedroom. The dog looked like a Doberman, with short ears and short hair, but it appeared as a shadow with no face. When the child screamed, the dog simply disappeared. The same thing happened a few nights later:

This time, the dog disappeared when a light was turned on. The dog was not a pet, and it was never seen again.

Houdini the Terrier

Famous magician Harry Houdini promised his wife that if he could visit her from the Other Side, he would. Apparently, Houdini wasn't able to pull off that stunt—but a woman's pet terrier (which was named for the illusionist) did. After the 13-year-old dog died rather suddenly, his family was understandably grief-stricken. One night, the woman heard Houdini's footsteps following her down the hallway, just like he did in life. Her daughter also heard the footsteps and heard scratching too, but no one actually saw the phantom pooch. Houdini's ghostly visits gave the woman and her family comfort, but they finally decided that they should let him move on: The woman told the dog that she loved him but that he should go into the light. They did not hear the dog after that, but they believe that they'll be reunited with him one day.

A Spectral Black Cat

Home renovations can unearth treasures from the past. That's what happened to a family when they created a loft in the old house that had once belonged to the wife's mother. One night, the wife saw a skinny black cat walking down the stairs. Although the family did have a cat at the time, it was an orange tabby that was about ten pounds heavier than the feline she saw. The woman forgot all about the cat until her daughter said that she wouldn't play in the loft anymore because she didn't like seeing the black ghost-cat dart past. No one else ever saw the phantom feline, but an old photo of the wife's mother as a young girl showed her posing in the backyard holding a small black cat in her arms.

Kemway

Sonja was in Kenya with the Peace Corps when she had an unusual experience with her dog Kemway. One day, she left to help a friend, so she locked her two dogs in an outdoor pen. But when she realized that she had forgotten something, she headed back home. On the way, her car had a flat tire. When she got out

of the vehicle, she found herself staring into the eyes of a rabid hyena. Then she heard a low growl behind her: It was her dog Kemway. The dog and the hyena circled each other, pouncing and growling. Sonja realized that neither animal would make it out alive, so she drove home to get her shotgun. When she arrived, her neighbor ran outside, apologizing profusely and begging for her forgiveness: He had been driving down the road when he accidentally hit Kemway, who died instantly. He showed Sonja the dog's body by the road. It seems that Kemway's ghost appeared from out of nowhere to save his beloved owner.

Cindy the Dog

Some pets return to haunt people other than their masters; such was the case with Bon and Cindy, the neighbor dog. Cindy's family was often away, so she would play with Bon and her dogs. Cindy especially liked to come over when she knew that a storm was brewing. One day after Cindy passed away, Bon heard a familiar scratching at the front door when a storm was approaching. Bon opened the door, half-expecting to find Cindy; of course, nothing was there. But the family still hears Cindy scratching at the door whenever a storm rolls in.

Cheddar the Cat

One year on Halloween, a woman found a stray kitten by the side of the road. She took it home to meet her other cat, Biscuit; however, Biscuit wasn't fond of the new cat, which the woman named Cheddar. Biscuit hissed at Cheddar and cowered in a corner whenever she was around. Nevertheless, after a few months, the woman took a photo of the two pets together. Soon after, Cheddar meowed to go out  and she left—never to return. When the woman had the photos developed, Biscuit was there, but there was absolutely no sign of Cheddar. Did someone forget to say "cheese?"

Do You Pay Half the Rent if Your Roommate Is a Ghost?

Upon first glance, the 1856 Gothic Revival town house at 14 W. Tenth Street in New York City looks like any other apartment building on a quiet street in Greenwich Village. Shaded by trees, the red brick structure blends in with the expensive brownstones and other town houses that line the block. But its quaint facade masks the sinister activities that took place inside.

A plaque on the building explains that famed author Mark Twain resided there in 1901. However, it does not note that Twain may not have left, as his ghost reportedly haunts the stairwell—and he's not alone. Over the years, 22 people have died in the building—many in horrific ways—and all are said to haunt the place.

One of the first grisly occurrences at the so-called "House of Death" was a murder/suicide that took place in the early 1900s. In the 1930s, a young girl was tortured and starved to death by her immigrant parents. Among the many abuses they heaped upon her, she was forced to walk around the apartment while tied to a chair. Not surprisingly, she died due to mistreatment and neglect.

Then, on November 1, 1987, criminal defense attorney Joel Steinberg beat and terrorized his partner Hedda Nussbaum and their adopted children, Lisa and Mitchell. Authorities found Mitchell tied to his playpen with a rope. Six-year-old Lisa was discovered unconscious with a fractured skull; Joel had beaten her during a crack-induced rage and left her on the bathroom floor for hours. Like the young girl in the building five decades earlier, Lisa died at the hands of her abuser.

The ghosts of 14 W. Tenth Street have many reasons for hanging around; rent control and the high cost of living elsewhere in the city, unfortunately, aren't among them. The hallways and stairwell abound with sightings of the immigrant girl, Mark Twain, Lisa, and many other spirits that don't want to leave their former residence. The ghosts don't seem to bother anyone, but potential renters and visitors should beware.

The Unhealthy Mansion

Violent, unexpected deaths are likely to produce ghosts, and shipwrecks are no exception. And when drowning deaths are combined with injustice, it's pretty much a given that a few restless spirits will remain earthbound. That was exactly the recipe for the haunting at the Mansion of Health.

Built in 1822, on New Jersey's Long Beach Island, the Mansion of Health was the largest hotel on the Jersey Shore upon its completion. This sprawling three-story structure featured a sweeping top-floor balcony that ran the length of the building and provided an unencumbered view of the glistening ocean, which was just a few hundred feet away. However, on April 18, 1854, the sea was anything but sparkling.

On that day, a violent storm turned the water into a foaming cauldron of death. Into this maelstrom came the *Powhattan,* a ship that was filled with more than 300 German immigrants who were bound for new lives in America. Unfortunately, the ship never had a chance. As it approached the coast of Long Beach Island, the storm tossed the boat onto the shoals and ripped a hole in its side. Passengers tumbled overboard, and later, dozens of bodies washed up on the shore.

Stealing from the Dead

Back in those days, a person known as a "wreck master" was responsible for salvaging cargo from shipwrecks and arranging the storage of those killed until the coroner took charge of their bodies. The wreck master for Long Beach Island was Edward Jennings, who was also the manager of the Mansion of Health. Accordingly, all of the bodies from the *Powhattan* that had come ashore were brought to the beach in front of the Mansion of Health.

When the coroner arrived hours later, he examined the bodies, although it didn't take a medical degree to determine that they had died from drowning. However, the coroner did find something peculiar: None of the dead had any money in their possession. It seemed unusual to him that immigrants who were coming to America to start new lives didn't carry any cash. Money belts were fashionable at the time, yet not a single victim was wearing one.

Suspicion immediately fell upon Jennings, who was the only person who'd had access to the bodies for many hours. However, no one had any proof of such a crime occurring, so the accusations died down.

The Long Arm of the Ghostly Law

Four months later, another storm revealed a hole near the stump of an old tree on the beach near the Mansion of Health. In the hole, dozens of money belts were found; they were all cut open and empty.

When word of this discovery got out, Jennings took one look at the writing on the wall and hightailed it out of town, narrowly evading the long arm of the law. But there are some things that you can't escape, as Jennings found out the hard way. Supposedly, he became a broken man and was haunted by nightmares that destroyed his sleep and ruined his life. He died several years later in a barroom brawl in San Francisco.

However, the spirits of the *Powhattan* victims were not content to simply haunt Edward Jennings. Shortly after the accident, strange things began to happen at the Mansion of Health: Disembodied sobs were heard at night, and ghostly figures were seen walking across the hotel's expansive balcony. Guests also reported feeling uneasy, which is not exactly the best advertisement for a place that was supposed to be restful and encourage good health.

The Haunted Mansion

Eventually, the Mansion of Health became known as the "Haunted Mansion," and people avoided it like the plague. Soon, the building was abandoned; the brooding hulk of a structure that towered over the beach slowly began rotting away.

During the summer of 1861, five young men who had more bravado than brains decided to spend the night in the gloomy structure. After cavorting through the empty halls and dashing around the balcony without seeing a single spirit, the men decided to sleep on the allegedly haunted third floor. After most of the young men had drifted off to sleep, one who remained awake suddenly noticed the luminous figure of a woman bathed in moonlight standing on the balcony; she held a baby in her arms. The apparition was gazing sadly out to sea, as if mourning the life that had been taken away from her so abruptly.

The startled young man quietly shook each of his companions awake, and all five gazed in disbelief at the figure. Each of them observed that the moonlight passed right through the woman. Then, suddenly and without warning, the woman vanished.

The young men quickly gathered their belongings and fled the building, and from then on, not even vandals dared to enter the Haunted Mansion.

In 1874, fire destroyed the Mansion of Health. But the hotel's real end had come years earlier, when Edward Jennings made the unfortunate decision to tamper with the dead.

Downtown Houston, Texas, may be haunted by 19th-century madam Pamelia Mann. According to staff members and patrons at establishments such as La Carafe, the late Ms. Mann is a nightly visitor. Dressed in a white Victorian gown, she has reportedly been seen outside on Congress Avenue and inside some of the buildings. She also frequents the ladies' rooms on the block of Market Square where her brothel once stood.

Spooks That Roam the Stacks

While at work, librarians strive to maintain volume levels that can be described as "tomblike." But if those whose corporeal forms actually reside in tombs want to raise a ruckus, no librarian in the world can stop them.

Raritan Public Library (Raritan, New Jersey)

Built in the early 1700s, General John Frelinghuysen's historic house became the Raritan Public Library in the 1970s. When the library is closed, an unseen presence likes to turn on the lights and move the books. The ghost of an elderly woman is often seen in a window and in the library's garden. In 1999, paranormal investigators verified that several spirits haunt the building.

New Hanover County Public Library (Wilmington, North Carolina)

A ghost that is apparently obsessed with researching the Civil War spends a lot of time in the North Carolina Room at the New Hanover County Public Library. On several occasions, librarians have come to work in the morning to find files scattered on a table despite the fact that everything was put away the night before. People have heard the rustling of pages turning even though they are alone, and once, the glass door of a locked bookcase began shaking violently on its own.

Steubenville Public Library (Steubenville, Ohio)

Ellen Summers Wilson served as the first librarian at the Steubenville Public Library when it opened in 1902. Tragically, she died of tuberculosis only two years later at age 31. Almost immediately after her death, people began hearing footsteps and creaking floorboards coming from the library's attic, which was empty. In subsequent years, air-conditioning equipment was placed in the attic, but it repeatedly and mysteriously turned off on its own. Eventually, the AC unit was moved to another room, and the ventilation problems ceased.

Easton Area Public Library (Easton, Pennsylvania)

The Easton Area Public Library might be the most haunted library in the United States. When the Carnegie Foundation offered Easton $50,000 to build a public library if the town would contribute the land, the most suitable site was already occupied by an old cemetery. The grounds were cleared, and most of the graves were relocated, but some were interred in a vault that is now located underneath the back exit of the library's parking lot. Two marked graves are also present on the site: those of William Parsons, the founder of Easton, and Elizabeth "Mammy" Bell Morgan, who ran a local hotel and was helpful to townspeople who had legal issues. Since the library opened in 1903, articles in the local newspaper have reported that it is haunted. Some people have claimed to see a lady with a glowing head floating in a window; others have witnessed a headless woman wandering the grounds and glowing lights traveling throughout the building. Even today, mysterious sounds and sensations are credited to the spirits, including that of Mammy Morgan.

James D. Hoskins Library (Knoxville, Tennessee)

After hours at the James D. Hoskins Library on the campus of the University of Tennessee can be scary. Maintenance workers have heard doors shut on their own and the footsteps of the spirit of a former graduate student known as the "Evening Primrose." This ghost apparently likes to cook late at night, as custodians and other employees have reported the inexplicable scent of cornbread baking.

Sweetwater County Library (Green River, Wyoming)

It's not surprising that the Sweetwater County Library is haunted; after all, it's built on the site of a graveyard. Since the mid-1980s, lights have mysteriously turned on and off by themselves, and orbs of light have been known to move along the walls inside the art gallery, even when it's empty. Strange flapping sounds are heard throughout the building at night, and two old electric typewriters once began operating on their own. The paranormal activity at the library is so common that in 1993, staff members started a "Ghost Log" to document their experiences.

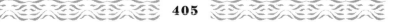

Spirits Shine On at the Stanley Hotel

The Stanley Hotel—a beautiful Georgian-style resort in Estes Park, Colorado—was the inspiration for the Overlook Hotel in Stephen King's famous novel The Shining *and the movie adaptation, which starred Jack Nicholson. Fortunately, unlike at King's fictional inn, the ghosts of the Stanley Hotel are not malicious. But rest assured, there are definitely ghosts at this famous hotel.*

How It All Began

In 1903, F. O. Stanley—inventor of the Stanley Steamer automobile—was suffering from tuberculosis and was told that he had just months to live. That year, Stanley and his wife, Flora, visited Estes Park hoping to find some relief in the thin mountain air. They fell in love with its majestic Rocky Mountain landscape and decided to move there permanently. Shortly thereafter, construction began on the Stanley Hotel, which was completed in 1909. (Stanley died in 1940 at the ripe old age of 91, so apparently the mountain air did the trick.)

Nestled in the mountains, the resort offers a spectacular view. Many notable guests have stayed at the Stanley Hotel, including John Philip Sousa, President Theodore Roosevelt, Japanese royalty, members of the Hollywood set—including Jim Carrey, Rebecca De Mornay, and Elliott Gould—and, of course, writer Stephen King.

Friendly Ghosts

King stayed in Room 217, which is the haunted room in *The Shining*. However, most of the paranormal activity at the Stanley seems to occur on the fourth floor, specifically in Room 418. There, guests have heard children laughing and playing, but when they complain that the children are too loud, no children are ever found.

In Room 407, a ghost likes to play with the lights. However, it's apparently a reasonable spook: When guests ask it to turn the lights back on, it does.

During his stay, Stephen King alerted the staff that a young boy on the second floor was calling for his nanny. Of course, the staff

members at the Stanley were well aware of the ghostly boy, who had been spotted throughout the hotel many times over the years.

But the two most prominent spirits at the resort are those of F. O. Stanley and his wife. Flora makes her presence known by playing the piano in the ballroom. Even those who haven't seen her claim to hear piano music coming from the ballroom when it's empty, and some have seen the piano keys move up and down of their own accord.

F. O. Stanley's specter most often manifests in the lobby, the bar, and the billiard room, which were apparently his favorite spots in the building when he was alive.

A Ghostly Visitor

When Jason Hawes and Grant Wilson from the television show *Ghost Hunters* stayed at the Stanley Hotel in 2006, their investigation hit paranormal pay dirt. Hawes stayed in Room 401—purportedly one of the most haunted guest rooms—and set up a video camera to record anything that occurred while he was asleep. Although the picture is dark, the camera captured the distinct sounds of a door opening and glass breaking—all while Hawes was sound asleep. When he got up to investigate, he noticed that the closet door had been opened and a glass on the nightstand was broken. Later, the camera recorded the closet door closing—and latching—with no humans in sight.

Wilson had his own paranormal experience in Room 1302: He was sitting at a table with some other team members when the table lifted off the ground and crashed back down—all of its own accord. When the group tried to raise the table, they found it to be so heavy that it took several people to lift it even a few inches.

During a follow-up session at the Stanley Hotel, those in attendance were also treated to paranormal activity. K-2 meters were used to detect changes in the electromagnetic field (which indicate that a ghost is nearby), and they lit up time and again. Clear responses to questions directed at the resident spirits were also captured on audio recordings.

Meet the Spirits

The Stanley Hotel offers ghost tours to educate visitors about the paranormal activity within its walls. Or if you'd rather just stay in your room, you could always watch a movie—*The Shining* runs continuously on the guest-room televisions.

The Amityville Horror:
Haunted House or Horrible Hoax?

It seems that nearly every town has a haunted house—the one home that animals and locals avoid like the plague. But when it comes to haunted houses that can chill your bones with just one glance and give you nightmares for weeks, nothing can hold a ghostly candle to the foreboding Dutch Colonial in Amityville, New York, which once glared down at passersby with windows that seemed to resemble demonic eyes.

Brutal Beginnings

Most hauntings begin with tragic circumstances, and the house at 112 Ocean Avenue is no exception. In the early morning hours of November 13, 1974, someone fatally shot six of the seven members of the DeFeo family—parents Ronald Sr. and Louise and four of their children: Mark, John, Allison, and Dawn. The only family member to escape the massacre was 23-year-old Ronnie "Butch" DeFeo, who was arrested and charged with all six murders. He eventually confessed and was sentenced to 25 years to life in prison. During the trial, rumors suggested that demonic voices had directed DeFeo to commit the murders, although prosecutors claimed that he was merely trying to collect the family's $200,000 life insurance policy.

The DeFeo house stood unoccupied until December 1975, when new owners came calling.

The Horror Begins

George and Kathy Lutz knew that they had found a bargain when their realtor showed them the house at 112 Ocean Avenue. It had six bedrooms, a pool, and even a boathouse—all for the unbelievable price of $80,000. Of course, an entire family had been murdered in the house, and some of their belongings were still inside, but the Lutzes decided that it was too good a deal to pass up. So George and Kathy moved in with their three young children: Daniel, Christopher, and Missy. Shortly thereafter, the Lutzes' nightmare

began. It quickly became obvious to them that demonic forces were at work inside the house. Here is some of the paranormal activity that allegedly took place there:

- George had trouble sleeping and continually woke up at exactly 3:15 A.M., which was believed to be the time that the DeFeo murders took place.

- Daughter Missy began talking to an imaginary friend—a girl named Jodie, who sometimes appeared as a pig. Standing outside the house one night, George looked up and saw a giant pig with glowing red eyes staring back at him from Missy's room. Later, cloven hoofprints were found in the snow outside the house.

- Even though the family moved in during the middle of winter, certain rooms in the house—especially the sewing room—were constantly infested with flies.

- A small room painted blood-red—which was dubbed "the Red Room"—was found hidden behind shelving in the basement. The Lutzes felt that an evil force inhabited the room; even the family dog refused to go near it.

- During an attempt to bless the house, a priest suddenly became violently ill and heard an inhuman voice tell him to "Get out!" When George and Kathy attempted to bless the house themselves, they heard voices screaming, "Will you stop?"

- Green slime oozed out of the toilets and dripped from the walls.

- George unintentionally began to take on the mannerisms of Butch DeFeo; he even grew a beard, which caused him to resemble the murderer. Apparently the likeness was so uncanny that when Lutz walked into a bar that DeFeo used to frequent, patrons thought he *was* DeFeo.

On January 14, 1976, unable to cope with the unseen forces at work in the home, George and Kathy Lutz gathered up their children and their dog and fled the house in the middle of the night. The following day, George sent movers to collect their belongings. The Lutzes never again set foot inside the house at 112 Ocean Avenue.

Searching for Evil

In an attempt to understand exactly what had happened to his family inside the house, George hired paranormal experts Ed and Lorraine Warren, who arrived at the house with a local news crew on March 6, 1976. Lorraine said that she sensed a very strong evil presence in the house. Several years later, the Warrens released time-lapse infrared photographs from the investigation; they seem to show a ghostly boy with glowing eyes standing near one of the staircases.

Jay Anson's book *The Amityville Horror: A True Story* was released in September 1977. The book, which chronicles the Lutz family's harrowing ordeal, was compiled from more than 40 hours of tape-recorded interviews with George and Kathy and became a best-seller almost immediately. After the book became a cultural phenomenon, however, people started taking a closer look into what really happened at 112 Ocean Avenue.

Controversy Begins

When people started to scrutinize the specifics in Anson's book, the story began to fall apart. For example, a check of weather conditions showed that no snow was on the ground when George claimed to have found the strange cloven footprints in the snow. Likewise, windows and doors that ghostly forces had supposedly broken were found to be intact. Reporters who interviewed neighbors along Ocean Avenue found that not a single person could remember seeing or hearing anything strange going on at the house. And despite the book mentioning numerous visits by the local police to investigate strange noises at the Lutz house, the Amityville Police Department publicly stated that during the time that the Lutzes lived at 112 Ocean Avenue, they never once visited the home or received a single phone call from the family.

The Lawsuits

In May 1977, George and Kathy Lutz filed a series of lawsuits against numerous publications and individuals who had either investigated 112 Ocean Avenue or had written about the reported hauntings there. They alleged that the accused had invaded their privacy and caused their family mental distress. There was one other name in the lawsuits that raised more than a few eyebrows: William Weber, Butch

DeFeo's defense attorney. Even more surprising was that Weber filed a countersuit for $2 million for breach of contract.

Weber contended that he had met with the Lutzes, and "over many bottles of wine," the three made up the story of the house being haunted. When Weber found out that the Lutzes had taken their story to Jay Anson and essentially cut him out of the book deal, he sued. In September 1979, U.S. District Court Judge Jack B. Weinstein dismissed all of the Lutzes' claims and made some telling remarks in his ruling, including his belief that the book was basically a work of fiction that relied heavily upon Weber's suggestions. Weber's countersuit was later settled out of court for an undisclosed amount.

What Really Happened?

Even though it's been decades since the Lutzes occupied the house at 112 Ocean Avenue, many questions still remain unanswered. A series of books and films bearing the name *The Amityville Horror* continued to blur the lines between what really happened in the home and what was fabricated. In 2005, a remake of the original *Amityville Horror* movie added many new elements to the story that are unsubstantiated, including a link between the house in Amityville and a man named John Ketcham, who was reportedly involved in witchcraft in Salem, Massachusetts.

Kathy Lutz died of emphysema in August 2004, and George passed away of complications from heart disease in May 2006. Both went to their grave claiming that what they said happened to them at 112 Ocean Avenue was not a hoax.

The house itself still stands. One would think that a building as infamous as the "Amityville Horror" house would be easy to find; not so. In order to stop the onslaught of trespassing curiosity seekers, its address has been changed, so 112 Ocean Avenue technically no longer exists. Also, the distinctive quarter-moon windows have been removed and replaced with ordinary square ones.

Since the Lutz family moved out, the property has changed hands several times, but none of the subsequent owners have reported anything paranormal taking place there. Some have acknowledged being frightened from time to time, but these scares are usually caused by trespassers peering into the windows, trying to get glimpses of the inside of this allegedly haunted house.

Westover Plantation's Friendly Ghost

🪦 🪦 🪦 🪦

She said that she wanted to return in a nice way, so as not to frighten anyone. And in the afterlife, Evelyn Byrd seems to have gotten her wish to become a friendly ghost.

Love Byrd

Evelyn Byrd was born in 1707; her father was William Byrd II, who founded the city of Richmond, Virginia. When she was ten years old, Evelyn was sent to school in England. While she was away, she fell in love with someone whom her father disliked—as young girls sometimes do. And as fathers often do, William forced the lovebirds to end their relationship. A few years later, when a brokenhearted Evelyn returned to her father's Virginia estate—which was known as Westover Plantation—she simply withdrew from life. She only maintained contact with a friend named Anne Carter Harrison; the two girls met almost daily in a nearby poplar grove.

This continued for several years until one day, Evelyn confided to Anne that she felt the approach of death. However, she urged her friend to continue going to the poplar grove; she said that after her death, they would still meet there. Evelyn insisted that she would return but not in a scary sort of way.

The Genial Ghost

Evelyn's prophecy was correct: She died shortly thereafter at age 29. One day soon after, Anne was in the poplar grove when she saw Evelyn wearing a stunning white dress and strolling through the trees, just as she had in life. Evelyn smiled at Anne and then vanished. Thus began the sightings of Evelyn, both on the grounds of Westover and inside the house. What sets Evelyn apart from most ghosts is that she's often seen as a three-dimensional figure that's only identified as a ghost when she vanishes.

Once, when a workman walked into a bedroom at Westover to complete some repairs, he was startled to see a woman sitting in front of a mirror combing her hair. Surprised that the room was occupied, the workman told the homeowner about it. When they returned to the room, it was empty.

Clearly, Evelyn wants to be as unobtrusive as possible while still making her presence known. On another occasion, a girl visiting Westover awoke to see Evelyn—resplendent in her white dress—staring benignly at her. Another visitor woke up in the middle of the night, casually gazed out the window, and saw Evelyn standing on the front lawn. Evelyn motioned the woman away from the window, as if to say, "Go away. You've got all day. This is my time now." The guest obediently closed the drapes.

Sometimes, Evelyn just seems to want to be a part of the action at Westover, such as the time when she began following a person out of the house. Thinking that it was a friend, the person turned and gazed back to see a woman with black hair wearing a beautiful white dress. As soon as the two made eye contact, the woman in the white dress disappeared.

Byrds of a Feather Haunt Together

Evelyn does not hold a ghostly monopoly at Westover. Her sister-in-law, Elizabeth Hill Carter Byrd, had an unhappy marriage and died tragically in her bedroom when the heavy chest of drawers that she was searching for evidence of her husband's infidelity fell on top of her and crushed her. Even today, people hear horrible disembodied screams coming from her old bedroom; it is believed that Elizabeth is doomed to forever reenact her agonizing death.

Still another Westover ghost is that of Evelyn's brother, William Byrd III, who committed suicide in his bedroom in 1777 after he lost the family fortune due to his gambling. Once, a person who was spending the night in that room felt an icy cold presence enter and then watched it glide over to a chair. After that, the room was filled with an oppressive atmosphere, which the visitor suspected was caused by the spirit of William Byrd III.

But it's Evelyn, the friendly spirit, who holds the most sway at Westover, which proves that nice ghosts don't necessarily finish last.

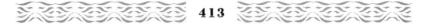

Spending Life—and Death—Behind Bars

Life is difficult for those who are incarcerated. But not even death could grant the following phantoms reprieves from spending eternity confined to prison.

Andersonville Prison (Andersonville, Georgia)

Known to Confederate soldiers as "Camp Sumter," this remote prison was built in the 1860s to hold captured Union soldiers. Henry Wirz, who served as captain of the site, immediately established what he called the "Dead Line"; anyone proceeding beyond that point was gunned down. As in most prison camps, sickness overtook many of the men and morale was poor. Today, visitors can still hear gunshots and sense the devastation that was felt by those prisoners of long ago. A foul odor is often detected, and many people have observed ghosts walking across the grounds.

New Mexico State Penitentiary (Santa Fe, New Mexico)

A riot at the New Mexico State Penitentiary in 1980 resulted in more than enough trauma to create unsettled spirits. In a rebellion that was driven by rage rather than well-thought-out plans, 33 inmates lost their lives. Twelve guards were taken hostage, and more than 100 people were injured.

If heightened energy and emotions are the ingredients for paranormal activity, then the New Mexico State Pen should be one of the most haunted prisons in the world. And perhaps it is. Doors have been observed opening and closing on their own, lights turn on and off by themselves, unusual noises are heard, and visitors report a general feeling of unease when entering Cellblocks 3 and 4, where the worst fighting of the riots occurred. New Mexico's governor closed the prison in 1998 because of its "uncontrollable disturbances"; it has since been used in the production of films such as *The Longest Yard* (2005).

Cornwall Jail (Cornwall, Ontario)

One of the oldest buildings in Ontario, this *gaol* was built in 1833, and it was used for detention until 2002. Today, the jail is a tourist

attraction that allows visitors to see what prison life was like in another era—and maybe glimpse a ghost or two.

Nowadays, the prison system separates criminals by several factors, such as age, gender, and severity of crime. But that was not the case at the Cornwall Jail. In the 1800s, inmates there included both criminals and the criminally insane. Men, women, adults, and minors were all housed under one roof. Living conditions were poor, which resulted in many deaths over the years. When renovations took place in recent years, at least ten unmarked graves were found. Nearly a dozen executions by hanging and two suicides also took place on the grounds. Tourists who visit the site have heard disembodied humming and other strange noises. Doors that are locked at night are open in the morning. And some visitors report feeling the presence of a young woman and her child.

Wyoming Frontier Prison (Rawlins, Wyoming)

Known as "The Old Pen," the Wyoming Frontier Prison was built in 1901 and was used until 1981. Today, the building is a national historic monument that houses a museum. The Old Pen was known for the use of severe torture and the mistreatment of its inmates. Fourteen prisoners were executed on the premises, and several more were killed during a botched escape attempt when death-row inmates hit a gas line while trying to tunnel their way to freedom; someone lit a match to identify the obstruction and the men died instantly. They may have been the lucky ones, however: Nine other death-row prisoners were victims of a poorly constructed gallows. The contraption didn't drop the men far enough to break their necks, and they ended up dying slow, agonizing deaths by strangulation.

The Old Pen is now the site of several residual hauntings that feed off the negative energy of the place. Residual hauntings often create an atmosphere of unpleasantness, as if the agony that occurred there still lingers. People have reported unusual odors, screams, wailing, and a sense of intense fear. Because these are mostly residual hauntings, the spirits at the Old Pen don't seem to acknowledge the living at all, which is probably a good thing.

The Ghostly Tales of Stephen Crane

🪦 🪦 🪦 🪦

Stephen Crane's classic Civil War novel The Red Badge of Courage *is often praised for its honest and intense depiction of war. Although Crane had never experienced battle himself, war was one subject that he obviously knew something about . . . another was ghosts. He wrote about phantoms in two stories that appeared in* The New York Press: *"Ghosts on the New Jersey Coast" (November 11, 1894) and "The Ghostly Sphinx of Metedeconk" (January 13, 1895).*

In the late 1880s and early 1890s, Stephen Crane worked as an assistant to his brother Townley at a news bureau in coastal New Jersey. At the time, the Jersey Shore was a lonely, wild, and untamed place, populated predominantly by sand dunes and seagulls. Crane knew of the region's reputation for mysterious hauntings and unexplained phenomena. "A man had better think three times before he openly scorns the legends of the phantoms," he warns solemnly in "Ghosts on the New Jersey Coast."

Is That Your Final Answer?

Crane's "The Ghostly Sphinx of Metedeconk" concerns a ghostly lady in white—"a moaning, mourning thing of the mist"—that prowls the beaches of the Metedeconk area (near what is today the northern end of Barnegat Bay) late at night, when clouds float past the face of the moon and the air is thick with salty spray. Her hair is described as wild and disheveled, falling about her shoulders like unruly serpents. Dressed all in white, she walks with her hands clasped, seeking out humans who are unlucky enough to cross her path. When she finds someone, she gazes at him or her and asks if they know the whereabouts of her lover's body. Those who don't reply immediately in a coherent manner are fated to die before the next morning. Grown men who normally faced down the dangers of the sea with a sneer and a snarl have been known to turn and run rather than face this awful specter.

In life, the woman lived with her husband—a sea captain—in a house on the beach. One day, as the captain was preparing for a voyage, the woman complained about the length of his upcoming absence. Even before his ship had disappeared from view, the woman longed for his return.

As she pined for her lover night after night, the woman became a pale, emaciated shadow of her former self. One night, a terrific storm caught a ship and tossed it onto the shoals near the woman's home. The vessel was battered mercilessly until it broke apart, leaving those on board helpless. Eventually, the ferocious waves began yanking bodies off the boat and washing them onto the beach. The woman, who had been anxiously walking along the shore, saw something rolling in the surf. Suddenly, a giant wave brought it crashing right in front of her, and she saw that her lover had indeed come home to her—although not in the manner that she had hoped. But she had gotten her wish: Never again would he leave her.

The shock of this was all too much, and the woman died shortly thereafter. But it wasn't long before her spirit began walking the beach, asking anyone she met her eternal question. She may be there still, threatening any nocturnal beachgoers with her unearthly presence.

Blue Light Special

In "Ghosts on the New Jersey Coast," Crane tells of the November 1854 shipwreck of the German vessel *New Era,* which was one of the worst disasters to occur on the Jersey Shore. Nearly 250 people drowned after the ship ran aground near Deal Beach and the captain and crew abandoned her, leaving the passengers at the mercy of the wind and water.

The victims were collected and buried in a mass grave, and soon after, rumors began to suggest that the dead had been buried with an untold amount of gold that they'd brought with them from Europe. However, the grave was said to be guarded by a dim blue light that floated above it and attacked anyone who tried to disturb the peaceful rest of those just below.

Fighting Phantoms

Another incident that Crane relates in "Ghosts on the New Jersey Coast" that continues to resonate to this day took place on the beach just south of where the famed Barnegat Lighthouse now stands.

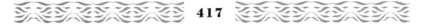

There, in 1782, a band of about 20 American privateers found an abandoned British ship run aground. The men worked all day salvaging cargo from the ship, and when night fell, they were so tired that they decided to sleep on the beach. However, a crew of Tories snuck over from a nearby island and murdered the men as they slept.

According to Crane, the hideous ghost of the Tory leader haunts the beach, and anyone who sleeps there will wake to find a phantom holding a knife to his or her throat. No matter how fast the person tries to run away, he or she hears the ghostly crunch of invisible footsteps right behind and knows that the evil creature is close by.

Even today, strange occurrences are reported on this beach late at night. The sounds of moaning, laughter, and yelling are often faintly heard, as if the surprise attack of centuries ago is being replayed.

Too Much Salt Is Indeed Harmful

Another tale from "Ghosts on the New Jersey Coast" concerns a Native American who had been dead for hundreds of years when the story was published. His restless spirit walked the beaches at night searching for the young wife he had killed because she had displeased him by using too much salt while cooking. This apparition had a daggerlike glance that would send shivers down the spine of even the bravest soul. Once, a few young men with alcohol-fueled bravado decided to try to follow this spirit. However, when they spotted the Native American, he simply turned around and looked at them with his fearsome stare. With their liquid courage rapidly evaporating, the men turned and ran away as if the devil himself was after them . . . and perhaps he was.

Dutch Treat?

Most coastal regions have their own versions of the famous *Flying Dutchman* ghost ship (see page 443), and Crane told of New Jersey's, which is often seen in a sparsely populated area behind the Shark River near Asbury Park. The large vessel easily cruises in just inches of water and carries a crew of skeletons, whose terrifying visages peer out at bystanders.

Nothing but a Hound Dog

This tale of a phantom black hound is another of Crane's scary stories. After a shipwreck, marauders waited for the dead to wash

ashore so that they could rob them of their valuables.

Suddenly, the bandits saw a large black hound emerge from the roiling surf; the beast was dragging the body of a man behind it. The man was still and lifeless, but the dog hopefully laid the body of his master on the beach and nudged his hands a few times.

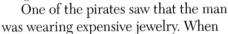

One of the pirates saw that the man was wearing expensive jewelry. When the scavenger reached for it, the hound bared its teeth and growled, ready to defend its master. A few moments later, however, another man struck the animal with a fatal blow, and it crawled onto the body of its master to die.

However, death was just the beginning for the hound. Soon after, fishermen returning home late at night saw the phantom beast on the beach. The spectral hound had blood dripping from its head and foam oozing from its mouth; the creature's eyes blazed with demonic fire. The dog is often seen scampering along the beach with its nose down, as if trying to pick up a scent.

The Barnegat region in which this story is set is still there— a little more developed and a little more crowded but still primarily ocean and sand. It's very possible that the hound is still there too, searching for the person who did it wrong but quite possibly not caring who it encounters, as long as it's human. As Crane advised, if you come across the hound (or any of these other specters), run.

"It is wonderful that five thousand years have now elapsed since the creation of the world, and still it is undecided whether or not there has ever been an instance of the spirit of any person appearing after death. All argument is against it; but all belief is for it."

—British author Samuel Johnson

FRIGHTENING FACTS

Celebrity Hauntings

- *The Avalon Hollywood theater—formerly the Palace Theater and Hollywood Playhouse—sees a lot of paranormal activity in the wee hours of the morning. It's home to both male and female ghosts that are musical, conversational, and always playful and good-hearted—yet no one knows their identities.*

- *Paramount's studios have more than one resident ghost. Rudolph Valentino (who seems to get around in death as much as he did in life) hangs around the costume department and the soundstages. Also, an unidentified spirit likes to walk the overhead catwalks.*

- *Orson Welles had a special table at Ma Maison—now Sweet Lady Jane—on Melrose Avenue in West Hollywood. According to those who have seen his caped specter or smelled his brandy and cigars, Welles just can't bear to leave what was once—and apparently still is—his favorite haunt.*

- *The internationally known Palace Theatre on Broadway is said to be home to more than 100 spirits, including that of singer Judy Garland, who apparently still lingers by the stage door— perhaps waiting for her fans. However, there's one ghost that no one wants to encounter: the acrobat who broke his neck onstage. According to legend, anyone who sees him will die soon afterward.*

- *Thelma Todd's film career survived the transition from silents to talkies, but in 1935, she died of carbon monoxide poisoning in her garage at age 29. Her death was ruled accidental, but some believe that she was murdered. Today, those in the empty garage can hear a phantom engine running and smell exhaust fumes.*

- *William S. Hart (a star of Westerns during the silent-film era) and his wife Mary Ellen lived in a mansion in Santa Clarita, California. The building now houses the Hart Ranch & Museum, which is dedicated to Western art and Hart's career. Tourists visiting the museum have reported that their cameras malfunction there; they've also claimed to have seen Hart in the living room and Mary Ellen near her bed.*

- *While filming* The Sheik *(1921), Rudolph Valentino stayed at a cozy beach house in Oxnard, California. The house still stands, and some have reported seeing a dark figure that resembles Valentino pacing the porch.*

- *How many places can one icon haunt? Rudolph Valentino often stayed in Room 210 of the Santa Maria Inn in Santa Maria, California, for some rest and relaxation. These days, if you want peace and quiet while staying at the hotel, you should avoid Room 210 because Valentino's ghost is said to knock on the room's door and walls at all hours of the day and night. Some guests have also reported feeling the mattress depress while they're lying on it, as if someone else had just sat down.*

- *Buxom blonde starlet Jean Harlow once lived in Westwood, California, not far from UCLA's campus. Subsequent residents of her house heard sobs and soft feminine whispers calling for help, smelled perfume for no explainable reason, and witnessed lights turning on and off by themselves.*

- *Before he was killed in 1980, at the Dakota apartment building in New York City, John Lennon told his son Julian that if he ever saw a white feather floating across a room, it would be his spirit. Julian believes that since his death, his father has indeed stopped by. Paul McCartney also claims that he felt Lennon's spirit in a recording studio in 1995 and saw him in the form of a white peacock at a photo shoot.*

- *From 1964 to 1968—during her heyday as a sexy siren of films and pinups—Elke Sommer lived in a Beverly Hills home that was haunted by a well-dressed man. Sommer and hubby Joe Hyams sold the place after a suspicious kitchen fire.*

- *In 1959, George Reeves—television's first Superman—died of a single gunshot wound to the head at his home on Benedict Canyon Drive. Ever since then, those living in his former abode have spotted a spectral Reeves (who is sometimes wearing his Superman costume) roaming the grounds. His death was ruled a suicide, but some say that his ghost has come back to tell people that he was actually murdered.*

The Ghosts of Yosemite National Park

*Anyone with an ounce of supernatural savvy knows
that anything connected with Native American burial
grounds and/or curses is like a flashing yellow caution
light saying, "Warning: Paranormal Activity Ahead."*

The Creepy Canyon

Back in the 19th century, the ability of Native Americans to marshal
the wrath of the spirit world was dismissed as superstitious mumbo-
jumbo. That's unfortunate, because if it had been taken more seriously,
people might have feared the consequences of the words of Chief
Tenaya of the Ahwahneechee tribe. In 1851, when white settlers
were trying to force his people out of the Yosemite Valley in what is
now Yosemite National Park, Chief Tenaya put a curse on the land.

It turns out that the chief wasn't just making an idle gesture. In the
park's Tenaya Canyon, a disproportionate number of tragic incidents
have occurred: Visitors to the area have become lost, drowned, fallen
to their deaths, and died of hypothermia. Once, a pilot who was looking for an injured hiker was purportedly overcome by vertigo and
nearly flew his chopper into the side of the canyon. Not even Yosemite
champion John Muir was spared from the alleged curse: During his
first visit to the canyon, Muir fell and was knocked unconscious while
scaling cliffs in "the Bermuda Triangle of Yosemite," as Tenaya Canyon
is sometimes called.

Apparently, Tenaya is not above more forceful demonstrations to
exact his revenge. In 1996, a Native American who had been born in
the park and had spent his entire life working there as a maintenance
technician was preparing to retire. At that time, park officials were
told that Ahwahneechee legend warned that the last Yosemite-born
Indian's departure from the park would bring disaster. But in late
December 1996, with their heads firmly buried in the sand, park
officials let the man retire and leave the confines of the park.

A few days later, on January 1, a freak storm resulted in a flood
that caused $178 million in damage to the park. Some months later

(and possibly with a nervous nod to Tenaya), park officials agreed to establish a traditional Native American village in Yosemite Valley.

Sometimes Tenaya steps aside and allows others to do the supernatural heavy lifting at Yosemite. Visitors to the park have reported seeing and even speaking with Native American apparitions. Legends tell of a ghost boy that inhabits the waters of Grouse Lake; he reportedly likes to grab the legs of swimmers and pull them underneath the water. It is also said that an evil spirit wind inhabits Bridalveil Fall and that this wind is always ready to send an unsuspecting soul plummeting into the falls to his or her death.

A Ghostly Group

Some standard hauntings round out the supernatural smorgasbord at Yosemite. According to legend, a lonely camper once hung himself in his tent; late at night, his body can supposedly still be seen slowly swinging forlornly from the tent frame. Also, a young couple who drowned near Stoneman Bridge has been seen on or near the span on many occasions.

Yosemite's Ahwahnee Hotel is the park's own "Apparition Inn." The building was used as a convalescent home for soldiers during World War II, and it is believed that many of its ghosts are the spirits of those troops. The hotel's former operator, Mary Curry Tresidder, lived in the building for many years until she died in the 1960s, and apparently, she isn't letting a little thing like death force her to check out: She's still seen on the sixth floor, perhaps making certain that the guests are comfortable.

However, for sheer spiritual star power, nothing can top the phantom rocking chair that appears from time to time on the third floor. In 1962, President John F. Kennedy stayed in a third-floor suite, and the hotel placed a rocking chair in the room for his comfort. The chair was removed after Kennedy left; however, since his assassination in 1963, housekeepers have witnessed a rocking chair slowly swaying back and forth in the room in which he stayed. When they glance away from the chair, it disappears.

If it is indeed JFK still enjoying the pleasures of Yosemite, he's obviously not alone. From Native Americans to presidents to plain folks, Yosemite is a difficult place to leave for both the living and the dead.

 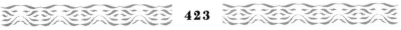

Guest Ghosts Are the Norm at Austin's Driskill Hotel

Southern hospitality abounds at the Driskill Hotel in downtown Austin, Texas. Built in 1886 by local cattle baron Colonel Jesse Lincoln Driskill, this lodging is hardly short on amenities. As a member of Historic Hotels of America and Associated Luxury Hotels International, the Driskill offers every comfort imaginable: From fancy linens and plasma-screen TVs to fine dining and complimentary shoeshines, this Austin institution has it all—including a few resident ghosts.

Since it opened, the Driskill has been a magnet for the rich and famous: Lyndon and Lady Bird Johnson had their first date at the hotel's restaurant, and Amelia Earhart, Louis Armstrong, and Richard Nixon have all sought respite there. At the Driskill, the upscale clientele mixes with the invisible guests that reside there full-time—the true spirits of the hotel.

Meet the Ghosts

Considered one of the most haunted hotels in the United States, the Driskill is the eternal home of many spirits. First and foremost would have to be the ghost of Colonel Driskill himself. He makes his presence known by entering random guest rooms and smoking the cigars that he once loved so dearly. Driskill is also said to play with the lights in bathrooms, turning them on and off for fun.

Hotel guests and employees have seen water faucets turn on and off by themselves; some have even reported hearing the sound of noisy guests coming from an empty elevator. Others have felt as if they were being pushed out of bed, and some wake in the morning to find that their room's furniture has been rearranged during the night.

A Ghost with Fashion Sense

When singer Annie Lennox stayed at the Driskill Hotel in the 1980s while performing in Austin, she laid out two dresses to consider after

she got out of the shower. When she emerged from the bathroom, only one dress was still on the bed; the other was once again hanging in the closet.

A ghost dressed in Victorian-era clothing has been seen at night where the front desk used to stand, and guests have detected the scent of roses in the area. This is believed to be the spirit of Mrs. Bridges, who worked at the Driskill as a front-desk clerk in the early 1900s.

The spirit of a young girl haunts the lobby on the first floor; she is believed to have been the daughter of a senator. In 1887, she was chasing a ball on the grand staircase when she tripped and fell to her death. Today, her ghost is often heard laughing and bouncing a ball up and down those same stairs.

The spirit of Peter J. Lawless might still be residing in Room 419, where he lived from 1886 until 1916 or 1917. Although the house-keeping crew cleans and vacuums that room like all the others, they often report finding rumpled bedclothes, open dresser drawers, and footprints in the bathroom—after they've already cleaned the room. Lawless is typically blamed for this mischievous behavior, and his specter is also often spotted near the elevators on the fifth floor. He pauses to check his watch when the doors open—then he promptly disappears.

In the Spirit of Things

A more modern ghost that hangs around the Driskill is the "Houston Bride." When her fiancé called off their wedding plans in the 1990s, the young woman did what many other jilted brides would be tempted to do: She stole his credit cards and went shopping! She was last seen on the hotel elevator, loaded down with her packages. Retail therapy was apparently not the cure, however: She was found dead a few days later, the victim of a gunshot wound to the abdomen. Some guests have seen her apparition with her arms full of packages; others have spotted her in her wedding gown. Oddly, it seems to be those guests who are at the hotel for weddings or bachelorette parties that are most likely to see her. And even stranger, some brides consider it good luck to catch a glimpse of the tragic "Houston Bride" before their own weddings. Maybe she counts as "something blue."

The Ubiquitous Lady in White

"So there I was, sitting in the empty hallway, when all of a sudden I felt like a cold wind was blowing through me. I felt a chill down to my bones, and then I looked up and saw a woman in a long white dress walking down the staircase without touching the ground."

No one knows why so many ghostly women wear white dresses (or, for that matter, exactly why ghosts wear clothes at all), but stories of ladies in white go back hundreds of years. In fact, tales of some of the spectral women in white that supposedly wander the forests of New England were among the very first American ghost stories.

Today, when paranormal investigators interview witnesses who talk about seeing women in white, they tend to be instantly skeptical. But these stories didn't just come from out of nowhere. Some say it's an image of ghosts that was created by Hollywood or by Victorian-era novelist Wilkie Collins (whose hit novel *The Woman in White* wasn't even about a ghost). However, such stories have actually been common in supernatural lore for centuries, and these spectral women are reported—often by reputable witnesses—more and more every year. Ladies in white were following children in dark woods, stalking the lonely hallways of old buildings, and wandering the streets of small rural towns long before movies could have created such images.

Forever Awaiting His Return

One of the more venerable ladies in white is the White Lady of the Bridgeport Inn, which was built in 1877 for Hiram Leavitt and his family in the mining town of Bridgeport, California. There, a woman in white has been seen in Room 19 so often that she's mentioned on the building's historical marker.

The most common story surrounding the origin of this ghost is that she was the fiancée of a young miner during the late 1800s. After a particularly good day of prospecting, the miner decided to walk from the room that he'd rented from Leavitt to the nearest bank—which was several miles away—to trade his gold for cash. His fiancée

wanted to go with him, but they didn't call it "the Wild West" for nothing: The young miner knew that he risked being robbed while carrying so much gold, so he told her to wait in their room (Room 19) at the inn. And so she waited . . . and waited . . . and waited. . . .

After several hours of listening for his footsteps and hearing nothing but the howling of the wind, she began to fear the worst. Finally, her fears were realized when she heard the news that her fiancé had been robbed and murdered by highwaymen.

In her grief, the poor woman hanged herself in Room 19, where her ghost has been seen ever since—often wearing a long white wedding gown.

Connecticut's Lady in White

In Easton, Connecticut—on the other side of the country from Bridgeport—is Union Cemetery, a burial ground that dates back to New England's earliest settlers, who arrived nearly 400 years ago. Dressed in a long white dress and a bonnet, Easton's Lady in White is sometimes seen at the graveyard or on the road outside of it,

which stretches between Union Cemetery and the nearby Stepney Cemetery.

Countless witnesses—including police officers and firefighters—have reported hitting a woman in white with their vehicles on the road that connects the graveyards. They slam on their brakes when she mysteriously appears in front of their cars, but it's too late: The terrified drivers hear the dreadful thud of the impact and watch her limp body fly away from their vehicles to the side of the road. They pull over, rush to the side of the road, and find nothing. The woman has vanished, leaving nothing but an imprint in the snow where her body landed. In 1993, a collision with the ghostly woman even left a dent in a firefighter's car. Roadside phantoms that vanish after being hit are not uncommon, but for them to leave behind such physical evidence is quite unusual.

So common were sightings of Easton's Lady in White that paranormal experts Ed and Lorraine Warren—founders of the New
England Society for Psychic Research and one of the first couples to
turn ghost hunting into a profession—used Union Cemetery as the
subject of their 1992 book *Graveyard*.

During their research, the Warrens spoke with a man whose late
wife had been buried in Union Cemetery. One evening, while he
was visiting his wife's grave, he heard something rustling the leaves
behind him. When he turned, he saw the Lady in White looking
down at him.

"I wish," she said, as he knelt frozen in place, "that my husband
had loved me as much as you loved your wife." Before he could reply,
she disappeared.

Others have seen the Lady in White surrounded by darker forms,
with whom she appears to be engaged in a heated argument. When
she vanishes, the dark shadows disappear along with her.

No one is sure who this Lady in White was in life, but sightings of
her were not reported before the late 1940s, despite the fact that the
cemetery dates back to the 1600s. Ed Warren speculated that it is
the spirit of a woman who was murdered shortly after World War II.

Ed also claimed to have captured video evidence of the Lady in
White, but in 2008, his widow, Lorraine, told reporters from NBC
that she keeps it under lock and key "because it's so valuable." He's
hardly the only person to photograph her, though—several ghost
hunters have taken photographs that feature strange phenomena at
the cemetery.

The Lady in White may not be the only ghost at Union Cemetery.
Many paranormal investigators have encountered an entity there
known as "Red Eyes," which is exactly that: a pair of glowing red
eyes that keep watch over the cemetery.

The fame of Connecticut's Lady in White has spread throughout
the ghost-hunting community, so much so that the town of Easton
has had to take steps to protect the cemetery from vandals: It is
closed after dark, and the police vigilantly keep trespassers from
entering it after hours. But it's not unheard of for officers to see a
pale, glowing form behind the gates in the middle of the night.

Near-Death Experience or Dream?

The notion of dreaming about death seems a bit depressing, but having a near-death experience (NDE) can actually seem like a dream. In the 1970s, little was known—or at least reported—about NDEs. Marjorie Floor initially thought that her experience was just a dream—until she read that many NDEs feature exactly the same scenario.

When Marjorie had her first child in 1976, a difficult labor led to an emergency C-section. She was put under anesthesia, and when she awoke, she was the proud mother of a baby boy.

A few days later, Marjorie started to remember a dream that she'd had while she was under. In it, she felt herself traveling down a cavernous tunnel. "It was like being inside a mountain cave," she recalled. "I could see a light near the opening of the cave, and when I got to that spot, I looked down and saw a beautiful land below."

She said that she was then approached by a spectral figure. "It might sound corny, but that's the best way to describe him," she said. He asked her if she wanted to choose life or death. "Of course, I chose life," Marjorie said, "but the figure warned me, 'Be careful. It's a trick.'" As a new mother, she couldn't imagine leaving her baby, so she chose life and found herself back in her hospital bed.

Marjorie said that she really didn't think much more about the "dream" until after a friend loaned her a copy of Dr. Raymond Moody's 1975 book *Life After Life*. She had never even heard of a near-death experience until then, so imagine her surprise when she read the recollections of dozens of people who had been declared clinically dead and were later revived. These were stories told by complete strangers—and they all had very familiar details. Upon their deaths, a bright light led these people to a land more beautiful than anything they could imagine. But Marjorie could imagine it; in fact, she knew exactly what they were talking about.

"Whether or not it was real," she said, "I know I'll never be afraid of dying."

School Spirits

*When a death occurs at a college or university, it's a tragic
event—it scars students emotionally, and it can also leave
a psychic imprint on the building in which it occurred.
So it's not surprising that institutions of higher learning
are among the most haunted places in America.*

Hamline University (St. Paul, Minnesota)

About 4,900 students—and several ghosts—attend Hamline
University, a liberal arts college in St. Paul, Minnesota. In Old
Main—the school's oldest building—a janitor reported seeing a
disembodied head with a noose around its neck float past him.
Two dormitories on campus also have paranormal connections.
Manor Hall has a resident ghost that likes to play tricks, especially
on the third floor, where lamps, fans, and TVs mysteriously turn
themselves on and off. And then there's Drew Hall, where a
sensor malfunctioned and caused an elevator door to slam shut on
a student's hand in the 1960s. The young man survived but lost
his hand; the phantom appendage is said to wander the dorm in
search of its body. This story may sound absurd, but try telling
that to the numerous students who have reported feeling
"icy fingers" touch them during the night.

Henderson State University (Arkadelphia, Arkansas)

The ghost of Henderson State University is said to be the victim
of a sad lover's tale. Around 1920, a young woman attended
Ouachita Baptist University; her boyfriend was a student at
Arkadelphia College (which is now Henderson State)—the
Methodist college across the street. They were in love . . . or at least
she thought so. But the young man decided that the differences
between their religions and schools were too much to overcome.
When he invited another girl to the Homecoming Dance, the
Ouachita student killed herself in despair. Now, each year during
Homecoming Week, she is seen drifting through the women's
dorms at Henderson, perhaps searching for the young lady who
stole her man's heart.

Illinois State University (Normal, Illinois)

Just like in *Ghostbusters,* books in a storage area of Williams Hall at Illinois State University used to fall off shelves and mysteriously rearrange themselves into tall, precarious stacks. Students there also reported feeling icy chills, and some even saw a ghostlike entity drift through the stacks. Who was this ethereal being? Most believed it was the spirit of Angie Milner, the school's first librarian, who died in 1928. Recently, when the books were moved to a new location, the paranormal activity ceased.

Nebraska Wesleyan University (Lincoln, Nebraska)

In 1912, Clarissa Mills was chosen to head up the music department and teach piano at Nebraska Wesleyan University. She was well liked by students and her peers, but in 1940, she died of unknown causes at her desk in the C. C. White building. For more than 20 years thereafter, all was normal, but in 1963, faculty member Coleen Buterbaugh stepped into Clarissa's old office and was never the same again. First she smelled the odor of gas, and then she felt an unknown presence in the room. In front of her stood the ghostly image of a tall, frail woman—Clarissa Mills. But that wasn't all: When she looked out the window, everything modern was gone. There were no paved streets, and a recently built sorority house was simply no longer there. Clarissa continued to haunt the building until it burned down in 1973. Buterbaugh, however, quit her job and moved to Colorado.

Olivet College (Olivet, Michigan)

Established in 1844, Olivet College—and the surrounding village of Olivet—hosts a ghost (or ghosts) with a sense of humor. Specters have been seen and photographed passing through walls and peering out of windows. Faint music is heard, but every time someone searches for its source, the music stops. And both students and town residents have often come home to find their possessions mysteriously moved or hidden. Although these incidents have occurred for more than a century and a half, no one seems to know why they started or who these prankster poltergeists might have been in life.

Samuel Clemens's Psychic Dream

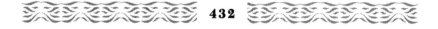

*One night in the late 1850s, Samuel Clemens—better known as
Mark Twain—woke up clutching the sheets on his bed; his palms
were sweaty and his heart was pounding. It had been so real, he
thought . . . so vivid. Had it really been just a dream, or did it actually
happen? And if it was indeed a dream, it was more like a nightmare.*

In the late 1850s—before he was world-renowned author and
humorist Mark Twain—Samuel Clemens worked as an apprentice
riverboat pilot on the *Pennsylvania*. His younger brother Henry also
worked on the vessel as a "mud clerk"—a hard and dreary job that
was barely one step above indentured servitude. But Henry stuck
with it, perhaps enticed by the possibility of a promotion to a superior
position on the steamboat.

While the ship was docked in St. Louis, Samuel stayed with his
sister and brother-in-law, who lived in town, and Henry would often
drop by to visit before returning to his shipboard duties. In May 1858,
Henry was unusually solemn as he prepared to return to the
Pennsylvania; it was not like him to be so somber.

Did That Really Just Happen?

That night, Samuel saw images in a dream that was frighteningly
realistic. He saw Henry lying in a coffin that was balanced on two
chairs in the sitting room of their sister's house. Henry was wearing a
suit of Samuel's, and in his hands—which were folded on his chest—
he held a bouquet of white roses with one red rose in the middle.

When Samuel awoke, he didn't know whether he had just had a
dream or if the events were real. Was his brother dead? His mind
spun; he decided that he must find out. Samuel leaped out of bed
and charged into the sitting room where he had seen the coffin
during his dream. To his relief, the room was empty.

Later that day, as he piloted the *Pennsylvania* down the
Mississippi River to New Orleans, Samuel couldn't get the dream out
of his mind. Unfortunately, on the trip downriver, Samuel got into

an argument with the owner of the steamer and was relieved of his duties when the *Pennsylvania* reached New Orleans; however, Henry remained on board.

A Nightmare Becomes Reality

Several days later, the *Pennsylvania* left on its return trip to St. Louis. As it approached Memphis, the boat's boilers exploded with a titanic roar. Dozens of people on board were killed and wounded.

Samuel heard about the horrible accident and quickly made his way to Memphis. After he arrived, he searched high and low for his brother until he found him on a mattress in a warehouse that had been turned into a hospital to treat the accident victims. Henry had inhaled red-hot steam and was not expected to live. But somehow he fought back, and his condition slowly improved.

One night, the agonizing screams of those in the makeshift hospital were getting the best of Henry, so a physician ordered a small dose of morphine to help him sleep. But the person who administered the drug gave Henry too much: He overdosed and died before morning broke.

The body of Henry Clemens was dressed in one of Samuel's suits, placed in a coffin, and displayed in a viewing room at the makeshift hospital. As Samuel was mourning near his brother's casket, a woman placed a bouquet of white roses with one red rose in the center in his dead brother's hands.

Samuel was stunned. His chilling dream—or rather nightmare— had come true.

Henry's coffin was sent back to his sister's house in St. Louis. Samuel arrived there just before the coffin was placed in the sitting room. There, two chairs sat spaced apart, waiting to receive the coffin. It was the final detail of Samuel's psychic dream come true.

Samuel Clemens was so deeply affected by his prophetic dream that foreshadowed his brother's death that 24 years later, he joined the Society for Psychical Research, a British group of supporters of paranormal studies.

Slave Spirits Still Seek Freedom on the Underground Railroad

In the first half of the 19th century, some landowners staged a concerted effort to help slaves escape bondage in the South and find freedom in the North. These strangers in hostile territory enabled slaves to escape their torment via the Underground Railroad. This, of course, was not an actual mode of transportation but rather a series of tunnels and hidden rooms in which escaped slaves were able to hide for a day or two, get a good meal, and travel onward toward freedom. Their journeys were fraught with fear, stress, and sometimes illness or injury. And if caught, the slaves were not only returned to their owners, they were also punished severely, and some were killed on the spot. So it goes without saying that many of the houses, farms, forests, and passageways of the Underground Railroad are still haunted by slaves who didn't succeed in their quest for freedom.

Deadman's Hill (Willmar, Minnesota)

Located in Willmar, Minnesota, Deadman's Hill is far north of areas that are typically associated with slavery, but for many of the escapees of the mid-1800s, the state was a stop on the way to Canada. Considered a free state, Minnesota outlawed slave ownership, but unfortunately, it was legal at the time for slave traders and bounty hunters to catch escaped slaves anywhere in the country and return them to their "owners." That was the case of one slave who was captured by a bounty hunter and chained to a fence post. The resourceful slave managed to escape by pulling the post out of the ground. A fence post makes for some pretty cumbersome luggage, however, and the bounty hunter caught up with the slave again. A fight ensued, and the slave killed his captor with the man's own sword. But the slave was injured in the fight, and his body was later found on a farmer's doorstep amidst a pool of blood and the uprooted fence post. Both men were buried on the property: The bounty hunter rests atop Deadman's Hill, and the slave is buried next to the farmhouse. Although the runaway slave's ghost has never

been seen, plenty of people have heard his moans, the rattle of chains, and the distinct sound of something heavy being dragged.

Hannah House (Indianapolis, Indiana)

It was indeed a sad situation when slaves who tried to escape to better lives died in the process. That's what happened at Hannah House, which was a well-known stop on the Underground Railroad. Slaves waiting in the cellar of the mansion were taken by surprise when someone accidentally tipped over a lantern. Flames engulfed them and trapped them in the basement; they all died within a few minutes.

Since then, visitors have heard voices, moans, and the rattling of chains coming from both the basement and the attic. People have also detected the smell of burning bodies, which has burdened Hannah House with the unpleasant moniker "the house that reeks of death." While no full-bodied apparitions have been spotted there, plenty of unexplained phenomena have been experienced: Doors open and close by themselves, people report feeling cold breezes even when the windows are closed, and objects move to new locations with no human assistance.

In 2006 and 2007, Indy Ghost Hunters—a local paranormal investigation team—visited Hannah House and recorded numerous EVPs (electronic voice phenomena), including mysterious voices imploring them for help and warning them to "Get out!" Cameras also captured a shadow moving across the attic, even though all living beings were well out of their range.

Hanson Home (Alton, Illinois)

As if having the Underground Railroad stop at the Hanson Home wasn't enough, the site on which it stood is where the Enos Sanitarium was built for tuberculosis patients in the early 1900s. In 1857, when Nathaniel Hanson built his home on a bluff just above the Mississippi River, he created underground rooms and

tunnels out of limestone, specifically for the purpose of assisting slaves to reach their freedom. Unfortunately, many slaves lost their lives on this journey, and some of their spirits may have remained at the Hanson Home.

The structure is now used as an apartment building, and many residents have had their belongings—keys, books, jewelry, and even a bottle of wine—disappear; they almost always reappear a day or so later in an entirely different spot. Like most ghosts, these spirits like to open and close doors and turn the lights on and off, and people often report hearing footsteps when no one else is around. Much of this activity seems to take place on the building's upper floors (where the sanitarium was located), but the basement has its own set of ghosts—spirits of slaves that cry out in despair.

Hickory Hill (Equality, Illinois)

Hickory Hill—which is also known as "The Old Slave House"— is one of the most haunted places in the state of Illinois. Its first owner, John Hart Crenshaw, amassed a fortune during the abolition years by operating what is known as a "reverse underground station": Slave catchers and bounty hunters captured escaped slaves and took them to Hickory Hill, where Crenshaw then sold them back into bondage or put them to work in his salt mines. Visitors to this place have felt cold drafts and the soft brushes of spirits passing by; they've also heard crying and moaning mixed with the rattling of chains. (Read more about this terrifying tale on page 14.)

Wedgwood Inn (New Hope, Pennsylvania)

If you're a 12-year-old girl, you may just be in luck if you're hoping to meet a ghost in this small Pennsylvania town. On her way to freedom in the mid-1800s, a 12-year-old slave girl named Sara stayed at the house that is now the Wedgwood Inn. No one knows the cause of her death, but the building's owners uncovered her remains while renovating the place in 2000. Sara's spirit seems to have remained at the hotel in order to tell her story to other girls her age—many young girls have reported meeting her at the inn, and when they recount the details of her life as a slave and how

she escaped by using the Underground Railroad, their stories are eerily similar.

Prospect Place (Trinway, Ohio)

A prime stop for slaves heading to Canada, the basement of Prospect Place was a temporary safe house for hundreds of escapees. Built by George W. Adams—a prominent mill owner and abolitionist—this 1856 mansion has 29 rooms, not counting the secret ones located below ground. Today, it is thought to be haunted by both slaves and the generous souls who lived on the property.

One story about the ghosts of Prospect Place centers on a girl who fell to her death from an upstairs balcony one winter during the early 1860s; her body was kept in the basement until the ground thawed in the spring. Her ghost is thought to wander the house and has been heard crying in the basement. The girl's mother died of pneumonia soon after the girl passed, and her spirit roams the house as well. The girl's ghost has been seen on the balcony, in the old servants' quarters, and in the basement, and another slave who died at the house has been seen standing in the basement, as if guarding the girl's body. Also, a husband and wife who were separated while escaping seem to search various areas of the property trying to find each other. And in true poetic justice, in the barn, farmhands hung a bounty hunter who searched for escaped slaves; his ghost still haunts the place where he met his death.

Riverview Farm (Drexel Hills, Pennsylvania)

The land on which Arlington Cemetery stands today was once part of Riverview Farm—the home of Thomas Garrett Jr., an abolitionist who reportedly helped as many as 2,700 slaves on the road to freedom. While no specific incident would have caused spirits to remain there, evidence suggests that they did. When taking pictures at a nearby home, a photographer captured the aura of something ghostly hovering in the background of an image. Could it be the spirit of one of these brave men and women who were searching for a better life?

Lincoln's Ghost Train

Abraham Lincoln's funeral train appears to have been much like the president himself: uncommonly determined and larger-than-life.

Final Journey

When President Lincoln was assassinated in April 1865, the nation was understandably plunged into a state of mourning. Swept away was the "Great Emancipator," who had not only put an end to slavery but also preserved a fractured American union. For everything that he had done for the nation, it was decided that Lincoln's funeral procession should be as great as the man himself. In order to bring the president close to the citizens who loved and mourned him, his funeral train would trace the same route—in reverse—that Lincoln had traveled when he went to Washington, D.C., four years earlier as president-elect. Covering a vast 1,654 miles, the procession left Washington on April 21, 1865, and finally pulled into Springfield, Illinois, on May 3. Officially, this was Lincoln's last ride—but unofficially, some say that Abe and his funeral train have never stopped chugging along.

First Phantom

In April 1866, one year after Lincoln's assassination, the first report of the ghost train surfaced. The sighting occurred along a stretch of railway in New York's Hudson Valley. Witnesses told a fantastic tale of a spectral train that whooshed by them without making a sound. They identified it as Lincoln's funeral train after they observed the president's flag-draped coffin on board. Surrounded by black crepe, the casket was identical to the original but with one notable difference: This time, a *skeletal* honor guard stood at attention beside it. Witnesses also recalled an equally skeletal band playing what must have been a dreary funeral dirge; that no sounds were emitted from their musical instruments also seemed bizarre. A strange bluish light surrounded the train as it chugged silently northward. Witnesses recalled that a blast of warm air could be felt and that

clocks inexplicably stopped for six minutes as the train slowly passed by. Over time, this vision would be reported surprisingly often along much of the original train's route.

Mass Hysteria?

With a tragedy of such immensity seizing the national psyche, it was almost a given that sightings of Lincoln's ghost would occur. Psychologists attribute such phenomena to denial—the subconscious act of refusing to let go. Lincoln had saved the union and restored peace to a nation whose future had hung precariously in the balance. It seemed extremely unfair that he should be taken away in such a brutal fashion. And yet, he had been.

Still, what can be said of a phantom train that appears to numerous people along so vast a route? While shock and denial might account for individual sightings of a spectral president, it seems doubtful that an entire funeral train could be hallucinated by scores of people at precisely the same time. And how could the details of such sightings match so closely from person to person and region to region?

Just Passing Through

If witnesses are to be believed, Lincoln's ghost train still chugs along on its seemingly endless journey. Sightings of it generally occur in April (the month in which the original funeral train began its trek), and details of eyewitness accounts are surprisingly similar to each other. But a few differences in these sightings have been documented. Some people say that the spectral train contains several cars that are all draped in black; others say that it only consists of an engine and one flatbed car that holds the dead president's coffin. And every so often, someone claims to hear a shrieking whistle coming from the phantom locomotive.

Despite such detailed accounts, naysayers exist. In his book *The Lincoln Funeral Train,* author Scott Trostel discusses his belief that these accounts are simply the products of people's "vivid and fertile imaginations." Perhaps, but how is it that different people in different states have such similar vivid and fertile imaginations? Like Lincoln himself, the question belongs to the ages.

The Cashtown Inn

🪦 🪦 🪦 🪦

*Located near Gettysburg, Pennsylvania's historic battlefield, the
Cashtown Inn is considered one of the region's hot spots for
paranormal activity. That's no small feat in an area
renowned for its otherworldly inhabitants.*

The Setting

The Battle of Gettysburg is perhaps the most famous of all Civil War
conflicts. This hard-fought confrontation—which was waged from
July 1 to 3, 1863—served as a turning point in the war that divided
the nation. Union troops earned a decisive victory, but it came at a
cost: The battle resulted in nearly 51,000 total casualties, including
nearly 8,000 deaths.

Not surprisingly, Gettysburg has become "Civil War central" to
historians and tourists. But paranormal activity is off the charts in
these parts, so much so that a cottage industry has sprouted up in the
form of ghost tours, ghostly Gettysburg memorabilia, and the like.
And the Cashtown Inn, which is located eight miles west of the
battlefield, is revered by fans of the supernatural as one of
Gettysburg's most haunted hotels. With much of the building's
history stained by the bloody battle, this comes as no surprise.

Three Days of Hell

The town of Cashtown served as a Confederate base of operations
before and during the Battle of Gettysburg. Soon after the blue and
the gray traded fire, wounded Confederate soldiers were brought
to the Cashtown Inn's basement, which had been turned into an
operating room. So many surgeries were performed there that a
nearby stream allegedly turned red with blood. Small mountains of
severed body parts were scattered about the inn, and screams and
moans permeated the premises. By July 4, the mood at the camp had
turned somber: Realizing that they had suffered a major defeat, the
Confederates knew that it was time to collect themselves, physically
and mentally, and retreat to Virginia.

Stirrings

After the battle, the Cashtown Inn returned to serving guests and remained successful through 1948, when a bypass rerouted traffic (and tourists) away from the hotel. Over the next few decades, the inn's condition worsened. Finally, in 1987, the building underwent a major restoration; shortly thereafter, tales of supernatural sightings began to come as quickly as musket fire. From ghostly silhouettes of men dressed in Confederate uniforms to the sound of phantom footsteps, the Cashtown Inn experienced paranormal activity in every one of its rooms. Some of these incidents were frightening, others were puzzling, and still others were downright laughable. Room 4, in particular, seems to have a lock on the latter.

Ghosts and Other Practical Jokers

In a lighthearted variation of the old "knock, knock" prank, playful poltergeists have been known to rap loudly on the door of Room 4. When occupants answer the door, no one is there.

Sounds of men on horseback once woke a guest in Room 4; when he checked to see what was causing the commotion, nothing was found. But the noises persisted. In the morning, the perturbed guest complained to the proprietor. When the man returned to his room, his suitcases were fully packed. This prompted him to ask if it was customary for the staff to pack guests' bags. "No," the innkeeper assured the man. "No one under my employ packed your bags."

Of course, not all of the ghosts at the Cashtown Inn are this helpful. More morose spirits that are dressed in full Confederate uniform have been seen lingering around the inn. They tend to frighten guests, but they are simply part of the scenery to employees.

Proof or Consequences

The Atlantic Paranormal Society (aka TAPS)—the stars of television's *Ghost Hunters*—put the Cashtown Inn to the test in 2008. During their four days of intense surveillance, they recorded the sound of boot-clad footsteps coming from the unoccupied floor above them and filmed a picture frame moving across a tabletop by itself. This can mean only one thing: The ghosts of the Cashtown Inn are still up to their old tricks.

Spectral Ships and Phantom Crews

Ghost ships seem to have the ability to slip back and forth between this world and the next, often making appearances that foretell of impending doom. Come with us as we set sail in search of some of the most famous ghost ships in maritime history.

The *Mary Celeste*

The *Amazon* was cursed from the day she left port: During her maiden voyage, the ship's captain died. After being salvaged by an American company that renamed her *Mary Celeste,* the ship left New York on November 7, 1872, bound for Genoa, Italy. On board were Captain Benjamin Briggs, his family, and a crew of seven.

On December 4, the crew of the *Dei Gratia* found the *Mary Celeste* abandoned. There was plenty of food and water on the ship, but the only living soul on board was a cat. The crew and the captain's family were missing, and no clues suggested where they went. The last entry in the captain's log was dated almost two weeks prior to the ship's discovery, so the vessel had somehow piloted itself all that time.

What happened to the *Mary Celeste* and those on board remains a mystery. Many believe that a ghostly crew sailed the ship and kept her safe until she was found.

The *Iron Mountain*

A ship disappearing on the high seas is one thing, but on a river? That's exactly what happened to the *Iron Mountain.* In June 1872, the 180-foot-long vessel left New Orleans on its way to Pittsburgh on the Mississippi River with a crew of more than 50 men. A day after stopping at Vicksburg, Mississippi, to pick up additional cargo, which was towed behind the ship on barges, the *Iron Mountain* steamed its way north and promptly vanished. Later that day, the barges were recovered, but the *Iron Mountain* and its crew were never seen nor heard from again. For years after it disappeared, riverboat captains whispered about how the *Iron Mountain* was simply sucked into another dimension through a ghostly portal.

The Palatine

According to legend, shortly after Christmas 1738, the *Princess Augusta* ran aground and broke into pieces on the coast of Block Island, Rhode Island. Roughly 130 years later, poet John Greenleaf Whittier renamed the European vessel and told his version of the ship-wreck in his poem *The Palatine*, which was published in *The Atlantic Monthly*. Today, strange lights are still reported in the waters around Block Island, especially on the Saturday between Christmas and New Year's Day; they are said to be the fiery ghost ship.

The Edmund Fitzgerald

When it comes to ghost ships, the *Edmund Fitzgerald* is the biggest—literally. More than 720 feet long, the freighter shuttled iron ore across the Great Lakes beginning in the late 1950s. On November 10, 1975, the mammoth ship sank during a violent storm without ever issuing a distress signal. All 29 members of the crew were presumed dead, but their bodies were never found.

Nearly ten years to the day after the *"Fitz"* sank, a strange dark ship was seen on Lake Superior. One look at the monstrous vessel was all that witnesses needed to recognize it as the *Edmund Fitzgerald*.

The Flying Dutchman

Stories say that during the 1800s, Captain Hendrick Vanderdecken was attempting to sail the *Flying Dutchman* around the Cape of Good Hope when a violent storm blew up. Rather than pull into port, the stubborn captain claimed that he would navigate around the Cape even if it took him all of eternity to do so. The ship and its crew were lost in the storm, and, as promised by Vanderdecken, they were condemned to sail the high seas for all eternity.

Almost immediately thereafter, people all over the world began spotting the Dutch ship moving silently through the ocean, often cast in an eerie glow. Because of the legend associated with Captain Vanderdecken, sightings of the *Flying Dutchman* are now thought to be bad omens. Case in point: One of the most recent sightings of the spectral vessel occurred off the coast of North Carolina's Outer Banks just prior to Hurricane Isabel's arrival in 2003.

Prison Poltergeists

Spirits Live On at the West Virginia Penitentiary

The fact that all of West Virginia's executions used to take place at the West Virginia Penitentiary is only one of the reasons why this prison has more than its fair share of ghosts. Torture, violence, murder, and suicide were all common occurrences during its 119 years in operation, so it's no wonder that some of the people who lived there still roam its dank, dark halls.

With the Gothic look of a spooky storybook castle, the West Virginia Penitentiary in Moundsville was built in the late 1800s. It was originally designed to house 480 inmates, but its population grew from 250 prisoners when it opened in 1876 to 2,400 in the early 1930s. With as many as three men sharing one tiny five-foot-by-seven-foot cell, living conditions there were atrocious.

Beaten Spirits

Wardens at the West Virginia Penitentiary—which was once listed by the Department of Justice as one of the Top Ten Most Violent Correctional Facilities in the nation—issued severe punishments for those inmates who misbehaved: Prisoners were tortured, whipped, and beaten. One spirit that lingers there is believed to be that of Robert, an inmate who was beaten to death.

Over the years, many deaths occurred within the prison's walls. Some were brought on by violent treatment, poor living conditions, and illness; additionally, a total of 94 men were executed there: 85 by hanging and 9 via the electric chair. One execution began with a mishap when a man who had been sentenced to hang fell through the floor before the noose could be fixed around his neck; he had to be picked up and taken back upstairs, where he was then hung successfully. It is said that his spirit still wanders around the gallows where he died.

As early as the 1930s, folks at the prison began seeing ghosts and reporting an eerie feeling that an invisible entity was standing close by. One specter that is often seen is that of a tattletale maintenance man who spied on the inmates and liked to get them in trouble. He met his end when a group of prisoners attacked him in a bathroom, which is where his earthbound spirit remains today.

Ghostly activity has also been observed in the shower area, in the chapel, along death row, and at the execution site. And don't forget the front gate, where the turnstiles move by themselves—perhaps admitting a "new" batch of inmates.

One particularly frightening spirit at the West Virginia Pen is that of the "shadow man," whose misty shape has been spotted lurking in the dark, giving off a menacing feeling to those who see him. In fact, many of the spirits there are intimidating; they often leave people with a sense that they are being watched or even followed.

Unruly Spirits

One area of the prison that investigators have found to be teeming with paranormal activity is known as "the Sugar Shack"—an area where inmates went to exercise. Although there is no official record of a death occurring there, many people have felt cold spots and heard unexplained noises, such as screams and arguing voices. Some visitors have even felt unseen hands poking them in the back or stroking them on the cheek.

If you like ghosts or history—or both—the West Virginia Pen is well worth the trip. But beware of this group of spirits: They were unhappy in life and are still unhappy in death. So if you feel the touch of something that you can't see, it might be a good idea to run.

Ghosts of Glensheen

In 1905, self-made millionaire Chester Congdon was one of Minnesota's richest men. When the banking and iron-mining magnate and his wife, Clara, moved into their stupendous mansion on the shore of Lake Superior in 1908, they never dreamed that their elegant home would someday be famous for murder... and ghosts.

The Congdons named their sprawling estate "Glensheen." The brick lakefront house features multiple gables and chimneys and 39 richly furnished rooms. The Congdons spared no expense on their state-of-the-art abode, equipping it with electricity, running water, and a humidification system and covering the grounds with lush gardens where they entertained Minnesota's elite with impressive parties.

Chester only lived in his dream home for eight years: He died in 1916 at age 63. The estate passed to Clara and then to the couple's youngest daughter, Elisabeth. To this day, the house retains most of the family's original furnishings, which makes the area where a grisly double murder took place seem even eerier to visitors.

Family Ties, Lies, and Sighs

In 1977, Elisabeth was 83 years old and was partially paralyzed. She had never married, although she had adopted two girls: Jennifer—who married a businessman and led a quiet life in Racine, Wisconsin—and Marjorie, the black sheep of the family. Elisabeth's life of luxury ended violently when an intruder smothered the helpless woman in her sleep with her own pink satin pillow; he also bludgeoned Elisabeth's protective night nurse, Velma Pietila, with a candlestick.

Suspicion immediately fell on Marjorie, but it was her husband, Roger Caldwell, who was charged with killing the elderly heiress to obtain Marjorie's $8 million share of the estate; Marjorie was charged with aiding and abetting him in the crime. Caldwell went to prison and later confessed to the crime, but Marjorie was acquitted. In fact, the trial's jurors felt so sorry for her that they threw her a posttrial party!

That was a nice gesture, but even being honored so highly was not enough to change Marjorie's basic nature. Although she did get her hands on a pile of her dead mother's money, her life deteriorated further thereafter. In 1981, she married Wallace Hagen (without divorcing Roger Caldwell), and in 1984, she was convicted of arson and insurance fraud in Minnesota. By 1992, Marjorie and Hagen, were living in Arizona, where she was again found guilty of arson. After her conviction but before she went to jail, Hagen died of a mysterious drug overdose. Marjorie was arrested and charged with his murder, but the charges were later dropped.

Marjorie was released from prison in 2004, but in 2007, she was arrested again—this time on charges of committing fraud and forgery. In 2010, she again made headlines when she tried to get her probation dropped so that she could move into an assisted-living facility in Arizona.

A Soft Sheen of Spirits

Meanwhile, Glensheen remains as grand as ever. Now owned by the University of Minnesota-Duluth, the mansion is used for art fairs and theatrical productions, including readings of the macabre stories of Edgar Allen Poe during Halloween season. The house and gardens are also open for public tours. And although its tour guides are reportedly tight-lipped about hauntings, it is believed that the spirits of Elisabeth and Velma have never left the place. People have seen misty figures floating about, heard unidentifiable noises, and felt cold chills when viewing the room in which Elisabeth died.

In one story that was recounted in *The Minnesota Road Guide to Haunted Locations,* an employee felt something pulling on his ankles while he was standing on a ladder. Thinking that a coworker had snuck up the ladder to play a prank, he turned to face the culprit, but no one was there—at least, no one that he could see.

Who could blame Elisabeth and Velma for lingering at the Glensheen Mansion? It's certainly a beautiful place to spend eternity.

Five years before Elisabeth Congdon was killed, Patty Duke starred in a dark thriller filmed at Glensheen. The movie's title? *You'll Like My Mother.*

More Haunted Restaurants

The next time you enjoy a meal at your favorite restaurant, know that you may be dining with some unseen guests. Here are a few eateries where a ghostly good time is always on the menu.

Stone's Public House (Ashland, Massachusetts)

Since 1834, Stone's Public House has been serving up food and drinks to area residents and visitors alike. Should you stop in for a bite, take a good look at the photo of John Stone that hangs over the bar's fireplace so that you'll be sure to recognize his ghost when it manifests. Stone's spirit is said to be one of a handful that haunt the pub; other resident ghosts include that of a man who Stone accidentally murdered in an argument over a card game. Stone and several friends allegedly buried the man in the basement and have been condemned to spend eternity haunting the scene of the crime along with their victim. The spirits make their presence known by breaking glasses, causing cold breezes, and appearing as shadowy figures.

Vino's Brewpub (Little Rock, Arkansas)

Vino's is a brewery, a pizza parlor, and a great place to hear live music. After the establishment opened in 1990, it attracted a following among the living—but it has quite a group of nonliving fans too. The source of the haunting is unknown, but employees say that the building—which was constructed in 1909—has a creepy vibe. It features several spots that are permanently cold for no scientific reason, and other cold spots move around. When the building is relatively quiet, banging noises, thumps, and creaking are heard in seemingly empty parts of the building. After closing, staff members stack up the chairs to mop the floors and then leave them that way overnight; but when employees arrive the next day, they often find the chairs scattered around the restaurant.

Historic White Horse Inn (Metamora, Michigan)

Advertised as "Michigan's Oldest Restaurant," the historic White Horse Inn has been in business since 1850, when Lorenzo Hoard

opened Hoard House to serve hungry and weary travelers. Hoard is believed to be among the building's many ghosts: He typically waits upstairs until the restaurant becomes lively, and then he makes his presence known by causing lights to flicker or a dessert tray to crash to the floor. Patrons and staff members acknowledge his presence by saying, "Hey Lorenzo!"

Orbs are common in photos that are taken at the restaurant, and sometimes, in an antique mirror in the hallway, Lorenzo can be seen smiling next to a living person's reflection. Doors that are left closed overnight are found open in the morning. And each night, the owners leave Lorenzo's riding boots at the top of the stairs—just in case he wants to check out the town overnight. Staff members have heard heavy footsteps clomping around above them late at night when no one else is in the building, and some mornings, Lorenzo's boots have mysteriously moved to another location.

Country House Restaurant (Stony Brook, New York)

Like many haunted eateries, the Country House Restaurant occupies a former residence with a troubled past. The structure was originally built in 1710; during the Revolutionary War, the family who owned the house fled for New Jersey and left a woman named Annette Williamson in charge of the property. Shortly thereafter, British soldiers occupied the house, and Annette was killed—although it is unclear whether she was killed by the British, who thought she was a spy, or by her neighbors, who accused anyone who didn't fight the British of colluding with them.

Nevertheless, Annette's spirit lingers at her former home. Many people have seen her looking out the window of the room in which she was reportedly killed, but she typically hangs out in the kitchen area and by the stairs. When she's around, unexplainable footsteps can be heard and objects seem to move on their own. Annette's apparition has blonde hair and blue eyes, and she wears a white Colonial-style dress. She is generally friendly, and children at the restaurant often ask their parents if they can play with the pretty young woman. However, she is not to be messed with: She once threw a glass of wine in a skeptic's face!

Ghost:
The Movie That Haunted Romantics

In 1990, romantics and lovers of the supernatural united to make the film Ghost *a giant hit. The movie—which was produced on a $22-million budget—grossed more than $200 million in the United States alone. Audiences swooned as sexy specter Sam Wheat (played by Patrick Swayze) tried to solve the mystery of his murder and save the woman who he loves, Molly Jensen (portrayed by Demi Moore).*

Learning to Be a Ghost

After they attend a performance of *Macbeth,* Sam tells Molly that he leads a charmed life, quoting a line that Macbeth utters in the play right before he is killed. Just then, a mugger confronts Sam and Molly, and although the couple complies with his demands, he shoots Sam and kills him. When a bright light appears to him, Sam turns away from it, which effectively traps his spirit in the world of the living.

What follows is an introduction to the spirit world: Sam discovers that good souls are welcomed into the bright light and evil ones are taken by angry, screaming shadow demons to be punished for their misdeeds on earth. Stuck in the world of the living but unable to communicate with Molly, Sam feels helpless. A tense scene ensues when Sam's killer enters the apartment that Sam shared with Molly. Despite his efforts, the best Sam can do is convince the couple's cat to scratch the intruder's face; fortunately, this scares the man off before he can hurt Molly. After that, Sam meets a paranoid ghost on the New York City subway that teaches him how to move objects and reach out to the living.

Help from the Living

For all of its romance and drama, the film has some humorous moments as well. Comedian Whoopi Goldberg portrays Oda Mae Brown, a medium who had been faking her psychic abilities and conning people who were desperate to reach their deceased loved ones on the Other Side. When Sam approaches her for help, Oda Mae

is horrified to discover that she really does have "the gift." Suddenly, spirits (including Sam) that are eager to talk to their friends and family members one last time begin harassing Oda Mae night and day. She reluctantly agrees to help Sam find his killer.

Ultimately, Sam discovers that his friend Carl orchestrated the murder to profit from illegal trading. Sam uses Oda Mae to foil the scam; hijinks ensue, and a panicked Carl decides to take matters into his own hands. Sam and Oda Mae try to persuade a skeptical Molly that Sam's spirit can help her. During an epic battle between Carl and Sam (who has finally mastered the use of his ghostly powers), Carl is killed. Sam, Molly, and Oda Mae watch in horror as the dark shadows collect Carl's terrified spirit and carry it off to its doom.

Together One Last Time

Then, for a few moments that tugged at the tear ducts of audiences worldwide, Oda Mae allows Sam to possess her body to be with Molly one last time. They reunite to the strains of The Righteous Brothers' "Unchained Melody," and Sam uses the opportunity to tell Molly that he loves her, something that he never said to her when he was alive. "Ditto," she says, using the word that Sam had uttered whenever she told him that she loved him. The bright light appears with shadowy but peaceful figures that beckon Sam to join them. There was rarely a dry eye in the house as Sam walked into the light.

This is one ghost story that continues to haunt the hearts of romantics everywhere. The movie garnered five Academy Award nominations (including Best Picture) and won two of the coveted Oscars—Best Original Screenplay and Best Supporting Actress, for Whoopi Goldberg's outstanding performance.

"He's stuck, that's what it is. He's in between worlds. You know it happens sometimes that the spirit gets yanked out so fast that the essence still feels it has work to do here."

—Oda Mae Brown (Whoopi Goldberg's character in *Ghost*)

Flagler College: Hosting Ghosts in Style

A dorm at Flagler College in St. Augustine, Florida, was once a hotel, which may explain why it's now the eternal haunt of several spirits.

Tycoon Henry Morrison Flagler certainly makes his presence known at his former luxury hotel, which is now home to Ponce de León Hall on the campus of Flagler College. The building houses the school's administrative offices and a women's dormitory. Flagler's second wife, his mistress, and several other earthbound spirits also join him there.

An eccentric businessman, Flagler retired to Florida in the late 1800s and built his hotel. Fascinated with death, he instructed hotel staffers that when he died, the doors and windows were to be left open so that his spirit could easily cross over. However, when Flagler passed away in 1913, a janitor unknowingly shut every door and window, and it is said that in its haste to leave, Flagler's spirit bounced off a closed window and landed on a floor tile, where his face is allegedly still seen to this day. He also reportedly plays pranks on students at the college that bears his name.

Flagler's second wife, Ida Alice, was mentally unstable and spent the last years of her life in an institution. These days, she's seen lingering in the former hotel's halls and staring at its old paintings.

Flagler was known as a philanderer, and the ghost of one of his mistresses still roams the building. To keep his wife from finding out about the affair, Flagler locked the mistress away one too many times: She hung herself from the chandelier in a room on the fourth floor, where her presence is still felt today. Students who later lived in that room heard screams and watched items fly off the walls.

If that trio isn't enough to scare you, look for two other ghosts. One is a pregnant woman in blue, who is believed to have been the mistress of a hotel guest. In despair over her situation, she ran up the stairs, tripped on her skirt, and broke her neck. And although the cause of his death is unknown, a spectral young boy has been seen wandering the premises. With all the paranormal activity in this building, one wonders how students get any work done there.

Ghost Dogs

Cynophobia is the fear of dogs. But the canines discussed here are ghostly dogs that have stuck around after passing away. The following is a list of places where, if you're not careful, you might find yourself staring down a phantom hound.

Colebrook Furnace

It is a horrifying tale that dog lovers everywhere hope is merely a legend: A Pennsylvania man who was furious at his pack of hunting dogs ordered his servants to throw all 40 of the hounds into the roaring flames of Colebrook Furnace, a massive structure that was used to melt iron ore. As the story goes, shortly after the heinous deed, ghostly howls and cries began emanating from the furnace. Even after the structure was dismantled in the 1850s, the sounds could still be heard. In addition, a pack of phantom dogs has been seen running through the woods nearby. Those reports continue today, although with a minor twist: Some believe that the strange cries belong to the ghost of the guilty man, who is forced to spend eternity in torment due to his inhumane actions.

Woodland Cemetery

There's something to be said for the unconditional love that's shared between a boy and his dog. A prime example of this is the story of five-year-old Johnny Morehouse and his scruffy pooch. In the mid-1800s, Johnny could often be seen playing by the Miami & Erie Canal near Dayton, Ohio, with his faithful dog beside him. One morning in 1860, Johnny slipped and fell into the icy water. Seeing his master struggling, the dog jumped into the water and tried to save him. Even though the dog aided several men who pulled Johnny from the water, it was too late for the little boy.

Legend has it that after Johnny was laid to rest at Woodland Cemetery in Dayton, his faithful dog refused to leave the grave site; instead, he kept watch over his young master. When the dog passed away in 1861, a monument was erected at Johnny's grave; it depicts the boy sleeping while his dog stands watch over him. Many believe that, even in death, Johnny's dog is still watching

over him. Some say that the statue often comes to life and if you place your hand under the dog's nostrils, you can feel it breathing; others have reported seeing the ghosts of Johnny and his dog running together through the cemetery.

Peddler's Rock

If you ever find yourself in the historic town of Port Tobacco, Maryland, ask the locals to show you the way to Peddler's Rock, where you just might catch a glimpse of a spectral blue dog. Although the animal is not technically blue in color, it is said to be the spirit of a blue mastiff. A long-standing legend states that a man and his dog were brutally murdered at Peddler's Rock in the 18th century; the culprits were never caught.

Today, it is said that the ghost of the blue mastiff paces back and forth across the top of Peddler's Rock. Occasionally, its loud, bone-chilling howls are also heard cutting through the night air.

Borley Rectory

Often dubbed the "Most Haunted House in England," the Borley Rectory was built in the 1860s and quickly gained a reputation for being home to all sorts of ghosts. In the late 1930s, famous ghost hunter Harry Price rented the building and began an investigation that lasted many months. During that time, Price and his team encountered ghostly nuns, a headless specter, and flying bricks. Of course, no haunted house would be complete without a ghost dog, and Borley did not disappoint in that regard. On more than one occasion, Price and his team heard the eerie sound of a hound howling from somewhere inside the building; however, no dog was ever found. Several investigators also described seeing a large spectral canine walking slowly across the rectory grounds.

Bonaventure Cemetery

Bonaventure Cemetery is the largest city cemetery in Savannah, Georgia. But the graveyard's real claim to fame is that it was featured in John Berendt's best-selling novel *Midnight in the Garden of Good and Evil* and the 1997 movie that was based on the book. It's also a place where ghost dogs are said to prowl.

For many years, a pack of phantom dogs has been known to chase people out of the cemetery, especially if they are trespassing late at night. If the idea of being pursued by a pack of spectral canines isn't spooky enough, consider that no one has ever actually seen the dogs—not even those who have been chased by them; rather, only their barking and snarling is heard as they draw near. Those of you who'd rather not risk being run down by the phantom dogs should just roll down your windows as you drive by and listen closely—you just might hear the baying of the hounds.

Sunnybank

Albert Payson Terhune may be best remembered as an author who wrote books about dogs, but his devotion to canines went much deeper than that. In 1912, Terhune decided to take up full-time residence at Sunnybank, his family's summer home in Wayne, New Jersey; it was there that he began breeding and raising rough collies. Eventually, Terhune became so successful at breeding that he opened Sunnybank Kennels. Some of the dogs from these kennels later made their way into Terhune's books—including Rex.

Rex was different from most of the other dogs at the kennels: He was not a purebred, but rather a collie/bull terrier mix. Also, Rex had a large, unique scar on his head. Rex loved Terhune, and the feeling was more than mutual. It was often said that if you wanted to know where Terhune was, all you had to do was find Rex and Terhune wouldn't be far away. That was true even after Rex's death: Shortly after the dog's passing, friends reported seeing his ghost following Terhune around the property and even lying at his feet. Those who were unaware that Rex had died even mistook the apparition for the real dog. Incidentally, Terhune himself never claimed to see Rex's ghost.

After Terhune passed away in 1942, the kennels and the surrounding property fell into disrepair and were eventually sold. Much of the original estate is now maintained as a park that is open to the public. As visitors wander the grounds, they may come across the graves of many of Terhune's dogs. But while Rex is rumored to be buried there, his grave site was never marked. Still, many locals claim to see Rex's ghost wandering through the park at night.

The Rolling Hills Are Alive with Spirits

You can turn an asylum into a mall, but you can't take the spirits out of it. That seems to be the case in East Bethany, New York, a small town located between Rochester and Buffalo. The main attraction there is a building that used to be a poorhouse and has undergone many changes during the nearly two centuries since it was constructed. However, it seems that its former residents just don't understand that the Rolling Hills Asylum is no longer their home.

The Poorhouse

Opened in 1827, the Genesee County Poorhouse was a residence for a wide array of people: Paupers, orphans, widows, and unwed mothers shared space with drunks, the mentally ill, the criminally insane, and the physically disabled. The massive structure served this eclectic group for 125 years before it was transformed into a nursing home in the 1950s.

Imagine the number of people who must have died there over the years. Some sources list the number of deaths at 1,750, but experts estimate that it was actually much higher. It's hard to say, though, because the dead were often dumped into unmarked graves.

In the early 1990s, the building was converted into a group of specialty shops known as Carriage Village. It wasn't long before store employees and shoppers began to notice some strange phenomena. When paranormal investigators were summoned, they observed mysterious shadows and doors that seemed to be held shut by an invisible force, as well as disembodied voices and screams. The property was officially declared "haunted." In 2003, the building was renamed Rolling Hills Country Mall, and the following year, it was opened to the public for ghost-hunting purposes and became known as "Rolling Hills Asylum."

Bargain Hunters Give Way to Ghost Hunters

Rolling Hills Country Mall has since closed its doors to shoppers, but in 2009, Sharon and Jerry Coyle purchased the property; they

keep the building open as a paranormal research center, which hosts ghost tours and other special events.

Former owner Lori Carlson said that shadows and electronic voice phenomena (EVPs) are common occurrences at Rolling Hills, especially on the first and second floors of the East Wing—an area that was added to the building in 1958. Perhaps trying to avoid modern-day visitors, the spirits there seem to be most active between 3 A.M. and 5 A.M. And if you walk around the second floor of this wing, you might hear footsteps above you; the trouble is, the building has no third floor.

The apparition of an older woman has been glimpsed heading into the ladies' room just outside the former cafeteria area; a man with a goatee has also been seen walking around the same area. And a former meat locker nearby is a good place to catch a few EVPs.

Another paranormal hot spot is the building's old solitary confinement cell, which was added in 1828 to house violent residents. These segregated souls frequently show themselves today.

See for Yourself

Rolling Hills Asylum attracts ghost hunters from all over the country, but working there isn't for the faint of heart. Staff member Suzie Yencer tells of one paranormal investigation during which the researcher wanted to try an experiment. The group gathered in a basement area known as the Christmas Room, where toys are often seen moving by themselves. No lights or detectors were used; the only illumination came from a pink glow stick that was set in the middle of the circle of people. Only Suzie was allowed to speak in the eerily quiet room: She was asked to try to make contact with the spirit world . . . and it worked. To her surprise, the glow stick moved back and forth, and a toy rocking horse in the room started to sway. Suzie and several others actually saw a phantom arm that appeared to reach for a ball; then, just as suddenly, it was gone.

In 2010, the *Ghost Adventures* team devoted an episode to the spirits of the old asylum. When Zak Bagans,

Nick Groff, and Aaron Goodwin spent the night locked inside the old building, they heard disembodied voices and saw apparitions in their photos. Their experience, combined with the testimony of staff members and visitors, convinced them that Rolling Hills is a hotbed of paranormal activity.

Investigators from Central New York Ghost Hunters agreed. Members documented unexplained cold spots, phantom footsteps, hushed voices (which were captured on audio recorders), and actual physical contact, such as hair pulling and light taps or pokes.

The Naughty and the Nice

Visitors to Rolling Hills frequently report seeing the shadow of Roy, a former resident who suffered from gigantism, a disease that caused him to become unusually large. He grew to be over seven feet tall at a time when six feet tall was considered exceptionally large. Embarrassed by Roy's appearance, his parents left him at Rolling Hills in the late 1800s, when he was 12 years old; he lived there until he died at age 62. Roy was a gentle soul whose spirit emits friendly energy.

But not every entity at Rolling Hills is as benevolent as Roy. Nurse Emmie Altworth was known to abuse patients and was thought to practice the dark arts and black magic. Inmates and other staff members feared her. Modern visitors have reported a feeling of evil and unease in the building's infirmary—possibly due to Emmie's negative energy.

If you visit Rolling Hills Asylum, watch out for its many spirits—the friendly and the anguished alike. And when you get home, be prepared to sleep with the lights on.

"The death is not smooth. When there is trauma—an unacceptable accident or shock or surprise—this will, in some cases, cause the personality to go into a state of psychotic shock. In that state of shock, they are not aware that they've passed on. They are confused as to their real status because they can see everybody and nobody seems to be able to see them."

—Hans Holzer, on what causes some people to become ghosts

The Hoosac Tunnel

*By the mid-1800s, the train was the preeminent form of
transportation in America, and competition between railroad
lines was fierce. If a means could be found to shorten a
route, create a link, or speed up a journey, it was generally
taken to help ensure a railroad's continued profitability.*

In 1848, the newly formed Troy and Greenfield Railroad proposed
a direct route that would link Greenfield and Williamstown,
Massachusetts. In Williamstown, it would connect to an existing route
on which trains could travel to Troy, New York, and points west. The
time-saving measure seemed like a brilliant move, except for one not-so-
small detail: Between Greenfield and Williamstown stood a forbidding
promontory known as Hoosac Mountain. In order to tame it, the railroad would need to drill a tunnel—but not just any tunnel: At nearly
five miles in length, it would have to be the world's *longest* tunnel.

The Great Bore
In 1851, the project was set in motion. Almost immediately, trouble
arose when drillers learned that the soft rock stratum through which
they were supposed to be boring was, in fact, harder than nails. In 1861,
funding dried up, and by 1862—realizing that it had bitten off more
than it could chew—the Troy and Greenfield Railroad defaulted on its
loan. The state of Massachusetts stepped in to complete the tunnel.

With a steady infusion of cash and a government bent on
completing the project, the Hoosac Tunnel was finally finished in
1873; in 1876, the "Great Bore" officially opened for business. The
project had taken a quarter century to complete at a total cost of
$21 million. Nearly 200 lives were lost while the tunnel was built,
with 13 being the result of an incident that's legendary to this day.

Tragedy Strikes
It happened on October 17, 1867, inside the tunnel's central shaft—
a vertical hole that was drilled from atop the mountain to intersect

with the midpoint of the tunnel 1,028 feet below. The shaft would supply much-needed ventilation to the tunnel and allow drillers two more facings from which to attack, a measure that would greatly speed up operations.

On this particular day, the shaft reached into the mountain some 538 feet. While attempting to light a lamp, a workman accidentally ignited a gasoline tank. Within seconds, an inferno rocketed up to the surface, claiming the pumping station and hoist house located above, causing them to collapse into the deep pit. Unfortunately, 13 men were working in the shaft during the incident. As soon as was humanly possible, a miner was lowered into the smoldering cavity to search for survivors; he passed out during the long trip but managed to gasp "no hope" upon his return to the surface.

Without an operational pump, the cavity eventually filled to the brim with seepage and rainwater. It wasn't until a year later that the central shaft gave up its grisly contents. As it turns out, most of the victims hadn't died from the flames or from drowning: The stranded men had built a survival raft but were slowly asphyxiated by the poisonous gases and the oxygen-hungry flames raging above them.

Spirits Rise

In a 1985 article, Glenn Drohan—a reporter for the *North Adams Transcript*—told of strange phenomena at the tunnel, such as "vague shapes and muffled wails near the water-filled pit." Shortly after the accident occurred, workmen allegedly saw the ghosts of the lost miners carrying picks and shovels. The workers called out to the missing men, but they did not answer, and their apparitions quickly vanished.

Other tragic goings-on at the Hoosac Tunnel include the strange death of Ringo Kelley. In 1865, when explosive nitroglycerin was first used for excavation, experts Kelley, Billy Nash, and Ned Brinkman attempted to set a charge of nitro before running for cover. Nash and Brinkman never made it: Kelley somehow set off the explosion prematurely, burying his coworkers in the process.

Shortly thereafter, Kelley vanished. He was not seen again until March 30, 1866, when his lifeless body was found two miles inside the tunnel. Bizarrely, he had been strangled to death at the precise spot where Nash and Brinkman had perished. Investigators never

developed any leads, but workmen had an ominous feeling about Kelley's demise: They believed that the vengeful spirits of Nash and Brinkman had done him in.

Present-Day Poltergeists

If the preceding tales seem quaint due to the passage of time, it's worth noting that the tunnel still features its share of hauntings; standouts among these are railroad worker Joseph Impoco's trio of supernatural tales. In an article that appeared in *The Berkshire Sampler* on October 30, 1977, Impoco told reporter Eileen Kuperschmid that he was chipping ice from the tracks one day when he heard a voice say, "Run, Joe, run!" As Impoco tells it, "I turned, and sure enough, there was No. 60 coming at me. Boy, did I jump back fast! When I looked [back], there was no one there."

Six weeks later, Impoco was working with an iron crowbar, doing his best to free cars that were stuck to the icy tracks. Suddenly, he heard, "Joe! Joe! Drop it, Joe!" He instinctively dropped the crowbar just as 11,000 volts of electricity struck it from a short-circuited power line overhead.

In the final incident, Impoco was removing trees from the tunnel's entrance when, from out of nowhere, an enormous oak fell directly toward him. He managed to outrun the falling tree, but he heard a frightening, ethereal laugh as he ran; he was certain that it hadn't come from any of his coworkers.

Travel Tips

For the brave at heart, a visit to the Hoosac Tunnel can prove awe-inspiring and educational. The tunnel is still used, so walking inside it is strictly off-limits, but a well-worn path beside the tracks leads to the Hoosac's entrance. For those who are looking to avoid things that go bump in the night, a trip to the nearby North Adams' Hoosac Tunnel Museum in the Western Gateway Heritage State Park will reveal the incredible history of this five-mile-long portal into another dimension—and will do so far away from Ringo Kelley's haunts. All aboard!

FRIGHTENING FACTS

- *"The Unsinkable" Molly Brown, a* Titanic *survivor and self-made socialite, lived in Denver for years. The spunky woman's spirit remains in her beloved former home, which is now a museum that highlights her life and offers exhibits about Victorian-era culture. Her apparition has been spotted there wearing old-fashioned attire, and she likes to open and close doors.*

- *Former First Lady Dolley Madison, one of the most influential American women of her era, passed away in a house located at Madison and H Street NW in Washington, D.C. (which is now part of the National Courts Complex). But perhaps she hasn't quite completed her earthly journey: Since her death in 1849, so many people have seen her specter in the building that it has become customary to tip one's hat to her.*

- *Key West, Florida, is home to the Audubon House, which is now a museum that's dedicated to naturalist John J. Audubon. If you happen to catch a glimpse of a well-dressed phantom wearing a ruffly shirt, it's probably just Audubon, perhaps eager to paint more birds.*

- *Country star Conway Twitty once visited Cragfont Mansion in Castalian Springs, Tennessee, to check out the ghosts that were said to haunt the place. He lasted two hours in the gorgeous antebellum house before bailing out, stating that whatever was in there was throwing things at him.*

- *Contrary to the assumptions of many, "Johnny Appleseed" was a real person named John Chapman, whose "legend" is quite factual. His family's cemetery is located south of Dexter City, Ohio, and Johnny's big-hearted specter seems to visit there often. Look for a barefoot man in tattered clothing.*

- *Cornelius Vanderbilt II (who was named after his shipping- and railroad-tycoon grandfather) built The Breakers—the Vanderbilt family's Rhode Island mansion—as a model of order and efficiency. His wife, Alice, who passed away in 1934, seems quite settled there. Although the house is now a Gilded Age museum, visitors often sense Alice's presence, even though her apparition doesn't manifest.*

- *Ernest Hemingway loved Key West, which is why he lived there in the 1930s. His former residence is now a tourist attraction— and the eternal home of his ghost. Visitors and staff members have heard him hammering away on his manual typewriter and witnessed him waving from a second-story window. He's also been spotted nearby at Sloppy Joe's Bar. Even a ghost needs to get out of the house and socialize once in a while.*

- *In the early 19th century, the ghost of Nelly Butler was said to haunt the entire town of Sullivan, Maine. She would appear to anyone who wanted to see her, and she was known to give long-winded speeches about morals and religion. She also made prophecies and predictions that came true. Reverend Abraham Cummings was a skeptic until he met the spectral Butler himself; after that, he held her up as indisputable proof of the afterlife.*

- *In the 1880s, long before ghost hunters began photographing "orbs," tiny Diamond Island—which is located on the Mississippi River near Hardin, Illinois—was said to be home to a blazing ball of fire that changed into a spectral man and then back again. Wanting to see the mysterious object for themselves, a group of people came armed with guns and swords; ultimately, however, they were scared away by the frightening sight. It is believed that the strange phenomenon is the restless spirit of a man who was murdered on the island.*

- *In the late 1890s, several residents of Benton, Indiana, reported seeing a ghost roaming around a local cemetery. The phantom resembled a local hermit who had been murdered with a club ten years earlier, except that the spirit brandished a large wooden club himself and was said to be at least eight feet tall.*

- *A strange "demon cat" was said to haunt the Capitol in Washington, D.C. It appeared to be ordinary at first, but then it would grow to the size of an elephant before witnesses' unbelieving eyes. Sightings of the enormous phantom cat were so common that few people doubted its existence throughout much of the 19th century. However, a security guard seems to have scared away the beast when he shot at it in 1862.*

Moore Ghosts Gather in Villisca

Villisca was once a bustling town in southwestern Iowa. In the early 1900s, it was home to more than 2,500 citizens, a busy train station, and dozens of businesses. But on June 10, 1912, a local family was brutally murdered in their home. The crime was never solved, and the town has since dwindled in size to about half as many residents. You might say that Villisca has become a ghost town . . . literally.

How It All Began—and Ended

The home of Josiah Moore and his wife, Sarah, was much like many other houses of its time. Built in 1868, it was a well-kept two-story white house on a quiet street in the heartland of America. After attending a Children's Day event on the night of June 9, 1912, the Moores and their four children, as well as Lena and Ina Stillinger— two young neighbor girls who were sleeping over—returned to the house and went to bed.

The next morning, Mary Peckham, the Moores' next-door neighbor, went outside to hang her laundry and was struck by the silence that greeted her from the Moore house; after all, a family of six was rarely quiet. Peckham called Josiah's brother Ross, who then came over to check things out.

Bungled Bungalow

Ross unlocked the door and entered the parlor; the home was covered in a blanket of eerie silence. But when he opened the door to one of the bedrooms, he was confronted with a horrific sight: the bloody bodies of the Stillinger girls lying in a bed.

Peckham called the police, who arrived to find the lifeless bodies of Josiah, Sarah, Herman, Katherine, Boyd, and Paul Moore, as well as the Stillinger girls—they had all been brutally murdered with an ax, which had been wiped off and left by the door of the downstairs bedroom.

That the crime was never solved is no real surprise due to the mayhem that ensued. As word of the carnage spread, friends and hundreds of curious onlookers raced to the house, where police soon lost control of the crime scene. With all of this chaos and none of today's technology, police were unable to solve the case—a fact that haunted them for the rest of their lives.

The Suspects

Among the leading suspects was Frank F. Jones, a local businessman who was angry with Josiah for leaving his company and poaching one of its best clients. People who believe in this theory suggest that Jones hired hit man William Mansfield to do the dirty work. Although police were suspicious of the pair, they did not find enough evidence to prosecute either of them.

Another school of thought suggests that a drifter committed the murders. Two men fit the bill: Andy Sawyer, a vagrant who traveled with an ax, and Henry Moore, who was later convicted of killing his mother and grandmother with an ax and was a suspect in several other ax murders. But no evidence connected either to the Villisca murders.

Traveling preacher George Kelly was another prime suspect. A rather odd character, Kelly had been present at the Children's Day event at the Moores' church. He left town the morning that the bodies were discovered and reportedly told fellow train passengers that he'd had a vision that told him to "Slay and slay utterly." When he was arrested for another crime in 1914, he admitted to the Moore murders but later withdrew his confession. Nevertheless, Kelly was tried twice for the Moore murders: One trial ended in a hung jury, and he was acquitted in the other.

If You Renovate It, They Will Come

After the murders, the Moore house changed hands several times because, really, who wants to live in a house where eight people were killed? By 1994, the house was dilapidated and in danger of being torn down; that's when a realtor presented Darwin and Martha Linn with a proposal. The couple operated the Olson-Linn Museum in Villisca, and the realtor hoped that they'd be interested in purchasing the house to preserve another piece of the town's history; they were.

The Linns secured state funding to restore the house. Using old photographs, they remodeled and redecorated it with items from the early 1900s. They removed the electricity, water, and working bathrooms and restored the building to its 1912 condition. It was placed on the National Register of Historic Places in 1998.

After the renovation was complete, the Linns began giving tours of the house. On these tours, visitors get a glimpse of Villisca in the early 1900s and learn the details of the grisly murders. Other topics of discussion include possible suspects and how the crime and the eventual trial of Reverend Kelly affected the small town.

They're Baaaaack

With the house looking almost exactly as it had in 1912, it seems that the spirits of the Moore family were drawn back to it. Visitors have reported seeing apparitions and hearing voices whisper in their ears. Closet doors open and close by themselves, and balls mysteriously roll across the floor.

Darwin Linn said that he always felt a pull toward this house, and he'd heard stories about the spirits that linger there. But when the renovations went smoothly, he dismissed the idea . . . until he saw the youngsters who came through the house on tours: He saw them interacting with other children—children who weren't there. "That makes the hair stand up on the back of my head," he said. That's when he became convinced that the Moore family is still around.

Many ghost hunters and paranormal investigators have toured the house and found evidence of spirits there. Orbs have been captured in photos and mysterious voices have been recorded on audio devices. But some of the most interesting documentation was collected by Maritza Skandunas, who related her harrowing firsthand account on the TV show *My Ghost Story*.

1912 Again

Skandunas, the founder of San Diego Ghost Hunters, decided that if most people take tours of the Moore house, she'd like to go one step further and spend the night there. Darwin Linn said that he was a little surprised by the request, but he was open to the idea; he didn't even charge her for the lodging. So Skandunas and a couple of ghost-hunting friends settled in at the dark and primitive house.

"It felt like you went back a hundred years," she said. "You could almost relive what they felt and the screaming that must have been going on, and no one heard it." Skandunas said that she felt that pure "evil was [permeating] out of the walls."

As Skandunas and her friends walked through the house absorbing the energy, they were able to imagine what took place in each room. Soon, they noticed a black shadow following them; they believe that it was the spirit of the murderer. Skandunas said that it gave off "a very hateful energy."

In the master bedroom, Skandunas felt something touch her arm; that sensation was validated when she took a picture of the room's mirror and saw the image of Sarah Moore staring back at her in the photo.

In one of the children's rooms, the investigators discovered the spirits of youngsters who were hoping to interact with the living. When they asked Herman, the eldest, to open the closet door, the door opened, even though no one was near it. When Skandunas's friend suggested reading one of the children's books aloud, the ghostly excitement was palpable. But shortly thereafter, the black shadow appeared and the reader began to feel nauseated. The killer obviously didn't want any happiness in the house, but when the group left the room, an audio recorder captured the voice of a child saying, "Don't go."

When the investigators asked the kids if they knew who committed the murders, they said no, but added clearly that it was two people. It seems that the Moores may have stuck around to offer clues about that terrible night.

Evil Energy

Even a seasoned ghost hunter like Skandunas was shaken by the night's revelations. "I had goose bumps," she said. "I would never go into that house alone."

According to historical records, the town was named "Villisca" after a Native American word meaning "pleasant view." But others claim that the town was originally called "Wallisca," which means "evil spirit." Now that sounds about right.

Near-Death Experiences Are Not All Black or White

Nothing about a near-death experience (NDE) is black or white—except, of course, for the light at the end of the tunnel. No matter what you believe about the afterlife (or lack thereof), one thing is certain: We're all going to die someday. Some deaths are premature, however, and when this is the case, the person gets sent back to earth with a memory to last a lifetime.

In 2009, after enduring 30 years of back pain due to arthritis, Marcia Bergman decided that she'd had enough. Although there were plenty of doctors near her home in suburban Indianapolis, Marcia followed a friend's recommendation to see a doctor in Kentucky. That's where her unusual journey began.

A Change of Plans

Marcia's doctor scheduled her for back surgery, but when she underwent routine X-rays prior to the procedure, a small spot was discovered on her lung. The back surgery was immediately put on hold and the growth was biopsied; unfortunately, it was cancer. Suddenly, instead of preparing for back surgery, Marcia was facing an operation to remove a malignant tumor from her lung.

The tumor was small and the surgery went well, and the doctors were confident that they'd removed all of the cancer. The near-death experience happened later, when Marcia was almost ready to go home. In fact, the nurse had just removed the central line from Marcia's jugular vein. To make the blood clot at this site, the nurse was supposed to hold his thumb over the vein for five minutes. But he was apparently distracted by *The Oprah Winfrey Show,* which was on the television set in Marcia's room. Marcia started to feel a little funny and suspected that the process was taking too long. It was. Essentially, the nurse kept his finger on Marcia's jugular vein for too long, and his carelessness stopped the blood flow to her brain, causing her to die right there in the chair.

View from Above

The next thing that Marcia remembered was floating above her body. She heard the nurse call her name and she watched herself fall over.

Unlike some people who see a white light, Marcia said that she went from seeing herself in the hospital room to seeing nothing but black all around her. The next thing she knew, she was waking up in the intensive care unit—three days later.

Seeing the Light

"Looking back, I really think this all happened for a reason," Marcia said. "The doctor I saw later in Indiana doesn't take presurgical X-rays, so they never would have found the cancer." Two years later, Marcia was still cancer-free, and her back had also been repaired, allowing her to enjoy her favorite hobby: working in her flower garden.

Marcia said that her NDE may not have been as complete as some; after all, she didn't see a white light or reunite with dead relatives. But she said that the experience has made her more spiritual. "When I thought about this sort of thing, I always hoped I'd be a white-lighter," she laughed, "but I'm just happy to be here. I think each step I took led me to this place."

Part of the Plan

And if Marcia thinks about God and her life a little more now... well, that's only natural. After her NDE, she was sitting in front of her makeup mirror one day when she may have received another message from above. "I was deep in thought, thinking of God and of my father, who died when I was four," she recalled. "All of a sudden, the mirror's lights dimmed, went off, and then came back on, from low to medium and then back to high. The lights in the room never changed."

Marcia doesn't know what the message was supposed to be, but she said that she's not afraid of dying. And until that time, she said, "I guess I'm just not done planting flowers."

Ghostly Encounters by the Average Joe

There's something fascinating about a ghost story. And sometimes the scariest, eeriest, and most mysterious tales are about the personal encounters that regular people—people just like you—have with the paranormal. The following stories were shared on the television show My Ghost Story; *they'll leave you wondering what you'd do if you encountered a ghost.*

Footprints on the Bed

Unexplained noises and cabinet doors opening on their own were the first clues that Marci Smith's home in rural Maryland might be haunted. And it only got worse from there. She felt something move across her feet at night, but there were no signs of rodents, so she set up a video camera to record her bedroom while she was sleeping. What she documented convinced her that something otherworldly was sharing her house. A misty figure that looked like a phantom cat was seen jumping onto the bed. Later in the video, the blankets depressed as if an unseen presence was walking across the bed.

Marci called in paranormal investigators, who set up audio and video recorders in the house. Several voices were captured, ranging from children to elderly people. Marci said that the house seems perfectly normal during the daytime. But at night? Well, let's just say that she's never really alone.

One Cool Spirit

If anyone would be safe from a ghostly encounter, it would surely be someone in the security business, right? Wrong. A policeman of nearly 24 years, Ron Colbert had a supernatural experience while working security for the city of Anderson, South Carolina. One night, while monitoring security cameras in Anderson's municipal building with IT Director Mark Cunningham, Colbert saw a ghostly orb move across the deserted lobby of the city's credit union. The pair cleaned the camera, adjusted the blinds, moved a chair, and finally replaced the camera in an effort to explain the phenomenon, but the orb kept coming back, and employees

2**470**

became spooked. Incidentally, the lobby was the coldest room in the building, with temperatures never rising above 60 degrees. Perhaps the spirit was cold-hearted because after space heaters were brought in to warm up the room, the orb was never seen again.

The Spirited Giraffe

When Nicholas Honkoski's father acquired a two-foot-tall porcelain giraffe statue from Africa, life started to get a little weird in the family's house in San Gabriel, California. Nick and his cousin Cody heard strange noises, so they decided to set up a video camera to record while they were sleeping. They were astounded by what they saw when they reviewed the footage: The giraffe was moving across the floor by itself! They even captured a partial apparition: a ghostly arm that reached out to grab Cody. The pair also picked up EVPs (electronic voice phenomena), and Cody saw the reflection of Nick's deceased grandfather in a mirror. One morning, the giraffe figurine was mysteriously found shattered; after that, everything returned to normal. The cousins never did figure out the connection between the giraffe and the spirit world, but they weren't sad when the haunting ceased.

An Ordinary Guy Meets a Long-Dead Actress

After David Oman built a house next to the Los Angeles–area dwelling where five people were murdered by the Manson Family in 1969, he was "welcomed" by a few uninvited guests. During his first night in his new home, he awoke to see the full-bodied apparition of a man. He got up to investigate, and when he asked who was there, he was shocked to hear, "It's Sharon." That would be Sharon Tate, the actress who was eight-and-a-half months pregnant when she was brutally murdered by Charles Manson's followers. Items that disappear and reappear in other places, objects that crash to the ground on their own, a palpable energy, and a photo showing an orb within an orb (which indicates a pregnant spirit) are just some of the phenomena that David has encountered there. He said that he has learned to live with his invisible roommates, but his friends prefer to gather elsewhere.

Ghost Lights

The legends are similar, no matter the locale. It's whispered that mysterious lights that blink and wink in the night are the spirits of long-dead railroad workers, jealous and jilted lovers, or lost children. They go by many names: marsh lights, ghost lights, will-o'-the-wisp, feu follet, earth lights, and even, to the skeptical, swamp gas. They occur in remote areas, often near old railway tracks or power transmitters. Some are thought to issue from the geomagnetic fields of certain kinds of rock. But tales of lights that change color, follow people, foil electrical systems, or perform acrobatic stunts are harder to explain.

Mysterious Marfa Lights

The famed Marfa Lights of Marfa, Texas, have become almost synonymous with the term *ghost lights*. Since 1883, they have been spotted in an area southwest of the Chisos Mountains, some 200 miles south of El Paso. The lights appear almost playful in their gyrations, skimming over the fields, bobbing like a yo-yo, or chasing visitors. One woman reportedly witnessed a white ball of light three feet in diameter that bounced in slow motion alongside her car as she drove through the area one night. Some of the lights have been attributed to auto headlights miles away across the desert, but the Marfa Lights were witnessed long before automobiles were invented.

The Peculiar Paulding Light

According to legend, an old railway brakeman was killed near the Choate Branch Railroad tracks that used to run near Paulding, Michigan, along the northern Wisconsin-Michigan border. People have observed strange lights near the tracks for decades, and it is said that they're from the railman's ghostly lantern swinging as he walks his old beat. Others, armed with telescopes and binoculars, believe that the famed Paulding Light is actually caused by head-lights shining from a highway a few miles away.

Still, many claim that the lights behave like anything but distant reflections. The lights are said to change from red to green, zoom up close as if peering into people's cars, chase people,

flash through automobiles cutting off all electric power, and zigzag through the nearby woods. Crowds flock to the Robins Wood Road site off Highway 45 to see the phenomenon for themselves, and a wooden sign has been erected complete with a drawing of a ghost swinging a lantern.

The Fiery Feu Follet

During the mid-18th century, when Detroit was being settled by the French, aristocrats and working folks feared the *feu follet*—spirit lights of the marshy river area. One local legend tells of a rich landowner who nearly drowned one stormy night when the brilliant lights lured him into a swamp. Luckily, two guests staying at his house heard his terrified cries and managed to rescue him. At the time, the prevailing theory of the marsh lights was that windows had to be closed when the feu follet were near or they would enter the house, snake their way into the windpipes of those present, and choke them to death.

Baffling Brown Mountain Lights

Although scoffed at as nothing more than reflected train lights, the multicolored light show in the foothills of North Carolina's Blue Ridge Mountains has fascinated humans since an early explorer reported it in 1771, and even earlier according to Native American legend. Several centuries ago, many people were killed during a battle between the Cherokee and the Catawba tribes. Legend has it that the Brown Mountain Lights are the spirits of those lost warriors.

Another tale states that a plantation owner got lost hunting on Brown Mountain and that one of his slaves came looking for him, swinging a lantern to light his way. The slave never found his owner but still walks the mountainside with his eternal lantern. Still another legend claims that the lights come from the spirit of a woman who was murdered on the mountain by her husband in 1850.

Whatever the source of the colorful lights, they come in many shapes, from glowing orbs to trailing bursts to still, white areas. Crowds flock to at least three locations to view the lights, but one of the most popular is the Brown Mountain overlook on Highway 181, about 20 miles north of Morganton.

Ghost Hunters Extraordinaire: Ed and Lorraine Warren

There are paranormal investigators and demonologists and then there are psychic research soul mates. This describes Ed and Lorraine Warren, who are considered to be among the pioneers in the field of paranormal research. Ghosts and demons were their bread and butter for more than 50 years until Ed joined the spirit world in 2006.

Home Sweet Haunted Home

Ed Warren—who was born in Bridgeport, Connecticut, in 1926—lived in a haunted house from age 5 until age 12. His father—a police officer—took a commonsense approach: He explained away the mysterious sights and sounds. But even at a young age, Ed knew better. He heard rapping and pounding on the walls and footsteps roaming the hallways; he also saw ghosts. Although he was frightened, Ed was also fascinated by the phenomena going on around him, and he yearned to know more.

In 1945, Ed married Lorraine, his high-school sweetheart; they were both 18. In the early years of their marriage, Ed worked as an artist, painting landscapes, seascapes, and haunted houses; he sold his works for $3 or $4 each. But of course, you need to *find* haunted houses in order to paint them.

Coming of Age

Although Ed was exposed to spirits as a child, his specialty was demonology—the study of demons and fallen angels. Unlike her husband, Lorraine didn't immediately recognize that she had an affinity for the paranormal, but that soon changed. The pair was on a drive with another couple when they spotted a house near Henniker, New Hampshire, that was rumored to be haunted. Lorraine rang the doorbell and persuaded the caretaker to let them inside. There, Lorraine got more than she bargained for: her first out-of-body experience, during which she hovered near the ceiling.

This was not her imagination or an exaggeration. Since then, Lorraine has refined her abilities, and her skills have been documented by experts. She is what is known as a light-trance medium, meaning that she is able to communicate with spirits; she's also a clairvoyant, meaning that she senses phenomena that are beyond normal perception; in other words, she has a sixth sense. Lorraine can also see the auras—or energies—that surround the living.

A Match Made in Heaven

Simply put, Ed and Lorraine were the perfect couple—perfect for each other, at any rate. Together they investigated more than 4,000 cases, and they were the top psychic research team in the United States for more than 30 years. They lectured at colleges across the country and were interviewed on radio and television shows in the United States, Great Britain, Australia, and Japan. The Warrens were among the few paranormal investigators who were allowed into the "Amityville Horror" house, where they were permitted to take photos—something that only a handful of people were allowed to do.

Over the years, the Warrens' interest in the supernatural only increased; in fact, they founded the New England Society for Psychic Research (NESPR) in 1952. (As of this writing, Lorraine is still active in NESPR, which she operates with the help of her son-in-law Tony Spera, a noted demonologist who was trained by Ed.) They also opened the Warren Occult Museum in Monroe, Connecticut, which houses numerous items that are allegedly cursed or haunted, including a mirror that was used to conjure spirits and Annabelle the doll. (Read more about Annabelle the doll on page 101.)

The Warrens built their reputations through hard work and many years of investigating and documenting the paranormal. Keep in mind that when they began, the field was very small. There were no TV shows featuring ghost hunters, and technology was relatively arcane. The couple investigated with only their experiences and senses.

The Warrens' investigations have been detailed in ten books, two of which (*The Haunted* and *The Devil in Connecticut*) were made into TV movies. Every day, Lorraine receives as many as a dozen calls from people seeking help with paranormal activity. And it all began because Ed needed to find a few haunted houses to inspire his painting career. Looks like the spirits found *them*.

Ghosts Live On at the Clovis Sanitarium

Picture this scene at the emergency call center in Clovis, California: "Hello. 911. What's your emergency?" Dead silence. "Hello? Is anyone there?" More silence. So the dispatcher checks to see where the call is coming from and finds that it's 2604 Clovis Avenue: the former home of the Clovis Sanitarium—a building that has no electricity and no working phone. It's probably not a life-or-death situation, since whatever is making the call is already dead.

Oddly, this type of phone call is not uncommon in Clovis—a city of 95,000 that is located just northeast of Fresno. Nicknamed "the Gateway to the Sierras," Clovis was the home of Anthony Andriotti, who built a magnificent mansion for his family in 1922. Unfortunately, he miscalculated the cost of the building's upkeep, and he went bankrupt, turned to alcohol and opium, and died in 1929 at age 36.

The estate sat empty until it was reopened in 1935 as the Hazelwood Sanitarium for tuberculosis patients. In 1942, it became the Clovis Avenue Sanitarium, which was dedicated to serving the area's physically and mentally ill.

A Place to Die

Families whose loved ones suffered from dementia or schizophrenia brought these unfortunate souls to the Clovis Sanitarium to die. It is said that at one point, the death rate at the facility reached an average of one person per day. Still, the building soon became over-crowded, with ten beds to a room and one nurse overseeing two or more rooms. Former employees told sad tales of patients who were abused and neglected.

When patients died, their bodies were stored in the relatively cool basement until they could be removed. Locals started talking about strange happenings at the sanitarium, and rumors began to suggest that the place was haunted. But it wasn't all idle gossip: It seems that there *were* some pretty strange things going on at 2604 Clovis Avenue.

A Call for Help

In 1992, the Clovis Sanitarium closed; that's when the mysterious phone calls began. Sometimes neighbors or passersby would call the police regarding trespassers or vandals. But then there were the other calls—the ones that came directly from the vacant building that had no working phone line.

Unfazed by these odd stories, Todd Wolfe bought the property in 1997 with hopes of creating a haunted-house-type Halloween attraction. Initially a skeptic, Wolfe was surprised when his employees complained about spirits interfering with their work. They saw apparitions and reported being touched and grabbed by unseen hands. It wasn't until he had his own encounter in "Mary's Room"— where he actually saw a shadowy apparition—that Wolfe began to believe. Today, Mary's Room is furnished with only original furniture because it seems that "Mary" gets quite upset when changes are made. And a disturbed Mary leads to increased paranormal activity, including phantom breathing, shoving by an invisible force, and objects that move seemingly on their own.

Many paranormal groups have visited the Clovis Sanitarium, and all agree that it is indeed haunted. They've heard shuffling footsteps and strange voices, and many have reported feelings of being watched.

Energetic Spirits

When the *Ghost Adventures* team visited the Clovis Sanitarium in a 2010 episode, they were greeted by a laughing spirit and a spike in electromagnetic energy (in a building with no electricity). Later, in the basement, the crew used a state-of-the-art ultraviolet camera to record a mysterious purple form; the shape even appeared to sit on a couch for a while. The team also captured some amazing EVPs (electronic voice phenomena), including one that told the group to "Get out" and another that said it wanted their energy.

Investigator Zak Bagans observed that the ghosts of Clovis Sanitarium are an unusual bunch. The original owners were a family with young children who lived a lavish lifestyle, full of happiness and laughter. But combine those feelings with those of the mentally ill who were neglected and abused after being brought there to die, and the mix becomes volatile. As Bagans concluded, "That contrasting energy has to do something weird to the atmosphere."

 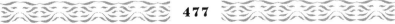

Stalked by an Invisible Entity

In November 1988, when Jackie Hernandez moved into a small bungalow on 11th Street in San Pedro, California, she was looking to make a fresh start. But her hopefulness quickly turned into what she described as the "nightmare of all nightmares."

From the time that Jackie moved in to her new place, she felt a presence in the house. At first, it made her feel safe—as if someone was looking out for her. But Jackie soon realized that the presence was less than friendly. Shortly after their arrival, Jackie and her young children heard a high-pitched screeching noise throughout the house. Then, in February 1989, Jackie's unseen houseguests manifested in the form of two separate apparitions: One was an old man that Jackie's friend also witnessed while she was babysitting in the home; the other was a disembodied head that Jackie saw in the attic.

Call in the Cavalry

In August 1989, Jackie asked a group of paranormal researchers to investigate the phenomena; parapsychologist Dr. Barry Taff, cameraman Barry Conrad, and photographer Jeff Wheatcraft had no idea how the case would impact their lives. On August 8, during their first visit to the Hernandez home, the group noted a foul odor in the house, heard noises in the attic, and captured glowing orbs of light in photographs. Skeptical of Jackie's claim of seeing a phantom head in the attic, Wheatcraft took several photos in the darkened space. But he left the room in terror after an unseen force yanked the camera from his hands. When he summoned the courage to go back into the attic (this time with a flashlight), he found the body of the camera on one side of the room and the lens on the other, inside a box.

Later that same evening, while Wheatcraft and Conrad were in the attic, Wheatcraft was violently pushed by an invisible hand. After they returned to the main level of the house, loud banging noises were heard coming from the attic, as if someone (or something) was stomping above them.

When the researchers returned to the house later that month, they observed a liquid oozing from the walls and dripping from the cabinets. Samples that were analyzed at a lab determined that the substance was blood plasma from a human male. Why it would be oozing from the walls was anyone's guess.

Get Out and Don't Look Back

The phenomena that Jackie and the investigators experienced on the night of September 4, 1989, shook them to their very cores. During the day, the poltergeist ramped up its attention-seeking behavior. After watching objects fly through the air and hearing mysterious moaning and breathing noises, Jackie called the researchers for help.

Wheatcraft and Conrad's friend Gary Boehm were inspecting the pitch-black attic and were just about to leave when Wheatcraft screamed. Boehm took a photo hoping that the flash would illuminate the room so he could see Wheatcraft and help him. Boehm's photo captured the spirit's latest attack on Wheatcraft, who was hanging from the rafters with a clothesline wrapped around his neck; the cord was tied with a seaman's knot. Boehm was able to rescue Wheatcraft, who was understandably shaken by his encounter with the evil entity that seemed to have a personal vendetta against him.

After observing several other paranormal phenomena that night, Jackie and the researchers left the San Pedro house, never to return.

You Can Run but You Can't Hide

Frightened for the safety of her young children, Jackie moved her family nearly 200 miles away to Weldon, California. But it didn't take long for the poltergeist to find her. The haunting started with unusual scratching noises that came from a backyard shed; then, a black, shapeless form was spotted in the hallway of the home. As had been the case in San Pedro, others witnessed the phenomena as well: While moving an old television set out of the storage shed, Jackie's neighbors saw the ghostly image of an old man on the screen.

In April 1990, when the researchers heard that the paranormal activity had followed Jackie to her new home, they drove to Weldon to continue their work on the case. Besides, Wheatcraft had a personal interest in the matter: He wanted to know why the entity was focusing its physical attacks on him.

 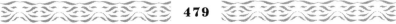

Hoping to provoke the spirit, Jackie, her friend, and the researchers decided to use a Ouija board. During the session, the table that they used shook violently, candles flickered, and the temperature in the room dropped dramatically. But the group may have received the answers it was seeking: Through the Ouija board, the spirit told them that he was a sailor who had been murdered in 1930 when his killer drowned him in San Pedro Bay. He also said that his killer had lived in Jackie's former home in San Pedro. When Wheatcraft asked the spirit why he was being targeted, the entity said that Wheatcraft resembled his killer. It then picked up Wheatcraft and threw him against the wall. He was naturally frightened, but he was not injured.

After that, Conrad searched old newspaper records to see if the information that they'd received from the spirit could be verified; it was. In 1930, sailor Herman Hendrickson was found drowned in San Pedro Bay. Although he'd also suffered a fractured skull, his death was ruled accidental. Perhaps Hendrickson's spirit was trying to make it known that his death was not accidental but that he was murdered.

Spirit Stalker

In June 1990, Jackie moved back to San Pedro and rented an apartment on Seventh Street. This time, she had a priest bless the place before she moved in. Nevertheless, the glowing orbs of light returned.

Later that year, Conrad's home was also infested with poltergeist activity, which he witnessed along with Boehm and Wheatcraft. Objects were mysteriously moved to new locations, burners on the gas stove turned on by themselves, scissors flew across the kitchen, a broom was left standing on top of the stove, and scissors were found underneath pillows in the bedroom. Also, Wheatcraft was again pushed by the invisible force, which left red scratch marks on his back.

The phenomena greatly diminished after that, although subsequent residents of the house on 11th Street in San Pedro also claimed to witness poltergeist activity; since then, it is said that no one has lived in the house for more than six months.

Although Jackie was terribly frightened by the mysterious activity at the time, she later said that she was grateful to have had a first-hand encounter with the Other Side, which not many people get to experience. Although some folks might welcome a visit from a ghost, few would want it to be as distressing as what Jackie went through.

Ghost Talk

"An idea, like a ghost, must be spoken to a little before it will explain itself."
—Charles Dickens

"What terrified me will terrify others; and I need only describe the spectre which had haunted my midnight pillow."
—Mary Shelley, *Frankenstein*

"There is no death. It is only a transition to a different sphere of consciousness."
—Tangina (Zelda Rubinstein's character in *Poltergeist*)

"Of all ghosts, the ghosts of our old lovers are the worst."
—Sir Arthur Conan Doyle, *The Memoirs of Sherlock Holmes*

"Never believe anything you hear from an inhuman haunting."
—Jason Hawes of The Atlantic Paranormal Society (TAPS)

"I would not participate in [a séance] under any circumstances. Not even if my wife died and a medium said she had a message from my wife.... We are too close as it is to a world that is incomprehensible."
—Stephen King

"The basic idea of an apparition is twofold: The consciousness must survive and it must be able to communicate or interact somehow with living people."
—Loyd Auerbach

"Ghosts, like ladies, never speak till spoke to."
—English novelist Richard Harris Barham (aka Thomas Ingoldsby)

"It is true with love as it is with ghosts; everyone talks about it, but few have seen it."
—Francois de La Rochefoucauld

"The oldest and strongest emotion of mankind is fear, and the oldest and strongest kind of fear is fear of the unknown."
—H. P. Lovecraft

Index

Contributing Writers

Jeff Bahr is a regular contributor to the Armchair Reader™ series. He is also well acquainted with the unexplained. "When I enter a room, people tend to scream; especially my long-suffering girlfriend, Maria," he said.

Mary Fons is a seasoned writer and performer. She once met a ghost and reprimanded it for being vague. Check out maryfons.com to read her juicy blog, PaperGirl.

Linda Godfrey is an author and artist who lives near a haunted forest in the creature-infested Kettle Moraine of southeastern Wisconsin. She has written more than a dozen books on the strange and unusual and is noted for her works about werewolves. She lives with her husband and attack dog—a Lhasa Apso named Grendel.

J. K. Kelley has contributed to numerous Armchair Reader™ books. He lives with his wife Deb, his conure Alex, and their dogs, Fabius and Leonidas.

Suzanne Reisman lives in Manhattan with her husband and is the author of *Off the Beaten (Subway) Track: New York City's Best Unusual Attractions*. Her writings about the city, public policy, and feminism have appeared in print and online.

Michael Riedlinger lives in Racine, Wisconsin, with the love of his life and their three spooky children. A member of the Horror Writer's Association, he hopes to encounter a ghostly nun at St. Mary College in Milwaukee, where he is completing his MA in writing.

Russell Roberts is an award-winning freelance writer who has written and published more than four dozen books for both children and adults. Show him a creepy graveyard or a mysterious light and you've made a friend for life . . . and beyond. He lives in New Jersey with his family and a diabolical cat named Rusti.

Adam Selzer is the author of roughly a dozen fiction and nonfiction books. He lives in Chicago and knows enough about the history of grave robbing in the city that his neighbors regard him with suspicion. He is a member of the American Ghost Society and a contributor to ChicagoUnbelieveable.com.

Sue Sveum lives in Madison, Wisconsin, where she satisfies her haunted curiosity by reading and watching programs, both paranormal and historical. Sue has coauthored two nonfiction books and contributed to many others. She lives with her very real family and a golden retriever that haunts her every move.

Don Vaughan ain't afraid of no ghosts, though he's hard-pressed to explain why he still sleeps with a night-light. He has written extensively about the paranormal for *The National Examiner* and the *Weekly World News* and has tackled more staid subjects for *Military Officer Magazine, Cure Magazine, Mad Magazine,* and other publications. Don lives in Raleigh, North Carolina, with his wife, Nanette, and their very spoiled cat, Rhianna.

James Willis has been involved with more than a dozen books on the strange and spooky, including five in the Armchair Reader™ series. He's also the founder of The Ghosts of Ohio (GhostsOfOhio.org), a nationally recognized paranormal research group. When not trying to drag the boogeyman out from under the bed or standing on a Crybaby Bridge waiting for "Bloody Mary," Willis resides in Columbus, Ohio, with his wife, daughter, a Queen-loving parrot, and three narcoleptic cats.